A Liberal Peace?

About the Editors

Susanna Campbell is a Research Fellow at the Centre on Conflict, Development and Peacebuilding at the Graduate Institute of International and Development Studies. She has fourteen years of experience researching peacebuilding interventions, and has written numerous publications on the subject, including those published by the Council on Foreign Relations, International Alert, International Crisis Group, *International Peacekeeping*, and the *Journal of Peacebuilding and Development*, and has contributed to several United Nations publications.

David Chandler is Professor of International Relations at the University of Westminster. He is the founding editor of the *Journal of Intervention and Statebuilding*. His recent books include *International Statebuilding: The Rise of Post-Liberal Governance* (2010) and *Hollow Hegemony: Rethinking Global Politics, Power and Resistance* (2009).

Meera Sabaratnam is a PhD candidate in the Department of International Relations at the London School of Economics, with previous degrees from Balliol College, Oxford and the LSE. Her current research applies post-colonial theoretical approaches to a critical appraisal of the liberal peace in Mozambique. She has formerly edited *Millennium: Journal of International Studies* and currently teaches a Masters' course on Conflict and Peace Studies. She is co-editor of the collection *Interrogating Democracy in World Politics* (2011).

A Liberal Peace?

The Problems and Practices of Peacebuilding

**edited by Susanna Campbell,
David Chandler and Meera Sabaratnam**

ZED BOOKS
London & New York

A Liberal Peace? The Problems and Practices of Peacebuilding was first
published in 2011 by Zed Books Ltd, 7 Cynthia Street, London N1 9JF, UK
and Room 400, 175 Fifth Avenue, New York, NY 10010, USA

www.zedbooks.co.uk

Editorial Copyright © Susanna Campbell, David Chandler and Meera Sabaratnam 2011
Copyright in this collection © Zed Books 2011

The rights of Susanna Campbell, David Chandler and Meera Sabaratnam to be identified
as the editors of this work have been asserted by them in accordance with the
Copyright, Designs and Patents Act, 1988

Typeset in Bembo by Swales & Willis Ltd, Exeter, Devon
Cover designed by www.alice-marwick.co.uk
Printed and bound by CPI Group (UK) Ltd, Croydon, CR0 4YY

Distributed in the USA exclusively by Palgrave Macmillan,
a division of St Martin's Press, LLC, 175 Fifth Avenue, New York, NY 10010, USA

All rights reserved. No part of this publication may be reproduced, stored in a
retrieval system or transmitted in any form or by any means, electronic, mechanical,
photocopying or otherwise, without the prior permission of Zed Books Ltd.

A catalogue record for this book is available from the British Library
Library of Congress Cataloging in Publication Data available

ISBN 978 1 78032 003 8 hb
ISBN 978 1 78032 002 1 pb

Contents

About the Contributors   vii

Introduction: The Politics of Liberal Peace   1
Susanna Campbell, David Chandler and Meera Sabaratnam

PART I   Introducing the Debate

1 The Liberal Peace? An Intellectual History of International Conflict Management, 1990–2010   13
  Meera Sabaratnam

2 Critiques of Liberal Peace   31
  Roland Paris

PART II   Not Such a 'Liberal' Peace? Rethinking Intervention

3 The Effects of Peacebuilding: Sovereignty, Patronage and Power   55
  Ole Jacob Sending

4 The Liberal Peace: A Tough Sell?   69
  Christoph Zürcher

5 Routine Learning? How Peacebuilding Organisations Prevent
   Liberal Peace   89
   Susanna Campbell

6 Promoting Women's Rights in Afghanistan: The Ambiguous
   Footprint of the West   106
   **Torunn Wimpelmann Chaudhary, Orzala Ashraf Nemat
   and Astri Suhrke**

7 Neither Liberal nor Peaceful? Practices of 'Global Justice' by
   the ICC   121
   Adam Branch

8 Civil Society beyond the Liberal Peace and its Critique   138
   Thania Paffenholz

PART III Rethinking the Critique: What Next?

9 Alternatives to Liberal Peace?   159
   Roland Paris

10 The Uncritical Critique of 'Liberal Peace'   174
   David Chandler

11 A Reality Check for the Critique of the Liberal Peace   191
   Shahar Hameiri

12 Hybrid Peace: How Does Hybrid Peace Come About?   209
   Roger Mac Ginty

13 Resistance and the Post-Liberal Peace   226
   Oliver P. Richmond

14 Situated Critiques of Intervention: Mozambique and the
   Diverse Politics of Response   245
   Meera Sabaratnam

   Index   265

About the Contributors

Orzala Ashraf Nemat is a PhD candidate at the School of Oriental and African Studies, University of London, and a prominent civil society activist. Her research focus is on local governance and the understanding of power dynamics in the Afghan context. Orzala is the founder and executive director of Humanitarian Assistance for the Women and Children of Afghanistan (1999–2007). She has served on the board of directors of the Afghan Women's Network and other human rights networks in Afghanistan.

Adam Branch is Assistant Professor of political science at San Diego State University and Research Associate at the Makerere Institute of Social Research, Kampala, Uganda. His work examines the politics of humanitarian and human rights intervention into episodes of political violence in Africa. He is the author of *Displacing Human Rights: War and Intervention in Northern Uganda* (2011).

Torunn Wimpelmann Chaudhary is a PhD candidate at the School of Oriental and African Studies, University of London, and a researcher at the Chr. Michelsen Institute. Her current focus is the intersections between gender, violence and political and legal orders in contemporary Afghanistan.

Shahar Hameiri is Australian Research Council Postdoctoral Fellow and Research Fellow, Asia Research Centre, Murdoch University. He has written extensively on issues of statebuilding, non-traditional security, risk and risk management, regional governance, and Australian development and security policy, including *Regulating Statehood* (2010).

Roger Mac Ginty is Reader at the School of International Relations and Centre for Peace and Conflict Studies, St Andrews University. His recent publications include *Conflict and Development* (2009) and *No War, No Peace: The*

Rejuvenation of Stalled Peace Processes and Peace Accords (2006/2008). He has conducted field research in Bosnia, Croatia, Northern Ireland, Jordan, Sri Lanka, Lebanon and New Zealand.

Thania Paffenholz is a Lecturer on peace, conflict and development at the Graduate Institute of International Relations and Development, Geneva. Her recent books include *Civil Society and Peacebuilding* (2010) and *Aid for Peace* (2007). She is also a trained mediator and facilitator, and has participated in several UN missions, as well as being an advisor to different national and international organisations.

Roland Paris is University Research Chair in International Security and Governance and director of the Centre for International Policy Studies at the University of Ottawa. His book *At War's End: Building Peace After Civil Conflict* (2004) won the Grawemeyer Award for Ideas Improving Global Order as well as the ISA's prize for best book on multilateralism.

Oliver P. Richmond is Professor of Peace and Conflict Studies and Director of the Centre for Peace and Conflict Relations at the School of International Relations, St Andrews University. His recent books include *Peace in International Relations* (2008), *The Transformation of Peace* (2005/7) and *Liberal Peace Transitions: Between Statebuilding and Peacebuilding* (2009/2011).

Ole Jacob Sending is Senior Research Fellow at the Norwegian Institute of International Affairs. His research focuses on peacebuilding, global governance and the functioning of international organisations, and on the power of experts in international policymaking. He is the co-author of *Governing the Global Polity* (2010).

Astri Suhrke is a Senior Researcher at the Chr. Michelsen Institute. She has worked on the social, political and humanitarian consequences of violent conflict, and strategies of response. She is currently working on strategies of post-war reconstruction and statebuilding, with particular reference to Afghanistan. Her most recent books are *Roads to Reconciliation* (2005), *Eroding Local Capacity: International Humanitarian Action in Africa* (2003), and *The Path of a Genocide: The Rwanda Crisis from Uganda to Zaire* (1999).

Christoph Zürcher is Professor at the Graduate School of Public and International Affairs, University of Ottawa. His research and teaching interests include conflict research, methods of conflict research, statebuilding and intervention, international governance and development. He is author of *The Post-Soviet Wars: Rebellion, Ethnic Conflict and Nationhood in the Post-Soviet Era* (2007).

Introduction:
The Politics of Liberal Peace

Susanna Campbell, David Chandler and Meera Sabaratnam

With the end of the Cold War, it appeared that a new 'liberal' epoch of international relations had emerged, based on a consensus that democracy, the rule of law and market economics would create sustainable peace in post-conflict and transitional states and societies, and in the larger international order that they were a part of. But in the wake of the failure of international efforts to create liberal governments through the peace operations of the 1990s (i.e. in the Former Yugoslavia, Timor-Leste, Sierra Leone, Haiti, Côte d'Ivoire, Kosovo, DR Congo and Burundi, among others) and the most recent high-profile failures (i.e. in Iraq and Afghanistan), sustained debate has emerged in both academic and policy circles around the value and validity of the 'liberal peace' approach to international intervention (see, for example, PRIO 2010; Mac Ginty and Richmond 2009; Newman et al. 2010; Tadjbakhsh 2011). This debate has often been polarised between the 'critical voices', who reject the premise that 'liberal peace' can or should be created through intervention, and the 'problem solvers', who study the faults of current peacebuilding and statebuilding efforts, but do not necessarily question their inherent value. This book advances our understanding of peacebuilding intervention beyond this unhelpful dichotomy by assembling chapters that present empirical research that investigates the degree to which the liberal peace is, in fact, imposed on post-conflict and transitional states and societies, and enters into dialogue with authors who suggest that we need to transcend conceptually the 'liberal peace' categorisation in order to develop more nuanced and empirically informed critical approaches. Through adding a richer and more nuanced range of investigations, this collection is designed to give the reader a comprehensive framing of the ways in which liberal peace has been understood in relation to interventions at the same time as it presents new frameworks for reconceptualising the liberal peace problematic.

The scholarly debate about international peacebuilding and statebuilding has increasingly become dominated by critical voices, in fact, so much so, that it is not difficult to find edited collections entirely devoted to critical frameworks and approaches to liberal peace, all varieties on the theme of problematising the alleged imposition of liberal forms upon the non-liberal or a-liberal Other. In one such collection, Tadjbakhsh and Richmond (2011, 232–3) argue that the critical approaches are so diverse that they can usefully be broken down into a typology consisting of at least five key types: communitarian critiques – problematising liberal assumptions of universal values; social constructivist critiques – arguing that liberal peace approaches are too technical and depoliticised, ignoring the role of values and identity; critical international theory approaches – highlighting the hegemonic power relations and interests involved in international interventionist missions; post-modern frameworks – which deconstruct the liberal assumptions of universalising progress towards a single form of modernity, the technocratic frameworks of liberal rationality, and the inscriptions of hegemonic forms of sovereignty; and post-colonial critiques – which challenge the divisions between the global and the local, focus on local context, and highlight the hybrid nature and outcomes of interventionist practices. Whilst it is a useful exposition of the diversity and richness of critical positions united around the liberal peace problematic, the current framing of the debate does not allow for an interrogation of the problematic itself, despite pointing to its many interpretations. This volume seeks to develop such an interrogation through prising apart the fictions and realities of intervention.

In structuring this volume, we include authors who are articulate representatives of the most critical approaches (see, for example, the pieces by Oliver Richmond and Roger Mac Ginty). These critics have a shared understanding of liberal peace policy practices, which they see as represented in a highly polarised international sphere, divided between liberal interveners (with liberal agendas) and non-liberal and a-liberal recipients (who do not share or resist these forms of alien imposition). Once this dichotomy is in place, they critically deconstruct it to show the hybrid and complex nature of peace operations and to suggest that policy makers should respond to this diversity of needs and interests by being more local or context-dependent, giving more than lip service to ideas of local participation and 'ownership'.

Also included in this collection are authors who claim that this critical framing of the problem of 'liberal peace' can be seen to have reached an impasse, despite the fact that the critique of liberal peace is now central to so many authors working across different perspectives. Roland Paris suggests that this impasse has been reached because the debate on 'liberal peace' has increasingly departed from the study of international intervention itself. It often seems that the critique has a life of its own, only vaguely related to the analysis of policy practices and implementation and seemingly happy to squeeze every problem of peacebuilding and statebuilding into the framework of the critique of the liberal character of interventions.

We bring these authors together in discussion with a range of positions that are much more sceptical about the assumptions underlying the 'liberal peace' debate itself. These include empirically driven chapters which suggest that the shared starting point – that international intervention can be adequately described as a liberal project of universalising transformation – is in need of critical re-examination. For example, Christoph Zürcher finds that liberal democracies cannot be created unless the local elites desire their creation, therefore challenging the critics' assumption that liberalism can be imported in a non-consensual way. In her chapter, Campbell supports Zürcher's finding that the imposition of liberal peace is not feasible, arguing that because of sticky bureaucratic routines and path dependency, intervening international organisations, international non-governmental organisations and bilateral donors are most often incapable of imposing significant change on dynamic post-conflict institutions. Analyses of Afghanistan (in Chaudhary, Ashraf and Suhrke's chapter) and Uganda (in the chapter by Branch) suggest a much deeper ambiguity at the heart of intervention politics, arguing that the desire for control and influence is incompatible with the liberal policy aims. In demonstrating the vast gulf between the ambitions and rationales for intervention on the one hand and the ultimate effect of intervention on the other, these analyses beg the question of whether it is useful to characterise these missions as if they were ideologically coherent.

This collection also assembles authors who suggest that 'hyper-critical' approaches have become dominant because the focus on 'liberal peace' has shifted from empirical analyses of interventions to debate over the imputed 'liberalism' of intervening actors (see the chapters by Chandler, Hameiri and Sending). The study of post-conflict interventions, in this reading, has been displaced by, or risks becoming a vehicle for, epistemological critiques that are less concerned with the analysis of external intervention than with problematising or deconstructing the 'liberal' assumptions of Western modernity. It would appear that the understanding and assessments of peacebuilding and statebuilding have become a field through which a rather different debate has arisen. This is a debate around the nature of liberalism itself and the ways in which liberal universal assumptions – of progress, of rationality, of instrumentality, of the understanding of humanity itself – should or could be renegotiated in a globalised, post-colonial or post-political world.

In an academic and policy context, where the dominant framing of the problems of intervention has become that of the critique of the 'liberalism' of the interveners, those authors who are more cautiously sympathetic to the goals of liberal peace approaches suggest that even the staunchest or most 'hyper-critical' of critics (see Roland Paris's chapters, 'Critiques of Liberal Peace' and

'Alternatives to Liberal Peace?'), in fact, share the assumptions of liberalism. As a result, the critique of the 'liberal peace' is misplaced and counterproductive. This defence of liberal peace has elicited clear responses from those theorists who are more critical, enabling them to articulate their distance from a liberal framework by arguing that liberalism could only, in fact, 'be saved' if it were to 'reinvent itself as a non-universalising political idea which preserves the traditional liberal value of human solidarity without undermining cultural diversity' (Tadjbakhsh and Richmond 2011, 237). Until such time, however, 'it is the hope of critical thinkers that bringing in context, the local and the everyday, will eventually take the "liberal" out of liberal peace' (ibid., 237).

It appears that for some authors (see Richmond, 'Resistance and the Post-Liberal Peace') the critique of liberal peace is the starting point for developing post-liberal frameworks of international intervention. Interventions which seek to articulate ways in which the recognition of difference can be the key to creating sustainable peace: 'Treating the a-liberal populations with dignity, without trying to render them liberal, starts with recognising their equal worth, even if they may be needy of interventions to end violence and restore peace' (ibid., 238). Here, it is respect for the 'Other' that should guide international intervention. This respect includes the reluctance to impose universal models onto these societies or develop external goals.

While some authors suggest that this critical and emancipatory approach is a radical challenge to power and policy-making, other authors suggest that privileging difference over universality is not inherently emancipatory or transformative. As Meera Sabaratnam indicates, analysing the concrete politics of critique in sites of intervention, rather than through the necessarily generic and reductionist critique of liberal peace, can be a better way of engaging the problem of domination, if that is its principal objective.

Once the *critical* nature of the critics of liberal peace is a subject of reflection, it appears that, in the debate over 'liberal peace', surprisingly little is at stake with regard to peacebuilding and statebuilding policy and practice. Nonetheless, the intellectual heat generated over the critique and defence of 'liberal peace' conceals a large area of political consensus. First, both the authors who are more sympathetic to the liberal peace and those who advocate a post-liberal or hybrid peace emphasise the binary division of the world into, on the one hand, a set of liberal actors with problem-solving agency and interventionist capacities and, on the other, a set of non- or a-liberal actors in post-conflict or transitional countries who are seen to provide the problem in need of resolution and are increasingly viewed as responsible for this resolution. Second, both advocates and opponents of the 'liberal peace' view liberal universalist assumptions as at the heart of the problem of post-conflict peacebuilding and share a desire to alter these assumptions and become more context-sensitive. Third, in many cases, both advocates and opponents of 'liberal peace' seek to support and facilitate international intervention in the cause of peace- or statebuilding. Both argue that interventionist policies are *necessary*, regardless of the fine-grained distinctions in how such interventions should be conducted to overcome the universalising liberal assumptions of how polities, societies and economies operate. The 'liberal peace' problematic thereby poses the risk of constraining and limiting critical political engagement with the policies and practices of international intervention, allowing critical theorists to operate within dominant policy frameworks, rather than *critiquing* these frameworks.

This collection seeks to put the politics back into the discussion of 'liberal peace' by unpacking the current state of the debate and suggesting alternative approaches beyond the original critique of liberal peace. To do so, it examines the validity of the critiques of contemporary peacebuilding and statebuilding practices through several in-depth case studies. It investigates the underlying theoretical assumptions of liberal peacebuilding and statebuilding, further critiquing the most fundamental of these assumptions. It also provides new theoretical frameworks through which to examine current peacebuilding and statebuilding interventions. The chapters are written by some of the most prominent scholars in the liberal peace and peacebuilding effectiveness debate, in addition to several new scholars who are making cutting-edge contributions to this rapidly growing interdisciplinary field of study.

Chapter Breakdown

The book is organised in three sections. The chapters in the first section introduce the volume's theme through a historical account of the liberal peace critique and an influential account of the impasse. The second section presents findings from field research, which investigate the relevance of the critique to current peacebuilding and statebuilding interventions. The chapters in the third section revisit the liberal peace debate in the light of case study findings and outline new theoretical frameworks that advance the discussion beyond the initial dichotomous debate between liberal peace's critics and proponents.

Part I of the book – *Introducing the Debate* – sets the stage for the volume by situating the historical and contemporary debates on the liberal peace. In the first chapter, Meera Sabaratnam narrates an intellectual history of the changes in international conflict management over the last twenty years, putting both the changes and the academic critiques of these developments into the context of historical events. She concludes that the idea of 'peacebuilding' appears to be disappearing altogether, as policy actors seek to focus on states and regional security. Roland Paris then offers a critical analysis of the impasse in the discussion of liberal peace, highlighting the shortcomings of some of the most influential critiques, arguing that critics have mischaracterised and confused various other aspects of Western intervention with the practices and objectives of liberal peacebuilding.

Part II – *Not Such a 'Liberal' Peace? Rethinking Intervention* – brings together a wide range of authors whose work suggests that the 'liberal peace' framework for post-conflict environments, understood as externally driven liberal reform, may be overly narrow or misleading in focus. Three of the chapters point to the limited ability of external actors to promote reform, and three others show that there may be perverse and contradictory outcomes despite supposedly liberal intentions.

In his chapter, Ole Jacob Sending argues that both 'critical' and 'problem-solving' approaches to intervention have systematically failed to understand or acknowledge the extant power and agency of actors within the society in determining the outcomes of intervention. In this sense, they miss the actual social infrastructure of power and sovereignty that largely shape the effects of peacebuilding activity. Sending suggests that state-society relations should be the principal focus for understanding post-war interventions. Relatedly, Christoph Zürcher argues through different case studies that the emergence of liberal democracy in post-war environments only occurs where local elites demand that these institutions be created. Accordingly, peacebuilders have little influence on the degree of liberal democracy achieved in a post-conflict or transitional country, in spite of their assumptions or otherwise. The primary lesson for peacebuilders is that they must reduce their liberal ambitions, and focus instead on achieving the best possible outcome from the bargains that they make with local elites. Susanna Campbell's chapter deepens the line of argument that intervening organisations cannot determine outcomes in post-conflict environments. These organisations lack the learning or adaptive capacity necessary to force significant behaviour or institutional change on complex and dynamic transitional environments. Instead, they must negotiate and bargain with the local and national actors who are the fundamental determinants of the liberal outcomes that they claim to pursue.

These and other limitations to the behaviour of external actors in transformative intervention projects result in situations which cannot really be described as liberal. In their chapter, Torunn Wimpelmann Chaudary, Orzala Ashraf Nemat and Astri Suhrke show through an analysis of legal reforms in Afghanistan that the presence of interveners has resulted in seemingly contradictory laws that both uphold and deeply limit women's rights. The authors show that international actors working on women's rights lack coherent action, have little political impact and fail to develop an overarching objective to achieve this most symbolically important of liberal values. They describe the footprint of the West as deeply ambiguous, and in so doing argue that liberal peacebuilding is not inherently progressive. In a pointed analysis, Adam Branch claims that the attempt to institutionalise international law in conflict and post-conflict environments through the activities of the ICC is highly selective and politicised. In examining the contribution of the ICC to the peace processes in Uganda, the chapter makes the case that this selective legal disciplining of the Lord's Resistance Army has rendered the political conflict harder to address, by framing it as part of a campaign for global justice and the institutionalisation of liberal norms. Indeed, he argues that this framing itself inhibits rather than progresses this agenda in any meaningful sense. Thania Paffenholz's chapter also problematises the 'global' lens that proponents and critics of the liberal peace use in their analysis of 'civil society' support. She argues, through a functional analysis of the different roles played by civil society organisations, that they are highly diverse, with no inherently 'good' agenda. Critics and supporters have tended to engage only with urban elite NGOs; however, more attention needs to be paid to the vulnerable and excluded parts of society who are often most affected by the conflict, but currently left out of the 'liberal peace' debate.

In Part III – *Rethinking the Critique: What Next?* – we introduce perspectives that recognise the contributions of the liberal peace debate but seek to get beyond the 'liberal peace' as a basic framework for analysing intervention and answering some of the questions. In doing so we aim to present new research agendas for approaching intervention, based on alternative readings of the political.

Roland Paris opens this section with a piece arguing that we need to go beyond the liberal peace debate as, to date, the critics of liberal peace have not been able to offer alternatives to liberal frameworks that help us to understand the need for intervention or the problems to be addressed. He concludes that the limited alternatives presented by the critics suggest that, despite its well highlighted shortcomings, in a broad sense there is no viable or attractive alternative to the liberal peace. David Chandler's chapter argues that the 'liberal peace' debate has become less about the questions that emerge from experiences of intervention than a critical validation of interveners' own fictions, in which they are agents of a liberal world order. In this, both power-based and ideas-based critiques of the liberal peace end up arguing in different ways that the problem encountered by the liberal peace is the existence of a non-liberal Other, which is either culturally or politically not amenable to liberal transformations. What is lacking is a conception of the political subject that might enable a more critical approach to the limiting statebuilding transformations that interventions do in fact effect. Shahar Hameiri's chapter extends this focus on the actual impact of interventions. He argues that debates on the liberal peace have focused on the absence of liberal transformations rather than the emergence of other constellations of power. Through analysing the case of Cambodia, he demonstrates the critical purchase of seeing intervention as establishing a multi-level regime of regulatory governance. This framework offers an understanding of the dynamic between interventionist and elite political actors, as well as an understanding of the social forces that bind them.

In his discussion of the hybrid peace, Roger Mac Ginty offers a clear account of how this framing changes the focus in analyses of intervention. He argues that an engagement with hybridity allows researchers to acknowledge and explore the interstices of co-operation as well as the differences that our normal categorisations paper over. Through identifying four different sites of interaction with the liberal peace, the chapter offers a framework for analysis that highlights the connections rather than the divisions between interveners and domestic agents. Oliver Richmond's chapter suggests that the alternative to the liberal peace should be the 'post-liberal peace' which is characterised by a recognition and respect for difference. He argues that this is a hybrid of liberal and local modes of being which focuses on the everyday as a site of politics and struggle. This involves the re-negotiation of the liberal peace in line with the traditional and customary to create a post-liberal peace. Meera Sabaratnam's chapter, by contrast, looks at the question of the liberal peace through the lens of anti-colonial critiques in the twentieth century. She argues that these radical and activist critiques of power pointed out deprivation, hypocrisies and inconsistencies in the concrete practices of empire through subverting and redeploying supposed universals rather than highlighting cultural difference as the root of failure. Through engaging with the politics of critique in Mozambique, she argues that this is a more useful and progressive frame for analysing intervention than one which turns on trying to manage the difference between the liberal and the local.

Conclusion

The editors of this collection have intentionally decided not to provide a concluding chapter. It is to be hoped that the different positions and perspectives gathered here will enable the reader to undertake their own reflections upon the material. The purpose of the collection is to bring together a range of authors engaged in the analysis of 'liberal peace' framings of international intervention. Out intention was to co-ordinate this debate, not to force the authors to speak with one voice or to assimilate their views. We have organised the collection in a way which makes the different perspectives accessible and enables the reader, if they so choose, to follow the chapters as if a debate were being held in front of them.

Bibliography

Mac Ginty, R. and O. P. Richmond (eds) (2009) *The Liberal Peace and Post-War Reconstruction: Myth or Reality?*, London: Routledge.
Newman, E., R. Paris and O. P. Richmond (2010) *New Perspectives on Liberal Peacebuilding*, New York: United Nations University Press.
PRIO (2010) Liberal Peace and the Ethics of Peacebuilding, Peace Research Institute Oslo project, http://www.prio.no/Research-and-Publications/Project/?oid=64922.
Tadjbakhsh, S. (ed.) (2011) *Rethinking the Liberal Peace: External Models and Local Alternatives*, London: Routledge.
Tadjbakhsh, S. and O. P. Richmond (2011) 'Conclusion: Typologies and Modifications Proposed by Critical Approaches', in S. Tadjbakhsh (ed.) *Rethinking the Liberal Peace: External Models and Local Alternatives*, London: Routledge.

PART I

Introducing the Debate

I

The Liberal Peace? An Intellectual History of International Conflict Management, 1990–2010

Meera Sabaratnam

In this volume, the term 'the liberal peace' is understood as the dominant critical intellectual framework currently applied to post-Cold War policies and practices of post-conflict intervention. However, as Heathershaw observes, its use within analysis has sometimes tended, misleadingly, to claim that the liberal peace has had only a singular logic or set of assumptions (2008a: 603), gradations of this logic notwithstanding. Both he and Call and Cousens (2008) note that different ideas are at work in the movements between peacebuilding and statebuilding as modes of conflict management. This chapter gives an alternative historical overview of these developments and locates the academic critiques in the context of these changes, giving a sense in which academic critique and political practice have co-evolved. These shifts and expansions reflect something rather more complex, and perhaps more opaque, than a hardening or deepening of a *liberal* logic in intervention – rather they reveal a reflexive anxiety about inadequacy of this logic to address seemingly intractable challenges of conflict, insecurity and underdevelopment. By tracking the recent evolution of these discourses and the critiques of the paradigm, this chapter sets the stage for the other contributions to the volume which interrogate and broaden empirically and conceptually the problem of 'the liberal peace'.

The chapter begins through exploring the intellectual and political climate of the early 1990s and the founding principles of 'peacebuilding' as articulated by the UN. It then shows how these were lost almost immediately in the mid-1990s, both to unfolding global events and to new discourses about failing and collapsed states. This had important linkages with changing discourses in other aspects of institutional intervention, including the policy turn within the international financial institutions towards the question of 'governance'. Connected to a resurgent interest in 'grassroots' and 'bottom-up' interventions, however, therapeutic discourses and practices dealing with trauma, healing and reconciliation became a central element of peacebuilding. At this time an increasingly broad set of actors, including humanitarian and transitional justice agencies, became involved. In the last ten years, however, renewed interest in the question of state fragility and the principles of statebuilding has become pervasive not just in responses to conflict but the governance of the global South more generally. In conclusion the chapter offers some reflections on the current historical juncture and how this might shape future understandings of conflict management.

UN Peacebuilding, the Early Years: From Social Justice to State Collapse

In the early days of the practice, third-party post-war interventions were seen as the basic preserve of the UN. The end of the Cold War was a watershed moment for the organisation, and in particular for its Department of Peacekeeping Operations (DPKO). Having been paralysed from all but minimal activity due to the exercise of Security Council vetoes, it found itself launching fourteen new operational missions between 1988 and 1992, compared to none in the previous ten years (DPKO 2010a). Whilst some of these operations followed the logic of traditional peacekeeping – mainly ceasefire monitoring, others began to foreshadow the more comprehensive, multidimensional and transformative operations that would become the hallmark of post-conflict peacebuilding. Early apparent successes in Nicaragua (1990) and Namibia (1990), involving relatively light-touch and well-defined missions in already-post-conflict environments, emboldened the organisation to take a more proactive stance in shaping the nature of the peace to come, through shepherding elections and demobilisation.

It was in this context that Boutros-Ghali's groundbreaking 1992 *Agenda for Peace* statement was delivered. Taken widely as the foundational text for the policy of 'post-conflict peacebuilding', it defined it as 'action to identify and support structures which will tend to consolidate peace and advance a sense of confidence and well-being among people' (1992: 32). In this text could clearly be seen an understanding of conflict that was based on structural violence and social grievance as the generative causes, with economic development and political freedom intended as the appropriate remedies:

Our aims must be ...
– To stand ready to assist in peace-building in its differing contexts: rebuilding the institutions and infrastructures of nations torn by civil war and strife; and building bonds of peaceful mutual benefit among nations formerly at war;

– And in the largest sense, *to address the deepest causes of conflict: economic despair, social injustice and political oppression.* (Agenda for Peace, 1992, emphasis added)

Indeed, in defining the term 'peacebuilding', the *Agenda for Peace* was about re-envisioning a role for the UN as a progressive, autonomous agent of peace, development and global justice after years of marginalisation. This theme is reinforced in the text itself through an explicit connection of the peace agenda to the contemporaneous Rio Summit and the proposed World Forum for Social Development. Establishing 'peacebuilding' as a defined and distinctive activity, grounded in the apparently universal aspiration of solving conflict, was intended, perhaps successfully in the short term, to channel growing Western attention towards these issues into a blossoming multilateral progressive consensus for peacemaking, development and social justice.

However, this new mandate became almost immediately besieged by events which demonstrated the split between its transformative ambitions and the shape of political events. Even as Boutros-Ghali gave his speech in June 1992, the violence in Bosnia was accelerating, and five months later Savimbi would defect from the UN's carefully chaperoned electoral process in Angola, prompting extensive caution and delay in the Mozambique mission. In 1993, UN troops and humanitarian workers would be ambushed in Somalia, leading to the re-deployment of US troops and the Black Hawk Down incident, resulting in the US withdrawal and little appetite to involve itself in international peacemaking. The tragic and egregious failures of the UN Assistance Mission for Rwanda in early 1994 seemed to underscore the gulf between Boutros-Ghali's projections for building peace and the mood of the contributing states, whilst the massacre at Srebenica in 1995 seemed to call into question the point of UN peacekeeping altogether. In particular, cracks were beginning to show between the expanded mandate for peacekeeping forces and their attempts to deliver humanitarian and political projects, which were clearly limited.

These peacekeeping failures had a knock-on effect on the ideas governing the expansion of peacebuilding, as the implications of a more ambitious peace operations agenda became clearer. Strangely, however, this was not a pull-back from the extended agenda, but a ramping-up of activity, ambition and response. More actors were involved, and asked to undertake a wider range of tasks. As reflected in the rather less exuberant *Supplement to the Agenda for Peace* (Boutros-Ghali, 1995), failures were rationalised through the perception that the nature of conflict was changing, from interstate to intrastate, and into chaotic, unmanageable situations where state institutions had collapsed:

Another feature of such conflicts is the collapse of state institutions, especially the police and judiciary, with resulting paralysis of governance, a breakdown of law and order, and general banditry and chaos. Not only are the functions of government suspended, its assets are destroyed or looted and experienced officials are killed or flee the country. This is rarely the case in inter-state wars. *It means that international intervention must extend beyond military and humanitarian tasks and must include the promotion of national reconciliation and the re-establishment of effective government.* (1995: section 13, emphasis added)

Nonetheless, Boutros-Ghali attempted to maintain and protect a traditional UN discourse that these were necessary precursors to addressing the injustices that underlay conflict:

As I pointed out in 'An Agenda for Development' (A/48/935), *only sustained efforts to resolve underlying socio-economic, cultural and humanitarian problems can place an achieved peace on a durable foundation.* (1995: section 22, emphasis added)

As such, the ideological and political foundations for an altogether more comprehensive, wide-ranging and co-ordinated effort at the transformation of state and society through multilateral multi-dimensional peace operations were being laid, even at this early stage, in the political arena. What we see in the *Supplement* is Boutros-Ghali trying to maintain the UN vision whilst accepting this more pessimistic account of conflict dynamics, which produces the idea that intervention has been insufficient rather than overambitious. This movement towards a comprehensive reform agenda in post-conflict societies was noted at an early stage by academic commentators, who pointed out its potentially radical implications (Bertram 1995).

Managing Global Chaos? The Emergence of a Field

Simultaneously with this new departure in UN thinking, the silos that that had been established in academia between 'peace studies' and 'security studies' through the 1970s and 1980s had begun to break down. In particular, peace studies was rescued from its political obscurity and engaged in the service of this new international agenda for peace. In particular, theories of human need (Burton 1987) and social grievances (Azar 1986) informed these early, Third World-friendly readings of conflict held by multilateral organisations. These readings of conflict held out the promise of peaceful resolution of conflict along politically emancipatory lines. Importantly, they corresponded with the Democracy and Development Agendas of the UN that underpinned the *Agenda for Peace,* and provided a scholarly rationale for how and why peace*building*, envisaged as progressive social transformation, was necessary.

New avenues of research were facilitated by this more expansive peacebuilding programme, which argued for broadening the intervention agenda for a more comprehensive peace programme. Academic debates about conflict prevention and early warning (Lund 1996), the management of spoilers (Stedman 1997), mediation processes (Touval and Zartman 1985), the involvement of humanitarian actors (Prendergast 1996) and the importance of human rights underpinned the much wider and deeper role peacebuilding practices were beginning to assume around conflict. Slowly, this set of concerns began to develop independent momentum as an industry, with various funding streams and research streams coalescing around this agenda. For example, large collaborations such as the UNRISD War-Torn Societies Project (1994–1998) and the Carnegie Commission on Preventing Deadly Conflict (1994–1999) were tasked with developing and bringing together work on conflict prevention and resolutions specifically to address what was seen as the worrying increasing prevalence of intrastate conflict.

The substance of the first United States Institute of Peace collected volume *Managing Global Chaos* (Crocker et al. 1996) gives us an interesting snapshot of the moment and captures some of the core intellectual trends which supported this expansion of the notion of peacebuilding, as understood by the peace studies community. The volume itself is divided into sections on the sources of conflict, with prominence given both to 'structural' explanations and social-psychological explanations, a large second section on traditional means of diplomacy, collective security, peacekeeping and humanitarian intervention, a sizeable third section on conflict management via mediation, conflict prevention and problem-solving, and a final, briefer section on the consolidation of peace and the need for custodianship of the post-settlement phase. The drawing together of these questions in a single textbook volume announced assertively the presence of a coherent, professional and focused field of conflict analysis and peace-based interventions, and strongly echoed the political climate in which it was believed that improving knowledge of conflict and peace processes would enable a willing international community to resolve these problems. At the time, critique of the paradigm, such as it existed, was highly focused on the technical questions of sequencing and speed, albeit with some consciousness of its politics.

However, the optimism of these approaches in foreign policy circles was also tested by the events of the 1990s, even as the field began to cohere. The intellectual and policy climate in Washington on conflict and post-conflict situations grew darker, beginning to reflect a growing perception of global collapse and chaos. A parallel worldview began to emerge in this period, particularly from the security community during and after the problems of Somalia and Rwanda, in which it was argued that the UN apparatus was ill-equipped to deal with conflict. Publications in this vein included the influential and provocative article on 'Saving Failed States' in (1992) *Foreign Policy* by ex-US Government advisers Helman and Ratner, Robert Kaplan's 'The Coming Anarchy' (1994) and Zartman's (1995) edited *Collapsed States: The Disintegration and Restoration of Legitimate Authority*. Although arguing in different modes, they collectively signalled a belief in a world that was, outside the West, subject to deep disorder and spinning further adrift from the state authority and order of the Cold War era. These states were seen as no longer 'transitioning' but 'failed' or 'failing', presenting a threat to regional and global security.

Although ostensibly coming from different places, these different intellectual traditions – peace studies and security studies respectively – nonetheless pushed international multilateral policy on conflict in a more or less consistent direction: on the basis of superior knowledge, deeper involvement, more commitment and the use of force where necessary, the international community could and should undertake more comprehensive and extensive interventions to secure global peace. This broad consensus became a basic truism of what came to be understood in later years as 'the liberal peace' by its critics.

Institutionalisation: The Turn to Governance, Responsibility and Transitional Administration

Whilst the new preoccupations with peacebuilding and state failure were beginning to animate the peace and security intellectual communities during the 1990s, the economic development community was also beginning to move in a similar direction. As Williams and Young (1994) note, in the early 1990s the international financial institutions, and particularly the World Bank, became quickly and deeply interested in questions of 'good governance', which it characterised as pertaining to the technical functional requirements of modern statehood, moving the institution towards a much more maximalist interpretation of its mandates for promoting 'efficiency'. This allowed it, in the framework of articles forbidding involvement in non-economic affairs, to become involved in legal reforms, reforms within the state, the promotion of civil society and so on. These were significant departures in terms of both the ideas and practices of the Bank that underscored the end of an uncontrolled market orthodoxy and a shift towards a more regulatory approach. This shift precipitated a rapid expansion of sectoral activities and a much deeper embedding in the governments of recipient states, such that they became part of the permanent state apparatus itself (Harrison 2004).

There were clear parallels between the expansion of this agenda and the expansion of the peace and security agendas, which connected the phenomena of conflict and underdevelopment to the fact that they had their roots in a malfunctioning political society in need of detailed and externally driven reform. Indeed, in practice these structures of external governance were deeply connected at the level of national missions, with powerful co-ordination mechanisms being established, such as the International Committee for the Reconstruction of Cambodia, which brought together the peacekeeping mission structures with the international financial institutions and other donor governments' agencies (DPKO 2010b). Although in theory these mechanisms were subordinate to national governments, in practice they were often the centre of political decision-making in the post-war periods (Harrison 2004).

Connected with this practical merger between conflict management and economic reform was also the growth of international political discourses about sovereignty as responsibility (see Deng 1996), which sought to provide a legal-political orientation for the increasingly interventionist climate. A symptom of this new discourse was the establishment of the International Commission on Intervention and State Sovereignty (ICISS). Informed by the need for 'no more Rwandas' as well as the memory of Srebenica, this eminent group of lawyers and experts represented the attempt to find a way to square the problem of the norm of non-intervention with the apparent moral need to intervene (ICISS 2001). As such, the *Responsibility to Protect* aimed to provide a standing basis for humanitarian and other forms of intervention. These conceptual adjustments to the political status of sovereignty followed on from, amongst other events, the rapid growth of the *de facto* role of the Office of the High Representative in Bosnia from 1995, which took on a increasing number of binding governmental powers as part of the Bonn Agreement in 1997, and the establishment of the UN protectorates in Kosovo and East Timor in 1999. The mandates for the presence in Kosovo and East Timor were unprecedented in terms of powers being comprehensively and indefinitely devolved to the UN Special Representative of the Secretary-General until such time as self-government could be established. Yet they were continuous with and perhaps the logical conclusion of the discourses that had been developing over the previous years, both in terms of the primacy of the 'governance' agenda within the peace, security and development institutions and the notion of sovereignty as responsibility.

Turbulent Peace? Reconciliation and Healing in the Wake of Conflict

Whilst the lofty discourses of the duties of liberal internationalism and changing sovereignty norms took place on the stage of international politics (see Blair's Chicago speech, Blair 1999), other themes of trauma, illness and healing informed a parallel and more doveish academic and practitioner discourse towards conflict, which sought a more conciliatory and therapeutic approach to intervention. Indeed, this discourse was also present in the *Supplement*

(Boutros-Ghali 1995), which referred to the potential for peacebuilding for 'healing the wounds after conflict has occurred' (ibid., section 49). This began to inflect the core peacebuilding literature. For example, Krishna Kumar, writing from within the United States Agency for International Development, framed peacebuilding essentially as the political, economic and social 'rehabilitation' to address the needs of 'countries shattered by war' (Kumar 1997: ch. 1), reflecting very much how certain kinds of practitioners saw their role.

The notion of 'rehabilitation' was consistent with the medicalisation of 'war-torn societies' as patients or wards of the international community, essentially incapacitated and unable to manage (Hughes and Pupavac 2005). In these discourses, the international community's presence was also viewed as curative and restorative in the wake of conflict: a position which resonated with the way that NGOs in particular had come to see their expanded presence in the global South. This conceptualised peacebuilding as being essentially continuous with humanitarian assistance, administered to the needy out of an ethic of care and based on a Burtonian framework of human needs (Tschirgi 2004). This then became compatible with the tradition whereby peacebuilding, alongside humanitarian assistance and other forms of care work, had roots in a sense of practical moral vocation as well as, or perhaps instead of, a political intervention. In many senses this was a substantive critique of the geopolitics that had determined Western assistance strategies in the past.

A cognate emphasis on reconciliation and healing also emerged from practitioners such as John Paul Lederach who had come from a Christian humanist background and worked at 'grassroots' levels in Central America. Lederach in particular advocated for a multi-modal and multi-level form of peacebuilding in which all levels of society, comprising the elites, mid-level and grassroots, would engage in different forms of peacebuilding and reconciliation (1997). This kind of rationale was applied by many practitioners to their interpretations of Rwanda's famous *gacaca* trials, which could be seen as a form of community-level healing process (Clark 2007). More generally, these kinds of discourses provided the basis for an increased role for transitional justice and human rights mechanisms under the umbrella notion of 'sustainable peace', which emphasised a need to remake post-conflict social relations and deter future human rights abuses (see ICTJ 2003).

For a brief time this approach was included more prominently in mainstream thinking about conflict management. The second edition of the USIP textbook *Turbulent Peace* (Crocker et al. 2001) amended its last section to reflect this new focus, calling it 'Peacebuilding: From Settlement to Reconciliation', and included pieces from Lederach and others working on the reconciliation and rehabilitation paradigms. Although motivated by a distinctive view of conflict and the needs of post-conflict societies and by ideas of peacebuilding these approaches fit with existing deliberations on conflict management insofar as they tended to validate in a different way a need for third party involvement in post-conflict societies, whilst simultaneously emphasising the need for this to be a 'grassroots' affair. In this vision, third parties play the roles of counsellors or therapists, facilitating a process of self-knowledge, or of advocates in the search for justice. Importantly, this was not received in practice as incompatible with the existing views that third parties should be seen as experts in conflict management, governance and political order. Rather, the emphasis on holism underpinned a diversification of third party approaches and the expansion of opportunities for intervention. In this sense, they worked as a complement to the Blairist interventionism in high politics. If *Managing Global Chaos* was a disciplinary intervention to reinforce the potential of conflict management strategies, *Turbulent Peace* seemed to demonstrate that approaches from different traditions might nonetheless be brought together under the same intellectual and practical umbrella.

Questioning the Liberal Peace: Ideology, Hegemony and (Dys)functions

However, it was not long before more substantial academic critiques of the peacebuilding paradigm emerged from various quarters. One of the most prominent of these was Roland Paris's critique of liberal peacebuilding as being excessively concerned with political and economic liberalisation (1997, 2004). Framed as a response to the 'liberal peace' debate within International Relations around Michael Doyle's work (1983), Paris argued that practices of early liberalisation in post-war environments could be destabilising for divided societies, who required institutionalisation before liberalisation (IBL). This approach seemed to confirm academically the orientation that had already been adopted in practice in Bosnia, Kosovo and East Timor. Paris however also argued that structurally liberal peacebuilding constituted an internationalisation of a particular form of government – free market liberal democracy, albeit one with which he was ultimately comfortable despite some similarities with colonialism (2002, also chapter 3 in this volume). Although the implications of Paris's critique could be seen in earlier discussions of conflict management, such as those of Ball and Halevy (1996), the emphasis on the problems posed by what were identified as its *liberal ideological* groundings also became a touchstone in a different kind of debate on the liberal peace amongst its critics, as we argue in the introduction to this book.

Duffield for example used the term the 'liberal peace' to describe international activity resulting from post-war interventions but did not limit this to a subset of UN missions in the 1990s as Paris had done. Rather, the scope of the critique included the growing inter-relationship at the institutional and practical levels between international regimes of economic governance, increasingly intimate programmes of aid and development, modes of conflict-related intervention and global economic flows (2001). Duffield argued that the liberal peace was not ultimately emancipatory or transformative in ambition or practice: rather it was a regulatory network of governance, the aim of which was to control and stabilise disorder in the global South. The 'liberal peace' as such was a radicalisation of development and in part flowed from the effects of globalisation which had eroded state control. As such, consideration of the 'liberal peace' needed to deal with the broader processes and networks of intervention in which overt interventions were embedded.

The intellectual background to Duffield's critique was the literature on complex emergencies that had become of interest to development, humanitarian and conflict analysis practitioners, the political economy of conflict and new wars (Berdal and Keen 1997; Cliffe and Luckham 1999; Kaldor 1999). This work, emerging from academics working closely in conflict environments, fundamentally challenged the paradigms of conflict that had informed peacebuilding to date, which had argued that continuing violent conflict was the result of socioeconomic grievances (Berdal and Malone 2000). Rather, work focusing on the political economy of war argued in a detailed and empirical way that war was its own alternative system of profit, power and protection (Berdal and Keen 1997; Keen 1998), in which the collapse of states provided the context for new forms of socioeconomic order linked to the global economy. In a related vein, Pugh argued that reconstruction continued to be informed by neoliberal economic models that systematically removed forms of social protection in post-war economies, causing people to engage in illicit economic activity as a means of survival (2002).

Whilst understanding 'the liberal peace' in ways that differed in both conceptual framing and scope, it is noteworthy that both Paris and Duffield located their work in the context of 'globalisation' debates which were highly topical and widespread at that juncture in the political and academic worlds (Held et al. 1999; Giddens 2000). For Paris, globalisation entailed the internationalisation of a particular form of liberal democratic polity that should be more responsibly and strategically managed by the international community, whereas for Duffield it represented the ongoing dismantling of government and politics as formerly understood, giving rise to new forms of regulation. In this sense we can see that this historical-intellectual juncture contributed substantially to the formulation of two influential conceptions of the 'liberal peace', which are understood as different facets of 'globalisation'. Thinking about the critiques in this way brings to the fore the contemporary preoccupations shaping the ideas, and sheds light on what future critiques might raise.

Leashing the Dogs of War! 9/11 and Statebuilding Reloaded

9/11 and the subsequent official securitisation of 'failed states' in the US's National Security Strategy had a definitive effect on the intellectual and political direction of intervention and the globalisation debate. Whereas in the immediate run-up to this period, the conflict management field had taken a turn towards the conciliatory and holistic, in its aftermath there was a comprehensive turn towards the ideas of 'statebuilding' as policy and practice. As shown earlier, concerns about 'failed states' had formed part of academic and institutional conflict management discourses since the mid 1990s and in this sense were not 'new'. What was different in this period was their rapid ascendance to prominence through a clear integration in the policies of the United States in its most interventionist period of recent years.[1] This was further compounded through an apparent expansion of expertise in questions of governance amongst the international financial institutions (IFIs). As such, discussion of 'statebuilding' as an independent object of concern greatly expanded. Although this change initially corresponded with a depiction of the regimes in pre-invasion Baghdad and Kabul as 'failed', it was the experience of suddenly disbanding Iraqi state personnel and watching the ensuing chaos that renewed interest in how to 'fix' failed states.

This new focus on statebuilding and governance was pronounced amongst the policy community, with governmental agencies such as USAID and the UK's Department for International Development (DfID) both issuing new guidelines and frameworks about engaging with 'fragile states' (USAID 2005; DfID 2006) which came to dominate their political activity and funding streams for research. The World Bank adopted 'statebuilding' as one of the principal objectives for the organisation, and also began to fund initiatives that would extend its competence in the area (UNDP 2010). In a move that symbolised the new hierarchy, the OECD began to define good governance and peacebuilding as activities which were to be understood as activities falling under the general umbrella of statebuilding (OECD 2007).

Quite suddenly, the field of conflict management became overwhelmed by rapidly proliferating literature on the question of statebuilding, state failure and its implications for potential interveners (see Rotberg 2003; Fukuyama 2004; Chesterman et al. 2005; Call et al. 2008; Ghani and Lockhart 2008). In this literature, there was a general consensus that 'statebuilding' meant constructing 'effective, legitimate institutions of governance' (Paris and Sisk 2009), though there were disagreements about the meaning of each of these terms, and what constructing them would entail. For example, Rotberg defined governance as 'the effective provision of political goods to citizens' (2007: 85). Such a reading seemed to be at odds with standing definitions used in organisations such as the World Bank, which defined it as 'the traditions and institutions by which authority in a country is exercised' (World Bank 2007). As the statebuilding debate continued, there was also something of a sociological backlash to the co-optation of Weber's definition of the state into a more narrowly defined conception of legitimacy based on liberal democracy (e.g. Schlichte 2005). This was perhaps unsurprising given the ongoing failures of the new regimes in Baghdad and Kabul to win popular support despite the widely touted electoral processes.

Once more this change in intellectual direction in the field was reflected in USIP's compendium on conflict management (Crocker et al. 2007). In its content, this third volume, *Leashing the Dogs of War: Conflict Management in a Divided World*, strongly echoed the turn that had been occurring intellectually and politically regarding the preoccupation with statebuilding as the appropriate response to crises. The last section, entitled 'The Uses and Limits of Governance in Conflict Management' focused on the compromises between democracy, stability and sovereignty in dealing with failed states, and tellingly jettisoned any reference to 'peace' or 'reconciliation'. Indeed, this turn away from 'peace' was a self-conscious one, according to the editors, based on the challenges of a new security environment characterised by 'terrorism, weapons of mass destruction, rogue states and conflict' (2007: 4). In exploring these phenomena as primary drivers of conflict and pushing issues such as political grievances, resource scarcity and economic opportunities further down the list, the volume captured the mood of an intellectual climate that was altogether more focused on the perceived security threats to the West than on the 'resolution' of conflict.

This new framing of conflict management techniques and concerns had a clear knock-on effect for understandings of peacebuilding, where they still existed, which sought to maintain the historic discourse that had framed past actions, whilst attempting to capture evolving understandings of conflict. This can be seen most clearly in the way in which the new UN Peacebuilding Commission (from 2005) framed its missions. Whilst on the one hand this body was the inheritor of the older doctrines of peacebuilding from Boutros-Ghali, its latest orientations show the changes in the intellectual environment. For example, in the strategy document for Burundi, one of its few selected cases for sustained activity, 'good governance' is the first listed priority for peacebuilding, coming above even the maintenance of the ceasefire, and above concern for economic and social reform to address political grievances (UNPBC 2007). As Le Billon notes, concern to fight corruption in particular became mainstreamed in peacebuilding practices following high-profile arguments from the IFIs that linked governance, security and conflict (2008). This was a key move in the concretisation of the new governance agenda and became a hallmark not just of peacebuilding operations but of the developmental agenda more broadly.

Since 2001, the overt re-configuration of mainstream academic and political discourses and practices of conflict management away from peace and reconciliation towards governance and statebuilding has been substantial and systematic, in no small part catalysed by a new security agenda, the substantive political problems faced by the coalition in Iraq and Afghanistan, and changing political discourses about the origins of conflict. In this sense, earlier critical discussions of the security-development merger (e.g. Duffield 2001) proved prescient of the trend which would come into fruition in statebuilding discourses, although they could not have anticipated the urgency with which this would accelerate. Historically speaking though, it is consistent with the trends in conflict management as a changing set of lenses through which international elite actors have sought to diagnose the sources of instability in the South.

The 'Liberal Peace' Debate as Meta-critique

More recent scholarly critiques of the 'liberal peace' have sought to analyses these discursive evolutions under one paradigm, which operate as a kind of meta-critique of contemporary projects of conflict management. As this has evolved, the debate has become increasingly distant from the concerns of the policy discourse. Richmond (2005) for example argued that the 'liberal peace' was a composite of different Enlightenment discourses comprising the victor's peace, the institutional peace, the constitutional peace and the civil peace which had been evolving over the centuries in the liberal European imagination, and found recent expression in the 'peacebuilding consensus'. Incorporated in this general problematic were the principles of the rule of law, constitutional democracy, human rights, neoliberal development and the civil peace, as implemented by an 'alphabet soup' of organisations who delivered 'peace-as-governance'. Building on the critiques of Duffield as well as other forms of critical IR theory, this general formulation became an important touchstone in an increasingly polarised debate (see Paris, this volume), which began to challenge the nature of the 'liberal peace' in a number of different ways (see introduction, this volume). Nonetheless, there was a consensus that the liberal peace represented a single and coherent object of inquiry (Mac Ginty and Richmond 2007) which acted as the point of departure for this discussion.

Yet this meta-critique, which has been stimulating and illuminating in its form and content, generally downplayed the ways in which the composition of conflict management discourses and practices rapidly shifted over time to incorporate a set of changing ontologies, values and methods in a reflexive manner.[2] This itself reflected different priorities and power shifts amongst would-be interveners which is a key underlying condition for these changes. In this sense there has been a growing disconnection between policy debates seeking to refine methods and academic debates centring around the politics of intervention. Whilst interesting debates have emerged about the extent to which practices are really 'liberal' (Chandler, this volume), relatively little attention has been paid to the disappearance of 'peace' from the dominant discourses. Yet this is in some senses the more striking question when thinking about the recent history of conflict management, and in particular when thinking about the substantive role that notions of 'peace' played in legitimating interventions in the past. Furthermore, although the framing of interveners is important, a critique which mainly looks at this can overstate the extent to which Western conflict management practices do in fact effect transformation (Heathershaw 2008b).

The contributions to this volume develop a number of sustained arguments about the limitations and new possible directions of this meta-critique. Calls to engage, re-discover or promote the 'hybrid' (Mac Ginty, this volume), 'everyday' and 'post-liberal' (Richmond, this volume) aspects of these practices respond by turning towards a more distinctively humanist basis for critique, articulated in distinction to a more ideologically driven liberal or neoliberal peace. It is clear that in some senses this shows continuities with the early concerns of the peace studies movement, which, as argued in this chapter, originally informed conceptions of peacebuilding. Yet others challenge in a more fundamental sense whether the 'liberal peace' has in fact deserved this title. This opens the possibilities for a much deeper problematisation of the ways in which world order over the last few years can be understood.

Conclusion: Looking Back and Thinking Ahead

What we have seen over the last twenty years has been a series of changing ideas and discourses about international conflict management, which have been premised on the basis of the global North bringing peace to the South through modes of social and political transformation. Critiques of these approaches have identified them in large part as 'liberal' in orientation and 'global' in scope. This chapter has shown that particular historical and intellectual junctures were influential in shaping both practices of conflict management and their critiques.

At the time of writing, we await the publication of a fourth USIP volume by Crocker et al. – *Rewiring Regional Security in a Fragmented World* (2011). Early material indicates a lateral step away from the themes of the first three volumes, which all imagine a global, Western-led form of conflict management and political transformation, towards a more minimalist and fragmented set of security regimes. This may be a strong indication that the ambitious and expansive 'peacebuilding' project has finally fallen out of public political favour as the international community feels increasingly unable to commit to its demands and objectives. Signs are that the US in particular feels itself in a mode of transition and is retrenching its prospects and priorities.

What is also clear is that the next iteration of the important debate will also have to speak to an increasingly confident global South, which shows scepticism towards traditional forms of assistance and the presumed better capabilities of the North. Many of the contributions in this volume demonstrate how, across various contexts and spaces, the 'liberal peace' has been more or less marginal to a number of outcomes, particularly where other aid partners play an important role. It will be interesting to see what a future role for the conflict management industry might be in disorderly environments, and whether the short history of 'peacebuilding' might remain a unique episode in a changing global order.

Notes

1 See Mallaby (2002) for a widely circulated and clear exposition of the political rationale connecting state failure and US interventionism.

2 An exception to this trend is Bendaña (2005), as well as Heathershaw (2008a) and Call and Cousens (2008).

Bibliography

Azar, E. (1986) 'Ten Propositions on Protracted Social Conflict', in E. Azar and J. W. Burton (eds) *International Conflict Resolution: Theory and Practice*, Brighton: Wheatsheaf.

Ball, N. and T. Halevy (1996) *Making Peace Work: The Role of the International Development Community*, Washington, DC and Baltimore, MD: Overseas Development Council.

Bendaña, A. (2005) 'From Peacebuilding to State Building: One Step Forward and Two Steps Back?' *Development* 48(3): 5–15.

Berdal, M. and D. Keen (1997) 'Violence and Economic Agendas in Civil Wars: Some Policy Implications', *Millennium: Journal of International Studies* 26(3): 795–818.

Berdal, M. R. and D. Malone (2000) *Greed and Grievance: Economic Agendas in Civil Wars*, Boulder, CO: Lynne Rienner.

Bertram, E. (1995) 'Reinventing Governments', *Journal of Conflict Resolution* 39(3): 387–418.

Blair, T. (1999) 'Doctrine of the International Community', Speech made to the Economic Club of Chicago, Hilton Hotel, Chicago, April 22.

Boutros-Ghali, B. (1992) *An Agenda for Peace: Preventive Diplomacy, Peacemaking and Peacekeeping*, Report of the Secretary-General pursuant to the statement adopted by the Summit Meeting of the Security Council on 31 January 1992, New York: United Nations.

Boutros-Ghali, B. (1995) *Supplement to An Agenda for Peace*, New York: United Nations.

Burton, J. W. (1987) *Resolving Deep-rooted Conflict: A Handbook*, Lanham, MD and London: University Press of America.

Call, C. and V. Wyeth (2008) *Building States to Build Peace*, Boulder, CO: Lynne Rienner.

Call, C. T. and E. M. Cousens (2008) 'Ending Wars and Building Peace: International Responses to War Torn Societies', *International Studies Perspectives* 9(1): 1–21.

Chesterman, S., M. Ignatieff and R. Thakur (2005) *Making States Work: State Failure and the Crisis of Governance*, Tokyo and New York: United Nations University Press.

Clark, P. (2007) 'Hybridity, Holism, and Traditional Justice: The Case of the Gacaca Courts in Post-Genocide Rwanda', *George Washington International Law Review* 39: 765–838.

Cliffe, L. and R. Luckham (1999) 'Complex Political Emergencies and the State: Failure and the Fate of the State', *Third World Quarterly* 20(1): 27–50.

Crocker, C. A., F. O. Hampson and P. Aall, eds (1996) *Managing Global Chaos: Sources of and Responses to International Conflict*, Washington, DC: United States Institute of Peace Press.

Crocker, C. A., F. O. Hampson and P. Aall, eds (2001) *Turbulent Peace: the Challenges of Managing International Conflict*. Washington, DC: United States Institute of Peace Press.

Crocker, C. A., F. O. Hampson and P. Aall, eds (2007) *Leashing the Dogs of War: Conflict Management in a Divided World*, Washington, DC: United States Institute of Peace Press.

Crocker, C. A., F. O. Hampson and P. Aall, eds (2011) *Rewiring Regional Security in a Fragmented World*, Washington, DC: United States Institute of Peace Press.

Deng, F. M. (1996) *Sovereignty as Responsibility: Conflict Management in Africa*, Washington, DC: Brookings Institution Press.

DfID (2006) *Making Governance Work for the Poor*, White Paper, London: Her Majesty's Stationery Office.

Doyle, M. W. (1983) 'Kant, Liberal Legacies, and Foreign Affairs', *Philosophy & Public Affairs* 205–235.

DPKO (2010a) 'List of Operations', Retrieved 6 January 2011, from http://www.un.org/en/peacekeeping/list.shtml.

DPKO (2010b) 'United Nations Transitional Authority in Cambodia (Background)', Retrieved 5 January 2011, from http://www.un.org/en/peacekeeping/missions/past/untacbackgr2.html.

Duffield, M. R. (2001) *Global Governance and the New Wars: The Merging of Development and Security*, London: Zed Books.

Fukuyama, F. (2004) *State-building: Governance and World Order in the 21st Century*, Ithaca, NY: Cornell University Press.

Ghani, A. and C. Lockhart (2008) *Fixing Failed States: A Framework for Rebuilding a Fractured World*, Oxford and New York: Oxford University Press.

Giddens, A. (2000) *Runaway World: How Globalization Is Reshaping Our Lives*, New York: Routledge.

Harrison, G. (2004) *The World Bank and Africa: The Construction of Governance States*, London: Routledge.

Heathershaw, J. (2008a) 'Unpacking the Liberal Peace: The Dividing and Merging of Peacebuilding Discourses', *Millennium: Journal of International Studies* 36(3): 597.

Heathershaw, J. (2008b) 'Seeing like the International Community: How Peacebuilding Failed (and Survived) in Tajikistan', *Journal of Intervention and Statebuilding* 2(3): 329–351.

Held, D., A. McGrew, D. Goldblatt, and J. Perraton (1999) *Global Transformations*, Stanford, CA: Stanford University Press.

Helman, G. B. and S. R. Ratner (1992) 'Saving Failed States', *Foreign Policy*: 3–20.

Hughes, C. and V. Pupavac (2005) 'Framing Post-conflict Societies: International Pathologisation of Cambodia and the post-Yugoslav States', *Third World Quarterly* 26(6): 873–889.

ICISS (2001) The Responsibility To Protect. Ottawa: International Development Research Centre.

ICTJ (2003) 'Transitional Justice: Conflict Closure and Building a Sustainable Peace', *Dispute Resolution*, from http://www.ictj.org/en/news/coverage/article/426.html.

Kaldor, M. (1999) *New and Old Wars: Organized Violence in a Global Era*, Stanford, CA: Stanford University Press.

Kaplan, R. (1994) 'The Coming Anarchy: How Scarcity, Crime, Overpopulation and Disease Are Threatening the Social Fabric of Our Planet', *Atlantic Monthly* 44–74.

Keen, D. (1998) 'The Economics of Civil War', Adelphi Paper No. 320, Oxford: Oxford University Press, for the International Institute for Strategic Studies.

Kumar, K. (1997) 'The Nature and Focus of International Assistance for Rebuilding War-Torn Societies', in K. Kumar, *Rebuilding Societies after Civil War: Critical Roles for International Assistance*, Boulder, CO: Lynne Rienner, pp. 1–17.

Le Billon, P. (2008) 'Corrupting Peace? Peacebuilding and Post-conflict Corruption', *International Peacekeeping* 15(3): 344–361.

Lederach, J. P. (1997) *Building Peace: Sustainable Reconciliation in Divided Societies*, Washington, DC: United States Institute of Peace Press.

Lund, M. S. (1996) *Preventing Violent Conflicts: A Strategy for Preventive Diplomacy*, Washington, DC: United States Institute of Peace Press.

Mac Ginty, R. and O. Richmond (2007) 'Myth or Reality: Opposing Views on the Liberal Peace and Post-war Reconstruction', *Global Society* 21(4): 491–497.

Mallaby, S. (2002) 'The Reluctant Imperialist: Terrorism, Failed States, and the Case for American Empire', *Foreign Affairs* 81(2): 2–7.

Malone, D. and M. R. Berdal (2000) *Greed and Grievance: Economic Agendas in Civil Wars*, Boulder, CO: Lynne Rienner.

OECD (2007) 'Principles for Good International Engagement in Fragile States and Situations', April, www.oecd.org/dac/fragilestates, accessed 4 January 2011.

Paris, R. (1997) 'Peacebuilding and the Limits of Liberal Internationalism', *International Security* 22(2): 54–89.

Paris, R. (2002) 'International Peacebuilding and the *"mission civilisatrice"'*, *Review of International Studies* 28(4): 637–656.

Paris, R. (2004) *At War's End: Building Peace after Civil Conflict*, Cambridge and New York: Cambridge University Press.

Paris, R. and T. D. Sisk (2009) *The Dilemmas of Statebuilding: Confronting the Contradictions of Postwar Peace Operations*, London: Taylor & Francis.

Prendergast, J. (1996) *Frontline Diplomacy: Humanitarian Aid and Conflict in Africa*, Boulder, CO: Lynne Rienner.

Pugh, M. (2002) 'Postwar Political Economy in Bosnia and Herzegovina: The Spoils of Peace', *Global Governance* 8(4): 467–483.

Richmond, O. P. (2005) *The Transformation of Peace*, Basingstoke: Palgrave Macmillan.

Richmond, O. P. (2006) 'The Problem of Peace: Understanding the "liberal Peace"', *Conflict, Security & Development* 6(3): 291–314.

Richmond, O. P. (2009) 'A Post-liberal Peace: Eirenism and the Everyday', *Review of International Studies* 35(03): 557–580.

Rotberg, R. I. (2003) *When States Fail: Causes and Consequences*, Princeton, NJ: Princeton University Press.

Rotberg, R. I. (2007) 'The Challenge of Weak, Failing and Collapsed States', in C. A.

Crocker, F. O. Hampson and P. Aall, *Leashing the Dogs of War: Conflict Management in a Divided World*, Washington, DC: United States Institute of Peace Press.

Schlichte, K. (2005) *The Dynamics of States: The Formation and Crises of State Domination*, Aldershot: Ashgate.

Stedman, S. J. (1997) 'Spoiler Problems in Peace Processes', *International Security* 22(2): 5–53.

Touval, S. and I. W. Zartman (1985) *International Mediation in Theory and Practice*, Boulder, CO and London: Westview Press with the Foreign Policy Institute, School of Advanced International Studies, The Johns Hopkins University.

Tschirgi, N. (2004) *Post-conflict Peacebuilding Revisited: Achievements, Limitations, Challenges*, New York: International Peace Academy.

UNDP (2010) 'BCPR Transitional Governance', retrieved 11/12/2010, from http://www.undp.org/cpr/we_do/trans_governance.shtml.

UNPBC (2007) *Strategic Framework for Peacebuilding in Burundi*, PBC/1/BDI/4. New York: United Nations Peacebuilding Commission.

USAID (2005) *Fragile States Strategy*, Washington, DC: United States Agency for International Development.

Williams, D. and T. Young (1994) 'Governance, the World Bank and Liberal Theory', *Political Studies* 42(1): 84–100.

World Bank (2007) 'World Governance Indicators', Retrieved 3 March 2008, from http://info.worldbank.org/governance/wgi2007/.

Zartman, I. W. (1995) *Collapsed States: The Disintegration and Restoration of Legitimate Authority*, Boulder, CO: Lynne Rienner.

2

Critiques of Liberal Peace

Roland Paris[1]

Introduction

The global experiment in post-conflict peacebuilding, underway since the end of the Cold War, has arrived at a crossroads and it is uncertain how it will proceed.[2] While the United Nations (UN) and its member states continue to reaffirm their support for peacebuilding and to mount new missions aimed at helping countries emerging from civil wars, observers have questioned the effectiveness and legitimacy of these missions. Many of these criticisms are warranted: the record of peacebuilding has indeed been disappointing. Efforts to promote liberal democratic governing systems and market-oriented economic growth, both core elements of the prevailing liberal peacebuilding model, have been more difficult and unpredictable than initially expected, in some cases producing destabilising side effects (for evaluations of the mixed record, see Berdal 2009; Howard 2008; Fortna 2008; Sambanis 2008; Call and Cousens 2008; Doyle and Sambanis 2006). It is crucial for scholars and practitioners to gain a better understanding of the underlying tensions and contradictions of peacebuilding (recent works exploring these include Paris and Sisk 2009a, 2009b; Jarstad and Sisk 2008; Baranyi 2008), including by using 'critical' methods of enquiry that dissect the assumptions of these operations.[3] But recent years have also witnessed the emergence of what might be called a 'hyper-critical' school of scholars and commentators who view liberal peacebuilding as fundamentally destructive or illegitimate. Some of these critics maintain, for example, that the post-conflict operations of the past two decades have done more harm than good. Others go further, portraying these operations as a form of Western or liberal imperialism that seeks to exploit or subjugate the societies hosting the missions.

In this chapter, I shall argue that such claims tend to be just as exaggerated as the rosy pro-liberalisation rhetoric that dominated the peacebuilding discourse in the early-to-mid-1990s, when democratisation and marketisation were portrayed as almost magical formulas for peace in war-torn states. To borrow a phrase from Alan Greenspan, former chair of the US Federal Reserve, early peacebuilding commentary was 'irrationally exuberant' about post-conflict liberalisation strategies. The problematic record of peacebuilding in subsequent years chipped away at this enthusiasm as scholars began to dissect the assumptions and challenges of consolidating peace after civil wars (recent surveys include Williams forthcoming; Fortna and Howard 2008; Goetze and Guzina 2008), including assumptions about the relationship between liberalisation and peace in post-conflict settings (Paris 2004). Like a swinging pendulum, however, criticism of peacebuilding has recently carried past the point of justified questioning and, in some quarters, now verges on unfounded scepticism and even cynicism. Careless conflation of multilateral peace operations with the US-led 'war on terror' has accelerated this pendulum swing, as I shall argue below, but whatever the explanation may be, such denunciations of liberal peacebuilding are both unwarranted and imprudent. They are unwarranted because such missions, in spite of their many flaws, have done more good than harm; and they are imprudent because the failure of the existing peacebuilding project would be tantamount to abandoning tens of millions of people to lawlessness, predation, disease and fear. In short, there is a need to clarify and rebalance existing academic debates over the meaning, shortcomings and prospects of 'liberal' peacebuilding.

Nearly two decades ago, Gerald Helman and Stephen Ratner (1993) wrote a seminal article titled 'Saving Failed States' in which they identified collapsing states as an emerging international security and development priority, and called for new multilateral methods to assist such states. Despite the passage of time, the challenge of aiding countries beset by internal unrest and instability remains urgent – as regional conflicts centred in the Democratic Republic of Congo, Sudan and elsewhere attest. But whereas a few years ago it was irrational exuberance about liberal peacebuilding that needed tempering, today the entire peacebuilding enterprise is being called into question. If the practice of providing large-scale assistance to post-conflict societies is to continue, peacebuilding will need to be 'saved' from this exaggerated backlash.

Saving peacebuilding does not mean blindly defending current international practices. On the contrary, the principles and methods of these missions need to be challenged and analysed continuously. Scholars have an important role to play in this process: their writings help to inform debates, to confirm or to disconfirm assumptions, and to frame understandings about what these missions are and what they do. But not all criticism is equally valid or sound. Critical perspectives themselves need to be subject to ongoing scrutiny and review.

As it turns out, many hyper-critical writings have been based on questionable logic and evidence. Saving liberal peacebuilding thus involves both: (1) continuing to press forward with efforts to dissect and understand the paradoxes and pathologies of peacebuilding, and (2) ensuring that this critical enterprise is well-founded and justified.

Critical studies of peacebuilding are 'critical' in the sense that they ask probing questions about underlying assumptions that might otherwise be taken for granted. However, this deeper questioning does not, in itself, lead to any particular conclusions about the merits, morality or advisability of a given peacebuilding paradigm. More precisely, nothing in critical theory or critical scholarship per se implies that liberal peacebuilding, broadly defined, should be rejected. Nevertheless, for one reason or another, critical peacebuilding studies have come to be associated, if not equated, with sweeping rejections of liberal peacebuilding. This is unfortunate, because the tools of critical analysis could just as easily be used to explore alternatives within liberal peacebuilding (see Roland Paris, 'Alternatives to Liberal Peace', this volume).

The Pendulum Swing: From Exuberance to Denigration

At the end of the Cold War, there was a widely shared conviction that political and economic liberalism offered a key to solving a broad range of social, political and economic problems from under-development and famine, to disease, environmental degradation and violent conflict. A record number of countries held elections during this period, and a broad ideological shift took place in the world's leading international organisations towards more open and enthusiastic support for liberal forms of government (based in the idea of elections, constitutional limits on governmental power, and respect for civil and political rights). For example, many international organisations, including the UN, the Organisation for Security and Cooperation in Europe and the Organisation of American States, created specialised democracy-promotion and electoral-assistance offices at this time. Such changes reflected the spirit of liberal triumphalism echoing in the pages of academic and popular publications, and perhaps best symbolised by Francis Fukuyama's claim that humankind had reached the (liberal) endpoint in its ideological evolution (Fukuyama 1993).

It was during this period that the UN launched its first flurry of peace-building operations to help implement peace settlements in war-torn countries, including Namibia, El Salvador, Nicaragua, Mozambique and Cambodia. Not surprisingly, given the prevailing zeitgeist, these missions pursued a strategy of promoting peace by encouraging political and economic liberalisation of the host states. The intellectual origins and theoretical foundations of international peacebuilding in the 1990s have been described in detail elsewhere, one of which is a key assumption that informed these missions: that rapid liberalisation would create conditions for stable and lasting peace in countries emerging from civil conflict (Paris 2004). Like modernisation theorists of the 1950s and 1960s, the practitioners of peacebuilding in the 1990s seemed to think that 'all good things go together' (Pakenham 1973): that democratisation and marketisation were mutually reinforcing and that, once these processes were initiated, they would be largely self-perpetuating.

As the years went by, however, the challenges of post-conflict reconstruction – and the limitations of rapid liberalisation strategies – became increasingly apparent. Rather than creating conditions for stable and lasting peace, efforts to hold a quick set of elections and economic reforms did little to address the drivers of conflict and in some cases produced perversely destabilising results. Peacebuilding missteps in the early 1990s were well documented: in Angola, for example, the UN oversaw post-war elections in 1992 that provoked one of the former belligerents to resume fighting, in part because there were no institutional mechanisms established to resolve disputes over the election, no adequate international and local forces to uphold the results and no serious measures to disarm the factional forces before the elections took place. In Rwanda, plans for power-sharing and democratic elections were scuttled in 1994 when extremist members of the Hutu government orchestrated genocidal violence against their political and ethnic enemies, the Tutsis. In Cambodia, international peacebuilders organised a relatively successful set of elections in 1993, declared the mission a success, and left the country, only to watch from a distance as the results were subverted by the country's long-time strongman, Hun Sen. In El Salvador and Nicaragua, political reforms were largely effective but the economic dimension of the peacebuilding mission, which prescribed far-reaching economic liberalisation, served to exacerbate socio-economic distributional inequalities that had been among the causes of the conflict in the first place. In Bosnia, the 2005 Dayton Accords prescribed a quick set of elections which reinforced the power of the most nationalist elements in the society who were the least committed to pursuing inter-ethnic reconciliation. Economic liberalisation in Bosnia also produced unexpected problems: in the acute institutional vacuum of that country after the war, internationally mandated privatisation efforts reinforced war-time black markets and enriched extremist groups. Meanwhile, in Liberia the outcome of peacebuilding efforts paralleled those in Cambodia: post-conflict elections were held successfully in 1997, the peacebuilding operation was declared a success and wrapped up, but the winner of the election, Charles Taylor, immediately began to dismantle the democratic elements of the state and repressed his political rivals, which triggered a new round of fighting.

Although most of the countries hosting operations in the 1990s did not experience a return to large-scale conflict, searching questions were rightly raised about the sustainability of the results, including the degree to which rapid liberalisation could produce the conditions for durable peace. These questions appeared not only in academic publications but also in the internal deliberations of major peacebuilding agencies including the UN, and served to temper earlier excitement and optimism about the peace-producing effects of liberal peacebuilding strategies. By the end of the 1990s and early 2000s, the UN itself was acknowledging the need for more comprehensive and longer-lasting approaches to peacebuilding, based on the principle of 'no exit without strategy' and on the need to pay greater attention to building or strengthening governmental institutions in the host countries as a means of consolidating, or 'locking in', post-war political and economic reforms (UN 2001). This emphasis on institutional strengthening came to be known as 'statebuilding' (see Paris and Sisk 2009b; also Ghani and Lockhart 2008; Call and Wyeth 2008; Fukuyama 2004).

In 1999, three more operations were launched in Sierra Leone, Kosovo and East Timor, this time with more explicit statebuilding mandates and more open-ended timeframes. Rather than holding an election and then concluding the mission within the first two or three years, these new missions embraced a broader set of goals, including more extensive efforts at disarmament, demobilisation and reintegration of factional forces, establishing functioning judicial and administrative structures within the host state (structures that have always been necessary for the functioning of democratic governance and a market economy) and promoting the growth of civil society groups within the state including human rights NGOs and political party organisations. But whether these measures went far enough remained a matter of disagreement. In East Timor, for example, the peacebuilding mission ended in 2002 and was widely touted as a resounding success, even though several observers warned at the time that the job of reforming the judicial sector and police had only just begun and that continued weakness in these sectors posed a threat to the stability of the country. As it turned out, fighting between elements of the security forces triggered a new round of violence in 2006, prompting then-UN Secretary General Kofi Annan to acknowledge that the earlier peacebuilding mission had been terminated prematurely and to recommend the deployment of a new mission to East Timor (UN 2006: paras 40, 142).

As peacebuilding strategies evolved and reflected more realistic understandings of the limitations of existing approaches (including the faulty assumption that peace-through-liberalisation could be easily achieved) a different set of critiques gained attention. For some observers, the principal problem in peacebuilding was not its brevity or superficiality, but quite the opposite: that peacebuilders exercised such expansive powers that they effectively squelched genuine political participation and locally driven reforms. David Chandler's analysis of the Bosnia mission offered a good example of this argument.

Chandler maintained that the extensive decision-making powers of international officials were 'undermining Bosnian institutions and creating relations of dependency' and consequently 'had done little to facilitate democracy and self-government in Bosnia' (Chandler 1999: 3, 154). Similar criticisms levelled at international peacebuilding efforts elsewhere, including East Timor (Chopra: 2000, 2002) and Afghanistan (Suhrke 2009), contributed to a growing belief, both inside and outside the UN, that greater 'local ownership' of peacebuilding processes was needed.

These observations raised difficult problems for peacebuilding practitioners, who were confronted by two competing imperatives. On one hand, for reasons outlined above, they were under pressure to expand the scope and duration of operations in order to build functioning and effective governmental institutions in war-torn states, and to avoid the problems of incomplete reform and premature departure seen in East Timor and elsewhere. On the other hand, they were also under pressure to reduce the level of international intrusion in the domestic political processes of the host states. Achieving the first goal seemed to require a relatively 'heavy footprint', or a large and long-term international presence with extensive powers, particularly in cases where governmental institutions are dysfunctional or non-existent; whereas the second goal seemed to require a relatively 'light footprint', a small and unobtrusive presence that would maximise the freedom of local actors to pursue their own peacebuilding goals. Squaring these two objectives became – and remains today – a crucial conceptual and strategic challenge for practitioners. Simply put, if both the heavy footprint and the light footprint are problematic, what is the 'right' footprint?

Other commentators, however, were more deeply sceptical about the prospects for peacebuilding reform, and some opposed the very idea of deploying international missions into war-torn countries. Jeffrey Herbst, for instance, argued that seeking to restore war-torn states in parts of Africa could backfire by freezing in place political arrangements that did not reflect underlying social patterns and were therefore unsustainable. His advice was to 'let states fail', in some cases allowing new forms and centres of political authority to emerge through conflict and cooperation, without outside direction or intrusion, and then to redraw national boundaries where necessary to reflect these new arrangements, rather than seeking to perpetuate the untenable fictions of many existing states (Herbst 2003; see also Herbst 1996; Atzili 2006). Pierre Englebert and Denis Tull made a related argument with regard to Somaliland and Uganda, which, in contrast to countries hosting major peacebuilding operations, underwent their own largely 'indigenous state reconstruction efforts' and 'have fared better than their externally sponsored counterparts' (2008: 111, 135). Similarly, Jeremy Weinstein endorsed a strategy of promoting 'autonomous recovery' that would allow states to achieve 'a lasting peace, a systematic reduction in violence, and postwar political and economic development in the absence of international intervention' (2005: 5). He maintained that international efforts to end wars through negotiated settlements, and to rebuild states on the basis of these settlements, could serve to 'freeze unstable distributions of power and to provide a respite from hostilities for groups that are intent on continuing the conflict when the international community departs' (ibid.: 9). Instead, allowing conflicts to take their natural course (which would sort out the winners from the losers) would sometimes provide a surer basis for a lasting peace.[4] This argument also built on other researchers' findings that civil wars ending in military victories tend to produce longer-lasting peace than those ending in negotiated ceasefires (for example, Luttwak 1999; see also Toft 2003, 2009; and, for a critique of this finding, Hartzell and Hoddie 2007).

Herbst and Weinstein questioned current approaches to peacebuilding on the prudential grounds that such missions were unlikely to succeed, and that allowing conflicts to burn themselves out might, in some circumstances, offer a better strategy for achieving lasting results. Others, by contrast, have based their objections on moral criteria: arguing, for example, that peacebuilding is a form of Western or liberal imperialism. One such writer, William Bain, denounced international administration as 'alien rule' that denies the 'human dignity' of the people who live in these countries (2006). David Chandler, extending his earlier work on Bosnia, characterised international statebuilding missions as the practice of 'empire in denial' in which external actors 'colonise' non-Western state institutions (2006; 2007: 176). Michael Pugh criticised liberal peacebuilding on the grounds that it is part of a larger 'hegemonic' project whose 'ideological purpose' is 'to spread the values and norms of dominant power brokers' (2008; see also 2005, 2006a, 2006b). According to William Robinson, peacebuilding activities in countries such as Nicaragua and Haiti represent an effort by 'the core regions of the capitalist world system' to maintain 'essentially undemocratic societies' which facilitates the continued exploitation of the global poor by the global rich (1996: 6–7). For all of these commentators, liberal peacebuilding was hiding a deeper and more destructive purpose: imperial or quasi-imperial domination.

The reaction of the US to 9/11 – including the declaration of a 'war on terror' and the invasion of Afghanistan and Iraq – added fuel to these peacebuilding-as-imperialism arguments. After all, the Bush Administration justified its invasions partly on liberal grounds: as a means of providing the benefits of democracy and freedom to oppressed societies. Efforts to stabilise Iraq after the invasion also bore at least a partial resemblance to liberal peacebuilding strategies pursued elsewhere by the UN and by other international agencies in countries emerging from civil wars. Elections, constitutional processes, market-oriented economic adjustment and institution-building were central to the US plan in Iraq and also part of the standard formula for UN-mandated peace operations. Given these apparent similarities and the disastrous effects of the Iraq invasion, it was not long before commentators began equating the Iraq war and international peacebuilding missions as a part of an abhorrent phenomenon of 'democratic imperialism' (Encarnacion 2005) or 'imperial nation-building' (Bendaña 2005). In the words of Wolfram Lacher, 'statebuilding and reconstruction practices in Iraq are in continuity with international operations during the post-Cold War era and beyond' because they have all involved 'the reproduction and expansion of hegemonic international order' (2007: 247). Alejandro Bendaña also portrayed the Iraq war as a natural extension of 1990s-era peacebuilding operations, which had promoted the 'external economic and strategic interests' at the expense of such principles as justice and self-determination, thereby 'opening the door to Washington's subsequent savagery' in Iraq (2005: 6). Similarly, John Gray insisted that liberal peacebuilding and the Iraq invasion were based on the same flawed methods and assumptions: the 'liberal interventionism that took root in the aftermath of the Cold War was never much more than a combination of post-imperial nostalgia with crackpot geopolitics', as events in Iraq definitively demonstrated, in his view (2007; for similar arguments see Jacoby 2007; Duffield 2007b; Heathershaw 2008: 620).

Frustration at America's 'regime change' invasion of Iraq thus seemed to contribute to a mounting backlash against all forms of liberal interventionism including UN-sponsored peacebuilding. It also deepened scepticism about the legitimacy and feasibility of promoting democracy and market-oriented economics as a remedy for civil conflict. Instead of simply critiquing the manner by which international agencies support liberal democratic transitions in war-torn states, some commentators began to dismiss the entire enterprise as 'futile' (Scheuer 2008: 37), 'folly' (Bain 2006; Encarnacion 2005: 47), 'delusional' (Gray 2007), 'hubristic' (Cooper 2007: 610; Richmond and Franks 2007), and destined to produce 'enemies instead of allies and [to heighten] insecurity instead of enhancing security' (Jahn 2007: 12). Similarly, rather than simply examining the similarities between old-style colonialism and modern peacebuilding, some commentators went further and claimed that liberal interventionism was colonialism or imperialism, now 'comprehensively discredited in the killing fields of Fallujah and Samarra' (Milne 2008). Thus, measured scepticism about the difficulties or appropriateness of promoting liberalisation in specific post-war circumstances gave way, in some quarters, to an almost indiscriminate indictment of such efforts, which contributed to what Neil Cooper has called a 'crisis of confidence and credibility . . . in the Western liberal peace project' (2007: 605).

In summary, the pendulum of peacebuilding analysis swung from one extreme to another. After a period of irrational exuberance about the almost magical effects of liberalisation, the study of this field entered a phase of constructive scepticism about the effectiveness or propriety of liberal peacebuilding strategies, but the pendulum kept on swinging, driven in part by 9/11 and the

Iraq war. Today, expressions of distrust, pessimism and even cynicism about liberal peacebuilding have become more common.

There are interesting parallels between the heady optimism of the early 1990s and the current 'crisis of confidence' in the strategy of promoting peace through liberalisation. Both of these positions can be viewed as reactions to major opinion-shaping events in international affairs. In the former instance, it was the end of the Cold War and the apparent 'victory' of liberalism that informed the early optimism about liberal peacebuilding. In the latter period, it was the Bush Administration's actions (and its appropriation of the language of liberalisation to rationalise and justify its own destructive unilateralism) that contributed to a turn towards pessimism. Both positions, moreover, reflected the zeitgeist of their respective times. In the early 1990s there was a widely shared view that liberal democracy had emerged 'the only model of government with any broad legitimacy and ideological appeal in the world' (as evidenced by the more than three dozen countries that adopted liberal democratic constitutions for the first time between 1990 and 1996; Diamond et al. 1990: x), whereas the 2000s witnessed democratic reversals in Africa, South America and elsewhere, leading many to lament the 'sobering state' of democracy in the world (Carothers 2004).

However, both of these extremely positive and extremely negative views of liberal peacebuilding have been based on exaggerated claims about the benefits (in the early 1990s) or the liabilities (in the late 2000s) of these missions. While the mixed record of more than 20 operations to date has shown that democratisation and marketisation are not all-purpose elixirs for societies emerging from civil conflict, the recent backlash against liberal peacebuilding is just as immoderate and mistaken as the earlier optimism. It is also reckless, as I shall argue below.

Critiquing the Critiques

The real shortcomings of liberal peacebuilding have been widely discussed. They include: inadequate attention to domestic institutional conditions for successful democratisation and marketisation; insufficient appreciation of the tensions and contradictions between the various goals of peacebuilding; poor strategic coordination among the various international actors involved in these missions; lack of political will and attention on the part of peacebuilding sponsors to complete the tasks they undertake, and insufficient commitment of resources; unresolved tensions in relations between the military and non-military participants in these operations; limited knowledge of distinctive local conditions and variations across the societies hosting these missions; insufficient 'local ownership' over the strategic direction and daily activities of such operations; and continued conceptual challenges in defining the conditions for 'success' and strategies for bringing operations to an effective close. This is just a sampling of the serious challenges that continue to face the practitioners of peacebuilding.

But some critiques – including claims that peacebuilding missions have done more harm than good, or that they are essentially exploitative or imperialist – have gone too far. Many of these arguments rest on flawed information and fail to make important distinctions between different forms of liberal intervention. In what follows, I describe five mistakes that underpin several such analyses.

Mistake 1: Conflating post-conquest and post-settlement peacebuilding

As noted above, several commentators have characterised the US invasion and subsequent occupation of Iraq as equivalent to, or a natural extension of, the multilateral peacebuilding missions of the post-Cold War era. According to this perspective, supporters of liberal peacebuilding as well as US neoconservatives who pushed for 'regime change' in Iraq have all suffered from the same delusions and hegemonic impulses, which have led to dangerous and futile efforts to impose democracy by force. Less extreme versions of this argument make distinctions between UN-sponsored and unilateral types of intervention, but nevertheless suggest that the practice of post-war peacebuilding 'open[ed] the door' to American liberal imperialism in Iraq and Afghanistan (Bendaña 2005: 6). Given the dreadful effects of the Iraq war, such assertions have the effect of raising serious doubts about the entire peacebuilding enterprise.

Although the post-conflict stabilisation mission in Iraq and other peacebuilding missions share some characteristics in common, including a sometimes naïve belief in the salubrious effects of holding quick democratic elections, their differences should not be ignored. Most importantly, the US operation in Iraq began with an external invasion – a war of conquest – followed by peacebuilding and counter-insurgency efforts, whereas most peacebuilding missions since the end of the Cold War have been deployed at the request of local parties after the negotiation of peace settlements to civil wars.[5] These 'conditions of birth' are important. When peacebuilding follows conquest, foreign peacebuilders are more likely to be viewed as occupiers, particularly when they are the same parties that invaded the country in the first place; and any new governing arrangements established during this period are more likely to be viewed as external impositions (Suhrke 2009). Although all peacebuilding missions involve a measure of foreign intrusion in domestic affairs, destroying a regime through external invasion is hardly equivalent, in degree or kind, to deploying a mission at the request of local parties with the goal of helping these parties to implement a peace settlement (Edelstein 2009). To be sure, there are examples of post-Cold War peace operations that began in less-than-consensual conditions – most notably, the mission in Kosovo, which followed NATO's bombing of Serb targets in that territory – but the vast majority of missions have not involved forcible entry: they have been examples of post-settlement, not post-conquest, peacebuilding. Blurring this distinction invites false analogising between UN peacebuilding and the American-led 'war on terror'.

Mistake 2: Equating peacebuilding with imperialism or colonialism

Although there are similarities between European colonialism and today's post-settlement peacebuilding operations, such comparisons should also not be taken too far. To be sure, both types of intervention have involved powerful external actors seeking to refashion the domestic structures of weaker societies in accordance with prevailing notions of good or 'civilised' governance. In this sense, today's post-conflict missions may be viewed as a modern version of the old mission civilisatrice – or the belief that European colonial powers had a duty to improve the people living in their overseas possessions – now translated into contemporary parlance of 'capacity building' and 'good governance'. Furthermore, as many have pointed out, international administrators have exercised extraordinarily broad powers in several modern missions, including the right to dismiss local officials from office who allegedly violate the terms or spirit of a peace agreement.

To some commentators, these powers resemble the far-reaching authority of colonial administrators and create similar relations of dependency and domination. However, the old and new versions of civilising mission also differ in important respects – differences that are often elided by those who portray peacebuilding as a form of imperialism (Paris 2002; see also Ottaway and Lacina 2003). First, colonialism was practiced largely to benefit the imperial states themselves, including through the extraction of material and human resources from the colonised society.[6] In spite of the self-proclaimed civilising mission including the purported benefits of colonialism for the colonised, the most enduring and 'unquestioned' assumption of French colonial policy, for instance, was that colonies must benefit France itself: both materially and strategically (Aldrich 1996: 91; Ch. 5). The same was true of Britain, where nineteenth century debates over the costs and benefits of colonialism focused not on whether to get rid of the colonies, but rather, on 'how to organize them so as to make the best use of them with a minimum of effort and expense' (Hyam 1976: 31–32). While modern UN-sponsored missions still reflect the interests of the world's most powerful countries – and therefore cannot be viewed as 'innocent assistance' (Meyer 2008: 573) – they have not principally been motivated by efforts to extract wealth from their host societies.[7]

On the contrary, the predominant flow of resources in contemporary peacebuilding has been in the opposite direction: from international actors to the host state. Moreover, those who claim that post-settlement peacebuilding serves the interests of 'transnational capitalism' have yet to demonstrate that either the expectation or the desire for economic gain has driven the decision to launch any such operations. Second, although the various European colonial powers differed on the prospects and desirability of their respective colonies moving towards independence, it was not until the twentieth century that the ethic of 'national self-determination' fully discredited the traditional view of colonies as imperial possessions. Put differently, shifts in the normative environment of international affairs gradually made colonialism impossible to justify or continue. As Neta Crawford points out: 'Colonialism – the political control, physical occupation, and domination by one group of people over another and their land for purposes of extraction and settlement to benefit the occupiers – was considered a "normal" practice until the early 20th century.' (2002: 131) The anti-colonialist ethic continues to predominate today and shapes the normative environment in which modern peacebuilding operations have unfolded (Paris 2003). Even the longest-lasting and most intrusive missions of recent years have been designed to exercise temporary and transitional authority in their host states, and to create the conditions for effective self-government in those states.

To be clear, I am not suggesting that colonialism was wholly self-interested or that modern peacebuilding is wholly altruistic. Both practices involved complex mixtures of motivations and effects.[8] For this reason, it is interesting to compare and contrast these practices. But observing that there are echoes of colonialism in peacebuilding is quite different from asserting their equivalence. Not only is the colonialism–peacebuilding analogy overstated, but it also serves to discredit and delegitimise peacebuilding by establishing an 'interpretive frame' in which these missions are portrayed as exploitative, destructive, and ultimately disreputable forms of international intervention and assistance.[9] Further, such characterisations make it difficult to distinguish between different types of peacebuilding, some of which have stronger echoes of imperialism than others.

Mistake 3: Defining the 'liberal peace' too broadly

Many problems of peacebuilding appear to stem from contradictions within the objectives of peacebuilding itself, including complex tensions between different 'liberal' reform objectives (see Paris and Sisk 2009; Chesterman 2004). On one hand, liberalism contains a universalist (and universalising) vision of emancipation through political and economic liberalisation, but it simultaneously embraces an ethic of individual and collective choice or self-government, which can conflict with universalist formulas. Some interesting recent scholarship on peacebuilding has explored these tensions and contradictions – within liberalism itself, and between liberalism and other peacebuilding objectives (see, for example, Richmond 2005).

However, there is a danger of defining liberalism (or the liberal approach to peacebuilding) too broadly. If such definitions include elements of peacebuilding that have little to do with liberalism, they can lead to dubious conclusions about the viability or the legitimacy of the 'liberal peace'. Oliver Richmond, for example, argues that liberalism includes the idea of a 'victor's peace', or the notion that 'a peace that rests on a military victory, and upon the hegemony or domination of a victor peace, is more likely to survive' than one based on a negotiated settlement or ceasefire (2006: 293). The assertion that liberalism contains a penchant for military victory over negotiated settlement, however, is dubious on both theoretical and an empirical grounds. Theoretically, this belief is more accurately associated with the realist project, as Richmond acknowledges elsewhere.[10] Empirically, there is little support for the claim that peacebuilding operations rest on a preference for military victory. As noted above, most of these missions have been deployed to implement and uphold negotiated settlements to civil wars, not military victories. Once in the field, moreover, international peacebuilders have generally sought to prevent formerly warring parties from remobilising or renewing their attempts to defeat their rivals – in other words, they have stood in the way of military victories – which is why commentators who view military conquest as a surer foundation for peace have tended to criticise peacebuilding on these very grounds. They have argued that peacebuilders display a reflexive preference for negotiation and compromise, which, they claim, is less effective as a strategy for building peace than allowing (or actively helping) one party to achieve victory over its rivals.[11] This is not a minor point: treating the victor's peace as a core element of peacebuilding serves to blur the distinction, once again, between post-conquest and post-settlement peacebuilding.

Another example comes from the writing of Beate Jahn (2007). By tracing the lineage of modern peacebuilding, Jahn offers an interesting analysis of the continuing relevance of modernisation approaches, but she then takes this argument to extraordinary lengths. Specifically, she suggests that post-settlement peacebuilding is an expression of the same liberal modernisation ethic that gave rise to realist balance of power and 'containment' policies during the Cold War, including US covert and overt interventions against authoritarian and liberal regimes alike. This claim is problematic. As one of Jahn's readers has noted: '[T]he inclusion of such a wide range of foreign policy motivations and activities under the liberal rubric makes the very idea of a particularly liberal foreign policy hard to specify.' (Tansey 2008: 89) Such definitional stretching is especially unfortunate because it elides critical distinctions between different forms of external intervention and thus invites misleading interpretations of post-conflict peacebuilding as being yet another instance of imperial meddling.

Mistake 4: Mischaracterising the peacebuilding record

If the purpose of peacebuilding is to create the conditions for self-sustaining peace, most missions cannot be judged to have fully succeeded, and for this reason important questions have been raised about the sustainability of peacebuilding outcomes (Krause and Jütersonke 2005). But recognising the many shortcomings of these missions and their sometimes troubling effects does not, in itself, demonstrate that peacebuilding has on balance been harmful to the societies into which these operations have been deployed. Most of these countries are probably better off than they would have been without such missions.[12]

Consider the specific case of Bosnia. Many commentators have criticised the international role in that country – and with good cause. Rather than taking the time to design an electoral system that would encourage inter-factional compromise, international peacebuilders rushed ahead with elections that served to reinforce ethnic divisions and the power of the most recalcitrant nationalist leaders. In effect, international agencies wound up supporting 'the dysfunctional political structures that emerged from the war, while failing to buttress the development of alternative political and social projects in civil society' (Belloni 2007: 5). This is just one of several criticisms, including the one raised by David Chandler and others: that peacebuilders have been too dirigiste and have done too little to ensure democratic accountability or to foster genuine political participation within the population (Chandler 1999, 2006; also Caplan 2005).

Acknowledging the validity of these criticisms, however, tells us little about the overall impact of the Bosnia mission. Although the Wilsonian assumptions informing this mission did not produce the hoped-for results, the fact that Bosnians are no longer killing each other, and have not been doing so for well over a decade, should figure prominently in any calculus of the 'net' effects of the operation. Even the specific criticism that international administrators have exercised excessive power in Bosnia needs to be interpreted with caution. Not all of Bosnia's problems – from unemployment and corruption to the passivity of the country's political class – can be attributed to the international administrator's robust authority. On the contrary, some of the most important postwar achievements can be traced to the very exercise of these powers, including internationally driven measures to allow the return of refugees and displaced persons, to create a Bosnian central bank and currency, and to remove ethnic identifiers from official documents including passports. As Sumantra Bose puts it: 'Virtually all developments in [Bosnia] since the end of the war that contribute to a slightly better present for its citizens and open up better prospects – however tenuous – for their future have been due to international effort, often very intensive and protracted.' (2005: 331) Bose's attribution of 'virtually all' major developments to international efforts may be debatable, but the broader point is that a balanced analysis of peacebuilding behaviour would consider both the costs and benefits of an assertive international presence, and that we stand to learn more from such an analysis than from caricatures of peacebuilders as a new 'Raj' (Knaus and Martin 2003).

This point also applies to the larger peacebuilding record. Most of the countries that have hosted missions are no longer at war. This is not, in itself, an adequate measure of success, because the absence of fighting is not equivalent to stable peace. (Indeed, peacebuilders have devoted too little attention to the longer-term requirements for sustainable peace). But the record does not support claims that liberal peacebuilding, on the whole, has been 'counterproductive' (Jahn 2007) or 'nonsensical' (Gray 2007). It is impossible to say how many lives would have been lost if not for these interventions, but there is compelling evidence that peace agreements endure longer, and societies are less likely to slip back into internecine violence, when major peacebuilding missions are deployed (Doyle and Sambanis 2006). The economic benefits of peace are also difficult to calculate, but one recent Oxfam study estimated the cost of Africa's armed conflicts from 1990 to 2005 as $284 billion, or approximately 15 per cent of GDP for the countries that experienced wars (Oxfam International 2007). Compared to peaceful countries, moreover, African states in conflict have 50 per cent more infant deaths, 15 per cent more undernourished people, five years less life expectancy, 20 per cent more adult illiteracy, 2.5 times fewer doctors per patient, and 12.4 per cent less food per person on average (ibid.). If and when international actors help to prevent such conflicts from reigniting, these human and developmental costs may be avoided. In other words, the specific problems of peacebuilding need to be considered in the light of the overall effects of these operations.

Mistake 5: Oversimplifying moral complexity

Mark Duffield is one of several commentators who dispute the moral foundations of international peacebuilding. Intervention in post-conflict societies and other fragile states, he argues, reflects the 'liberal urge to deepen the west's external sovereign frontier' and represents a new and noxious kind of 'international occupation', tinged with 'cultural racism' (2007a: 27; 2007b: 230). Duffield's analysis of peacebuilding – and of the larger security and development paradigm – is fascinating and insightful, but overstated and one-sided. He uses sharply reproving metaphors (occupation, racism) to characterise international development and peacebuilding efforts, while paying comparatively little attention to the positive effects of such interventions, or to the moral implications of not intervening in crisis situations. Nor does he spell out a clear alternative to current liberal peacebuilding practices, other than offering attractive but vague appeals for 'a new formula for sharing the world with others' (2007a: 227–234; 2007b: 242).

William Bain, who focuses on missions involving the international administration of war-torn territories, is also interested in the ethics of promoting democratisation and self-government through external intervention (2006: 78). Although Bain is more willing than Duffield to give credit to the humanitarian rationale of such operations, he nevertheless portrays internationally run transitional administration as a destructive enterprise that 'subjects' local people to 'alien rule' and thus leads to a kind of 'moral corruption' that 'augurs the breakdown of social life' – due, in part, to contradictions between the stated liberal goals of peacebuilding and de facto illiberal actions of the peacebuilders (ibid.: 536–538). Like Duffield, Bain is a sophisticated observer who exposes uncomfortable and important tensions within the liberal peacebuilding project, but his ethical calculus is constricted and incomplete. If international administration of war-shattered territories is 'folly', as he concludes, surely this judgment should be based on a more complete evaluation of the various benefits of peacebuilding, not just its moral costs.

It is a truism to observe that there are elements of 'folly' in every human institution, including international peacebuilding. If we accept this as a given, the more important ethical issue is whether international peacebuilding, viewed as a whole, not just in fragments, remains a justified and worthwhile enterprise. Among other considerations, answering this question requires careful assessment of possible alternative courses of action (or inaction). To arrive at sweeping moral judgments about peacebuilding based on fragmentary analysis is not only methodologically suspect, but it is ethically problematic in itself, given how much is at stake in debates over how and when to provide assistance to societies emerging from conflict.

Conclusion

Liberal peacebuilding has become the target of considerable criticism. Although much of this criticism is warranted, a number of scholars and commentators have come to the opinion that liberal peacebuilding is either fundamentally destructive, or illegitimate, or both. On close analysis, however, many of these critiques appear to be exaggerated or misdirected. At a time when the future of peacebuilding is uncertain, it is important to distinguish between justified and unjustified criticisms, and to promote a more balanced debate on the meaning, shortcomings and prospects of liberal peacebuilding.

In this chapter, I have attempted to show that some of the most sweeping critiques of liberal peacebuilding have rested on dubious claims and logic, including the conflation of post-conquest and post-settlement peacebuilding; un-nuanced analogies of peacebuilding and colonialism or imperialism; definitions of the liberal peace that are too broad; mischaracterisations of the peacebuilding record; and oversimplifications of the moral complexity of peacebuilding. Considered in this light, the purported crisis of liberal peacebuilding appears to be less severe and less fundamental than some have claimed.

Notes

1 An extended version of this chapter was published as 'Saving Liberal Peacebuilding', *Review of International Studies* 36 (2010), pp. 3337–3365, and the material is republished with kind permission.

2 In this chapter, 'peacebuilding' refers to efforts 'to identify and support structures that will tend to strengthen and solidify peace in order to avoid a relapse into conflict' (UN 1992: para 21). For different definitions, see Barnett et al. 2007; Chetail 2009.

3 On the distinction between 'critical' and 'problem-solving' approaches, see Cox 1986. On the importance of critical analysis in the study of peace operations, see Richmond 2007; Bellamy and Williams 2004; Paris 2000.

4 However, Weinstein also noted that 'the conditions under which autonomous recovery is likely to occur are rare and difficult to create' (2005: 5).

5 It is also worth noting that the Bush Administration's decision to invade Iraq was initially justified on the grounds of pre-emptive self-defence. Only later, when weapons of mass destruction were not discovered in Iraq, did the Bush Administration rationalise the invasion as a means of 'liberating' the Iraqi people and spreading democracy to the Middle East.

6 As Bernard Waites writes, 'It was no secret that the modern colonial empires were acquired for the advantages they brought the European states.' (1999: 222)

7 There have been cases of international personnel accused of corruption and malfeasance, but these activities have not been sanctioned by peacebuilding agencies, which sets these transgressions apart from the colonial powers' systematic and deliberate exploitation of the territories they occupied. Indeed, for those who believe that only national interests (and not humanitarianism) should justify the deployment of military forces, it may seem 'strategically irrational' to contribute troops to a UN peacebuilding mission (see Walton 2009).

8 For example, national interests play a role in the decisions of individual countries to contribute troops to specific international operations (see Neack 1995).

9 For a discussion of 'interpretive frames' and their role in shaping understandings of particular issues or phenomena, see Benford and Snow 2000.

10 Although the boundaries between liberalism and realism are diffuse, Richmond himself writes that the 'victor's peace' is associated more with realism than liberalism, yet he nevertheless maintains that the preference for military victory is 'a key aspect' of the liberal peace (2006: 310).

11 See, for example, the discussion of Jeffrey Herbst's and Jeremy Weinstein's writings above.

12 Determining what conditions would have been in the absence of a peacebuilding mission is a very difficult analytical task, but the evidence strongly suggests that peacebuilding missions have contributed to preserving peace in most countries that have hosted these operations; see Fortna 2008; Doyle and Sambanis 2006; Gilligan and Sergenti 2008; Quinn et al. 2007: 184–185.

Bibliography

Aldrich, R. (1996) *Greater France: A History of French Overseas Expansion*, London: Macmillan.
Atzili, B. (2006) 'When Good Fences Make Bad Neighbors: Fixed Borders, State Weakness, and International Conflict', *International Security* 31(3): 139–173.
Bain, W. (2006) 'In Praise of Folly: International Administration and the Corruption of Humanity', *International Affairs* 82(3): 525–538.
Baranyi, S. (ed.) (2008) *The Paradoxes of Peacebuilding Post-9/11*, Vancouver: University of British Columbia Press.
Barnett, M., H. Kim, M. O'Donnell and L. Sitea (2007) 'Peacebuilding: What's In a Name?', *Global Governance* 13(1): 35–58.
Bellamy, A. J. and P. D. Williams (2004) 'Conclusion: What Future for Peace Operations? Brahimi and Beyond', *International Peacekeeping* 11(1): 183–212.
Belloni, R. (2007) *State Building and International Intervention in Bosnia*, London: Routledge.
Bendaña, A. (2005) 'From Peacebuilding to Statebuilding: One Step Forward and Two Steps Back?', *Development* 48(3): 5–15.
Benford, R. D. and D. A. Snow (2000) 'Framing Processes and Social Movements: An Overview and Assessment', *Annual Review of Sociology* 26: 11–39.
Berdal, M. (2009) *Building Peace After War*, London: International Institute for Strategic Studies.
Bose, S. (2005) 'The Bosnian State a Decade After Dayton', *International Peacekeeping* 12(3): 322–335.
Call, C. T. and E. M. Cousens (2008) 'Ending Wars and Building Peace: International Responses to War-Torn Societies', *International Studies Perspectives* 9(1): 1–21.
Call, C. T. and V. W. Wyeth (eds) (2008) *Building States to Build Peace*, Boulder, CO: Lynne Rienner.
Caplan, R. (2005) 'Who Guards the Guardians? International Accountability in Bosnia', *International Peacekeeping* 12(3): 463–476.
Carothers, T. (2004) 'Democracy's Sobering State', *Current History* (December): 412–416.
Chandler, D. (1999) *Bosnia: Faking Democracy After Dayton*, London: Pluto Press.
Chandler, D. (2006) *Empire in Denial: The Politics of Statebuilding*, London: Pluto Press.
Chandler, D. (2007) 'The Other-regarding Ethics of "Empire in Denial"', in D. Chandler and V. Heins (eds) *Rethinking Ethical Foreign Policy: Pitfalls, Possibilities and Paradoxes*, London: Routledge, pp. 161–183.
Chesterman, S. (2004) *You, the People: The UN, Transitional Administration and State-Building* Oxford: Oxford University Press.
Chetail, V. (ed.) (2009) *Post-Conflict Peacebuilding: A Lexicon*, Oxford: Oxford University Press.
Chopra, J. (2000) 'The UN's Kingdom in East Timor', *Survival* 42(3): 27–40.
Chopra, J. (2002) 'Building State Failure in East Timor', *Development and Change* 33(5): 979–1000.
Cooper, N. (2007) 'Review Article: On the Crisis of the Liberal Peace', *Conflict, Security and Development* 7(4): 605–616.
Cox, R. (1986) 'Social Forces, States and World Orders: Beyond International Relations Theory', in R. O. Keohane (ed.) *Neorealism and Its Critics*, New York: Columbia University Press, pp. 204–254.

Crawford, N. C. (2002) *Argument and Change in World Politics: Ethics, Decolonization, and Humanitarian Intervention*, Cambridge: Cambridge University Press.
Diamond, L., J. Linz and S. M. Lipset (eds) (1990) *Politics in Developing Countries: Comparing Experiences with Democracy*, New York: Lynne Rienner.
Doyle, M. W. and Sambanis, N. (2006) *Making War and Building Peace: UN Peace Operations*, Princeton: Princeton University Press.
Duffield, M. (2007a) *Development, Security and Unending War*, London: Polity.
Duffield, M. (2007b) 'Development, Territories, and People: Consolidating the External Sovereign Frontier', *Alternatives* 32(2): 225–246.
Edelstein, D. (2009) 'Foreign Militaries, Sustainable Institutions, and Postwar Statebuilding', in R. Paris and T. D. Sisk (eds) *The Dilemmas of Statebuilding: Confronting the Contradictions of Postwar Peace Operations*, London: Routledge, pp. 81–103.
Encarnacion, O. G. (2005) 'The Follies of Democratic Imperialism', *World Policy Journal* 22(1): 47–60.
Englebert, P. and Tull, D. M. (2008) 'Postconflict Resolution in Africa: Flawed Ideas about Failed States', *International Security* 32(4): 106–139.
Fortna, V. P. (2008) *Does Peacekeeping Work? Shaping Belligerents' Choices After Civil War*, Princeton, NJ: Princeton University Press.
Fortna, V. P. and L. M. Howard (2008) 'Pitfalls and Prospects in the Peacekeeping Literature', *Annual Review of Political Science* 11: 283–301.
Fukuyama, F. (1993) *The End of History and the Last Man*, New York: Harper Perennial.
Fukuyama, F. (2004) *State-Building: Governance and World Order in the 21st Century*, Ithaca, NY: Cornell University Press.
Ghani, A. and C. Lockhart (2008) *Fixing Failed States: A Framework for Rebuilding a Fractured World*, Oxford: Oxford University Press.
Gilligan, M. J. and E. J. Sergenti (2008) 'Do UN Interventions Cause Peace? Using Matching to Improve Causal Inference', *Quarterly Journal of Political Science* 3(2): 89–122.
Goetze, C. and D. Guzina (2008) 'Peacebuilding, Statebuilding, Nationbuilding – Turtles All the Way Down?', *Civil Wars* 10(4): 319–347.
Gray, J. (2007) 'The Death of this Crackpot Creed is Nothing to Mourn', *Guardian*, 31 July.
Hartzell, C. and M. Hoddie (2007) *Crafting Peace: Power Sharing and the Negotiated Settlement of Civil Wars*, University Park, PA: Penn State University Press.
Heathershaw, J. (2008) 'Unpacking the Liberal Peace: The Dividing and Merging of Peacebuilding Discourses', *Millennium: Journal of International Studies* 36(3): 597–622.
Helman, G. B. and S. R. Ratner (1993) 'Saving Failed States', *Foreign Policy* 89: 3–20.
Herbst, J. (1996) 'Responding to State Failure in Africa', *International Security* 21(3): 120–144.
Herbst, J. (2003) 'Let Them Fail: State Failure in Theory and Practice: Implications for Policy', in R. I. Rotberg (ed.) *When States Fail: Causes and Consequences*, Princeton, NJ: Princeton University Press.
Howard, L. M. (2008) *UN Peacekeeping in Civil Wars*, Cambridge: Cambridge University Press.
Hyam, R. (1976) *Britain's Imperial Century, 1815–1914: A Study in Empire and Expansion*, London: B.T. Batsford.
Jacoby, T. (2007) 'Hegemony, Modernization and Post-war Reconstruction', *Global Society* 21(4): 534–535.

Jahn, B. (2007) 'The Tragedy of Liberal Diplomacy: Democratization, Intervention and Statebuilding (Part II)', *Journal of Intervention and Statebuilding* 1(2): 211–230.
Jarstad, A. K. and T. D. Sisk (eds) (2008) *From War to Democracy: Dilemmas of Peacebuilding*, Cambridge: Cambridge University Press.
Knaus, G. and F. Martin (2003) 'Travails of the European Raj', *Journal of Democracy* 14(3): 60–74.
Krause, K. and Jütersonke, O. (2005) 'Peace, Security and Development in Post-Conflict Environments', *Security Dialogue* 36(4): 447–462.
Lacher, W. (2007) 'Iraq: Exception to, or Epitome of Contemporary Post-Conflict Reconstruction?', *International Peacekeeping* 14(2): 237–250.
Luttwak, E. (1999) 'Give War a Chance', *Foreign Affairs* 7894): 36–44.
Meyer, J. (2008) 'The Concealed Violence of Modern Peace(-Making)', *Millennium: Journal of International Studies* 36(3): 555–574.
Milne, S. (2008) 'A System to Enforce Imperial Power Will Only be Resisted', *Guardian*, 28 February.
Neack, L. (1995) 'UN Peace-Keeping: In the Interest of Community or Self?', *Journal of Peace Research* 32(2): 181–196.
Ottaway, M. and B. Lacina (2003) 'International Interventions and Imperialism: Lessons from the 1990s', *SAIS Review* 23(2): 71–92.
Oxfam International (2007) 'Africa's Missing Billions: International Arms Flows and the Cost of Conflict', *Briefing Paper* 107 (October).
Pakenham, R. (1973) *America in the Third World*, Princeton, NJ: Princeton University Press.
Paris, R. (2000) 'Broadening the Study of Peace Operations', *International Studies Review* 2(3): 27–44.
Paris, R. (2002) 'International Peacebuilding and the "Mission Civilisatrice"', *Review of International Studies* 28(4): 637–656.
Paris, R. (2003) 'Peacekeeping and the Constraints of Global Culture', *European Journal of International Relations* 9(3): 441–473.
Paris, R. (2004) *At War's End: Building Peace After Civil Conflict*, Cambridge: Cambridge University Press.
Paris, R. and T. D. Sisk (eds) (2009a) *The Dilemmas of Statebuilding: Confronting the Contradictions of Postwar Peace Operations*, London: Routledge.
Paris, R. and T. D. Sisk (2009b) 'Introduction: Understanding the Contradictions of Postwar Statebuilding', in R. Paris and T. D. Sisk (eds) *The Dilemmas of Statebuilding: Confronting the Contradictions of Postwar Peace Operations*, London: Routledge, pp. 1–20.
Pugh, M. (2005) 'The Political Economy of Peacebuilding: A Critical Theory Perspective', *International Journal of Peace Studies* 10(2): 23–42.
Pugh, M. (2006a) 'Towards a New Agenda for Transforming War Economies' (co-authored with Mandy Turner), *Conflict Security and Development* 6(3): 471–479.
Pugh, M. (2006b) 'Peacekeeping as Constant Gardening by Other Means', paper prepared for the British International Studies Association conference, Cork, Ireland, 18–21 December.
Pugh, M. (2008) 'Corruption and the Political Economy of Liberal Peace', paper prepared for the International Studies Association annual convention, San Francisco, 26–28 March.
Quinn, J. M., T. D. Mason and M. Gurses (2007) 'Sustaining the Peace: Determinants of Civil War Recurrence', *International Interactions* 33(2): 184–185.
Richmond, O. P. (2005) *The Transformation of Peace*, London: Palgrave.

Richmond, O. P. (2006) 'The Problem of Peace: Understanding the "Liberal Peace"', *Conflict, Security and Development* 6(3): 291–314.

Richmond, O. P (2007) 'Critical Research Agendas for Peace: The Missing Link in the Study of International Relations', *Alternatives* 32(2): 247–274.

Richmond, O. P. and J. Franks (2007) 'Liberal Hubris? Virtual Peace in Cambodia', *Security Dialogue* 389(1): 27–48.

Robinson, W. I. (1996) *Promoting Polyarchy: Globalization, US Intervention, and Hegemony*, Cambridge: Cambridge University Press.

Sambanis, N. (2008) 'Short- and Long-Term Effects of UN Peace Operations', *World Bank Economic Review* 22(1): 9–32.

Scheuer, M. (2008) *Marching Toward Hell: America and Islam After Iraq*, New York: Free Press.

Suhrke, A. (2009) 'The Dangers of a Tight Embrace: Externally Assisted Statebuilding in Afghanistan', in R. Paris and T. D. Sisk (eds) *The Dilemmas of Statebuilding: Confronting the Contradictions of Postwar Peace Operations*, London: Routledge, pp. 227–251.

Tansey, O. (2008) 'Reply and Response to Jahn's "Tragedy of Liberal Diplomacy"', *Journal of Intervention and Statebuilding* 2(1): 87–98.

Toft, M. D. (2003) 'Peace Through Victory?', paper presented at the annual meeting of the American Political Science Association, Philadelphia, August 27–31.

Toft, M. D. (2009) *Securing the Peace: The Durable Settlement of Civil Wars*, Princeton, NJ: Princeton University Press.

UN (1992) United Nations, *An Agenda for Peace*, UN document A/47/277-S/24111 (17 June).

UN (2001) United Nations, 'No Exit without Strategy: Security Council Decision-Making and the Closure or Transition of UN Peacekeeping Operations', Report of the Secretary-General, UN document S/2001/394 (20 April).

UN (2006) United Nations, 'Report of the Secretary-General on Timor-Leste Pursuant to Security Council resolution 1690', UN Security Council document S/2006/628 (8 August).

Waites, B. (1999) *Europe and the Third World: From Colonialism to Decolonization, c. 1500–1998*, New York: St. Martin's.

Walton, C. D. (2009) 'The Case for Strategic Traditionalism: War, National Interest and Liberal Peacebuilding', *International Peacekeeping* 16(5): 717–734.

Weinstein, J. (2005) 'Autonomous Recovery and International Intervention in Comparative Perspective', Working Paper 57, Washington, DC: Center for Global Development.

Williams, P. D. (forthcoming) 'Peace Operations', unpublished essay prepared for the International Study Association's Compendium Project volume on Security Studies.

PART II

Not Such a 'Liberal' Peace?
Rethinking Intervention

3

The Effects of Peacebuilding: Sovereignty, Patronage and Power

Ole Jacob Sending

Introduction

In studying the social world, we have to presuppose some things as exogenously fixed. The trick is to choose what to keep constant carefully so as to allow for dynamism and the interplay of those factors that we have good reason to believe are most significant in accounting for any particular outcome or phenomena. I shall argue here that much of the literature on peacebuilding holds as exogenous or treats as marginal the interests, behaviour, and power of local actors. Peacebuilding outcomes in specific countries are used as ultimate tests or confirmation about claims either that peacebuilders fail or succeed, as if external actors are omnipotent and local actors have little or no power and agency.

Many different factors can help account for this state of affairs, including how the study of peacebuilding has been institutionalised as something of an inter-disciplinary sub-field in tandem with the expansion of the practice of peacebuilding. The object of analysis has not so much been the conditions for the emergence of peace, but assessing what external actors are doing and how to improve their effectiveness. One unfortunate consequence of this particular framing of the study of peacebuilding is either that local actors are seen to be relatively powerless, or that their power is used as an empirical basis for claiming that external actors cannot assume that social engineering-type of interventions will work. In neither case is there an explicit effort to model or account for *how* the power, agency, and interests of local actors shape peacebuilders' practices and their effects. Thus, both proponents and critics of the liberal peacebuilding model tend to assume the perspective of external actors, where the post-conflict country is an arena for observation, not its object.

Indeed, given the widely shared interpretation that peacebuilding generally fails to achieve stated outcomes, it is striking that analysts continue to analyse peacebuilding as if the key to the puzzle lies primarily with external actors. The critique of the liberal peace has brought out the importance of context-sensitivity, of local ownership, of 'bottom up' and 'hybrid' forms of peacebuilding. While these insights reflect an understanding of the limits of social engineering, they are used primarily as ammunition to criticise external actors' strategies and behaviour. This critique is a misguided one, due to the simplistic assumption that external actors, in fact, have it in their power to significantly shape outcomes. It appears that the goal is first and foremost to critique the political practices of intervention, and only secondarily, of it all, to understand or explain key dimensions of peacebuilding. To move beyond the simplistic critique of the liberal peace, it is necessary to develop analytical tools that can better capture and account for what peacebuilding can achieve or can contribute to peace, either through liberal or other approaches.

I argue that studies of peacebuilding would benefit from a shift in analytical and empirical focus that does not a priori privilege the power and behavior of external actors. While there is every reason to believe that external actors can and do shape developments in a post-conflict country, the point is that we cannot know how, through what mechanisms, and with what effects, they do so unless we also factor in the agency, interests, and power of different types of local actors. Thus, even if students of peacebuilding want to restrict their focus to the relative significance of external actors in the emergence of peace, even this cannot be adequately determined without making the power and agency of local actors endogenous to the analytical framework. One way to redress this limitation, I suggest, is a shift of focus to the character of the relationship between external and local actors, and to explicitly account for the interaction between them.

Omnipotent External Actors?

In a recent review of the peacebuilding literature, Roland Paris (2010) provides a list of core findings that reads as follows:

> inadequate attention to domestic institutional conditions for successful democratisation and marketisation; insufficient appreciation of the tensions and contradictions between the various goals of peacebuilding; poor strategic coordination among the various international actors involved in these missions; lack of political will and attention on the part of peacebuilding sponsors to complete the tasks they undertake, and insufficient commitment of resources; unresolved tensions in relations between the military and non-military participants in these operations; limited knowledge of distinctive local conditions and variations across the societies hosting these missions;

insufficient 'local ownership' over the strategic direction and daily activities of such operations; and continued conceptual challenges in defining the conditions for 'success' and strategies for bringing operations to an effective close. (Paris 2010: xx)

To this, we may add systematic marginalisation of the accountability of external actors vis à vis the local population (Chandler 2006); the pervasiveness of pre-conceived cognitive 'frames' that systematically privilege certain modes of intervention (such as democratic elections) over others (such as local conflict resolution) (Autesserre 2009); and the importance of organisational learning at the field level (Howard 2008). It is not, then, an undue stretch to claim that the study of peacebuilding tends to privilege the role of external actors.

This is not problematic in and of itself, of course, and there are good reasons why external actors' behavior has been singled out as central given the ambitious goals and strategies advanced by international organisations and bilateral donors. My concern is, however, that the theoretical framework and methods used are not well suited to produce robust findings: analysts often invoke *outcomes* of peacebuilding processes (relapse into conflict, lack of institutionalisation of liberal institutions, etc.) as a measuring stick for the effectiveness of what external actors are doing. This is tantamount to measuring the causal significance of only one among many possible core independent variables by looking at the value of the dependent variable (existence of peace, degree of institutionalisation of liberal principles, etc.) *without* demonstrating – either through empirical analysis or counterfactuals – the relative significance of other factors or actors in shaping these very outcomes. It is simply assumed that external actors control peacebuilding outcomes and hence that it makes sense to assess their effectiveness by looking at some of the key indicators of (liberal) peace in a country. As I seek to demonstrate below, this problem is found in works that differ significantly in terms of their conclusions about what peacebuilders should do.

Paris's *At War's End* (2004) assesses whether the lofty goals of external actors – acting according to the injunctions of the Wilsonian liberalisation thesis – are achieved, through a series of case studies ranging from El Salvador and Nicaragua in Latin America, Mozambique, Namibia and Liberia in Africa, and Cambodia and East Timor in Asia. In Angola, premature elections are said to have contributed to the fighting that erupted when UNITA did not recognise the results of the election. In Rwanda, economic liberalisation and early elections (political liberalisation) is similarly said to have contributed to the conditions that enabled the 1994 genocide to happen. In discussing those two cases where a relatively stable peace has been institutionalised and economic growth has been relatively steady – Mozambique and Namibia – Paris contends that these developments are *not* to be attributed to the success of a Wilsonian, liberal peacebuilding strategy. Rather, they had more to do with the nature of the conflict: more specifically, the fact that in both cases one of the main warring parties was from outside the country. Thus, when a peace agreement was signed, elections held, and a new government formed, there simply was not, as Paris puts it, much domestic 'demand' to continue fighting.

For East Timor and Kosovo, Paris turns the explanatory logic used to debunk the relative successes in Mozambique and Namibia, namely that it had to do with the relations between and resources of the warring parties, on its head: the primary cause of what then appeared to be relatively successful trajectories in East Timor and Kosovo – both of which had the UN assuming de facto sovereign powers – is located in the more assertive and institution-building focus of external actors in keeping with Paris's call for 'institutionalization before liberalization' (IBL). But there is no way of knowing from Paris's analysis whether it was, in fact, the IBL strategy that caused what then appeared to be positive development. In fact, Paris's causal argument is not primarily about peacebuilding understood as a political and social phenomenon. Rather, he identifies what policymakers, and liberal peace theorists, say and assume about 'liberalisation' as a conduit for peace, and then goes on to demonstrate that they are wrong in their assumptions: i.e. that liberalisation does not produce peace. It was, and is, an important corrective and critique of peacebuilding practice, and of liberal peace theorists. The problem, however, is that the finding that external actors' assumptions and objectives about liberalisation are flawed does not constitute an argument *for* 'institutionalization before liberalization'. This would only hold if we could demonstrate that external actors, in fact, had significant power to shape the outcome of post-conflict political processes. However, this is merely assumed rather than demonstrated. In discussing Sierra Leone, for example, Paris locates the central explanation for why fighting erupted after the election in 1996, and not after the election in 2002, in the fact that the interval period had seen extensive statebuilding measures taken by external actors. He assumes that the investment in security sector reform and in the training of civil servants to serve in the state apparatus may have contributed to the more peaceful trajectory that set in after the 2001 election. But to demonstrate the relative significance of external actors' efforts to this outcome would require an assessment of how external actors' interventions were effective or significant by the tracing their effects *on and through core domestic political actors*, upon their interests, their constituencies, and their power.

Similarly, Michael Barnett (2006) uses developments in Afghanistan and Iraq as illustrations for why a 'republican' peacebuilding model (Afghanistan) is to be preferred over a liberal one (Iraq). While the situations of Afghanistan and Iraq are used as illustrations, not as fully fledged case studies, the implication is that things looked better in Afghanistan and worse in Iraq *because* external actors had opted for a republican model in the former and a liberal one in the latter. However, Barnett's argument lacks any sustained discussion of the internal make-up of each country, and the practices and understandings of different local groups. Lise Howard's (2008) study of ten cases of so-called complex peacekeeping operations, including peacebuilding, finds that the factors that determine whether or not peacebuilding efforts are successful can be divided into three: situational factors; support, but not intense interest, from members of the UN Security Council; and the ability of peacekeepers to learn from and adapt to local circumstances, what Howard calls 'first-level organizational learning' (2008: 14–20). I concur with Howard's contention that those that place the explanatory power of successes and failures of peacebuilding efforts exclusively in situational characteristics miss the point (ibid.: 10): external actors do impact domestic peacebuilding trajectories.

But whereas Howard accords agency and interests to external actors (UNSC member states, and management and staff of peace operations), local actors figure under the heading of 'situational factors'; primarily as data points specified in terms of the degree to which both parties consent to a peace agreement, whether the peace agreement is specific or vague, how many were killed during the conflict, and so on. This category is not suited to capture on-going political dynamics in a country, only to add 'background' or contextual parameters for what external actors do. Thus, the domestic political scene is an arena for observation rather than its core object. This tendency is all the more surprising when we consider that what local actors are doing, the interests they may have, and the resources at their disposal, would intuitively appear to be the default explanation for why peace did or did not become institutionalised.

I am not claiming that students of peacebuilding should abandon their focus on the role of external actors. What I am claiming is that students of peacebuilding, in focusing on external actors, cannot uncritically use outcomes or trends in a particular country as evidence about whether external actors are causally significant in shaping those outcomes. To do so is to assume that external actors' goals and governance practices are *unaffected* by the interests and governance logics of local actors – as if implementing peacebuilding measures through and with local actors is smooth and relatively frictionless. Séverine Autesserre's (2009) analysis of the Congo exhibits a similar tendency of omitting to factor in the agency, power and interests of key local actors. She develops a robust argument about the discursive frame that shaped external actors' behavior, for example, illustrating how the doxic character of this discursive frame explained why external actors opted for national elections as a means to end the conflict, without recognising that they were dealing with a situation that was primarily a series of inter-linked local conflicts. Autesserre is cautious not to over-state her case. Nonetheless, would external actors have made progress in stalling the conflict had they adopted a different strategy? Would local conflict resolution organised by external actors have been effective? To answer these questions in an empirically robust way is central, I believe, to get at the heart of what peacebuilding is about. It is representative of the literature that these questions fall beyond the scope of Autesserre's otherwise excellent study.

To be sure, there are plenty of studies that do focus on the domestic dynamics of post-conflict societies. Here, the resources, strategies and actions of external actors takes the backseat to the contents and strength of already existing structures in post-conflict societies, such as patron-client networks (Reno 1997), the dynamics of 'regime survival' (Eriksen and Nordhaug 2006), and how, for example, African society 'works' (Chabal and Daloz 1999; Boone 2003). These studies are not concerned with peacebuilding, but with understanding and comparing the functioning of political systems in the global south. Students of peacebuilding typically draw on such findings in an effort to make arguments about how external actors could do better, for example, through calls for more emphasis on local ownership (Narten 2009), to develop a more general cautionary tale about the limits of social engineering (Suhrke 2009), or as a platform from which to make a charge 'against statebuilding' (Bhuta 2008). In most, if not all, of these works, the findings concerning local actors and relations are framed as important because the external peacebuilding actors have paid 'inadequate attention' to them.

There are exceptions. Empirically, Englebert and Tüll (2008) build explicitly on a broad range of insights from students of African political systems to produce a much more nuanced picture of the nature of the processes through which peacebuilding evolves, a process where – it is clear – local actors hold significant power. Theoretically, Barnett and Zürcher (2009) have modeled the dynamics of interaction between external and local actors (see also Zürcher, this volume). They posit that peacebuilders (external actors) aim for 'stability and liberalization', that state elites want to remain in power, and that rural elites want autonomy from the state and to remain in power locally. The crucial ingredient here, at least for the present purpose, is that the model explicitly recognises that: 'The ability of each actor to achieve its goals is dependent on the strategies and behavior of the other two' (2009: 24–25). From this, they posit four possible outcomes, finding that 'co-opted peacebuilding', where local elites and external actors negotiate peacebuilding measures that satisfy the latter's goal of stability and the former's goal of remaining in power, is the most common one. This is also in keeping with Miles Kahler's (2009: 292) observation, that to get a good grasp of how the 'preferences, resources, and strategies of the key players vary to produce success or failure in statebuilding' it is necessary to specify the political conditions under which external intervention takes place. Below, I seek to develop a generic framework that would capture such political conditions in terms of the rules of the game between external and local actors and the political economy of political survival among political elites in post-conflict countries.

It is important to note the key question at issue here: the assumption that external actors are much more powerful than local ones. The reason why there is so little sensitivity to context and to according ownership to local actors is the far-reaching assumption that there is an asymmetrical power relation in favor of external actors. Oliver Richmond, for example, discusses the concepts of the 'everyday' and local agency in critiquing the liberal peacebuilding model, and notes, for example, that 'resistance appears, at least from the local level, to offer the main avenue through which the shape the emerging political environment, though this is predicated on the overwhelming technical superiority, and to modify it marginally, or to mimic it' (2010: 685). He thus argues that the 'everyday forms of resistance' are where local agency is expressed 'despite overwhelming authority' (ibid.: 685). Below, I seek to substantiate the argument that external actors are not necessarily more powerful than local actors, and that they certainly do not constitute an 'overwhelming authority'. I argue for a shift in focus that models or renders endogenous the 'political infrastructure' through which external actors operate to try to build peace. In so doing, it should be possible to produce a more nuanced and specific account of the effects of external actors' peacebuilding efforts. I do so by first discussing different dimensions of power and subsequently by discussing how the institution of sovereignty is central to an appreciation of the character of the relation between external and local actors.

Sovereignty, Patronage and Power

Space does not allow an extended analytical discussion of the concept of power, however, the points can be made adequately by relying on a conventional relational understanding of power (Dahl 1961), where power can be defined as 'A's ability to get B to do something that he/she would otherwise not do'. Following Baldwin (2002) we can distinguish between the scope, domain, and costs of power. Scope refers to those aspects of B's behavior that A is in a position to affect. Domain refers to the constituent nature of B (for example, a government, a political elite, a broader set of social groups). Costs refer to how much resources it takes for A to get B to do certain things, and how much it costs for B to comply or not.

But even before such an analysis of the power of interacting actors can begin, we need to account for why it makes sense to speak of 'external' and 'internal' actors in the first place. To do so necessitates a discussion of sovereignty and how it shapes the very character of the relationship between external and internal actors. There is a sizeable literature on sovereignty and the liberal peace, mainly expressed through discussions of humanitarian intervention and the 'responsibility to protect' (Weiss 2004), and transitional administrations established by the UN in Kosovo and East Timor (Chesterman 2004). What has not received much sustained attention is how the institution of sovereignty structures the relationship between external and internal actors. Obviously, the institution of sovereignty is constitutive of the relationship between 'external' and 'internal' actors. It is expressed in Article 2, paragraph 7 of the UN Charter in terms of a specification that: 'Nothing contained in the present Charter shall authorize the United Nations to intervene in matters which are essentially within the domestic jurisdiction of any state.' But how, specifically, does the institution of sovereignty structure the interaction between external and internal actors? I argue that it accords much more autonomy and also power to internal actors than is recognised in the literature, reducing the domain and scope of external actors' power, and increasing the costs of enforcing compliance.

As an institution, sovereignty serves to undermine the alleged effectiveness of the power of external actors. This is so because, for all of its expertise, international legitimacy and resources, external actors have little choice but to act through and with the consent (explicit or implicit) of representatives of states (Neumann and Sending 2010). While colonial rule also relied on political elites as middle-men for governing, present-day peacebuilding efforts must – as a rule – operate through government representatives not always of their own choosing. The relation between the colonial power and the colony was based on suzerainty, not sovereignty.

While liberalism seeks to specify how sovereign power is to be exercised, sovereignty itself allows for a multitude of governance practices to flourish, such as patrimonial forms of rule. Thus, the ends and means of external actors are undermined by sovereignty, whereas key features of how local actors operate – for example, through patrimonial rule aimed at the 'politics of survival' – are not. The power potential of external actors is, in this way, undercut by the institution of sovereignty. And despite being seemingly dispossessed and having to consent to heavy international conditions, local actors have a range of strategies and resources at their disposal with which to mimic, evade, and ultimately undercut the ability of external actors to shape outcomes. This feature of the relation between external and local actors helps explain how and why, as Englebert and Tüll note:

> many African governments have skilfully evaded outside pressures for structural changes. State elites have frequently manipulated economic reform and used these reforms to recalibrate their power, notably in the realm of privatization of state-owned enterprises. (2008: 115)

Thus, rather than focusing on the behaviour of external actors and tracing their effects by looking at the overall developments in a post-conflict country, focus should be on how established forms of rule and socio-political organisation shape (and are also shaped by) efforts to introduce new governance practices by external actors. The institution of sovereignty establishes government representatives as the primary interlocutors for external actors. This is why it is necessary to study how existing forms of rule (such as patronage) are shaped by and reproduce the primary interests and constituencies of domestic political elites in order to understand the impacts of external actors' peacebuilding policy practices. While political elites may adopt the ideology and the rhetoric required by external actors for the purpose of attracting or continuing to receive financial and political support, they have considerable autonomy, and thus also power, to use and distribute resources in ways that serve their primary interests (Bates 1981; Boone 2003). This is not to say that domestic political elites are not interested in investing in statebuilding and in liberal reform. This is an empirical question. Swidler captures the ways in which the local political logic may very well undercut and render ineffective the power of external actors:

> Despite donors' prestige and financial heft, they have more difficulty penetrating and altering local patterns of governance than one might expect. Many kinds of institutional imageries, ideologies, and buzzwords are embraced with great enthusiasm by those whom [. . .] international organizations seek to transform. But what donor organizations offer is received (or seized) within a different social organization, where intended and actual effects differ. In order to understand the penetration of new models of governance, it is important to know how governance actually operates on the ground – what power, influence, and administrative authority actually consists of. Only attention to the actual characteristics of African systems of governance an help us understand why some . . . interventions take root and thrive, while others fail to take hold, or, even if they become embedded, fester rather than flourish. (2009: 197)

Against this backdrop, it becomes difficult, if not impossible, to make robust claims about the effects of peacebuilding efforts by external actors without tracing and specifying what happens when external actors' logic of governance hit the logic of governance which is already in place in a post-conflict country. For this reason, it has to be included and specified in the analytical framework. Thus, by shifting focus to the relationship and interaction between external and local actors, and specifying that relationship as being shaped by sovereignty practices, it is possible to assess the power of both external and local actors to shape outcomes and also to capture the dynamics of interaction between them. What I call the political infrastructure through which peacebuilding efforts operate is meant to capture this aspect.

In some of my own work (Sending 2009) I have tried to show that external actors fail in large part because they adopt an 'Archimedean' view of what they are doing: i.e. they perceive themselves as acting disinterestedly above and beyond the sphere of politics (understood to be a product of domestic contestation). While I still think that the argument is valid as an account of external actors' behavior and identity, I am now less sure about its significance for the effects of peacebuilding efforts. Or, more to the point, its significance depends on the particular political infrastructure for peacebuilding of the country in question. This political infrastructure is made up of the interests of the political elites, their core constituencies, and the relations between them. Thus, if political elites see their interests undermined by investments in good governance and state institutions, the Archimedean view of external actors will be of little significance. But if political elites are uncertain about whether their interests are best served by investing in state institutions, or if rival political groups can be co-opted or marginalised by it, then it would appear to matter whether there is an Archimedean view with its attendant lack of concern regarding context-sensitivity and ownership. Put differently, the significance of how external actors operationalise peacebuilding efforts also depends crucially on the socio-political basis that underwrites formal political institutions. As Evans (2004) has argued 'informal structures of power and practice render the formal structures ineffectual' (2004: 34).

Thus, the relative significance of external actors' strategy, sequencing, prioritisation, and coordination seems to depend crucially on the nature and functioning of these 'informal structures of power'. Against this background, claims about the lack of attention to ownership and context may be a generic or universal trait of external actors, but the *effects* of this trait must be determined empirically from case to case.

On the strength of the above, a generic analytical framework can be tentatively formulated as follows (drawing from Eriksen, Sundstøl and Sending 2010): the effects and success of peacebuilding efforts depend both on how the state is integrated with society and on how it is separated from it. The outcome of peacebuilding efforts is determined by the dynamic interaction between external and internal actors, where the former seeks to build capacity (transferring skills and resources) and the latter receives, selects, uses and also disregards elements of the donors' programmes. The character of state–society relations in a post-conflict country (which Munro usefully analyses as consisting of both the political and moral economy of the state, 1996), emerges as the principal analytical tool to understand how local actors perceive and use the resources accorded to them by external actors. In this way, a 'thicker' account is made of how local actors are situated socially, economically and politically. Thus, the 'recipients' of peacebuilding efforts are seen as actors with interests, identities and 'projects'; these concerns and practices are thereby central to any measure of whether peacebuilding reinforces, weakens or transforms state institutions. A guiding hypothesis for such studies is that peacebuilding does not fundamentally alter the relations between key political elites and their constituencies. Rather, it reconfigures pre-existing governing logics (such as patronage) and accords new skills and resources to some actors rather than others. I recognise that part of the challenge here has to do with methods and access to data: it is much more challenging to capture the evolving interaction between domestic political actors, and between these and external actors, than to focus squarely on the actions and declarations of external actors while holding constant the domestic political setting. But it can and should be done in order to analyse how the interests and strategies of external actors and of different local actors combine to produce a particular outcome (a good example of an analysis of this kind is found in Chaudhary et al., this volume).

Conclusion

Students of peacebuilding are not alone in fixing the analytical gaze on one set of actors in accounting for particular outcomes while ignoring or assuming as fixed the actions of others. Much of the literature on global governance is focused on the role and power of different types of non-state actors, whose power is said to be on the increase. Whether these actors are transnational advocacy groups (Risse et al. 1999), epistemic communities (Haas 1992), or international organisations (Barnett and Finnemore 2004), these actors are said to be central in shaping policy outcomes. Typically, the analytical story starts with the identification of a group that shares some characteristics, whether labelled as an advocacy group or expert group, and then moves on to retrospectively tracing the processes through which such groups influenced a policy outcome, generally concluding that the final outcome, for example, a new or changed international policy, can be attributed to the agency of these actors. In basing their claims about global governance on the power of particular types of actors, these accounts make unduly strong assumptions about the lack of power of *other* groups, whether these are state or non-state. The critique offered here of studies of peacebuilding is thus one of more general application, the central point being that while it is often convenient to structure empirical analyses around particular actors, the central analytical question is the character of the *relationship between* actors (Jackson and Nexon 1999).

There is also a much broader issue at stake here, which concerns how the study of peacebuilding can be linked much more directly to analytical and empirical work in neighbouring sub-fields of the social sciences. On *power*, work on its 'performative' aspect seems relevant, as it draws attention to how 'attributing 'power' to an issue immediately implies that 'we could have done things otherwise'. In other words, 'attributing power to an issue immediately raises the stakes of political justification for action or non-action' (Guzzini 2005: 497). Thus conceived, the study of peacebuilding is linked to the practice of peacebuilding by suggesting that how and where power is located in the study of peacebuilding has important effects on how peacebuilding practices are debated and justified. Moreover, insights from new institutional theory about the conditions under which established forms of rule may change and how the introduction of new governance practices are received and acted upon, given pre-existing institutional rules and resources, seem relevant (Powell and DiMaggio 1991). As regards theories of *global governance*, there is much to be said for a more sustained focus on how those that seek to govern – because they need authority – have their eyes fixed on constituencies with different, often conflicting, views and concerns (Avant et al. 2010). Peacebuilding seems to be a case of how the authority to govern on the part of both external and local actors is secured in and through very different and partly competing constituencies (Eriksen and Sending 2010a), with the result that peacebuilding is caught in a web of constituencies that have different and partly competing interests and concerns.

Bibliography

Autesserre, S. (2009) 'Hobbes in the Congo: Frames, Local Violence, and International Intervention', *International Organization* 63(2): 249–280.

Avant, D., M. Finnemore and S. Sell (eds) (2010) *Who Governs the Globe?*, Cambridge: Cambridge University Press.

Baldwin, D. (2002) 'Power in International Relations', in W. Carlsnaes, T. Risse and B. Simmons (eds) (2002) *Handbook of International Relations*, London: Sage, pp. 177–191.

Barnett, M. (2006) 'Building a Republican Peace: Stabilizing States after War', *International Security* 30(4): 87–112.

Barnett, M. and M. Finnemore (2004) *Rules for the World*, Ithaca, NY: Cornell University Press.

Barnett, M. and C. Zürcher (2009) 'The Peacebuilder's Contract: How External Statebuilding Reinforces Weak Statehood', in R. Paris and T. Sisk (eds) *The Dilemmas of Statebuilding: Confronting the Contradictions of Postwar Peace Operations*, London: Routledge, pp. 23–52.

Bates, R. (1981) *Markets and States in Tropical Africa: The Political Basis for Agrarian Policies*, Berkeley: University of California Press.

Bhuta, N. (2008) 'Against State-Building', *Constellations* 15(4): 517–542.

Boone, C. (2003) *Political Topographies of the African State: Territorial Authority and Institutional Voice*, Cambridge and New York: Cambridge University Press.

Chabal, P. and J.-P. Daloz (1999) *Africa Works. The Political Instrumentalization of Disorder*, Bloomington: Indiana University Press.

Chandler, D. (2006) *Empire in Denial: The Politics of Statebuilding*, London: Pluto Press.

Chesterman, S. (2004) *You, the People: The United Nations, Transitional Administration, and State-Building*, Oxford: Oxford University Press.

Dahl, R. (1961) *Who Governs: Democracy and Power in an American City* New Haven, CT: Yale University Press.

de Waal, A. (2009) 'Mission without End? Peacekeeping in the African Political Marketplace', *International Affairs* 85(1): 99–113.

Englebert, P. and D. Tüll (2008) 'Postconflict Reconstruction in Africa: Flawed Ideas about Failed States', *International Security* 32(4): 106–139.

Eriksen, S. S. and K. Nordhaug (2006) 'Politics of Survival in the Making of Weak and Strong States', *Forum for Development Studies* 33(2): 237–265.

Eriksen, S. S. and O. J. Sending (2010a) 'Capacity Building in Post-conflict Societies: Police Reform, Revenue-collection and the Politics of State Formation', memo, Oslo: NUPI.

Eriksen, S. S. and O. J. Sending (2010b) 'Where Is the Global Public?', working paper, Oslo: NUPI.

Evans, Peter (2004) 'Development as Institutional Change: The Pitfalls of Monocropping and the Potentials of Deliberation', *Studies in Comparative International Development* 38(4): 30–52.

Haas, P. M. (ed.) (1992) 'Knowledge, Power and International Policy Coordination', special issue, *International Organization* 46(1): 1–35.

Howard, L. M. (2008) *UN Peacekeeping in Civil Wars*, Cambridge: Cambridge University Press.

Hyden, G. (2006) *African Politics in Comparative Perspective*, Cambridge: Cambridge University Press.

Jackson, P. T. and D. Nexon (1999) 'Relations before States: Substance, Process, and the Study of World Politics', *European Journal of International Relations* 5(3): 291–332.

Kahler, M. (2009) 'Statebuilding after Afghanistan and Iraq,', in R. Paris and T. Sisk (eds) *The Dilemmas of Statebuilding. Confronting the Contradictions of Postwar Peace Operations*, London and New York: Routledge, pp. 287–303.

Krasner, S. (2004) 'Sharing Sovereignty: New Institutions for Collapsed and Failing States', *International Security* 29(2): 85–120.

Munro, W. (1996) 'Power, Peasants and Political Development: Reconsidering State Construction in Africa', *Comparative Studies in Society and History* 38(1): 112–148.

Narten, J. (2009) 'Dilemmas of Promoting "Local Ownership": The Case of Postwar Kosovo', in R. Paris and T. Sisk (eds) *The Dilemmas of Statebuilding. Confronting the Contradictions of Postwar Peace Operations*, London and New York: Routledge, pp. 252–283.

Neumann, I. B. and O. J. Sending (2010) *Governing the Global Polity: Practice, Mentality, Rationality*, Ann Arbor: University of Michigan Press.

Powell, W. and P. DiMaggio (eds) (1991) *The New Institutionalism in Organizational Analysis*, Chicago: Chicago University Press.

Paris, R. (2000) 'Broadening the Study of Peace Operations', *International Studies Review* 2(3): 27–44.

Paris, R. (2004) *At War's End: Building Peace after Civil Conflict*, Cambridge: Cambridge University Press.

Paris, R. (2010) 'Saving Liberal Peacebuilding', *Review of International Studies* 36(2): 337–365.

Paris, R. and T. Sisk (eds) (2009) *The Dilemmas of Statebuilding: Confronting the Contradictions of Postwar Peace Operations*, London: Routledge.

Reno, W. (1997) 'War, Markets, and the Reconfiguration of West Africa's Weak States', *Comparative Politics* 29(4): 493–510.

Richmond, O. P. (2007) 'Critical Research Agendas for Peace: The Missing Link in the Study of International Relations', *Alternatives* 32(2): 247–274.

Richmond, O. P. (2010) 'Resistance and the Post-Liberal Peace', *Millennium: Journal of International Studies* 38(3): 665–692.

Risse, T., S. Ropp and K. Sikkink (eds) (1999) *The Power of Human Rights: International Norms and Domestic Change*, Cambridge: Cambridge University Press.

Rueschemeyer, D., E. H. Stephens and J. D. Stephens (1992) *Capitalist Development and Democracy*, Cambridge: Polity Press.
Sending, O. J. (2009) 'Why Peacebuilders Fail to Secure Ownership and Be Sensitive to Context', *Security in Practice*, Report No. 1 Oslo: NUPI.
Stedman, S. (1997) 'Spoiler Problems in the Peace Process', *International Security* 22(2): 5–53.
Suhrke, A. (2007) 'Reconstruction as Modernization. The "Post-Conflict" Project in Afghanistan', *Third World Quarterly* 28(7): 1291–1308.
Suhrke, A. (2009) 'The Dangers of a Tight Embrace. Externally Assisted Statebuilding in Afghanistan', in R. Paris and T. Sisk (eds) *The Dilemmas of Statebuilding. Confronting the Contradictions of Postwar Peace Operations*, London and New York: Routledge, pp. 227–251.
Swidler, A. (2009) 'Dialectics of Patronage: Logics of Accountability at the African AIDS-NGO Interface', in David C. Hammock and Steven Jeydemann (eds) *Globalization, Philanthropy, and Civil Society*, Bloomington: Indiana University Press.
Weiss, T. (2004) 'The Sunset of Humanitarian Intervention? The Responsibility to Protect in a Unipolar Era', *Security Dialogue* 35(2): 135–153.
Zaum, D. (2007) *The Sovereignty Paradox: The Norms and Politics of International Statebuilding*, Oxford: Oxford University Press.

4

The Liberal Peace: A Tough Sell?

Christoph Zürcher

Introduction

All peacebuilding missions after the end of the Cold War have sought to bring not only peace to countries torn by civil war, but also democracy.[1] Two decades after the Cold War came to an end, democratisation is now firmly anchored in peacebuilding and has led to ever more ambitious and demanding agendas. It is no longer enough that war comes to an end. Rather, the international community seeks to build fully developed, democratic and economically viable states on the ruins of war. This not only bears witness to how ambitious and encompassing the post-Cold War peacebuilding agenda has become, but also to how deeply the international community chooses to believe that post-war societies can be socially engineered. Contemporary peacebuilding, in short, is statebuilding, though in a post-conflict context aimed at 'constructing or reconstructing institutions of governance capable of providing citizens with physical and economic security. This includes quasi-governmental activities such as electoral assistance, human rights and rule of law technical assistance, security sector reform, and certain forms of development assistance' (Chesterman 2004: 5). Much attention, then, is directed at attempting to invest the state with the capacity to deliver services and public goods that will enhance the welfare of society. But, importantly, peacebuilders are also interested in producing a particular kind of state – a liberal democratic state organised around markets, the rule of law, and democratic institutions. While I refrain here from discussing the reasons for this, it is clear that this preference is evident across the peacebuilding universe: contemporary peacebuilding operations, from Mozambique to Afghanistan, are deployed in order to secure the peace, and in order to build a liberal, democratic polity.

However, the evidence for successful post-war democratic transitions is not encouraging. Since 1989, the international community has launched nineteen major peacebuilding operations (see Table 4.1). These operations were reasonably successful in securing the peace, defined as an end to large-scale violent conflict, but they were less successful in establishing a democratic regime. Five years after the beginning of the peacebuilding operation, only one country was rated as a liberal democracy by Freedom House (a score between 1 and 2 denotes a liberal democracy). Six more countries, with a Freedom House score between 2.5 and 3.5, can be considered electoral democracies; they hold reasonably free, fair and inclusive elections, but civil liberties are considerably less developed and protected than in a liberal democracy. Finally, twelve countries

Table 4.1 Major multinational peacebuilding missions after 1989 and post-war democratic transitions[2]

Country	Year mission started	Freedom House Score five years after start of mission
Croatia	1996	2
Namibia	1989	2.5
East Timor	1999	3
Macedonia	2001	3
Liberia	2003	3.5
Mozambique	1992	3.5
Sierra Leone	1999	3.5
Burundi	2004	4.5
Bosnia	1995	4.5
Afghanistan	2002	5
Haiti	1994	5
Côte d'Ivoire	2003	5.5
Kosovo	1999	5.5
Tajikistan	1997	5.5
Angola	1995	6
Central African Republic	1998	6
DR Congo	1999	6
Cambodia	1992	6.5
Rwanda	1994	6.5

Source: Freedom House: Freedom in the World Comparative and Historical Data, Country status and ratings overview, FIW 1973–2010.

cannot be considered democracies at all, even though there are substantial differences within this group.

Also noteworthy is that none of the most recent major peacebuilding operations – East Timor, Bosnia, Kosovo, and Afghanistan – has resulted in the establishment of a fully democratic regime, East Timor being closest with a Freedom House score of 3. Why is it that peacebuilding missions so often fail to achieve their goal of creating a reasonably democratic peace?

A pessimistic line of thought maintains that it is simply not reasonable to assume that peacebuilders should be able to socially engineer, in a matter of years, a society which is capable of producing and maintaining a liberal democratic regime. In this view, bringing democracy to a war-torn country is simply the impossible dream, born out of Western hubris (Kaplan 2008).

A more optimistic view is that post-war democratisation is possible, but that it is extraordinarily rare because most post-war societies lack the resources and capacities to implement and maintain the complex and costly political institutions required for democratic governance. Civil war is highly destructive and leaves a legacy of poverty, destroyed infrastructure, weak political institutions and deep-seated mistrust between the ex-combatants (Jarstad and Sisk 2008). It may, therefore, be beyond the capacities of the local elites to build the institutions which are required to run a democracy, such as free media, an independent judiciary, a system of checks and balances for the separation of powers, and a strong civil society (Diamond 2006). Furthermore, local elites may lack the capacity to engage in meaningful cooperation with their former opponents if mistrust or hatred continues to dominate the political arena, and political institutions that could enable cooperation are weak or missing altogether (Collier 2009; Roeder and Rothchild 2005).

Another argument, often described as the problem-solving approach, is concerned with the policies of peacebuilding itself. This argument, by and large, still upholds the belief in the promises of liberal peacebuilding, but points to many flaws in the implementation of many peacebuilding missions (Paris 2008; Paris and Sisk 2009). Serious time and resource constraints are often thought to be the main culprit for the lack of success in democratic peacebuilding. The assumption is that missions with a larger footprint in terms of financing, manpower and mandate could perhaps achieve better outcomes. Furthermore, coordination problems among the myriad of peacebuilding actors and the peacebuilders' limited ability to learn are also quoted as causes for the modest track record of democratic peacebuilding. Another widespread complaint is that peacebuilders rarely adapt their strategies to the context, but tend to treat post-conflict democratisation generally as a problem that can be solved by mechanically implementing a series of known tasks in the correct order, resulting in an ahistorical and voluntaristic approach to democratic peacebuilding (Carothers 2004). In a related argument, Paris (2004) more specifically maintains that peacebuilders have taken an inappropriately uniform approach to post-conflict state reconstruction, based upon prioritising political and economic liberalisation over constructing the foundations of effective political and economic institutions.

None of these arguments is without merits, yet our findings show that none is systematically associated with success or failure across a substantial number of cases. For example, some successful democratic peacebuilding operations were launched in poor countries lacking domestic capacity (e.g. Mozambique and East Timor), whereas other operations failed in considerably affluent countries with a relatively high level of development and viable administrative structures in place (e.g. Bosnia and Kosovo). Some robust and highly intrusive operations failed (e.g. Afghanistan) and some succeeded (e.g. East Timor). On the other hand, operations with a low level of intrusiveness and a small footprint succeeded in some cases (e.g. Namibia) and failed in others (e.g. Tajikistan and Rwanda). Some peace operations contributed to democracy even after a very long and bloody war (e.g. Mozambique) and some did not even though the war was relatively short (e.g. Kosovo). From these examples it should be quite apparent that we lack a consistent explanation of post-war democratic transition.

In this chapter, I propose a conceptualisation of the peacebuilding process that may contribute to a better understanding of what causes failed or successful liberal peacebuilding. I am fully aware that the labels 'failed', 'successful' and 'liberal' are normatively highly charged categories, rather than ready-to-use analytical categories. For the moment, I will stick to the commonly used definition of a reasonably democratic regime (a polity score of 6 or higher, and a Freedom House score of 2.5 or higher) as a threshold for success. I readily concede that there may be better measures for democracy, that democracy may or may not be a necessary ingredient for peacebuilding success, and that the focus on 'liberal peace' in the context of peacebuilding mission actually may create more problems that it solves. In this chapter, however, I focus on an explanation of why peacebuilding missions rarely lead to democratic outcomes, and I do not, for the moment, engage in a discussion of measurements and normative standards and their potential detrimental effects.

I argue that existing approaches to post-war democratic transitions suffer from the fact that they ignore one of the most important and consequential aspects of contemporary peacebuilding, namely that peacebuilding is an interactive process not only between the former adversaries, but also between peacebuilders and the victorious elites of a post-war society, and that this interaction decisively shapes the process of the peacebuilding and its outcomes. By ignoring the interactive quality of peacebuilding, much of the literature seems to implicitly assume that the interests of the peacebuilders and of the government of the host country are typically aligned and therefore assumes that the process of peacebuilding is a problem of capacity and coordination, rather than a problem of cooperation. I take issue with this implicit assumption. I think that one of the major determinants of peacebuilding is indeed the differing of priorities of peacebuilders and local elites. In a nutshell, local elites may wish to benefit from the resources, both material and symbolic, that peacebuilders bring, while they may not be too keen to adopt democracy because they may perceive democratic reforms as endangering their security or their privileged access to power or predation. Peacebuilders, on the other hand, expect democratic reforms, but may be unwilling to commit too many resources or risk their own casualties. The outcomes of peacebuilding, I argue, depend to a large extent on the outcome of the informal bargaining by which peacebuilders and local elites try to sort out these differences and agree (or fail to do so) on the kind of peace they intend to build (Barnett and Zürcher 2009).

When peacebuilders deploy, they are met by a local political elite, which may share some aspects of the peacebuilders' vision but not others. On the surface, peacebuilders and local elites have a common objective – building peace – but this objective is loosely enough defined to trigger a constant bargaining over the exact contents of the peace, over allocation of resources, over who has the control over the process, over priorities and, most importantly, over the contents of reform polices. In short, what is at stake is not only how the peace is being built, but also what kind of state will emerge from this process.

So what do they want? Peacebuilders want to implement reforms that lead to a liberal peace: they want to deliver services and assistance that will create new institutions that (re)distribute political and economic power in a transparent, accountable and democratic way. However, peacebuilders typically operate under serious constraints which may temper their zeal for radical reforms that are needed in order to achieve these objectives. Peacebuilders operate with limited resources, and they operate under time constraints because voters at home may not support an expensive peacebuilding mission indefinitely (Bueno de Mesquita and Downs 2006). Most importantly, peacebuilders need to minimise casualties. Otherwise, their governments will lose the support of the electorate. Consequently, peacebuilders may prioritise stability over the kinds of structural reforms that are posited to produce the kind of liberal peacebuilding they desire. In addition, peacebuilders are highly dependent on domestic actors because their cooperation is essential for a smooth and stable implementation of the many peacebuilding projects. Without the consent and the support of local elites, peacebuilding programmes cannot be implemented, and security for international personnel cannot be guaranteed. This creates a strong incentive to cooperate with local elites, even when they are not committed to democratic reforms.

What do local elites want? I think it is plausible to assume that local elites in post-war situations want to preserve their political power and to ensure that the peacebuilding process either enhances or does not harm their political and economic interests. It is possible that local elites perceive it to be in their best interest to fully align with the peacebuilders' vision, as it was, for example, in the case of Namibia. However, it is more likely that local elites have priorities which differ from those of the peacebuilders. As a matter of fact, local elites may welcome peace, but not democracy, for various reasons.

To start with, introducing democratic rules endangers the militarily strongest party's grip on power, because it may lose in elections what was won in battle. Hence when a party that emerged as the winner on the battlefield risks losing its supremacy at the ballot box, it is likely to oppose democratic procedures (Jarstad and Sisk 2008). Second, liberal peace brings with it norms and rules of good governance that restrict the ability to arbitrarily reign, extort and expropriate. Elites that grew strong and rich during civil wars may hence oppose any reforms that endanger their ways of extortion, which may include racketeering, smuggling, illegal private taxing, drug cultivation and corruption.[3] Finally, and most importantly, democratic procedures and good governance threaten the very foundation on which the authority and often the survival of most regimes in post-conflict states are built: patron–client networks. Clientelistic networks are an endemic feature of weak states; arguably they are the most basic form of governance practiced in places where infrastructural power is weak. Clientelistic ties form the basis of support in many non-democratic systems where an ambitious elite cultivates ties with a subset of society in order to make an implicit bargain: political support in exchange for state jobs or targeted public goods (Bratton and van der Walle 1996; Eisenstadt and Roniger 1984; Ilkhamov 2007; van de Walle 2007; Kitschelt and Wilkinson 2007). Leaders may broaden their support by co-opting powerful actors into their network, a capacity that is especially essential in volatile post-war countries. A transition to good governance standards endangers these mechanisms, and it is no surprise that elites in states that are ruled predominately by patronage networks may oppose reforms that would make patronage more difficult and that would strip them of the possibility to co-opt potential contenders.

In short, local elites in a post-war country often fear that a transition to a more democratic regime might endanger their access to political power, their access to resources, and their way of ruling by means of patronage. In a volatile post-war situation where opposing political factions typically retain their capacity for organised violence, such concerns can quickly become very real security concerns: elites that lose political power may well lose their lives as well.

For all of these reasons, the transition to a liberal and democratic state can put considerable adoption costs on to elites in post-conflict zones. Thus, democratisation in the eyes of local elites is often a problem rather than a solution to a problem, and hence they may prefer the status quo to political reforms. They may therefore choose a strategy of balancing the opportunities that peacebuilders offer with the threats that the implementation of liberal peacebuilding poses to their survival strategy. They will attempt to steer international peacebuilders in a direction that furthers their interests: attracting as many resources – material and symbolic – as possible, while implementing as few reforms as possible in those areas where reforms might undermine their ability to rule and to extract resources.

What follows from this brief discussion is that unless the interests of the local elites and the peacebuilders are perfectly aligned, the trajectory of peacebuilding is determined by the priorities of the involved actors, their bargaining power and the resulting informal 'contract' between the parties.

At the heart of such a conceptualisation of the peacebuilding process are two claims that show that this bargain is not likely to create liberal democratic institutions. The first claim is that elites in post-war countries typically have a low demand for democracy because the liberal reforms that are part of a transition to democracy can undermine the elites' grip on power and resources. In other words, it is often risky and costly for local elites to adopt democracy, which reduces the demand for democracy. Without considerable domestic demand for democracy, peacebuilders' calls for more democratic reform are likely to fail. The second claim is that the engagement of peacebuilders is not enough to substitute for insufficient domestic demand for democracy, or generate new demand (Barnett et al. 2008; Barnett and Zürcher 2009; Zürcher 2011). Peacebuilders often tacitly accept that local elites are reluctant to adopt liberal reforms, and refrain from pressuring them. Even if peacebuilders do have leverage over local elites, which is often not the case, they do not push very hard for reforms because they prioritise stability over the risks that are associated with a transition to democracy. Our case study research in Afghanistan, Rwanda, Tajikistan and the Balkans provides important evidence to support both claims.

With regard to the lack of domestic demand for democracy, a very prominent recent case is Afghanistan. At the time of writing, the open tensions between President Karzai and his international backers about Afghanistan's increasingly undemocratic course were making headlines. Karzai came under heavy criticism after a fraudulent first round of presidential elections in the summer of 2009. Under international pressure, a second round run-off vote between incumbent President Hamid Karzai and his main rival Abdullah Abdullah was finally announced. However, Abdullah withdrew and Karzai kept the presidency, only to increase his personal control over the electoral process by further curbing the influence of the United Nations. The international community also pressured Karzai to fight the rampant corruption and to fire the most corrupt officials, among them Karzai's own brother. Karzai again resisted and increasingly distanced himself from his international backers, saying the coalition troops risked being seen as invaders rather than saviours of the country (New York Times 2010).

This deterioration in the relations between Karzai and the international community might be surprising given that the international community was willing to make Afghanistan the flagship project of liberal peacebuilding and that their Afghan partners, led by President Karzai, initially committed themselves to the same vision. But the new Afghan political elite was soon confronted with the fact that the vision of a democratic, centralised state did not resonate well with power holders in the provinces. Tribal leaders, warlords and regional strongmen saw the peacebuilders' vision as a threat to their autonomy and their fiefdoms. Soon the weakness of the government in relation to the provincial elite became apparent. Karzai had to rely more and more on patronage, clientelistic co-optation and ad hoc alliances in order to gain some influence in the provinces and to secure his own political and perhaps physical survival. He co-opted various regional strongmen into his entourage, among them the Tajik warlord Ismail Khan from Herat and the Uzbek warlord Rashid Dostum from northern Afghanistan.

When Karzai found himself caught between a powerful provincial elite that was inclined to defend its autonomy and an international community demanding more democratic reforms, he and his entourage increasingly abandoned their commitment to reforms and strengthened their clientelistic network, which became the backbone of Karzai's limited authority. The international community continued to support Karzai both politically and with generous amounts of aid money. By the end of 2009, donors had spent $36 billion and pledged $62 billion and had refrained from applying conditionality, despite the fact that Karzai had largely abandoned the liberal agenda (Donor Financial Review 2009).

Afghanistan may be an extreme case in so far as its democratic failure seems over-determined by so many adverse factors. Massive poverty, the destabilising effects of its geopolitical location and the ongoing Taliban insurgency are not conducive to democracy. At the same time, it is also evident that the Afghan political elite sees further democratisation as a threat to their ways of running a highly fragile country and resist pressure from the international community to make further democratic reforms. We observe the same dynamics at work in other peacebuilding operations.

In Rwanda, for example, there is little demand for democracy among elites. Against the backdrop of the disastrous outcomes of earlier attempts at democratisation which led to civil war and then to genocide in 1994, the political elite today is apprehensive about rapid democratisation. Five years after the end of the war, Rwanda stabilised as an undemocratic state, and it has not made significant progress since with regard to political openness. The regime has a paternalistic attitude to the population, seeing its role as nurturing notions of responsibility and accountability within a populace who continue to associate democracy with ethnic discrimination, majority rule and violence. The ruling elite's main concern is to avoid new ethnic division within the society, and a frequently repeated argument is that Western-style competitive democracy would widen these divides. As a result, there is hardly any elite-driven demand for more democracy. Donors' calls for more democracy are routinely fended off by pointing to the highly volatile situation in the country.

As in Rwanda, democracy is a concept that has a limited appeal among Tajik elites. Tajikistan is a fairly stable, authoritarian country, ruled by a dominant president and his entourage. Demand for democracy is very low. The population generally desires above all stability and trusts that the current regime can provide it. The ruling elite generally sees democratic changes as a threat to their way of running the country and to the political stability within Tajikistan. Since the civil war was prompted by the presidential elections of 1991 and the social forces it unleashed, the leadership has learned the lesson that an uncontrollable expression of grievances cannot be allowed and that opposition should be kept firmly in check. This perception is shared across the board by the elites and the population.

Even in the Balkans, where peacebuilding missions were overwhelmingly well resourced and the prospects of future EU membership provided incentives for democratic reforms, elites defied the peacebuilders' vision of a democratic peace. In Bosnia and Herzegovina, ethnic-based politics continued to dominate the political arena ten years after the Dayton Peace Agreement. In the context of thoroughly ethnicised politics, democratic openings are often perceived as zero-sum games by the parties. Consequently, political elites in Bosnia and Hezegovina have a substantial interest in limiting democratic competition. In Kosovo, as in Bosnia, it is the politicising of ethnicity and the de facto ethnic segregation which stands in the way of further democratisation. The local political elite has so far managed to resist international pressure for a more inclusive and more democratic regime. Formally, Kosovo's post-war political system is a multi-party parliamentary democracy with respect for human rights and the rule of law. Yet, the Kosovar polity and society are deeply segregated along ethnic lines, and corruption and patronage remain significant.

In reference to the first claim discussed above, these cases, on the one hand, show that the reasons why political elites in post-war countries are unwilling to embark on fully fledged democratic transitions vary from case to case. Furthermore, there may be additional factors beyond the political preferences of the elites which explain why democracy so rarely gains ground in post-war countries. In Rwanda and Tajikistan, it was the memories of horrendous atrocities that happened shortly after a democratic opening which darkened the prospects for democracy. In the case of Tajikistan, its autocratic course was backed by Russia's foreign policy, which traditionally has supported authoritarian leaders in Central Asia. In Bosnia and Kosovo, a lack of democracy is also partly caused by the dominant authority of the international administrators, although their influence has at least formally waned in the past several years. On the other hand, despite the many and meaningful differences between these cases, they also show that local elites often see further democratisation as not in their best interest and therefore resist international pressure for more reforms.

Let us now consider the second claim that the engagement of peacebuilders is not enough to substitute for insufficient domestic demand for democracy, or to generate new demand. Clearly, the massive resources and the prospects of political support which peacebuilders promise create considerable leverage over local elites, which could be used to push for more democratic reforms. But, interestingly, peacebuilders almost never use their leverage. Researchers would be hard pressed to identify cases of peacebuilding missions where peacebuilders used their often considerable leverage in order to push for more democratic reforms. Within the framework of a research project on post-war democratic transitions, we have closely analysed nine recent cases of major peacebuilding mission (see footnote 1). In none of the nine cases did we find that peacebuilders tried to use their leverage. They did not withhold aid or withdraw the peacekeeping forces, nor did they threaten to do so. Instead, we found that, confronted with the low demand for a liberal peace by local elites, peacebuilders actually often seemed to prefer stability to potentially disruptive liberal reforms, and cooperation with status quo-oriented elites over the vagaries of possible regime change. As a result, they compromised and tacitly accepted the new course set by local elites.

Indeed, peacebuilders may have good reasons not to push too hard for reforms. Democratisation can increase the risks of war. This is because the opening of domestic political space in the early stages of a democratic transition intensifies the competition between incumbent elites and challengers. The new democratic structures often are too weak to regulate political competition, and hence there is a risk that the mix of intense elite competition, mass political participation and underdeveloped democratic institutions triggers renewed conflict (Mansfield and Snyder 1995, 2002).

But this is not the only reason why peacebuilders tend to compromise. Peacebuilders are also highly dependent on domestic actors because their cooperation is essential for a smooth and stable implementation of the many development projects that peacebuilders seek to implement: emergency and humanitarian aid needs to be delivered, macro-economic stability needs to be achieved, the capacity of key ministries needs to be built up, the security sector needs to be reformed, the political institutions of the country need to be strengthened, and civil society needs to be nurtured. Contemporary peacebuilding missions assign hundreds of millions of aid money for these objectives. But without the consent and the support of local elites, these development programmes cannot be implemented, and the safety of international personnel working for these programmes cannot be guaranteed. Once peacebuilders are deployed, there is enormous pressure on them to implement their projects before the current budget cycle comes to an end. This creates a strong incentive to cooperate with local elites, even when they are not committed to democratic reforms.

For these reasons, peacebuilders may be reluctant to use their leverage. On numerous occasions, leaders in post-conflict states have capitalised on the peacebuilders' preference for stability and cooperation. Leaders in Tajikistan, Afghanistan, Bosnia, Rwanda and Kosovo have fended off reforms that the peacebuilders insisted on by claiming that these reforms would threaten the precarious post-war stability. In sum, peacebuilders might not always be the uncompromising promoters of democracy the public discourse often portray them to be. They may compromise their goals because they prioritise stability over democracy and because they need the cooperation of local elites. Indeed, there is much evidence that peacebuilders often come to accept a peace which is far from democratic.

A case in point is Rwanda, one of the largest recipients of official development assistance in Africa. Aid as a percentage of GDP was on average 42 per cent for the five years after the civil war (1993–1997), and the functioning of the central state administration was highly dependent on donor support. Yet, despite the considerable leverage that peacebuilders and donors had over the local elites, Rwanda remains an authoritarian country. Donors' calls for more democracy were routinely fended off by the local elites who pointed to the highly volatile situation in the country, and donors did not use their leverage over the government in order to push for liberal reforms. In sum, all parties settled for an outcome far short of a liberal democracy.

Another example is Afghanistan, where peacebuilders continue to support an increasingly inefficient and sclerotic regime with 100,000 soldiers and billions of aid money. Despite their heavy criticism of Karzai's undemocratic regime, the international community is clearly reluctant to use its considerable leverage, out of fear that the security situation might worsen if Karzai were weakened.

In Bosnia, peacebuilders tried to use their leverage to push the ethnic parties toward playing within the rules of the Dayton Peace Agreement, but despite their overwhelming resources, they could not overcome the ethnic barriers and have accepted de facto ethnic partition. And in Kosovo, peacebuilders gave in to the Kosovars' pressure for independence when the security situation threatened to deteriorate, thereby sacrificing the dream of a democratic, inclusive and multiethnic Kosovo. Today, more than a decade into the most ambitious, intrusive and costly peacebuilding operations of all times, neither Kosovo nor Bosnia are free societies with fully democratic regimes. This does not, however, imply that Kosovo and Bosnia are examples of a failed peacebuilding. Both countries are reasonably stable and the foundations for a democratic development are laid. This is no small achievement. But, the peacebuilding experience in the Balkans demonstrates that there is a certain limit to what even the most encompassing international engagement can achieve, given the lack of domestic demand for democracy.

So far I have offered an explanation of why peacebuilding rarely leads to democracy. This explanation emphasises the low demand for democracy among local elites and the unwillingness of peacebuilders to use their leverage. But what about the cases of successful democratic transitions? What factors enable a post-war democratic transition in the context of a peacebuilding mission? In order to explore this question, I will now take a close look at Namibia, Mozambique, and East Timor – cases of peacebuilding operations which are commonly seen as success stories because they led to peace *and* democracy.

Namibia gained its independence in 1989 after 23 years of violent struggle against the South African Apartheid rule, and ever since has been considered a liberal democracy. The victorious SWAPO (South West Africa People's Organisation), which was to become the new ruling elite in Namibia after two decades of armed struggle, had an overwhelming interest in the success of democratic peace because it saw universal suffrage as the precondition to an independent and sovereign Namibia. In a way, it saw democracy as a by-product of the long-desired independence and therefore gladly embraced it. Furthermore, gaining independence also meant that the SWAPO could simply take over the state. Since the previous administrators were 'foreign', they simply left and did not become a major obstacle for a post-war democratic transition. The peacebuilders supported this transition, but both military deployment and aid flows were modest. UNTAG (United Nations Transition Assistance Group) was launched in April 1989 with a peak military strength of 4,493.[4] During the first five years of independence, the country received a modest US$133 million per year (average during 1989–1993) (World Bank). But, the small, non-intrusive peacebuilding operation and the limited resources were, in the presence of a clear demand for democracy by local elites, enough to steer the country towards a stable liberal democracy.

The post-war democratic transition in East Timor was shaped by similar factors as in Namibia.[5] A highly articulated and organised popular and elite-driven demand for independence and democracy was the key factor in bringing about the end to Indonesian occupation. For many members of the new regime, both the demands for a 'Free East Timor' and '*Demokrasi*' went hand-in-hand. With the occupation regime gone, the rebels could take over the state. Without a major player against either independence or democracy and with international donors keen on supporting a democratic peacebuilding process, the adoption costs for the new regime were minimal. There were no veto players in East

Timor who opposed democracy, and there was an overall consensus to remain within the bounds of the constitutional order. Compared to Namibia and also Mozambique, the mission in East Timor was robust, and aid flows vast: 6,200 troops supported the mission and were fully in charge of administering the territory. In the beginning, all authority was concentrated in the hands of the UN transitional administration. But, after a series of riots, the international community revised its approach, and the local elite achieved a greater say in domestic politics. Since 1999, East Timor has received over US$4 billion in external assistance. The result is a democracy in making: there is still insufficient socio-economic progress and the politicisation of the security forces, corruption and a poorly functioning judiciary stand in the way of a fully liberal democracy. But the institutional foundations for democracy are in place, and there is a general acceptance that democracy is the only game in town. Clearly, the local demand for democracy and independence has set East Timor on a democratic course.

A third widely cited success story is Mozambique. After sixteen years of civil conflict, Mozambique experienced a successful transition to peace despite numerous social, political and economic conditions that were not conducive to peace or democracy. Many factors played a role in fostering this unlikely outcome. But crucial among them was a genuine desire by both warring parties, Renamo and Frelimo, for peace and democracy. The demand for democracy was nurtured by the fact that both parties saw a democratic power-sharing arrangement as the only way out of a mutually hurting stalemate. The two parties agreed on a peace agreement and on a democratic institutional framework because they were locked in a hurting stalemate, hence both parties had strategic reasons to support democracy. The war fatigue of the population supported the process. The system that emerged benefited Frelimo, because it won the election and continued to rule the country. However, Renamo too supported the democratic process, because the alternative was to become a marginalised party in an unwinnable war. Renamo successfully transformed itself into a political party and participated in the political process, a move which was greatly sweetened by assistance and support from the international donors. But as in Namibia, military deployment and aid flows were rather modest, especially compared to the subsequent peace operations in the Balkans. At its peak, the mission deployed less than 7,000 military personnel, and the total gross expenditure of the mission was US$492.6 million. This is not to say that peacebuilders did not play a highly decisive part. Mozambique's success was due in large part to the flexible, intensive and coordinated efforts of major donors, who were committed to making peace work and had long-standing relationships with the former belligerents. These long-standing relationships fostered mutual trust and understanding between external and internal actors and gave donors a good contextual understanding of the priorities and conditions that were necessary to successfully establish peace in Mozambique. But what drove the democratisation process in the end was the understanding of the former adversaries that a democratic power-sharing arrangement could unlock the mutually hurting stalemate.

So what can we learn from such a close reading of recent cases of post-war democratic transitions? Perhaps the clearest lesson, and one that should not come as a surprise, is that local elite demand for democracy is a crucial factor in explaining the outcome of post-war democratic transitions. Namibia, Mozambique and East Timor – the champions of post-war democratic transition – all display a high local demand for democracy. This demand, in turn, is partly a consequence of the fact that the costs of adopting democracy were seen by local elites as low. The ruling elites felt secure enough to move towards democracy, because they faced no political opposition (e.g. East Timor and Namibia), or because the opposition party was clearly committed to playing by the rules (e.g. Mozambique).

On the other hand, those post-war countries which did not emerge as liberal, or at least electoral, democracies display a clear lack of elite-driven demand for democracy. In these countries, elites perceived the adoption costs for democracy as high, for various reasons. In Rwanda and Tajikistan, the previous unsuccessful experiences with democracy and the fear of rising interethnic tensions to some extent explain the elites' apprehension of democracy. In Kosovo and Bosnia, moving to a more liberal democracy would have threatened the mono-ethnic fiefdoms on which elites built their power. But, in all cases, and most clearly so in Afghanistan, moving towards a more democratic regime would have threatened the very foundations on which the political authority in many of these post-war countries rests: an elaborate system of informal governance, of which widespread patronage and corruption are common manifestations.

The evidence from the case studies suggest that there are two situations in which adoption costs are untypically low and demand for democracy untypically high. The first such situation is in the context of a war for independence, when democracy is bundled with independence. Elites and the population are prepared to accept the adoption costs for democracy because they desire independence. Also, independence struggles tend to build high elite coherence and considerable popular support for the leadership which improves the chances for a successful democratisation process. When elites enjoy widespread support from the population, this further reduces the costs of a democratic transition, because elites can safely assume that they will prevail at the ballot box. Second, adoption costs for democracy are also low when democracy offers a way out of a hurting stalemate. If the parties to a war are convinced that neither can win on the battlefield, they may be inclined to accept the costs that are associated with the adoption of democratic rules of the game.

This is not to say that the usual suspects for explaining the success or failure of post-war democratic transitions, such as the duration and intensity of the war, the level of development within the country, the mandate and the resources of the peacebuilding missions and aid flows, do not influence peacebuilding outcomes. They do, but not in a mechanical way which consistently associates a set of factors with one particular outcome. Rather, these factors help to explain why the local demand for democracy, or the peacebuilders' willingness to use their leverage, may vary across cases.

The analysis presented in this chapter also suggests that the impact of peacebuilders on the democratic outcome is rather small, despite the often massive resources they deploy. The two factors which most influence the local demand and the adoption costs – independence struggle and hurting stalemate – are beyond the influence of peacebuilders' policies. This is not to say that peacebuilders have nothing to contribute to a democratic outcome. As the cases of Namibia, Mozambique and East Timor show, the support of external actors provided an additional boost to the democratic transition under way. Peacebuilders also succeed in providing stability when they deploy massively. Highly intrusive, high-cost missions bring an end to large-scale violence. But they do not bring liberal, democratic, self-sustaining peace when there is a lack of demand for it. Whether the missions were robust and highly intrusive, as in Kosovo, Bosnia and Afghanistan, or had a light footprint, as in Rwanda and Tajikistan, peacebuilders were not able to provide enough incentives to local elites to encourage further democratisation. Without a doubt, each of these cases poses its specific challenges to democratisation. Kosovo and Bosnia are prisoners of a highly ethnicised political landscape, and the different ethnic groups see democratisation as a winner-takes-all game. Afghanistan lacks all institutional infrastructure, is engulfed in a civil war and has a weak president that faces powerful regional potentates. In Rwanda, the elite and the population associate democracy with the horrors of the civil war and the genocide. The elite strives to build a system which offers some participation, but little competition. In Tajikistan, an authoritarian president, supported by a regional power, claims that a democratic opening would destabilise the country, and the population seems, by and large, to agree. But, whatever the reasons, when local elites perceive democracy as a problem rather than a solution, they resist pressure for democratic change, and they do it quite successfully.

As these cases reveal, local elites perceive democracy as a problem partly because peacebuilders are rarely prepared to play their hand well. The considerable potential leverage that their resources and military muscles give peacebuilders over local regimes is rarely put to use. Rather, we find that peacebuilders are often willing to compromise on their noble goals. This explains why peacebuilders often engage in peacebuilding missions with noble visions of a liberal, multiethnic, and democratic society, and why they may often be willing to compromise and settle for much less ambitious goals.

Should peacebuilders then give up their aspirations for a peaceful *and* democratic end state? I do not think so, but they should have more modest and more realistic expectations of what is feasible, and when. There are two aspects of a more realistic agenda. First, peacebuilders should lower their expectations with regard to a democratic outcome. Unless there is a high domestic demand for democracy, there is little reason to believe that the resources and leverage that peacebuilders can muster will be enough to commit local elites to democratic reforms that result in liberal democracies. Perhaps securing the peace is a demanding enough objective in many post-war countries, and there is no reason why peacebuilding policies should always be geared towards the immediate achievement of democracy in a post-war environment.

We should not easily discard the fact that local elites and the public in some post-war countries perceive democratisation as a real threat to stability, as is the case in Rwanda and Tajikistan. Also, a transition to a liberal democracy is, as we have seen, only achievable under rare circumstances, yet the international community continues to finance programmes for democracy promotion in many post-war countries. Perhaps these resources should be concentrated in countries which show real promise for a fast and sustainable democratisation, or else spent on less elusive goals.

More realistic expectations should also lead to a more realistic appraisal of the good things which peacebuilding can and has achieved (see Paris in this volume). While robust peacebuilding missions, perhaps, cannot socially engineer liberal democracies, they can secure the end of violence, create conditions for refugees to return home, provide much-needed emergency aid and help in rebuilding state capacities. All of this makes a dramatic difference in the lives of millions of people. Also, the fact that around one third of all recent major peacebuilding mission resulted in regimes where democratic elections are an important aspect of the political game is perhaps not such a bad track record, given the many challenges and constraints of democratic peacebuilding.

Finally, even though the impact of peacebuilders on democratic outcomes will be limited under the best of circumstances, peacebuilders can and should try to strengthen their hand. Given the fact that the democratic outcome of peacebuilding is to some extent the result of a bargaining process between local elites and peacebuilders, there may be room for better bargaining and hence for more democratic outcomes, even though the ultimate goal of establishing a liberal democracy may remain elusive.

How can peacebuilders strengthen their hand? First, peacebuilders should try and reach a comprehensive agreement with all players as far upstream as possible. The leverage of peacebuilders is greatest before they deploy. Once they have committed and deployed, they become dependent on local actors in order to implement their programmes, and the public at home will expect signs of activities, both of which reduce the credibility of a threat of withdrawal.

Second, peacebuilders can increase their resources and, perhaps more importantly, their perceived commitment. A high and credible commitment of peacebuilders provides incentives for local elites to bet on the final success of the peacebuilding operation. Peacebuilders have to make sure that local elites see them as valuable and trusted allies. Only then will local elites prefer a lasting alliance with peacebuilders to a pact with those segments of their society that are opposed to liberal reform. This can create an environment in which peacebuilders and local elites closely cooperate towards a common objective.

Lastly, the hand of peacebuilders is also strengthened when they speak with one voice and achieve internal unity with regard to their priorities. All peacebuilding operations are plagued by massive coordination problems among the myriad of actors which participate. At best, a lack of coordination hampers efficient delivery of aid and efficient implementation of development programmes. At worst, when a lack of coordination is caused by different actors pursuing different strategic objectives, the whole operation can be jeopardised. Greater cooperation among peacebuilders would increase their capacity to credibly use their leverage over local elites. But, as I have argued in this chapter, whether peacebuilders would actually want to use their leverage is a different question.

Notes

1 An earlier version of this essay appeared in the *Journal of Democracy*, vol. 22, 1, pp. 81–95. Reprinted by permission of The Johns Hopkins University Press.

The conceptual understanding of peacebuilding which I put forward here was developed together with Michael Barnett. See Michael Barnett and Christoph Zürcher 2009, pp. 23–52. With Songying Fang and Michael Barnett we developed a formal model of peacebuilding. See Michael Barnett, Songying Fang and Christoph Zürcher 2008.

The empirical material upon which the article builds stems from a comparative research project on post-war democratic transitions, conducted by the Freie Universität Berlin. An international team of country experts prepared nine structured cases studies between October 2007 and December 2008. The case studies closely followed a research template that consists of 101 questions, divided into four sections: outcome of the transitions; structural and war-related factors affecting the transition; nature and scope of the peacebuilding operation; and aid flows. Short versions of the case studies are published in the *Taiwan Journal of Democracy*, vol. 5, 1, July 2009. The long versions are accessible at the projects website http://aix1.uottawa.ca/~czurcher/czurcher/Transitions.html.

The following case studies were prepared: Afghanistan (Hamish Nixon and Brendan Whitty), Bosnia and Herzegovina (Kristie Evenson), East Timor (Henri Myrttinnen), Kosovo (Jens Narten), Macedonia (Tome Sandenvski), Namibia (Christof Hartmann), Mozambique (Carrie Manning), Rwanda (Rachel Hayman) and Tajikistan (Anna Matveeva). Sarah Riese and Nora Roehner contributed additional research. *The examples given in this chapter draw heavily on these case studies.*

2 The Freedom House score measures political rights and civil liberties. A rating of 1 indicates the highest degree of freedom and 7 the lowest. Counties with a score or 2.5 or above are rated as free, with a score of 3–5 as partly free, and with a score of 5.5–7 as not free. We define a major mission as a mission mandated by the UN or by another international organisation which is aimed at keeping the peace in a post-conflict situation and at inducing social change, with the ultimate goal of creating a stable and democratic country. A mission must be deployed for at least six months and have at last 500 military personnel in the field. We code a mission start only when these thresholds are met, even if the mission had been established and deployed earlier but was different in character and scope. Multiple simultaneous missions are collapsed into one observation. Subsequent missions within one country which are not separated by more than twelve months are also collapsed into one observation.

3 For a discussion of how entrepreneurs of violence may do well of war, see, for example Berdal and Malone 2000; De Soysa 2000; Sherman 2001; Ballentine and Sherman 2003; Collier and Hoeffler 2004; and Humphreys 2005.

4 UNTAG: http://www.un.org/en/peacekeeping/missions/past/untagF.htm (accessed 6 May 2010). By comparison, the mission in Kosovo costs so far US$44 billion, and the mission in Bosnia US$41 billion (Evenson 2009; Narten 2009).

5 Timor scores 6 points on the polity IV score, which is often used as the threshold for democracy, but it is still rated 'partly free' by Freedom House. But the democratisation of Timor, it seems, is constrained rather by the lack of capacities than by the absence of political will among the local elites.

Bibliography

Ballentine, K. and J. Sherman (2003) *The Political Economy of Armed Conflict. Beyond Greed and Grievance*, Boulder, CO: Lynne Rienner.

Barnett, M. and C. Zürcher (2009) 'The Peacebuilder's Contract. How External Statebuilding Reinforces Weak Statehood', in R. Paris and T. D. Sisk (eds) *The Dilemmas of Statebuilding: Confronting the Contradictions of Postwar Peace Operations*, London and New York: Routledge, pp. 23–52.

Barnett, M., S. Fang, and C. Zürcher (2008) 'The Peacebuilder's Contract. A Game Theoretical Approach', paper presented at the American Political Science Association Annual Meeting 28–31 August, in Boston, MA.

Berdal, M. and D. M. Malone (2000) *Greed and Grievance. Economic Agendas in Civil Wars*, Boulder, CO and London, Lynne Rienner.

Bratton, M. and N. van der Walle (1996) *Democratic Experiments in Africa: Regime Transitions in Comparative Perspective*, Cambridge: Cambridge University Press.

Bueno de Mesquita, B. and G. W. Downs (2006) 'Intervention and Democracy', *International Organization* 60 (Summer): 627–649.

Carothers, T. (2004) *Critical Mission: Essays on Democracy Promotion*, Washington, DC: Carnegie Endowment for International Peace.

Chesterman, S. (2004) *You, the People: The United Nations, Transitional Administration, and State-Building*, A Project of the International Peace Academy, Oxford and New York: Oxford University Press.

Collier, P. (2009) *Wars, Guns, and Votes: Democracy in Dangerous Places*, New York: Harper.
Collier, P. and A. Hoeffler (2004) 'Greed and Grievance in Civil War', *Oxford Economic Papers* 56(4): 563–595.
De Soysa, I. (2000) 'The Resource Curse: Are Civil Wars Driven by Rapacity or Paucity?', in M. Berdal and D. M. Malone, *Greed and Grievance. Economic Agendas in Civil Wars*, Boulder, CO and London: Lynne Rienner, pp. 113–137.
Diamond, L. (2006) 'Promoting Democracy in Post-Conflict and Failed States: Lessons and Challenges', *Taiwan Journal of Democracy* 2(2): 93–116.
Donor Financial Review (2009) Ministry of Finance, Islamic Republic of Afghanistan, Report 1388, November.
Eisenstadt, S. N. and L. Roniger (1984) *Patrons, Clients and Friends. Interpersonal Relations and the Structure of Trust in Society*, Cambridge: Cambridge University Press.
Evenson, K. D. (2009) 'Bosnia and Herzegovina: Statebuilding and Democratization in the Time of Ethnic-Politics and International Oversight', *Taiwan Journal of Democracy* 5(1) (July): 93–125.
Humphreys, M. (2005) 'Natural Resources, Conflict, and Conflict Resolution', *Journal of Conflict Resolution* 49(4): 508–537.
Ilkhamov, A. (2007) 'Neopatrimonialism, Interest Groups and Patronage Networks: The Impasses of the Governance System in Uzbekistan', *Central Asian Survey* 26(1): 65–84.
Jarstad, A. and T. D. Sisk (eds) (2008) *From War to Democracy: Dilemmas of Peacebuilding*. Cambridge: Cambridge University Press.
Kaplan, S. D. (2008) *Fixing Fragile States: A New Paradigm for Development*, Westport, CT: Praeger Security International.
Kitschelt, H. and S. I. Wilkinson (2007) 'Citizen-Politician Linkages: An Introduction', in H. Kitschelt and S. I. Wilkinson, *Patrons, Clients, and Policies: Patterns of Democratic Accountability and Political Competition*, Cambridge: Cambridge University Press, pp. 1–49.
Mansfield, E. D. and J. Snyder (1995) 'Democratization and the Danger of War', *International Security* 20 (Summer): 5–38.
Mansfield, E. D. and J. Snyder (2002) 'Democratic Transitions, Institutional Strength, and War', *International Organization* 56 (April): 297–337.
Narten, J. (2009) 'Assessing Kosovo's Postwar Democratization: Between External Imposition and Local Self-Government', *Taiwan Journal of Democracy* 5 (July): 127–162.
New York Times (2010) 'Afghan President Rebukes West and U.N.', 1 April.
Paris, R. (2004) *At War's End. Building Peace Atfer Civil Conflict*, Cambridge: Cambridge University Press.
Paris, R. (2008) 'Understanding the "coordination problem" in postwar statebuilding', in R. Paris and T. D. Sisk, *The Dilemmas of Statebuilding: Confronting the Contradictions of Postwar Peace Operations*, Abingdon and New York: Routledge, pp. 53–78.
Paris, R. and T. D. Sisk (2009) *The Dilemmas of Statebuilding: Confronting the Contradictions of Postwar Peace Operations*, Abingdon and New York: Routledge.
Roeder, P. G. and D. Rothchild (2005) *Sustainable Peace. Power and Democracy after Civil Wars*, Ithaca, NY and London: Cornell University Press.
Sherman, J. (2001) 'The Economies of War. The Intersection of Need, Creed and Greed. A Conference Report', *The Economics of War*, Washington, DC: International Peace Academy, Woodrow Wilson International Center for Scholars.
Van de Walle, N. (2007) 'Meet the New Boss, Same as the Old Boss? The Evolution of Political Clientelism in Africa', in H. Kitschelt and S. I. Wilkinson, *Patrons, Clients, and*

Policies: Patterns of Democratic Accountability and Political Competition, Cambridge: Cambridge University Press, pp. 50–67.

Zeeuw, J. de, K. Kumar and Nederlands Instituut voor Internationale Betrekkingen 'Clingendael' (2006) *Promoting Democracy in Postconflict Societies*, Boulder, CO: Lynne Rienner.

Zürcher, C. (2011) 'Building Democracy When Building Peace', *Journal of Democracy* 22(1): 81–95.

5

Routine Learning? How Peacebuilding Organisations Prevent Liberal Peace

Susanna Campbell

Introduction

What determines how international peacebuilding institutions and organisations interact with the national and local institutions and organisations that they aim to transform?[1] Certainly the money, skill and knowledge possessed by international peacebuilders play a role. The receptivity of national and local institutions to what the international peacebuilders are trying to sell matters a great deal as well. But these international–national transactions are also determined by the organisational routines, systems and cultures of the international organisations (IOs), international non-governmental organisations (INGOs) and government aid agencies engaged in liberal peacebuilding. More specifically, the routines and systems that govern how these international actors learn from and adapt to national and local contexts help to determine their impact on this context (Howard 2008). After all, peacebuilding actors today do not aim to sustain peace themselves, but rather to increase the capacity of national and local institutions to sustain peace (DfID 2009). As Sending (this volume) writes: 'The outcome of peacebuilding efforts is determined by the dynamic interaction between external and internal actors, where the former seeks to build capacity (transferring skills and resources) and the latter receives, selects, uses and also disregards elements of the donors' programmes.'

If international liberal peacebuilders were to achieve their transformative goals, they would need to develop a high degree of understanding of national and local institutions, adjust their understanding and approach as the dynamics governing these institutions change, and build cooperative relationships that enable national actors to sustain the desired results (Call and Wyeth 2008; International Alert 2004; Pouligny 2005). This chapter asks if this degree of organisational learning, adaptation and engagement is feasible.[2]

Constructive Critiques and the Importance of Organisational Adaptation and Learning

Peacebuilding problem-solving literature levels several important critiques at international peacebuilding efforts, all of which suggest that these efforts have a weak capacity to adapt to and learn from the national and local institutions that they aim to influence. It criticises liberal peacebuilding for applying a standard template of strategies, programmes and activities in each post-conflict country without consideration for each country's unique institutions and history (Ottaway 2003; Pouligny 2005; Woodward 2007). It finds that international peacebuilding stifles national peacebuilding capacity and local democratic processes, thus reducing each country's endogenous capacity to sustain peace (Barnett and Zürcher 2009; Fortna 2008; Suhrke 2007). It argues that international peacebuilding lacks the necessary knowledge of how to support state–society relations or catalyse the types of institutions that may, one day, embody liberal democratic norms (Barnett and Zürcher 2009). It points to numerous contradictions between the various programmes and strategies that comprise liberal peacebuilding, which can lead international peacebuilders to work at cross-purposes and wreak harm on the host state and society (Carothers 2006; Jarstad and Sisk 2008; Paris and Sisk 2007; Uvin 2001). Finally, it argues that the entire peacebuilding effort is doomed to fail because it aims to transplant a model of state–society relations and democracy that will never align with the institutions of state and society in countries emerging from years of civil war or violent conflict (Barnett 2006; de Waal 2009).

To address these challenges, the literature puts forward several prescriptions, all of which point to the importance of greater flexibility, adaptability and learning by peacebuilding organisations.

Peacebuilding organisations should question their theories of change and definitions of success. A minimum criterion for peacebuilding success is the absence of significant direct violence (Call 2008; de Waal 2009; Doyle and Sambanis 2006). Success is therefore defined as a 'non-event': the absence of something rather than its presence. While this definition makes the measurement of failure relatively easy, it provides no clear indication of how to achieve success. To compensate for this gap in knowledge, organisations develop their own visions of success and express them as *theories of change* (Church and Rogers 2006; OECD-DAC 2007). Peacebuilding scholarship argues that identification and evaluation of theories of change are necessary for the organisation to adjust outdated theories; to question theories of change derived from organisational mandates rather than empirical analysis; and to address the potential disconnect between the international norms expressed in these theories and the national norms and institutions that they aim to transform (Barnett et al. 2007; Woodward 2007). Questioning theories of change and adapting in response requires that an organisation investigate its underlying principles and whether or not they are appropriate to the context, or engage in the most challenging type of organisational learning, double-loop learning (Argyris 1992: 68).

Peacebuilding organisations should focus on incremental aims and a country's particular war-to-peace trajectory. Problem-solving peacebuilding scholarship recommends that peacebuilding organisations reduce their liberal peacebuilding ambitions and focus on incremental goals that correspond to each country's possible war-to-peace trajectories. Incrementalism requires that 'peacebuilders confess to a high degree of uncertainty' in what they are doing and how they will achieve the desired ends (Barnett and Zürcher 2009: 48). Admitting to this uncertainty, actively gathering information about the needs, capacities and perceptions of the post-conflict state and society, and developing corresponding strategies and activities requires a high degree of organisational learning and adaptation.

Peacebuilding organisations should increase local feedback and accountability. Several scholars recommend that peacebuilding organisations deal with the uncertainty about the war-to-peace trajectory in the countries in which they intervene by increasing the feedback that they receive from the local population (Barnett 2006: 110; Pouligny 2005). Accurate feedback from citizens on the contribution of an intervention is necessary for the organisation to improve its impact, and, yet again, requires an important investment in organisational learning capacities (Levitt and March 1988).

Peacebuilding organisations should increase linkages and coordination with other peacebuilding actors. Problem-solving literature also emphasises the interdependence of all international and national actors in a post-conflict context. According to Dan Smith, the trick is to combine the different peacebuilding activities (or the *peacebuilding palette*) together 'in ways that are specific to the country, region and conflict in question, for greater effect – like mixing paint' (Smith 2004: 27). With the right mixture, the aggregate whole becomes greater than the sum of the parts. According to advocates of greater coherence, peacebuilding outcomes not only depend on how these organisations interact with the state and society in which they intervene, but also on how they learn from and adapt to actions by other peacebuilding actors.

Peacebuilding organisations should catalyse and facilitate local and national social and institutional change. The problem-solving literature is largely in agreement that buy-in and ownership by the host state and society are essential for even a modicum of liberal peace (Call and Cousens 2008; Doyle and Sambanis 2006: 56). To achieve buy-in from the state and society, international actors have to understand the dynamics of the state and society well enough to develop approaches that will resonate and become 'owned'. Engaging with the various national actors in a way that encourages their buy-in and ownership requires a high degree of sensitivity and adaptation to the context, as well as a willingness to adapt peacebuilding aims.

Peacebuilding practitioners have drawn many of these same lessons. Foremost, they have learned that all peacebuilding must be context-specific, or 'conflict-sensitive'. The literature on peacebuilding practice argues that while all organisations should be sensitive to their positive or negative impact on violent conflict (Anderson and Olson 2003), peacebuilding organisations should to be conflict-sensitive in relation to their peacebuilding aims (OECD-DAC 2007: 8). Conflict sensitivity is the ability of an organisation to understand the context in which it operates, understand the interaction between its intervention and the context, and act upon the understanding of this interaction, in order to avoid negative impacts and maximise positive impacts (International Alert 2004: 1.1).

Interestingly, the *critics* of the liberal peace have a similar focus: the local and national actors, and the everyday reality that they live, should be the focus of any peacebuilding effort. For these authors, the main purpose of international peacebuilders is to negotiate with, empower and emancipate these actors. 'A post-liberal peace requires that international actors use a range of methods that enable local actors and the most marginalised to engage with a discussion of their own requirements for needs provision and their own understandings of rights and institutions' (Richmond, this volume). This bargain between the local and international actors (see Zürcher, this volume) may result in a very different institutional form than that envisioned by the most ardent liberal peacebuilders.

Most academics in the problem-solving camp share Richmond's hopes of a post-liberal peace that supports representative institutions, greater economic equality, and both formal and informal institutions that resolve conflict peacefully (Richmond, this volume). They argue that addressing the root causes of inequality and destitution is paramount, even if extremely difficult (Stewart 2010). Even policymakers argue that peacebuilding must be an endogenous process, and that peacebuilders' role is to support, rather than impose (DfID 2009; Ki-moon 2011; OECD-DAC 2007). In sum, within most of the problem-solving literature, much of the policy literature, and even some of the critical literature, there is a clear and consistent point of agreement: *for peacebuilding to be successful, it must help to support an endogenous change process that enables the existence of formal and informal institutions of state and society that can sustain a just peace.*

This vision of peacebuilding has significant implications for the IOs, INGOs and donor aid agencies trying to support it. It means that these organisations must be prepared to alter their specific organisational targets and their organisation's knowledge-base, or knowledge-laden routines, so that they can design and implement interventions that are appropriate to each context. They also have to be prepared to adapt both their intervention design and their goals in response to changes in the context. To achieve all of this, peacebuilding organisations would have to be highly adaptive learning organisations.

Lise Morje Howard's (2008) work supports this claim. She found that field-level learning is necessary for the UN because success 'is not based on learning discrete, concrete "rules of the game," because the game is constantly changing. When the UN learns on the ground, it acquires the ability to adapt to the changing contexts of civil wars – the organisation engages with its environment and invents mechanisms to understand it' (Howard 2008: 19).

Mark Duffield (Duffield 2001: 265) agrees, arguing that one of the primary barriers to the liberal peace agenda is the structure of the peacebuilding organisations themselves:

> Not only are many organisations culturally maladjusted to complexity, as the recent failure to significantly reform the UN would suggest, but this maladjustment is actively maintained by powerful groups and networks. Indeed, successful careers are often built out of the innovative reworking of failure. Rather than searching for better policy or commissioning more detailed forms of analysis, the real task is reforming the institutions and networks of global governance to address complexity. Without reform, policy failure and the associated pressure to turn liberal peace into liberal war will continue to shape the international scene. Reform would require turning rule-based bureaucracies into adaptive, learning and networked organizations.

If organisational adaptation and learning is so important for improved liberal peacebuilding practice, then why does much of the anecdotal evidence available indicate that so many peacebuilding organisations fail to learn?

The Complexity of Adaptation and Learning

What does the theoretical literature on organisational learning say about how peacebuilding organisations can be expected to learn?

Defining learning

Organisational learning is about identifying, and acting to correct, misalignment between an organisation's aims and the outcomes of its activities in relation to those aims.[3] It does not just refer to the intake and processing of information; action based on that information is also necessary. 'This distinction is important because it implies that discovering problems and inventing solutions are necessary, but not sufficient, conditions for organisational learning' (Argyris 1992: 62).

The literature on organisational learning distinguishes between two levels and two degrees (or loops) of learning. Double-loop learning occurs when individuals within an organisation openly and honestly examine the underlying assumptions and behaviours that may have caused gaps between the intended and actual outcome of the organisation's actions (Argyris 1992: 68). It is distinguished from single-loop learning in which no significant questioning of underlying assumptions or behaviours is necessary. As mentioned above, questioning the underlying assumptions and theories of change in liberal peacebuilding requires double-loop learning, which in turn requires that organisations process information about the relationship between intentions and outcomes in a non-defensive and transparent fashion (Argyris 1992).

Lise Morje Howard (2008: 19) describes 'first-level learning' as field-based learning and adaptation. Second-level learning, on the other hand, 'entails learning not within, but between missions' (Howard 2008: 19–20).

Challenges of organisational learning

Organisational learning and adaptation are challenging for all organisations. Entrenched routines, cultures and patterns of behaviour make quick change and adaptation difficult. Individuals have different interpretations of what should be learned, and in which direction change and adaptation should take place.

Organisations learn what they define and measure as successful

Organisations learn in relation to targets. Organisational behaviour depends on the relationship between the outcomes they observe and the aspirations, or targets, they have for those outcomes (Levitt and March 1988: 320). An organisation therefore learns what it defines and measures as successful. Measuring success in peacebuilding is particularly challenging because of the large number of factors that contribute to success and failure, the unique circumstances of each conflict environment, and the high degree of conflict sensitivity and organisational learning required to measure incremental success. When peacebuilding impact is measured, it usually takes place in the form of detailed evaluations carried out by academics after a project or programme is finished, leaving few opportunities to adapt and change an ongoing intervention. A catch 22 emerges. While organisational learning capacity helps to determine a peacebuilding organisation's capacity to measure success, improved capacity to measure success is essential for organisational learning. Consequently, better assessment of incremental impact on the causes of peace is likely to be critical in improving peacebuilding practice.

Organisations learn through historical frames and knowledge-laden routines

Organisational routines guide learning. Organisations learn 'by encoding inferences from history into routines that guide behaviour' (Levitt and March 1988: 319). Routines are the rules, 'procedures, technologies, beliefs, and cultures [that] are conserved through systems of socialisation and control' (ibid.: 326).

Action in organisations therefore 'involves matching procedures to situations more than it does calculating choices' (ibid.: 320). Because learning is based on 'interpretations of the past more than anticipations of the future,' peacebuilding organisations are likely to apply old solutions to new problems, whether they fit or not (ibid.). Because routines shape behaviour in organisations, organisational learning is limited to aspects of experience that are translatable into routines.

The routines – and the individuals who observe success and translate it into routines – largely determine, and limit, what an organisation can learn. Individuals make numerous mistakes in their attempts to interpret and draw lessons from history, leading to 'systematic biases in interpretation' (Levitt and March 1988: 323). As a result, an organisation's best practices may be difficult to capture fully, translate into routines and replicate. Because of the complexity of conflict environments, and the unique nature of each conflict, it is even more likely that interpretations of peacebuilding success that are integrated into routines will be flawed. Furthermore, because organisations learn from history, even when a lesson is learned it may not be the right lesson. Organisations are often taught the same lessons repeatedly and learn only the lessons they can easily translate into the language of pre-existing routines.

Organisational routines are representative of larger organisational frames (Eden 2004). Organisational frames are 'approaches to problem solving used by organisational personnel' (Eden 2006: 198), determining 'what counts as a problem, how problems are represented, the strategies to be used to solve those problems, and the constraints and requirements placed on possible solutions' (Eden 2004: 49–50) These criteria are developed during 'the creation of organisations, and during periods of organisational upheaval' when 'actors articulate organisational goals and draw on and modify existing understandings, or knowledge, of the social and physical environment in which they must operate' (ibid.: 49–50). These organisational frames are critical to organisational learning because they determine how organisations interpret and understand their experiences (i.e. histories) and thus encode them into knowledge-laden artifacts and routines. It is organisational frames, rather than historical facts, that determine how organisations act (Eden 2006: 199).

The role of routines and frames in organisational learning poses particular challenges for peacebuilding organisations because these organisations were largely designed to implement other types of activities (i.e. development, humanitarian, human rights or conflict resolution). These organisations will have difficulty encoding lessons learned about the impact of peacebuilding on routines that were designed to support and reward other types of programming. In addition, while routines can adapt incrementally, adaptation requires some proof of necessity, which calls for assessment of success or failure. Because of the difficulty of assessing the impact of peacebuilding efforts, there is weak evidence within many peacebuilding organisations of the need to change or adapt routines in order to improve peacebuilding practice, and thus few incentives to do so.

Because organisational learning is dependent on historical routines, it is largely path-dependent. According to Powell, 'Path-dependent models suggest that institutional arrangements are not likely to be flexible; they cannot change rapidly in response to perturbations in the environment' (Powell 1991: 193). In other words, organisational action and learning reinforce historical frames, which in turn influences what is learned and which actions are taken. An organisation's original institutional environment is particularly important, as it imprints the organisation with its routines, resources, knowledge, structure and culture, which new organisational forms must draw upon (Scott and Davis 2007: 252). The path-dependent nature of organisational learning is likely to have real significance for many peacebuilding organisations that were founded to achieve different aims, particularly in a less complex and dynamic environment.

Particular challenges of organisational learning in peacebuilding organisations

While learning is difficult for any organisation, it may be particularly challenging for peacebuilding organisations because of particular historical, normative, and structural barriers.

The challenge of unaltered routines

Each peacebuilding organisation chooses tasks that correspond to its original mandate and corresponding routines (Barnett et al. 2007). They are therefore likely to use the same organisational routines and implement peacebuilding activities in the same way as they approach their standard development, humanitarian, human rights, or conflict resolution programmes. How could they achieve different outcomes, if they do things in the same way?

The increasing professionalisation of peacebuilding would ideally have led to changes in organisational routines and culture that corresponded with these organisations' new peacebuilding aims. Unfortunately, research into seven prominent peacebuilding organisations has found that this is not often the case (Campbell 2009). Instead, the old routines have become mixed up with some new routines and packaged in peacebuilding jargon, creating increasingly complex organisational behaviours that often work at cross-purposes. As a result, even though these organisations may have clear peacebuilding aims, their routines often prevent them from obtaining the necessary knowledge or altering their incentive structures to enable action and adaptation that corresponds to these aims.

Bureaucracies reproduce themselves

There are also distinct barriers to learning in bureaucracies, which is the organisational form of many peacebuilding organisations. Barnett and Finnemore explain that international organisations (IOs), which are bureaucracies, tend to reproduce themselves. 'Solutions that involve regulation, arbitration, and intervention by rational-legal authorities (themselves or other organisations) appear sensible, rational, and good to IOs and so disproportionately emerge from IO activity' (Barnett and Finnemore 2004: 34). Instead of responding to the needs of the post-conflict state and society, international bureaucracies are likely to recreate institutions and programmes in their own image. 'The result is that what began as a relatively narrow technical intervention (training police) expands into a package of reforms aimed at transforming non-Western societies (where most peacebuilding takes place) into Western societies' (ibid.). Rather than catalysing a change process, bureaucracies are likely to try and do much of the work themselves in a manner that fits with their standards and approach (ibid.). These factors are likely to significantly inhibit the degree to which bureaucracies can be expected to learn from the particular post-conflict country in which they intervene, and design programmes that meet the needs and capacities of the post-conflict state and society.

External accountability and the broken feedback loop of international aid

Peacebuilding organisations are primarily accountable to actors that are external to the state in which they intervene, rather than to the beneficiaries that they claim to serve. A donor agency is accountable to its home government and its political constituency. An international organisation is accountable to its Member States. A non-governmental organisation is accountable to its donors. Peacebuilding organisations' incentive structures are aligned with the policies and systems of these external constituencies, not those of the host state and society.

This tendency toward external accountability is described by some as the broken feedback loop of international aid.

> [A] unique and most striking characteristic of foreign aid is that the people for whose benefit aid agencies work are not the same as those from whom their revenues are obtained; they actually live in different countries and different political constituencies. This geographical and political separation between beneficiaries and taxpayers blocks the normal performance feedback process. (Martens et al. 2002: 14)

While some monitoring and evaluation systems attempt to gather information about the beneficiaries' perception of the goods delivered, they often rely on easily measurable deliverables rather than impact or outcome (Ebrahim

2005: 64). They also have difficulty gathering accurate information from beneficiaries, who may be reluctant to voice displeasure with the services provided (Martens et al. 2002: 15). The cultural gulf between the taxpayer or donor and the beneficiary is enormously wide, and a great deal is lost in translation, when attempted (ibid.).

The problem of broken feedback loops applies to international organisations, donor governments and NGOs alike. Alnoor Ebrahim (2005: 61) argues that because NGOs' dominant emphasis is on upward accountability to donors, rather than accountability to the communities that they profess to serve. NGOs have a short-term focus on outputs and efficiency criteria causing them to 'lose sight of long-range goals concerning social development and change' (ibid.: 61). He concludes that too much upward accountability greatly compromises 'field-level learning and downwards accountability' (ibid.: 149).

The constraints of a normative agenda

Finally, the norms contained in the liberal peace agenda may actually prevent peacebuilding organisations from identifying and supporting the needs and capacities of the host country. Barnett and Finnemore point out that international organisations derive their authority from their normative mandate. Member States established international organisations to protect values that they could not protect on their own, and IOs therefore derive their authority from this delegation: 'IOs are thus authoritative because they represent the collective will of their members,' which is embodied in international law and human rights conventions (Barnett and Finnemore 2004: 22). If they were to pursue less ambitious normative aims than those contained in the liberal peace agenda, they could risk compromising their basis of authority.

Western donor agencies and NGOs also have normative missions and constraints. Western donor agencies are accountable to their governments and may find it difficult to compromise their own liberal democratic ideals for solutions that may be less palatable to their populations and legislative bodies (i.e. corruption, inequality, etc.). Or, if they do aim for stabilisation rather than liberalisation, they may be unwilling to collect valid information about their outcomes, which is a prerequisite for learning. Most NGOs also possess highly normative mandates (i.e. humanitarian, human rights, sustainable development, religious focus), although the degree to which they can compromise them is dependent on their organisational culture and their relationship with their donors.

The impossibility of enforcing or coercing a liberal peace

Staunch proponents of liberal peacebuilding often argue that their aims are achievable through the right combination of capacities, strategy and coordinated action (Covey et al. 2005; DPKO 2008). Staunch critics of liberal peacebuilding argue that it imposes a Western agenda on transitional and post-conflict countries. Between these poles, academics describe the complexity of liberal peacebuilding, catalogue its successes and failures, critique its faulty assumptions and lament its dysfunction. This chapter approaches these debates from a different perspective. Instead of asking whether the liberal peacebuilding endeavour is valid or not, it has asked whether it is feasible. Can the IOs, INGOs and donor aid agencies implement their own peacebuilding best practices and support an endogenously driven (i.e. by national and local actors) process that aligns with norms that are also exogenously acceptable (i.e. to the international community)? Do these actors actually have the capacity to ensure that transitional and war-torn countries develop liberal democratic institutions, grounded in the rule of law and a market economy, as both staunch critics and supporters of liberal peacebuilding claim?

The theory presented in the previous section points to the extreme difficulties that peacebuilding organisations are likely to face in carrying out the liberal peace agenda, at least in part because of their weak organisational capacity to learn from and adapt to complex conflict dynamics. Empirical research conducted with multiple types of peacebuilding organisations in Burundi confirms these theoretical propositions.[4] Through in-depth case study research, I have found that organisational and institutional barriers to the implementation of successful liberal peacebuilding projects are so great that when the determinants of liberal peace appear in transitional or post-conflict countries they should not be attributed solely, if at all, to liberal peacebuilding interventions. Peacebuilding organisations' 'path dependency' and upwardly accountable routines often make many liberal peacebuilders the guarantors of the status quo rather than the liberators of the oppressed. Even those liberal peacebuilders who do develop innovative locally driven and owned approaches often lose their relevance to the context as the actors and issues quickly change. The rules, routines and organisational culture of peacebuilding organisations are powerful predictors of how they are likely to engage with and influence transitional and post-conflict countries.

My findings show that the agency of the host government is much greater than imagined by both critics and proponents of the liberal peace, in part because of how peacebuilding organisations are structured to relate to it. An important organisational routine is created in peacebuilding organisations by the sovereignty of the host government. All international actors that implement activities in a transitional or post-conflict country have been granted permission to be there by the host government.[5] This permission can be quickly taken away if the international actor acts in ways that the government disapproves of. The governments of Sudan, Burundi and many others have repeatedly demonstrated their willingness to declare international staff *personae non gratae* or revoke an organisation's registration, forcing them to leave the country within a matter of days. This forced evacuation not only prevents the international peacebuilder or peacebuilding organisation from achieving its liberal aims, but can do significant harm to careers. It is a coercive tool that the government can use to ensure that international actors do not push the boundaries too far.

National agency and local agency are also present in the very notion of liberal peacebuilding. National and local actors determine the outcomes of all liberal peacebuilding activities because they must decide whether or not to engage in them or sustain them. If they do not support peacebuilding activities and attempt to sustain their outcomes, then these activities will not achieve liberal results (Campbell et al. 2010). National and local ownership are therefore integral to peacebuilding outcomes. That said, the focus of most bilateral and multilateral donors on direct engagement with the state privileges national ownership (i.e. by members of the state) over local ownership (i.e. by members of communities, local governments or civil society). The organisational routines that require agreement by the state therefore detract from ownership by other members of society, often leading to the empowerment of an illiberal state.

The bureaucratic routines of most peacebuilding organisations also tend to create a technocratic approach to liberal peacebuilding, removing norms, ideals and ideas from peacebuilding projects and programmes. While the aim to create the determinants of liberal institutions may be behind many peacebuilding programmes and projects, the professionalisation and bureaucratisation of peacebuilding has led to the creation of a standard menu of projects and programmes that are often devoid of the original concept or ideal. As a result, staff implementing these projects and programmes are often more concerned with implementing the project as designed rather than achieving the behavioural or institutional change necessary for the existence of liberal institutions (Campbell et al. 2010).

Upward accountability routines in the United Nations and many other peacebuilding organisations discourage accountability for liberal peacebuilding outcomes. Accountability mechanisms hold staff accountable for project delivery and spending budgets, not achieving liberal peacebuilding outcomes or impact (Campbell et al. 2010). When peacebuilding organisations do focus on accountability for outcomes, their desire to show an aggregate impact across all countries in which they intervene may lead them to condense all possible outcomes into a few general indicators, creating the incentive on the ground to fulfil these generic indicators (e.g. the Millennium Development Goals), rather than to achieve a specific conflict-sensitive outcome or impact.

There is also an apparent disconnect between 'liberal' and 'peacebuilding' that is perpetuated by the creation of standard peacebuilding routines and programmes. The increasing focus of peacebuilding organisations' routines on pursuing the same policies and outcomes from one country to the next makes the development of conflict-sensitive programmes more difficult. To be conflict-sensitive, a peacebuilding project must ask how it reinforces or mitigates the particular causes and manifestations of conflict in a particular country at a particular time in that country's history. While many peacebuilding organisations conduct conflict analyses, they often fail to analyse the particular institutions that they aim to influence, and adapt their projects and programmes to the information in this analysis. As a result, they may exacerbate the causes of conflict that they purport to be addressing. Furthermore, the focus on standardisation and professionalisation of liberal peacebuilding may lead to the prioritisation of 'liberal' above 'peacebuilding', resulting in a failure to achieve either.

In spite of the enormous organisational, institutional and contextual challenges facing peacebuilding organisations, they do, in fact, manage to achieve some outcomes that support behaviours and institutions that resolve conflict peacefully and improve the protection of rights of all citizens. These successes can largely be explained by the readiness of national and local actors to commit to and lead these efforts, and the willingness of staff of international peacebuilding organisations to manipulate organisational routines to help achieve their peacebuilding aims and outcomes, often with huge transaction costs in terms of time, resources and personal risk.

Even in the cases of successful incremental liberal peacebuilding, national actors may be more likely to decry the lack of effort by international actors to push for real institutional change, than criticise them for attempting to change too much, as many critics of liberal peace argue. This was certainly the case in Burundi, where the international community fully endorsed recent democratic elections in which only one party ran. Many Burundians were greatly disappointed that years of war and over a decade of peacebuilding had resulted in a one-party state that again used oppressive tactics to maintain power, and that the international community was neither willing nor able to do anything to change this.

Conclusion

This chapter has argued that the liberal peace debate fails to ask whether or not it is feasible for international actors to impose liberal institutions on post-conflict and transitional countries. Based on a review of organisational theory and preliminary findings from research into peacebuilding organisations in Burundi, I have argued that liberal peacebuilding cannot be imposed. Like Zürcher and Sending (this volume) I have argued that the determinants of liberal peace can only be created if national actors are both willing and able to create them. The organisational and institutional routines in peacebuilding organisations prevent liberal peacebuilders from applying the type of pressure or wielding the type of authority necessary to impose liberal peacebuilding. These same routines also often prevent these organisations from engaging effectively with national actors and institutions, which would require them to learn and adapt, thus altering their peacebuilding aims and/or their corresponding projects and programmes to fit each country context. While perfect learning organisations are rare in any field, they are likely to be particularly rare in peacebuilding. As a result, not only do the organisational and institutional barriers to learning and adaptation have important implications for the academic debate around the critique of the liberal peace, but they have significant implications for peacebuilding practice in general and those who study it, presenting an important area of future research, debate, and potential reform.

Notes

1. For the purposes of this chapter, a peacebuilding organisation is an external organisation – whether initially founded to implement humanitarian, development, political, security, conflict resolution, human rights or even peacebuilding programming – that 'adopts goals and objectives' intended to impact the drivers and causes of peace (OECD-DAC 2007: 8).
2. Earlier versions of this chapter were presented at the American Political Science Association Annual Meeting in 2009 and the International Studies Association (ISA) Annual Convention in 2010, and related arguments were published in Campbell 2008b.
3. Adapted from the definition by Argyris (1992: 67): 'Learning is defined as occurring under two conditions. First, learning occurs when an organisation achieves what it intended; that is, there is a match between its design for action and the actuality or outcome. Second, learning occurs when a mismatch between intentions and outcomes is identified and corrected; that is, a mismatch is turned into a match.'
4. These findings are based on research into the interaction between IOs, INGOs and donor aid agencies and the evolving conflict context in Burundi from 1999 to 2010.
5. The exceptions to this rule are the recent cases of international trusteeship: the former Yugoslavia, Timor-Leste and Kosovo.

Bibliography

Anderson, M. B. and L. Olson (2003) *Confronting War: Critical Lessons for Peace Practitioners*, Cambridge: The Collaborative for Development Action.
Argyris, C. (1992) *On Organizational Learning*, Cambridge: Blackwell.
Ayoob, M. (2007) 'State Making, State Breaking, and State Failure', in C. A. Crocker, F. Osler Hampson and P. Aall, *Leashing the Dogs of War: Conflict Management in a Divided World*, Washington, DC: United States Institute of Peace.
Barnett, M. (2006) 'Building a Republican Peace: Stabilizing States after War', *International Security* 30(4): 87–122.

Barnett, M. and M. Finnemore (2004) *Rules for the World: International Organizations in Global Politics*, Ithaca, NY: Cornell University Press.

Barnett, M. and C. Zürcher (2009) 'The Peacebuilder's Contract: How External Statebuilding Reinforces Weak Statehood', in R. Paris and T. Sisk, *The Dilemmas of Statebuilding: Confronting the Contradictions of Postwar Peace Operations*, London: Routledge, pp. 23–52.

Barnett, M., K. Hunjoon, M. O'Donnell and L. Sitea (2007) 'Peacebuilding: What Is in a Name?', *Global Governance* 13: 35–58.

Berman, B. (1998) 'Ethnicity, Patronage and the African State: The Politics of Uncivil Nationalism', *African Affairs* 97.

Call, C. T. (2008) 'Knowing Peace When You See It: Setting Standards for Peacebuilding Success', *Civil Wars* 10(2): 173–194.

Call, C. T. and E. M. Cousens (2008) 'Ending Wars and Building Peace: International Responses to War-Torn Societies', *International Studies Perspectives* 9: 1–21.

Call, C. T. and V. Wyeth (2008) *Building States to Build Peace*, Boulder, CO: Lynne Rienner.

Campbell, S. P. (2008a) '(Dis)Integration, Incoherence and Complexity in UN Post-Conflict Interventions', *International Peacekeeping* 15(4): 556–569.

Campbell, S. P. (2008b) 'When Process Matters: The Potential Implications of Organizational Learning for Peacebuilding Success', *Journal of Peacebuilding and Development* 4(2): 20–32.

Campbell, S. P. (2009) 'Organizational Barriers to Peace? Understanding the Interaction between International Peacebuilding and the Countries It Aims to Influence,' paper presented at the Annual Meeting of the American Political Science Association, Toronto, ON, September.

Campbell, S. P. (2010) 'Organizational Barriers to Peace: International Bureaucratic Routines and Modern State Formation,' paper presented at the International Studies Association (ISA) Annual Convention, New Orleans, LA, February.

Campbell, S. P. with L. Kayobera and J. Nkurunziza (2009) *Independent External Evaluation: Peacebuilding Fund Projects in Burundi*, Bujumbura: Joint Steering Committee of the UN Peacebuilding Fund Projects in Burundi, March.

Carothers, T. (2006) *Promoting the Rule of Law Abroad: In Search of Knowledge*, Washington, DC: Carnegie Endowment for International Peace.

Chabal, P. and J.-P. Daloz (1999) *Africa Works: Disorder as Political Instrument*, African Issues series, Bloomington: Indiana University Press.

Church, C. and M. M. Rogers (2006) *Designing for Results: Integrating Monitoring and Evaluation in Conflict Transformation Programs*, Washington, DC: Search for Common Ground.

Cousens, E. (2001) 'Introduction', in E. Cousens and C. Kumar, *Peacebuilding as Politics: Cultivating Peace in Fragile Societies*, Boulder, CO: Lynne Rienner.

Covey, J., M. J. Dziedzic and L. Hawley (2005) *The Quest for Viable Peace: International Intervention and Strategies for Conflict Transformation*, Washington, DC: United States Institute of Peace Press.

De Waal, A. (2009) 'Mission without end? Peacekeeping in the African Political Marketplace', *International Affairs* 85(1): 99–113.

DfID (2009) *Building the State and Securing the Peace*, Emerging Policy Paper, London: Department for International Development, June.

Dobbins, J., S. G. Jones, K. Crane and B. Cole DeGrasse (2007) *The Beginner's Guide to Nation-Building*, Santa Monica, CA: RAND Corporation.

Doyle, M. and N. Sambanis (2006) *Making War and Building Peace: United Nations Peace Operations*, Princeton, NJ: Princeton University Press.

DPKO (2008) *United Nations Peacekeeping Operations: Principles and Guidelines*, New York: United Nations Department of Peacekeeping Operations.

Duffield, M. (2001) *Global Governance and the New Wars: The Merging of Development and Security*, London and New York: Zed Books.

Ebrahim, A. (2005) 'Accountability Myopia: Losing Sight of Organizational Learning', *Nonprofit and Voluntary Sector Quarterly*, 34(1) 56–87.

Eden, L. (2004) *Whole World on Fire: Organizations, Knowledge, and Nuclear Weapons Devastation*, Ithaca, NY and London: Cornell University Press.

Eden, L. (2006) '"Getting It Right or Wrong": Organizational Learning About the Physical World', in M. L. Brown, M. Kenney and M. Zarkin, *Organizational Learning in the Global Context*, Aldershot: Ashgate, pp. 197–216.

Englebert, P. and D. M. Tull (2008) 'Postconflict Reconstruction in Africa: Flawed Ideas About Failed States', *International Security* 32(4): 106–139.

Fortna, V. P. (2008) 'Peacekeeping and Democratization', in A. Jarstad and T. Sisk, *From War to Democracy*, Cambridge: Cambridge University Press.

Galtung, J. (1969) 'Violence, Peace, and Peace Research', *Journal of Peace Research* 6(3): 167–191.

Goetschel, L. and T. Hagmann (2009) 'Civilian Peacebuilding: Peace by Bureaucratic Means?', *Conflict, Security and Development* 9(1): 55–73.

Howard, L. M. (2008) *UN Peacekeeping in Civil Wars*, Cambridge: Cambridge University Press.

International Alert, Saferworld and FEWER (2004) *Conflict Sensitive Approaches to Development, Humanitarian Assistance and Peacebuilding: A Resource Pack*, London.

Jarstad, A. K. and T. D. Sisk (2008) *From War to Democracy: Dilemmas in Peacebuilding*, Cambridge: Cambridge University Press.

Jones, B. (2002) 'The Challenges of Strategic Coordination', in S. J. Stedman, D. Rothchild and E. M. Cousens, *Ending Civil Wars: The Implementation of Peace Agreements*, Boulder, CO: Lynne Rienner, pp. 89–115.

Ki-moon, Ban (2011) 'Given Marked Increase of Institution-Building Mandates in United Nations Missions, More Must be Done to Ensure Engagement with Other Actors, Says Secretary-General', New York: United Nations, SG/SM/13358, SC/10161, PBC/76.

Lederach, J. P. (1997) *Building Peace: Sustainable Reconciliation in Divided Societies*, Washington, DC: United States Institute of Peace Press.

Levitt, B. and J. G. March (1988) 'Organizational Learning', *Annual Review of Sociology* 14: 319–340.

Levy, J. S. (1994) 'Learning and Foreign Policy: Sweeping a Conceptual Minefield', *International Organization* 48(2): 279–312.

March, J. G. (1999) *The Pursuit of Organizational Intelligence*, Malden, MA: Blackwell.

Martens, B., U. Mummert, P. Murrell and P. Seabright (2002) *The Institutional Economics of Foreign Aid*, Cambridge: Cambridge University Press.

OECD-DAC (2007) *Principles for Good International Engagement in Fragile States and Situations*, Paris: Organisation for Economic Cooperation and Development.

OECD-DAC (2008) 'Evaluating Conflict Prevention and Peacebuilding Activities', Factsheet, Paris: Organisation for Economic Cooperation and Development.

Ottaway, M. (2003) 'Rebuilding State Institutions in Collapsed States', in J. Milken, *State Failure, Collapse, and Reconstruction*, Malden, MA: Blackwell.

Paris, R. (2002) 'International Peacebuilding and the "Mission Civilisatrice"', *Review of International Studies* 28(4): 637–656.
Paris, R. (2004) *At War's End: Building Peace after Civil Conflict*, Cambridge: Cambridge University Press.
Paris, R. and T. Sisk (2007) *Managing Contradictions: The Inherent Dilemmas of Postwar Statebuilding, Research Partnership on Postwar Statebuilding*, New York: International Peace Academy.
Pouligny, B. (2005) 'Civil Society and Post-Conflict Peacebuilding: Ambiguities of International Programmes Aimed at Building "New" Societies', *Security Dialogue* 36(4): 495–510.
Powell, W. W. (1991) 'Expanding the Scope of Institutional Analysis', in W. W. Powell and P. J. DiMaggio, *The New Institutionalism in Organizational Analysis*, Chicago: University of Chicago Press.
Pressman, J. L. and A. Wildavsky (1984) *Implementation: How Great Expectations in Washington Are Dashed in Oakland*, 3rd edn, Berkeley: University of California Press.
Pritchett, L. and M. Woolcock (2004) 'Solutions When the Solution Is the Problem: Arraying the Disarray in Development', *World Development*.
Rueschemeyer, D. (2005) 'Building States – Inherently a Long-Term Process? An Argument from Theory', in L. Matthew and D. Rueschemeyer, *States and Development: Historical Antecedents of Stagnation and Advance*, New York: Palgrave Macmillan, pp. 143–164.
Scott, W. R. and G. F. Davis (2007) *Organizations and Organizing: Rational, Natural, and Open System Perspectives*, Upper Saddle River, NJ: Pearson Prentice Hall.
Serwer, D. and P. Thomson (2007) 'A Framework for Success: International Intervention in Societies Emerging from Conflict', in C. A. Crocker, F. Osler Hampson and P. Aall, *Leashing the Dogs of War: Conflict Management in a Divided World*, Washington, DC: United States Institute of Peace Press.
Smith, D. (2004) *Towards a Strategic Framework for Peacebuilding: Getting Their Act Together*, Overview Report of the Joint Utstein Study of Peacebuilding, Brattvaag: Royal Norwegian Ministry of Foreign Affairs.
Stewart, F. (2010) *Horizontal Inequalities and Conflict: Understanding Group Violence in Multiethnic Societies*, New York: Palgrave Macmillan.
Suhrke, A. (2007) 'Reconstruction as Modernisation: The "Post-Conflict" Project in Afghanistan', *Third World Quarterly* 28(7): 1291–1308.
Tadjbakhsh, S. and O. P. Richmond (2011) 'Conclusion: Typologies and Modifications Proposed by Critical Approaches', in S. Tadjbakhsh, *Rethinking the Liberal Peace: External Models and Local Alternatives*, London: Routledge.
Tilly, C. (1985) 'War Making and State Making as Organized Crime', in P. B. Evans, D. Rueschemeyer and T. Skocpol, *Bringing the State Back In*, Cambridge: Cambridge University Press.
Uvin, P. S. (2001) 'Difficult Choices in the New Post-Conflict Agenda: The International Community in Rwanda after the Genocide', *Third World Quarterly* 22(2): 177–189.
Woodward, S. (2007) 'Do the Root Causes of Civil War Matter? On Using Knowledge to Improve Peacebuilding Interventions', *Journal of Intervention and Statebuilding* 1(2): 143–170.

6

Promoting Women's Rights in Afghanistan: The Ambiguous Footprint of the West

Torunn Wimpelmann Chaudhary, Orzala Ashraf Nemat and Astri Suhrke

Introduction

The critique of the Liberal Peace is based on the assumption that Western countries attempt to impose 'their' values and models on war-torn countries (see Chandler, this volume). In reality, however, the effects of Western intervention are often far more complex, and often contradictory. This was the case even in Afghanistan, where the need for social transformation provided an explicit justification for the military intervention.

Western pledges to improve the conditions of Afghan women have been particularly prominent justifications for the intervention and subsequent military operations to defeat the Taliban. While the genuineness and, indeed, durability of these promises are debated, the main contention of this chapter is that the Western presence from the beginning had an ambiguous effect on the conditions of Afghan women. Rather than being one-directional, the intervention set in motion a number of contradictory processes that profoundly shaped the landscape and the strategies of those fighting to improve women's positions in contemporary Afghanistan. This chapter questions common assumptions about straightforward relationships between 'liberal peace' interventions and the effects on the society in question, whether positive (as its advocates maintain), or misguided (as critics argue).

The following analysis explores these contradictory processes through an examination on two important pieces of legislation that have preoccupied women activists in Afghanistan in recent time; the Shia Personal Status Law and the Law on Elimination of Violence against Women. The history of these two laws reveals four important dynamics at work in post-2001 Afghanistan. Together these dynamics render problematic the idea that outside interventions in fact translate into 'liberal effects' on the ground.

Background

As elsewhere, but with particular force in Afghanistan, the position of women is a highly symbolic and contested issue around which various political groups mobilise. In Afghanistan's kinship-oriented society, women and family have historically been keenly guarded against state intervention. The *nature* of state regulation of family matters has also been highly disputed, with various Islamic and secular oriented frameworks and their advocates competing for prominence. After 2001, another dimension was added as the position of Afghan women was made an explicit justification for the US-led military invasion (Abu-Lughod 2002).

In 2009, two laws which aimed in different ways to increase state regulation of the role and life of women intersected as they passed through the legislative process. The Shia Personal Status Law (hereafter: the Shia law) originated among a group of Afghan Shia clerics with ties to religious scholars in Iran and was formulated according to orthodox jurisprudence. The law defined personal law (property, marriage, divorce) for the country's Shia minority in terms that significantly restricted the rights of women and contained what many Afghan women and legal scholars felt was an excessive codification of personal life. Of particular concern in the West, the law established a legal understanding of marital relations where the wife's obedience, including in conjugal matters, was rendered in return for financial maintenance from the husband. This point was included in the version signed by President Karzai in March 2009, which provoked international outrage. The UN High Commissioner on Human Rights called it 'reprehensible'(United Nations 2009), President Barack Obama in a news conference chose 'abhorrent'.

By contrast, the Law on Elimination of Violence against Women (hereafter: the EVAW law) originated in a completely different Afghan milieu, framed by twentieth-century interpretations of women's rights, their codification in the Convention on the Elimination of All Forms of Discrimination against Women (CEDAW), and the views and experiences of progressive Afghan women. Many of these women had dealt with cases of violence against women through their work in the Ministry of Women's Affairs, women's NGOs, and the courts. The EVAW law was signed as presidential decree in 2009, and by late 2010 was still awaiting parliamentary ratification.

The parliamentary context at the time when the two laws were prepared and processed, (2005–2010), was decidedly conservative. There were more women in the Parliament than at any time before in Afghanistan's history, with 68 out of 249 members of the Lower House (Wolesi Jirga), and 23 of the 102 members in the Upper House (Meshrano Jirga). Yet the women did not form a coherent group, and were certainly not united in a pro-women agenda (Wordsworth 2007; Fleschenberg 2009). Among the male parliamentarians, clerics and ex-*mujahedin* commanders who likely would be conservative in religious and social matters were in the majority, totalling three-quarters of the male members of the Lower House, according to one careful estimate (Fleschenberg 2009; Wilder 2005).

Religious conservatives chaired five central committees in the House, including the Justice and Judiciary that was central in the Shia law case. The committee was chaired by Maulawi Ataullah Ludin, a Sunni Pashtun and high-ranking official of Hezb-e Islami, a movement and later a political party known for its Islamic militancy and in the period under consideration here a key political ally of the president. The Speaker of the House, Yunus Qanooni, a (Sunni) Tajik with a background in another *mujahedin* party, appeared as a broker among opposing interests in the legislative process involving the Shia and the EVAW laws, but who, on balance evidently favoured the conservatives.

The Shia Personal Status Law

The 2004 Constitution for the first time stipulated that courts were to apply Shia jurisprudence in family matters where both parties are Shia (Article 131). This formed the basis for efforts to draft a personal status law, led by the Shia scholar Sheikh Asif Mohseni. A Qizilbash Shia from Kandahar with close ties to Iranian religious scholars, Mohseni had a different background than the majority of Afghanistan's Shia population, which belongs to the ethnic Hazara minority. Mohseni's promotion of the law was perceived by many as a bid to position himself as a leader of the Shia population through an attempt to shift the primary identification of this group from ethnicity to religion (Oates 2009).

The minister of justice, Sarwar Danish, himself a Shia, reportedly shepherded the draft prepared by Mohseni's group through the Ministry of Justice for technical review before sending it to the Parliament in 2006. Here the draft was buried in committees for almost three years before being reported out to the floor and passed in early 2009. The slow passage reflected in part the opposition from a small but determined number of liberal parliamentarians who worked with civil society organisations to gain time to remove some of the law's most objectionable features. More important, there was concern among the Sunni religious scholars that a separate law for Shias would diminish the position of Sunni jurisprudence as the predominant Sharia source of legislation in the country. If passed, it would be the first law in Afghanistan's history based solely on Shia jurisprudence. At the same time, unrelated disputes involving the largest Shia group, the Hazaras, erupted over other matters. Conflict between Hazara farmers and Pashtun nomads over access to land, and disagreement over quota representation for Pashtun nomads in the Parliament, paralysed parliamentary proceedings for the better part of a month. In this situation, the parliamentary leadership was reluctant to bring to the floor a bill that could accentuate ethno-religious divides.

The delay gave the opponents time to organise. The most public and politically visible opposition formed around a few women parliamentarians and a civil society organisation who opposed it on grounds of human rights, women's rights and liberal interpretations of Sharia. An additional process was initiated by the Afghanistan Independent Human Rights Commission, which engaged Kateb University, a private university influenced by Hazara religious scholars, to review the law. The opponents succeeded in modifying the proposed law in three priority areas: raising the legal age of marriage (from 'minor', taken to mean 9 for girls, to 16 for girls and 18 for boys) the age at which the father can claim custody of children after divorce (raised from 2 to 7 for boys and 7 to 9 for girls) and giving the wife greater freedom of movement outside the house. The opponents had a much longer list of proposed amendments – a shortlist of 17 and a wish list of 96 changes, including the conjugal obedience item – but a powerful Sunni leader and ex-*mujahedin*, Abdul Rasul Sayyaf, who had been an initial opponent of the law, cut the discussion short. After his intervention the Lower House voted to approve the bill as a package without further debate on 7 February 2009. So apparently did the Upper House a little later[1] and the bill went to President Hamid Karzai for signature.

The opponents of the bill made no major effort to solicit international support until after the bill had been approved by the Lower House of Parliament. As the bill then was moving through the final stages of approval, however, some MPs and civil society approached internationals actors. An ad hoc coalition of Afghan opponents, Western donors and UN organisations started to meet in February and March to assess strategies to further modify the bill. At this point, items of priority were provisions governing polygamy and the wife's obedience to her husband. However, international actors hesitated to take a strong stand for several reasons.

First, the politics of the case were complicated. Seeing that the Shia elite, including the Minister of Justice, supported the law, some internationals feared being perceived as standing in the way of Shia desire for a separate law and hence partisan in Afghanistan's sensitive ethnic politics. In Parliament, sectarian lines were strongly evident. Some Shia MPs in Parliament openly said 'this is our law' and asked Sunni MPs not to intervene. All Shia women MPs voted for it, and Shia women activists were told not to spoil the Shia community's opportunity to get their own law. Particular issues could be sorted out later, they were told. Opponents were also warned that their opposition was un-Islamic, a serious charge that implied blasphemy or apostasy.

There were tacit political understandings and bargains. Sayyaf's eventual endorsement of the law was premised on a rejection of the Sunni parliamentarians' right to debate its content and effectively signalled an arrangement in which Sunni and Shia actors would recognise each other's exclusive authority on their respective jurisprudence. The implication was to preclude debate across sectarian lines in Parliament on any law of religious association. Conservative Sunni MPs supported the bill based on this understanding and once it was clear there would be no separate Shia courts and a provision for temporary marriage (inimical to Sunni jurisprudence) was removed. Yet many of them were brought to believe they were voting for an advisory document rather than a law. In a bargain of a different kind, rumours circulated that Karzai and Mohseni had made a deal whereby the latter would 'deliver' the Shia vote for Karzai in the 2009 presidential election in return for Karzai's support for the bill.

The UN itself was divided over how to respond. Whereas some officials, notably within UNIFEM, advocated a strong stance against problematic aspects of the law, others within the UN system argued that the issue was too sensitive and called for a lowering of UN activity on the issue to avoid 'destabilisation'. International officials on the Kabul human rights network – a group of human rights advisors organised around EU and the UN – asked themselves if it were wise for international actors to get involved in this thicket of thorny issues, and if so, how? They had earlier expended human rights capital on religious issues by opposing verdicts on blasphemy and apostasy, each time causing a massive public outcry and controversy.

Second, the process surrounding the drafting of the law was extremely complicated and opaque, making advocacy for change exceedingly difficult. Lack of knowledge constrained the Afghan opponents of the bill, and even more so the internationals. UNAMA had produced a preliminary translation of the bill, but there was no authoritative translation until April 2009, well after it had been passed by the Parliament and signed by Karzai. Translation was no simple matter. The bill was a complicated legal corpus of 249 clauses, with numerous words and concepts in Arabic. USAID had a dozen experts working for two weeks to produce an authoritative translation. Although international concern would be justified in terms of international human rights provisions, including CEDAW (which Afghanistan had signed in 2003), some donors felt ignorance of Shia jurisprudence was a constraining factor. The opaqueness of the Afghan political process and the failure of Western governments to invest in long-term country expertise (including language resources) meant that the internationals had quite limited information that was verifiable. By late March 2009, when the EU–UN network of international human rights advisors had moved to a more active stance, they did do not know which version of the law had been adopted by the Parliament, nor did they have an authoritative translation, or even a copy of the law itself. They did not know whether Karzai had signed it or not, or even if it was a law (the chairman of the House Justice Committee said it was only an advisory opinion for the Supreme Court). To complicate matters further, the UN community remained divided.

At this point unknown sources leaked a UNIFEM document assessing the law to the international press. The debate entered the Western public realm with consequent loss of nuance. International headlines proclaimed that the law legalised rape in marriage, citing a provision on conjugal obedience that required the wife to submit to sexual intercourse once every fourth night (Article 132). Information landing on the desk of a European foreign minister said the law sanctioned rape, house arrest and paedophilia. The UNIFEM document was leaked to coincide with the opening of a major international meeting on Afghanistan in the Hague on 31 March, called by the US government to solicit allied support for a stronger engagement in Afghanistan. Given their formal commitment to promote democracy and human rights in Afghanistan, news of the law created public outrage in NATO member countries. Western official reactions were predictable. With the credibility of the international mission at risk of being undermined in the eyes of their population, NATO governments issued strong statements condemning the law.

Faced with a storm of public international protest Karzai at first withdrew the law, claiming technical reasons and that he had not read it. He then announced that the Ministry would review the law and amend any articles in contradiction with Sharia or the Constitution.

The stronger international stance had also emboldened some of the Afghan opponents of the law. Several Shia women not connected to the Parliament or the core opposition staged a public protest. It was supported by Hazara leaders opposed to the influence of Mohseni and his suspected ambition to take credit for delivering the country's first law for the Shia minority. The demonstration dispersed in the face of strong counter-demonstrations organised by Shia clerics linked to Mohseni, who accused the women of being anti-Islamic, Western agents and prostitutes.

In the months that followed, Afghan women and civil society organisations, the UN and concerned embassies met repeatedly to agree on strategies on how to influence the review process of the law that had been announced by the Minister of Justice. Groups of Afghan women, including civil society activists and MPs, met several times with government officials to follow up the review. But with the Afghan government playing its cards close to its chest – the Minister of Justice was reportedly managing the review in person – it proved difficult for these actors to access and provide input to the process. An amended law was presented by the minister in early July. The revisions included changes in language relating to sexual obedience, but these and other changes were only minor and insufficient for the core opposition from the Parliament and civil society that had fought the bill from the start. Members of this coalition wrote an open letter to President Karzai expressing their concern. The amended law, they argued, failed to take into consideration their suggestions and as a result remained problematic on many issues, particularly relating to polygamy, women's rights to work and sexual obedience. The law nevertheless was signed by the President on 19 July in the presence of some women critics of the law. At that point, some groups took a more conciliatory stance. Most notably, the AIHCR issued a statement which declared that the efforts of civil society to bring the necessary changes to the law had been successful.

The Elimination of Violence Against Women law

The EVAW law originated in 2005 in the Afghan EVAW Commission, established by the Ministry of Women's Affairs (MOWA) with support of UNIFEM to address the problem of violence against women. Citing widespread and abhorrent cases of violence against women, the Commission argued that there was a need for a new law that could end impunity and provide stronger punishments.

The legal department of MOWA drafted the first version of the law. The department consulted various legal experts, other academics and government officials although concern to protect the law as an Afghan / MOWA item resulted in UNIFEM not being included at this point The MOWA draft was officially submitted to the Ministry of Justice (Taqnin section) on the International Women's Day in 2006 amidst national media coverage. A group of Afghan women's activists, however, felt that the law required significant improvements and started working on a revised draft, this time with the technical support of UNIFEM. Following a nine month process, their draft was submitted to the Taqnin through MOWA channels in late 2007. Yet another, parallel drafting process had started in the Parliament's Women's Affairs Commission, much to the dismay of the contributors to the previous drafts. This draft, a short and declaratory statement, was perceived by other participants in the process as an attempt by the main female MP involved to position herself politically at the cost of unity among women activists.[2]

The Taqnin now had three drafts and started working on creating a single version. But while Afghan efforts had been multiple and competitive from the start, international involvement – apart from UNIFEM support to the civil society draft and assistance to Taqnin to streamline the three drafts into one – was only evident late in the process. In early 2009, i.e. more than three years after the initiative originated in the EVAW Commission, a joint international-Afghan working group received a copy of the draft law through the Taqnin. The working group (Criminal Law Working Group, chaired by the UN Office on Drugs and Crime) included international legal experts with a mandate to ensure consistency and coherence in the criminal law area. Numerous laws had already been introduced, often at the initiative of international advisors schooled in their respective national legal traditions, creating incoherence in the legal corpus. Presented with a short deadline, the committee could only make small suggestions, most of which were not incorporated by the Taqnin.

By this time, concern over the Shia law was deepening and women activists and concerned internationals started to look to the EVAW law as a possible corrective to its problematic provisions. The EVAW law thus appeared on the agenda of the international-national advocacy coalition that was lobbying to amend the Shia law. In an evident concession to this group, President Karzai signed the EVAW law and the Shia law at the same time, on 19 July 2009.

As the EVAW law was sent back to the Parliament for review and ratification, women activists became increasingly worried that it would fail to get past conservative MPs in an acceptable form. Some argued that the only viable strategy was to furtively introduce the law in plenary on a day when key conservatives were absent. The Women's Affairs Commission in the Lower House that was tasked with leading the process sought instead to develop a consensus by taking the law to the Joint Commission composed of representatives of all 18 parliamentary commissions, before bringing it to a plenary debate

The parliamentary proceedings were an opening for international experts from the joint working group that previously had tried to modify the draft to re-enter the process. Having secured a copy of the law, they became concerned when discovering that technical weaknesses remained. Chief among them were a lack of coherence with the broader legal framework and confusion over legal categories. At this point, however, the logic of legal professionalism clashed with the logic of politics.

Women activists argued that the purpose of the law was in part political, that is, to bring the problem of violence and discrimination against women to political attention and send a strong signal against impunity for such crimes. They also feared that introducing changes at this point would complicate the matter and possibly give ammunition to the conservatives, especially if opponents could frame the law as a foreign creation. Undoubtedly, there was also a strong sense among the women who had worked on the bill for years that this was 'their' product and some resentment that unsolicited external advice was being offered at a late stage in the process. As a result, repeated efforts by the international legal experts to improve the technical language of the law did not succeed.

In the Parliament, meanwhile, the atmosphere in the Joint Commission became increasingly hostile. Conservative MPs accused women supporters of the law of being anti-family and under foreign influence. In the end meetings were suspended. Those who had worked on the law from the beginning now argued that it was better left as a presidential decree, and for the parliamentary process to be abandoned. There were concerns that the law would either be rejected or only get through Parliament in a severely butchered form. The new situation also revealed a split among the female MPs, with the initial backers of the law accusing key members of the Women's Affairs Commission of using the parliamentary ratification process to put their stamp on the law and claim credit for delivering it.

The international actors were becoming similarly fatigued over the parliamentary process. Previous attempts to lobby key parliamentarian powerbrokers on the law had not yielded results and there was a sense that salvaging it as a presidential decree might be better than nothing. By spring 2010, due to the efforts of its original supporters, the EVAW law had been taken off the parliamentary agenda for the time being, with its eventual acceptance there uncertain. Having lost patience with the long drawn-out process of getting the law past the Parliament, supportive government agencies, women's organisations and donors were implementing its provisions as a presidential decree. Scattered reports of prosecutions based on the EVAW law in courts started to emerge, and informal conversations suggested the law was well known and referred to by many provincial courts around the country.

The Ambiguous Western Footprint

Examining the processes of the EVAW and Shia law together reveals a number of effects of the Western presence in deep contradiction with proclaimed aims to systematically stimulate a liberally oriented set of social and political transformations. Whilst empirically overlapping, analytically these effects can be separated into four dynamics: Firstly, the Western presence directly empowered actors of an anti-liberal inclination. Secondly, the strong support for women's rights was to a large extent articulated for NATO's home audience, and the primary accountability was to this group and not to Afghan constituencies. Thirdly an increasingly unpopular Western presence indirectly shaped the political landscape by polarising faultlines alongside Western versus Islamic or Afghan lines. Finally, the heavy presence of the aid machinery reinforced personalised and top down dynamics, both in civil society and in the law-making process itself.

Empowering Anti-liberal Forces

A significant proportion of post-2001 powerholders had been associated with the Islamist or conservative Islamic movements – the *mujahedin* – that had formed with Western support in the 1970s and 1980s in opposition to (first) President Daoud and then the communists. Most of these *mujahedin* espoused a distinctively illiberal view when it came to gender and social issues, and many also had a history of human rights abuses. Having fallen out with the Taliban

– although some had fought them all along – these groups were mobilised by the 2001 US invasion and were made key actors in the post-Taliban political settlement (Azarbaijani-Moghaddam 2007).

Some appeared as governors on the local level, e.g. Gul Aga Sherzai in Kandahar and later Nangarhar, and Ismail Khan in Herat. Others moved into formal positions of power at the central state level (e.g. Marshal Fahim became Defence Minister and General Dostum initially his deputy). Yet others, having been contacted and funded by the US government at the eve of the overthrow of the Taliban government, entrenched themselves as important informal power-holders (Rashid 2008). For instance, Abdul Rasul Sayyaf emerged as a key powerbroker in the post-2001 order. Amongst other things he was able to exercise great influence through the appointment of his ally Fazl Hadi Shinwari as the first Chief Justice of the Supreme Court.

Shinwari was an outspoken religious scholar who marked his position on women's issues by refusing to appoint any women to the Supreme Court during his tenure (2002–2006), instead packing the court with judges who primarily had religious legal training. While the international community was divided on particular appointments, above all Shinwari, the overall inclination was to stabilise the post-invasion order by supporting local allies who controlled the means of violence or represented the religious conservatives.

These men – and they were all men – wielded enormous power by virtue of their capacity for physical violence or their authority to declare certain actions and activities contrary to Islam. Shinwari had set the tone in this respect: he wanted to restrict the role of women in the public sphere, sought to ban cable TV, supported the reintroduction of the Ministry for the Promotion of Virtue and the Prevention of Vice – an older institution that became infamous during the Taliban regime – and sent a clear signal about the limitations on freedom of speech in the new, post-Taliban order by agreeing in 2002 to hear a charge of blasphemy. The accused was the well-known reformer and outspoken Minister of Women's Affairs, Sima Samar. Although the court dismissed the case, it cast a chill over the public debate that deepened with three subsequent cases of blasphemy brought before the courts, a charge which carries a mandatory death sentence according to certain interpretations of Islamic criminal law. Similarly, the former *mujahedin*, who wielded significant control in Parliament, was also able to pass a controversial amnesty law, granting themselves immunity for the considerable abuses conducted during decades of war. In a rally in support for the law Sayyaf declared: 'Whoever is against *mujahedeen* is against Islam and they are the enemies of this country'. In sum, the post-2001 domination of the political arena by *mujahedin*-era strongmen meant that the situation was overwhelmingly stacked against women's rights advocates, despite Western pledges of support to their very agenda.

Accountability to 'Home' Audiences vs. Afghan Activists

As noted above, liberation of Afghan women was frequently cited as a justification for the Western commitment to create 'a liberal peace' in Afghanistan. In practice, international dedication in this respect was faltering, and at times markedly so compared to the commitment of Afghan reformers as demonstrated by the case of the Shia law. The Afghan activists had articulated their concerns about the law prior to international involvement and carried the main burden of trying to change it. The internationals initially hesitated to take a strong stand. It was only following Western media outrage that NATO governments made strong public statements on the law.

The sequence suggested that the condemnation of the law was primarily meant for Western domestic audiences. The primary 'stream' of accountability therefore was from NATO governments to their home populations. Only after Western governments were pressured by their own constituencies did they contact their representatives in Afghanistan to apply more pressure to modify the law. The public skirmish had its costs, however, by further polarising the debate inside Afghanistan as well. Many Afghan actors found a middle ground position untenable for various reasons. Some disengaged from the issue. Others declared themselves satisfied with the revised law, leaving those internationals actors who had come out strongly to oppose the Shia law both puzzled and embittered. This unwillingness and inability to commit to backing Afghan reform movements indicates again the contradictions that underpinned the pursuit of an avowedly liberal transformation agenda.

Polarisation of the Political Climate

More subtly, ongoing NATO military operations and related 'collateral damage', aid projects that were often misguided and poorly designed, and a political settlement that empowered former *mujahedin* commanders combined to undermine the appeal of Western models of reform in Afghan society at large. As is typical, opposition to Western frameworks crystallised around questions of women and family, which were made to serve as key bearers of culture and authenticity to be protected against outside corruption. Common Afghan themes of unruly and disobedient women as the ultimate signifier of incapable families and weak communities fed into local polemics where women's rights and autonomy were represented as tools of foreign domination. In turn such polemics were made more potent by the liberation of Afghanistan's women as an explicit justification for the NATO intervention. Thus, assertive Afghan women were in constant danger of inviting charges of being '*gharbi*' (westernised), with all the social stigma (including being an infidel) such charges implied in a highly charged political environment. Afghan men had considerably more leeway due to the prevalent gender roles and their escape from being the declared object of Western liberation.

This political landscape significantly shaped the strategies of both foreign and national actors attempting to steer the two laws in a progressive direction. Afghan reformers and Westerners were careful not to let the latter been seen as openly 'interfering' in Afghan affairs, in particular in the hypersensitive 'woman question'. Fear of counterproductive results was one reason why international actors initially hesitated to take a stand on the Shia law. A public Western position on the law only emerged once it reached the Western media, at which point it was politically impossible for NATO leaders to remain quiet. Afghan activists and politicians, for their part, attempted to publicly distance themselves from Western frameworks as well as Western support.

The polarised climate thus translated into an increasingly bifurcated discourse on women's rights, as was evident also in the case of the EVAW law. International lobbying for the law was discreet and informal, whereas the Afghan women who promoted it presented it as a *bona fide* Afghan creation – which in most respects indeed it was. In general Western policy makers usually referenced women's rights to international human rights and other secular-sourced instruments, such as CEDAW. Inside Afghanistan, however, as the political field became increasingly antagonistic to such discourses, Afghan women's rights activists, governmental and non-governmental gender programmes – whether for tactical reasons or out of genuine conviction – increasingly formulated gender rights within the discourse of Islam and liberal interpretations of Sharia. In Parliament, women MPs made frequent references to Islam, Sharia and protecting the family when arguing for the EVAW law, while carefully avoiding 'human rights' – the primary vocabulary of the internationals. As a result, many Afghan activists increasingly ventured into a territory where Sharia and Islam constituted the main reference points. While some found this empowering, others found that it put them at a disadvantage, because those trained in Islamic law were able to quote in Arabic, effectively 'owning' the debate.

However, their conservative opponents did not always meet the women activists with elaborate reference to Islamic law, instead accusing them of immorality, wanting to ruin the family or being under foreign influence. The polarised political climate, in which Afghan versus Western faultlines had crystallised around questions of women's position, greatly aided such discursive slippage, where Westernisation, anti-Islamism, immorality and support for women's rights were collapsed into a singular and interchangeable category.

The Impact of the Aid System: NGOisation and Fragmentation of Lawmaking

The unleashing of billions of aid dollars, projects and foreign consultants generated their own contradictions. The 'NGOisation' of civil society meant that technocratic requirements for programme design and reporting sometimes took priority over investing in local political mobilisation for social change. Often, development of technocratic capacity impeded or overrode political capacity building. Equally if not more important, competition for funding and fame within civil society tended to undermine coalition-building and information-sharing among civil society groups, especially when combined with the existing patronage logic of much of Afghan politics (Azarbaijani-Moghaddam 2006). The processing of both laws illustrated this.

As the momentum and international outrage against the Shia law gathered pace, original opponents were joined by more opportunistic figures, regarded by the former as attempting to position themselves as *the* main women's rights activists; that is, those deserving external funding, or alternatively, those whom the president should consult with to placate the West. The existence of three competing drafts for the EVAW likewise testified to the importance of claiming personal credit over collaborative efforts. Similar dynamics were at play when efforts were made to get the law through the Parliament.

The influx of foreign assistance also shaped the legislative process itself. As the post-2001 reconstruction gathered pace, so did the reforms in the area of 'rule of law'. Aid and international engagement in the justice sector created a dynamic similar to what could be observed in Afghanistan's nascent civil society. Large funds meant large programmes, the arrival of international consultants and the formulation of numerous policy strategies. Reporting demands from headquarters, a focus on measurable outputs and short-term timelines often translated into emphasis on cosmetic and isolated achievements that could illustrate success. Drafting laws was an ideal activity for this purpose, leading to what Hartmann and Klonowiecka-Milart (2011: 282) term 'resumé law reform' or 'summer project lawmaking'. Laws were relatively easy to produce, drafting could often be done with little Afghan input and associated messy negotiations, and they represented a tangible achievement. In effect, law reform was sometimes undertaken for a result-oriented Western audience rather than for the purposes of strengthening Afghanistan's legal framework overall.

Often, new laws were conceived and drafted in their entirety by actors outside of the Afghan government. Typically they were then enacted through presidential decrees, achieved by political pressure and the calling in of favours. Laws were typically stand-alone laws, and rarely engaged with other legislative reform efforts, or indeed existing laws, producing incoherence and inconsistency in the legal corpus as a whole (Hartmann and Klonowiecka-Milart 2011). While elements of such strategies are familiar parts of the lawmaking process everywhere, in Afghanistan they have become paramount. The ad hoc approach to lawmaking reinforced an opaque legislative process, which put a premium on informal connections with the executive and key powerbrokers to influence the outcome.

Conclusion

The Western presence in Afghanistan has often undercut the very objectives it was said to promote. To some extent this is already widely pointed out: NATO countries have been accused of double standards as they have promoted development, democratisation and women's rights in declaratory policy and at the same time supported 'warlords' and other illiberal characters in practice. However, the contradictions brought about by the NATO presence have additional and more subtle dimensions, as this chapter has sought to demonstrate.

The improvement of the conditions of Afghan women was at the forefront of Western declarations to transform Afghanistan – often in the language of 'liberation'. However, assuming that sustainable gains in women's positions requires a certain degree of open debate and some level of political constituency, the effect of the NATO engagement was often detrimental. A fragmented and non-transparent law-making process, a polarised political climate and a fragmented civil society were part of the context created in large part by the international presence. This context in turn rendered top-down, informal and covert strategies more expedient then broader debate and accommodation.[3]

With the EVAW law, many international actors clearly wanted to see it passed, even in an imperfect form. In this case the informal channels worked to their advantage, as combined international and Afghan pressure succeeded in getting the law passed as a presidential decree and later, prevented it from being rejected in Parliament (at least for the time being). In the case of the Shia law, by contrast, those mechanisms worked against both Afghan and international actors who tried to secure amendments. Arguably, they would have been better served by a transparent and rule-bound legislative process.

Moreover, while relying on external actors and links to the executive may lead to short-term goals, such political strategies also may have drawbacks. They lessen the need for developing broader and long-term bargains with national actors – in a word: political mobilisation. Without building political constituencies and institutions that can anchor social reform, individual gains might be tenuous, especially in a sensitive and unstable political context.

Notes

1 The government maintains the law was finally passed on 22 February, but there is no record of the Upper House discussing it that day or any other day.
2 Interviews with MPs and women's rights activists, Kabul September–December 2009.
3 Cheshmak Farhoumand-Sims (2009) notes how a similar dynamic may have been at play with Afghanistan's ratification of the CEDAW convention. The convention was signed in 2003 without any reservations, highly unusual for a Muslim country. F-S suggests that this may have been a result of US pressure and notes how Afghan activists now are reluctant to draw too much attention to the convention as this might lead to challenges to the validity of the ratification. In turn, this limits the effectiveness of the convention as an advocacy tool.

Bibliography

Abu-Lughod, L. (2002) 'Do Muslim Women Really Need Saving? Anthropological Reflections on Cultural Relativism and Its Others', *American Anthropologist* 104: 783–790.

Azarbaijani-Moghaddam, S. (2006) 'Gender in Afghanistan', Publication Series on Promoting Democracy under Conditions of State Fragility. Issue 1: *Afghanistan*, Berlin: Heinrich Böll Foundation.

Azarbaijani-Moghaddam, S. (2007) 'On Living with Negative Peace and a Half-Built State: Gender and Human Rights', *International Peacekeeping* 14: 127–142.

Farhoumand-Sims, C. (2009) CEDAW and Afghanistan. *Journal of International Women's Studies* 11: 136–156.

Fleschenberg, A. (2009) *Afghanistan's Parliament in the Making*, Berlin: Heinrich Böll Foundation in cooperation of UNIFEM.

Hartmann, M. and A. Klonowiecka-Milart (2011) 'Lost in Translation: Legal Transplants without Consensus-based Adaptation' in W. Mason (ed.) *Rule of Law in Afghanistan: Missing in Inaction*, Cambridge: Cambridge University Press.

Oates, L. (2009) *A Closer Look: The Policy and Law-Making Process Behind the Shiite Personal Status Law*, Kabul: Afghanistan Research and Evaluation Unit.

Rashid, A. (2008) *Descent into Chaos: The United States and the Failure of Nation-building in Pakistan, Afghanistan and Central Asia*, New York: Viking.

United Nations (2009) 'UN Human Rights Chief Says Afghan Law Restricting Women's Rights Is Reminiscent of Taliban Era', press release, 2 April, United Nations.

Wilder, A. (2005) *A House Divided? Analysing the 2005 Afghan Elections*, Kabul: Afghanistan Research and Evaluation Unit.

Wordsworth, A. (2007) *A Matter of Interests: Gender and the Politics of Presence in Afghanistan's Wolesi Jirga*, Issues Paper Series, Kabul: Afghanistan Research and Evaluation Unit.

7

Neither Liberal nor Peaceful?
Practices of 'Global Justice' by the ICC

Adam Branch

Introduction

Many of the International Criminal Court's liberal proponents celebrate the ICC for being a moral agent, a tool of good against evil, an essential component for the triumph of global justice over particular injustice. For these advocates, the ICC is valued for its ability to sweep in to emergency situations and punish those most responsible for violent atrocities, to uphold liberal ideals when they are most under threat.

Other liberal proponents of the ICC, however, see the court in a more institutionalist framework, not so much as a moral agent of justice but as a political agent of peace. The ICC's importance, in this view, derives not from its one-off triumphs over evil in specific instances, but from its helping to build a global rule of law in which criminal violence will be punished today for the sake of preventing it in the future. The ICC is thus valued for the long-term assistance it is thought to provide in establishing an institutional infrastructure of global liberal governance, one that guarantees peace by applying criminal law to individuals in such a way that ends current episodes of violence and prevents future episodes from occurring.[1] According to this view, the primary route through which the ICC fulfils its role is not through its own occasional prosecutions, but by catalysing the emergence of a transnational network of institutions at the international, national and local levels, at the pinnacle of which is the ICC, that promotes and enforces international criminal law. International criminal law as part of transitional justice has risen to the fore of the so-called 'liberal peace-building' agenda as part of the ideological framework for remaking societies (Sriram 2007). If international law has been conceived of as the 'gentle civilizer of nations' in the past, (Koskenniemi 2001) then international criminal law presided over by the ICC may be seen as the gentle civilizer of humanity today.

This institutionalist understanding of the ICC as an instrument of global liberal peace depends upon seeing the court through the lens of the *domestic analogy*. According to the domestic analogy, the ICC is the key judicial body for a global liberal rule of law that represents a scaled-up domestic liberal rule of law. Just as domestic liberal criminal law is thought to ensure peace within a given political community through the judgment and punishment of individuals transgressing that community's rules, so is the ICC thought to ensure peace globally through the application of criminal law to all members of the human community everywhere in the world. The ICC's champions are not alone in seeing the court as a key agent of global liberal governance on the basis of the domestic analogy. Indeed, many of its critics also frame the Court in just those terms even as they reverse the normative valence: instead of global liberal governance being an emancipatory project, it seen as a disciplinary project, with the ICC at the cutting edge of this repressive regime.

In the years since its establishment in 2002, however, the ICC has looked in practice to be anything but the midwife of a global liberal order, whether emancipatory or repressive. Instead, its prosecutions have appeared politicised, partial, unpredictable and ineffective. It has been anti-democratic, secretive and dismissive of criticism or dissent. It has intervened exclusively in a swath of East-Central Africa and, in those cases, targeted only a small handful of individuals based not upon objective legal criteria but upon the Prosecutor's own pragmatic self-interest. Far from realising the ideal of being a universal judicial body that deals with those most responsible for the worst crimes wherever they occur and that helps institutionalise global liberal peace, the ICC's practice has been determined by international power inequalities and has ended up institutionalising conflict, not peace. The ICC's practice, instead of embodying liberal values on the domestic analogy, has stood if anything in contradiction to those values.

All this the ICC's champions (and often its critics) ignore: instead of starting with the ICC's actually existing practice and consequences, they start with the ideology of the ICC as a universal court for a global community developing and enforcing a 'law of humanity' (Teitel 2001) and subsume scattered elements from its practice into that ideological framework. This, I argue, is illegitimate. In what follows, I first explore the understanding of the ICC as an agent of global liberal governance on the basis of the domestic analogy. Then I discuss the inapplicability of the domestic analogy to the ICC in terms of the ICC's structure and in terms of the effects of its interventions. I end by asking, given that the ICC is failing to spread a global liberal order of justice and peace, then what, in fact, is it doing – if it is doing anything at all.

The Domestic Analogy and the ICC

The domestic analogy casts international criminal law as a 'scaled-up' version of liberal domestic law, one that applies to individual members of the global community instead of to individual members of particular national political communities. The ICC is seen as the consummation of the development of this global rule of law, which is thought to have its antecedents in the jurisdictionally limited ad hoc tribunals of the 1990s. Like domestic law, global law is represented as characterised by both legitimacy and efficacy: the first deriving from the universality of the norms it enforces and the second proven by the successful prosecutions carried out by international tribunals.

By representing existing international criminal law as a scaled-up version of domestic law, in which the liberal qualities that characterise domestic criminal law are thought to be replicated at the global level, a number of assumptions are extracted from the domestic criminal law context and scaled up, including assumptions about the subjects of law, the nature of violence, and the legitimacy and consequences of prosecution. For one thing, the domestic analogy imagines the ICC to be a court for a global community of individuals, each of whom has a certain set of fundamental rights that, when violated, demands legal remedy. The liberal nature of the civil and political rights protected by the courts and police in the context of the state is assumed to scale up to the global level in the form of the fundamental rights protected by the ICC in the context of the international community.

At the same time, the understanding of violence employed by domestic criminal law frameworks is also scaled up and used to comprehend episodes of mass violence on the global level. In this way, by interpreting mass violence through the domestic analogy, international criminal law sees such violence as representing individual acts of deviance in violation of the global community's accepted, existing norm of general peace. This fiction of individual criminal responsibility for mass violence implies a self-evident distinction between perpetrator, victim and bystanders comprising the community whose rules have been broken. As this scheme is projected globally, so are each of these categories: the victim and perpetrator are individuals divorced from their immediate social or political contexts and made subject to universal norms, while the bystanders are the global community which is harmed by crimes against humanity, a community which has a stake in seeing perpetrators punished so as to re-establish its basic rules.

The domestic analogy also entails the assumption that the ICC, as the ultimate legal instance enforcing the norms of a global community, enjoys universal consent to its legitimacy, its authority, and its rules and procedures. It is thought that, simply by being human, people everywhere will consent to the judgments made by the ICC in the name of global justice, whether for them or against them. It enforces norms no member of the human community can reject without placing themselves outside of humanity itself.

When assessing international criminal law's conformity to the liberal ideals of equality before the law and the general and impartial enforcement of the law, the ICC's limited and partial practice thus far presents the domestic analogy with a challenge. It is overcome, however, by invoking an evolutionary narrative as the necessary corollary of the domestic analogy. This narrative declares today's selective justice to be merely a step on the way to tomorrow's truly universal justice and thereby translates the gap between the ICC's current partial practice and impartial justice into a temporal gap between the imperfect present and an inevitable future when the ICC will overcome the political interests of weak and strong states alike.[2] Universal global justice is *in statu nascendi*, it is declared, and we should not expect the ICC to be perfect yet. How long we will have to wait is uncertain, but there is faith that universal justice will eventually emerge and the ICC will, one day, redeem us all.

Among the many assumptions scaled up from domestic to international criminal law, perhaps the most important for the doctrine of global liberal peace is that international criminal law will help prevent violence in the future. As domestic criminal law is thought to deter future violence and underwrite social peace, so is international criminal law, according to the domestic analogy, to serve a deterrence function as states and non-state actors alike cease using violence for fear of punishment. Given the difficulty of proving the efficacy of deterrence, it is mostly anecdotes that are marshalled to support the claim. Chief Prosecutor Moreno-Ocampo, for example, has declared that the release of 3,000 child soldiers in Nepal was the result of the ICC's prosecution of Timothy Lubanga,[3] while others constantly repeat sanguine slogans such as that 'the era of impunity is over' or 'an age of accountability has begun', It is also widely held that removing key perpetrators will end specific instances of criminal violence, bringing peace to those places where the ICC intervenes.[4]

The liberal assumptions derived from the domestic analogy work their way as well into understandings of the consequences ICC interventions are thought to have for states and societies. As the global rule of law expands, states are to be disciplined into conformity with global liberal norms through the mechanism of 'positive complementarity'. This may occur as national legal systems have international criminal law built into them, but also through the presumed growing normative commitment to the global rule of law. States are not to be coerced but are to willingly become 'responsible' instantiations and enforcers of global norms. Global liberal governance will be institutionalised through 'good governance' within states as they conform to global norms, and the global rule of law presided over by the ICC will gently civilise national politics. In this vein, for example, Moreno-Ocampo in 2004 claimed that the ICC would quickly bring peace to northern Uganda (Clark 2008b: 42) and, in 2010 implied that ICC intervention would prevent future election violence in Kenya.[5]

This liberal global community is similarly presumed to gradually triumph within societies as well, undoing the conditions for conflict. The domestic analogy frames international criminal trials as building peaceful, liberal communities as people's narrow parochial interests and differences are transcended through the impartial application of global law. People everywhere are to become liberal subjects, empowered by the ICC. The law of humanity, protecting rights-bearing individuals, is to be institutionalised at the global level through ICC prosecutions, at the national level through state normalisation, and at the local level through spreading 'empowering' discourses among potential and actual victims of mass violence. People are to become aware of their rights through the interventions of the ICC, it is thought, and thus able to hold their states or victimisers accountable, leading to perpetual liberal peace.

The Inapplicability of the Domestic Analogy

It is only by taking the ICC's ideology at face value that international criminal law can be assumed to embody scaled-up versions of domestic law's liberal traits. This ideology leads ICC proponents to interpret a few scattered facts – an arrest warrant here, a prosecution there, a few unsubstantiated anecdotes – as evidence for the existence of a full-fledged international criminal legal regime, a regime expounded upon endlessly in the voluminous and often fantastical writings by legal scholars, practitioners and activists. Starting with the facts and not the ideology, however, leads instead to the conclusion that the liberal traits of domestic criminal law simply do not scale up, and that in fact there is little that is liberal about the ICC's practice or consequences.

While the liberal fiction of individual criminal responsibility may be widely accepted on the domestic level, the presumption that violence can be understood as representing individual acts deviating from agreed-upon norms, acts that harm both the immediate victim and the community of bystanders, cannot be scaled up to the global level. For one thing, the designation of individual perpetrators presents a serious obstacle on the global level since the forms of violence categorised as crimes against humanity, and thus subject to ICC jurisdiction, are precisely those forms of violence that cannot be reduced to individual acts deviating from an accepted norm.[6] Hannah Arendt, for example, has argued that genocide requires a state apparatus for its execution, and so the clear attribution of responsibility for genocide to a few individuals is made impossible by the widespread, even generalised, participation in and consent to this form of violence within states and societies – and possibly even among the victims themselves (Arendt 1963). Even in cases where the state is not instrumental in mass violence, the ICC will still find itself having to attribute individual responsibility to collective phenomena given that the Rome Statute declares its jurisdiction specifically over systematic and widespread violence. Furthermore, mass violence is embedded in international and global structures of domination and injustice, a fact ignored by the liberal focus on individual perpetrators. As numerous authors since Arendt have made clear, the attempt to reduce mass violence to individual criminal acts and to try those acts through law can lead only to a series of conundrums, both moral and practical. The ICC is thus uniquely unsuited to address the very acts which it was established to prosecute, and the insistence on the domestic analogy only obscures the divergence of the ICC from domestic criminal regimes.

The victim of mass violence who is to be redeemed through international criminal prosecution is qualititatively different to the liberal rights-bearing individual who is the subject of domestic criminal legal regimes. While the perpetrator targeted by international prosecution ends up being burdened individually with what is in fact a vast collective and structural responsibility, the victim under the domestic analogy is conversely reduced to a highly attenuated subject possessing a restricted set of rights. The rights of concern to international criminal law are not the full panoply of rights required for the autonomous, politically and socially active liberal subject, but rather are a basic set of rights having to do with physical survival – human rights merge with animal rights, as Slavoj Žižek puts it (Žižek 1997). More important than which rights are granted is the manner in which those rights are conceived of as being fulfilled: individuals who have experienced mass violence are represented as 'victims' with a certain set of 'victims' rights', in particular the rights to reparation and justice, fulfilled through criminal prosecution. When the ICC is put forth as the chosen agent for fulfilling these rights, the rights-bearing, active subject is displaced by a 'subject' whose rights imply only endless appeals to the international community and the privilege of waiting for international intervention (Chandler 2002). The sole 'entitlement' entailed is the hope that international human rights organisations will lobby on their behalf, carry out 'name and shame' campaigns, provide professionalised philanthropy: victims' rights are not enforced by right but by charity (Arendt 1963).

A process of depoliticisation can occur through international law enforcement as those denominated victims are told to wait for the ICC to intervene for their sake to realise justice (de Waal 1997). Those who have suffered violence are individualised into 'witnesses,' and the judgment as to whether an individual's experience of suffering deserves reparation is removed from that individual and from their the community, not to be arrived at through collective reflection, deliberation and organisation but through the ICC's non-transparent decision-making process. This general depoliticisation is consolidated through the mechanisms that promote victim 'participation', through 'outreach' by the

ICC and its allied organisations, and through the work of international human rights organisations, as human rights practice becomes a practice of individual testimony. These testimonies, made to investigators or human rights monitors, do not lead to the articulation and realisation of common grievances, interests and demands, but are divested of their capacity to produce meaningful collective action and become the raw material for the production of international law for international elite consumption (Koskenniemi 2002). This model of international human rights advocacy reduces the victim of violence to a natural resource, grist for the advocacy mills, in the form of testimony and images, to be exported and processed abroad by Western human rights organisations into human rights reports.

This points to the basic incongruity of the domestic analogy with international criminal law. The nation-state, ideally, is the political form in which law, including criminal law, is to define the relation between the population and decision-making instances, binding both. What the spread of global law does is to separate these, so that the location the population addresses through law is not the location where decisions affecting them are being made; the people are subject to decisions they did not consent to and must obey a law they did not make. At the same time, people translate their political demands into human rights claims made into a vacuum. Legal action on the part of the subjects of global law becomes merely the affirmation of their incapacity to act.

This disjuncture derives from the absence of a global community of mankind, the community that would be necessary for the domestic analogy and its liberal assumptions to hold on the global scale. Despite the claims of some cosmopolitans, the kinds of formal and informal modes of communication, collective organisation, action and representation needed to institutionalise a global community remain absent. The 'global community' remains metaphorical and far too thin a category upon which to base a universal responsibility to punish. Without the existence of such a political community, global law enforcement will always be arbitrary because it does not take place at the behest of an actually existing political community, nor is it accountable to any such community. Instead, law enforcement will be undertaken by those who happen have the power and will to appropriate the mantle to themselves. The idea that a global community sees its basic norms re-established through criminal prosecution of international criminals gets it backwards: international criminal law enforcement does not re-establish a harmed global community but invents the fiction of that community's existence (Tallgren 2002).

The domestic analogy's insistence that international criminal prosecutions will spread liberal, peaceful communities within states, as global norms triumph over particular national and sub-national identities, also fails to hold. The assumption that a global identity based upon adherence to certain liberal norms will expand and consolidate through criminal trials fails to recognise, once again, the collective and structural character of mass violence. The domestic analogy reduces mass violence to cynical acts undertaken by self-interested 'conflict entrepreneurs' who are thought to lead misguided or coerced followers. It ignores the affirmative character of identity-based violence and the way in which radicalised identity-based political forces will not be defused through punishing their leaders, but will often be further radicalised as punishment inflames divisions. Trials in cases of collective violence will often be seen not as the legitimate triumph of universal liberal norms, but as the illegitimate triumph of one's political antagonists – not as a compromise but as a provocation. Those being punished may see trials as no more than the continuation of war by legal means, as Hans Kelsen described the victors' justice of the Nuremberg Trials.[7] Trials can thus further fragment and polarise national political communities instead of building them on supposedly liberal grounds.

Finally, there is the issue of prevention, essential if the ICC is to be justified as contributing to liberal peace. The domestic analogy's insistence that international criminal prosecutions serve a deterrence function requires that two assumptions from domestic legal regimes be scaled up to the international legal arena: first, that collective violence represent individual acts of deviance from a widely accepted norm of non-violence; and second, that enforcement be general and impartial enough so that those committing or planning crimes see themselves running a significant risk of punishment. Neither assumption holds.

As to the first, the domestic analogy ignores the fact that in many contexts, participation in mass violence may not be seen as a deviation but instead as participation in a legitimate political project (Snyder and Vinjamuri 2004). Furthermore, the deterrence argument presumes a reductive portrayal of the psychology behind atrocity: it presumes that violence is committed by non-political, non-ideological, self-interested but risk-averse actors who are trying to maximise gains and minimise losses. This may fit with one version of the image of contemporary conflict – greedy warlords engaging in perfectly rational, non-political, behaviour – but the relation of this image to reality is, of course, highly contested, and especially in the situations of collective violence into which the ICC intervenes. As Koskenniemi points out, the international criminalisation of political leaders by those acting in the name of the global community may very well only further legitimate their violence in the eyes of the people instead of deterring it (Koskenniemi 2002: 8).

Second, even more importantly, the ICC has so little power that it cannot select cases or suspects based upon its own legalist criteria. Instead, the ICC Prosecutor must intervene based upon strategic political and pragmatic calculations. The result is that the liberal ideal of equality before the law is made a mockery of by the ICC. Its selectivity makes it totally unpredictable, both in terms of where it intervenes and whom it prosecutes where it does intervene

– or at least, its actions cannot be predicted according to objective legal criteria. Its interventions are so irregular and unpredictable that they have less in common with the rule of law and more with arbitrary, apparently vindictive acts of fate, of mysterious retribution from an unknowable source (Simpson 2007: ch. 5). Law is supposed to stabilise expectations and take some of the unpredictability and discretion out of politics, but the ICC does the opposite of this, degrading law in the process.

In short, the liberal dimensions of domestic criminal legal regimes simply cannot be scaled up to the global level. Mass violence is inherently collective, political and structural – it occurs in the midst of contestations between different political communities or around the very definition of political community, instead of being an exceptional, individual deviation from an established political community as the domestic analogy maintains. In situations of mass violence, where perpetrator and victim identities may be ambiguous and shifting and responsibility widespread, regardless of any moral legitimacy which may accrue to a criminal justice approach, its political legitimacy cannot be assumed, nor can its liberal character. International criminal justice values a particular kind of moral reasoning – one in which the moral claim of the individual victim, as interpreted by the ICC, trumps all other claims – and a particular kind of political 'community' – one in which the individual, whether perpetrator or victim, is conceived of as a member of a global community and is divorced from society, politics, history and culture, in need of punishment or redemption. Given the lack of any concrete global political community, interventions based on this reasoning end up being anything but liberal.

The lack of existing global political communities also leads, on the level of enforcement, to the ICC's reliance upon states for the coercion it requires to be effective. As I address in the next section, in the face-off between the ICC and states, it is not the ICC that gradually triumphs as a disciplining tool of global liberal governance, but rather states that triumph as they discipline the ICC.

The ICC in Practice: The Uganda Case

While many human rights activists, international law scholars and liberal interventionists seem to be convinced that the ICC will usher in a global rule of law and a regime of liberal peace, the leaders of many states in Africa – the continent to which ICC interventions have thus far been restricted – and in the West have shown that they are under no such illusion. They have seen that ICC enforcement is applied along political lines in contradiction to the ICC's own liberal ideology, and have noted the ICC's usefulness in legitimating certain forms of arbitrary power and violence. They have realised that the

ICC Prosecutor's relation to power has been one of accommodation, not contestation, and have taken advantage of the opportunity that provides.

The illiberal consequences of the ICC Prosecutor's accommodation to political power are on clear display on the international level in the Court's relation with the US. It is ironic that it was because of the Bush administration's hostility to the ICC that the Prosecutor came to conform his prosecution strategy to US interests (Mamdani 2008), as he appears to have calculated that the Court could best protect its viability and relevance by demonstrating to the US that the Court would not challenge it or its allies, which Moreno-Ocampo has done since the ICC's inception. This selectivity has been enabled by the broad discretion afforded to the Prosecutor by the Rome Statute and by the lack of transparency that characterises the Prosecutor's decisions as to where to intervene and whom to prosecute.

Because the ICC is increasingly monopolising the practice of international criminal justice in Africa, those African states and actors not prosecuted by the ICC because of their international political alignment become effectively immune from *any* criminal law enforcement. Ethiopian troops, for example, who, with US support, launched a bloody invasion and occupation of Somalia, are apparently effectively immune from human rights or international law standards, as are the mostly Ugandan African Union forces that have replaced the Ethiopians. Given this monopolisation and the infrequency of ICC intervention, the ICC's enforcement practice can thus entrench widespread impunity instead of the accountability promised by the liberal peace discourse.

This accommodation to US power and its damaging consequences stand to increase as the Prosecutor, in reaction to the difficulty of apprehending suspects, tries to convince the US to lead the way in enforcing arrest warrants. The Prosecutor has shifted from avoiding American censure to actively courting the US military for assistance: for example, in June 2009 at a public event in the US, Moreno-Ocampo declared the need for 'special forces' with 'rare and expensive capabilities that regional armies don't have', and said that 'coalitions of the willing', led by the US, were needed to enforce ICC arrest warrants.[8] If the ICC comes to rely heavily on American military capacity as its enforcement arm, in particular when the US continues to declare itself above the very law it claims to enforce, the ICC will end up trading what little independence remains in return for access to coercive force, a Faustian bargain that could ultimately help justify US militarisation in Africa at a dramatic cost to peace.

In short, the ICC's practice so far in Africa has already made clear, and its potential alignment with US military power would make it unquestionable, that the best way for an African state or armed force to be guaranteed immunity from criminal prosecution is not to avoid committing crimes, but to align itself with US security interests. Thus, far from ushering in an expanding regime of justice and global liberal governance in Africa, the ICC may be helping to create an expanding geography of impunity and violence, following most closely the contours of American interests.

Within African states, the ICC's accommodation to political power has come about as the Prosecutor has to depend upon alliances with unaccountable state elites to carry out investigations and prosecutions. These elites can in turn take advantage of the ICC's resources in order to bolster their own arbitrary power, a tendency clearly on display in Uganda. The Ugandan government has demonstrated its facility for manipulating the ICC; it seems well aware of the need to invoke the key buzzwords of the liberal peace discourse, as seen in its referral of the Lord's Resistance Army (LRA) to the Court:

> Having exhausted every other means of bringing an end to this terrible suffering, the Republic of Uganda now turns to the newly established ICC and its promise of global justice. Uganda pledges its full cooperation to the Prosecutor in the investigation and prosecution of LRA crimes, achievement of which is vital not only for the future progress of the nation, but also for the suppression of the most serious crimes of concern to the international community as a whole.[9]

Despite this lofty language, the Ugandan government stood to gain very secular benefits from ICC intervention if it could ensure that the ICC would prosecute only the rebel LRA. It managed to do so by making the ICC an offer the Prosecutor could not refuse: the perfect first case, a voluntary referral by an American ally that pledged its cooperation in pursuing a universally demonised group, the LRA. This offer appears to have come with the implicit – or perhaps explicit – condition that the ICC prosecute only the LRA, a condition made clear by the government since the beginning. For example, the 2003 referral cited only LRA crimes, as reflected in its one-sided title (Akhavan 2005), and the Ugandan government has since then consistently asserted that it would not be subject to ICC prosecution, and threatened several times to withdraw its referral to the court, implying that it would cease cooperating if its own military were to become subject to prosecution.[10] While the Ugandan government could not prevent prosecution by withdrawing its referral, an end to cooperation would, of course, effectively close down the investigation. This pressure on the Prosecutor to ignore possible Ugandan government crimes has come not only from Uganda but from the US itself (Perrot 2010). In response, the Prosecutor, despite occasional statements declaring that he was looking into actions by the Ugandan government, has issued arrest warrants only for LRA commanders and has openly enjoyed a close relationship with the Ugandan government, especially President Museveni.

This politicised approach has had negative consequences for peace and made the LRA insurgency, if anything, more difficult to resolve. Arrest warrants have removed the LRA command's incentive to leave the bush and, according to a statement by rebel leader Joseph Kony, kept him from signing the final peace agreement between the LRA and the government (Atkinson 2010). But more importantly, the ICC's one-sided intervention has allowed the Ugandan government to further militarise in the name of pursuing the LRA. Given that, according to many analysts, the Ugandan government and military have had significant interests in maintaining war in the north, it is not inconceivable that the Ugandan government referred the LRA to the ICC precisely so as to obtain support for its militarisation and even to entrench the war.

The arrest warrants have enabled the Ugandan government to justify its military approach to the conflict, an approach that has shown no success for over twenty years. ICC intervention was used to justify the President's amendment of the Uganda Amnesty Act which had granted a general amnesty to the LRA, including its top commanders, and had been passed only through intense mobilisation by Ugandan peace activists and political leaders. The ICC's rejection of the Amnesty shows again the ICC's need to rely upon unaccountable state elites to facilitate its intervention. More generally, the ICC intervention, by providing international legitimation to the government's military campaign in the name of enforcing international law, has cleared the way for militarisation, the effects of which are starkly apparent as Ugandan armed forces have spread out to three different countries – Sudan, Central African Republic and Democratic Republic of Congo – in the name of hunting down LRA leadership. The Ugandan government has also used the ICC intervention to further justify its domestic militarisation and repression of political dissent, as the government realised the utility of criminalising its political opposition. ICC arrest warrants have provided the Ugandan government with a tool to wield selectively against political opposition or to disqualify those calling for peace talks or for dialogue with the LRA.

Despite the claim by Payam Akhavan that, 'in the face of the continuing distrust between Uganda's north and south, the ICC could also become an instrument for national reconciliation' (2005: 410–11), the politicised and partial manner in which the ICC has intervened in Uganda has only increased mistrust and further revealed the impunity with which the government operates. Many Ugandans see the ICC as thoroughly captured by the Ugandan government, and so instead of ushering in liberal peace within Uganda by reconciling polarised political identities, the ICC has only intensified the national political crisis by deepening the political division between north and south and thus entrenching the conditions for possible future conflict. The ICC's involvement emphasises the Ugandan government's refusal to be held accountable for its legacy of violence and emphasises the international community's consistent failure to hold the Ugandan government to account while providing it with extensive support.

The ICC's intervention has also provided means for the Ugandan government to reconfirm its status as a key US security ally and significant beneficiary of US military support. Museveni has been the recipient of American military aid and diplomatic support for his own 'war on terror' against the LRA in exchange for serving as a conduit for support and resources to the Sudanese People's Liberation Army in southern Sudan, the front line in the American war on terror against the Khartoum government and now for his role as a US proxy in Somalia. Additionally, the Ugandan government has managed to dodge donor demands for the reduction of the military budget by citing the war against the LRA. The most significant manifestation of the US militarisation of Uganda as of 2010 has been Operation Lightning Thunder, a military attack carried out by the Uganda People's Defence Force with assistance from the US military intended to capture the LRA command and bring them to justice.

The ICC's intervention has not ushered in a liberal peace but has entrenched violence and provided resources and legitimacy to the Ugandan state elite with which it has further militarised, suppressed democracy and launched destabilising foreign adventures. The ICC prosecution provides support to Washington's proxy in the War on Terror and to the World Bank's neoliberal success story, building and legitimating arbitrary power nationally and internationally.

What the ICC Does Not Do

But are the destructive consequences of the ICC's intervention in Uganda representative, or are they an anomaly, a product of extreme prosecutorial misjudgment and state manipulation? Indeed, considering the overwhelming lack of results obtained by the ICC thus far in its near-decade of operation, a more convincing argument might be that the ICC's impact is negligible, and that those who attribute political significance to it are, once again, taking the sound and fury by human rights and international law professionals too seriously. As noted, the ICC has intervened into only five Central and East African countries, all of which already had significant levels of foreign intervention. It has issued public arrest warrants for a meagre total of fourteen people, of whom it has only four in custody and on trial and one awaiting transfer. It has yet to secure any convictions.

Even in Uganda, it is hard to definitively establish that the ICC is responsible for the breakdown of the Juba peace talks, or that the Museveni regime would not have found other ways of justifying its continued militarisation and foreign adventures without the ICC. Expectations voiced by critics and supporters alike for dramatic consequences from ICC interventions have generally proven hyperbolic, and Phil Clark's prediction concerning the ICC's pursuit of Bashir – 'if Ocampo indicts Bashir, nothing may happen,' – has more often appeared to be the rule (Clark 2008a).

Indeed, one might argue, following David Chandler, that the ICC is not a product of the West's effort to govern the rest of the world – whether for the sake of an emancipatory or repressive liberal peace – but is a symptom instead of Western withdrawal and lack of interest in intervention (Chandler 2009). The ICC thus is not a tool of Western states' coherent strategic interests, but rather has been fostered as a way for those states to avoid responsibility by passing off policy-making in situations of mass violence to an international body that is all too eager to take on that impossible task. This is why the ICC consistently fails to realise the lofty goals with which it has been burdened by its champions in the human rights industry – the Court was simply not designed to be effective as anything more than an alibi, a scapegoat. In practice, the ICC has appeared more as a parody of global power than the instrument of global liberal governance or governmentality.

However, I would argue that the ICC, whatever the circumstances that led to its establishment, today is an institution that clearly has the potential to be instrumentalised by states with what can be highly destructive consequences. The West may have set up the ICC as a way of avoiding responsibility for intervention – but this does not mean that factions within certain states, both in the West and where the ICC intervenes, will not instrumentalise the ICC to their own interests when it suits them, including as a justification for intervention. While the ICC is certainly not reducible to a tool of Western power, because it is vying to become one in an effort to establish its own relevance it may end up convincing certain states of its instrumental utility and be used in just that fashion.

Given the paucity of ICC interventions in practice and the fact that its interventions cannot be read simply as the strategic criminalisation of Western enemies, I would argue that far more important than what the ICC does, is what it does not do. What it does not do is important in the sense discussed above in that the ICC can effectively grant impunity by choosing to not investigate certain situations or not prosecute certain actors. But more fundamentally, the ICC's significance derives from what it does not do in the sense that it has come to define the terms in which justice itself is understood and, in doing so, closes off certain alternative possibilities for what justice may mean. What matters is not so much whom the ICC prosecutes, but rather that it frames justice as a matter of prosecution, and that people around the world consent to this definition – and not just cynical state elites, but more importantly human rights activists, political leaders and those who have themselves been affected by mass violence. When critics argue that the ICC should prosecute the Ugandan government in addition to the LRA, or prosecute Western and not only African countries, the ICC has already exercised its power by convincing people to consent to the conceptual framework it provides, to accept the definition of justice it has provided as the legitimate one – and then to argue only over the parameters of its application. Thus, it is not so much what the ICC does, and certainly not what the ICC does as a tool of Western power, that matters, but what it does not do, what possibilities it closes off by defining the debate over justice in terms of punishment and criminal law, and defining it in terms of *global* justice. The ICC has power not as a mode of coercive intervention, but as a generator of consent around a certain discourse on justice that ends up naturalised, that is, put beyond question or contestation.

This is particularly important today in Africa, where the ICC is quickly establishing a monopoly for international criminal justice as the primary form that justice can take. It and its supporters have defined justice for Africa as a goal that is to be pursued through the ICC and other formal legal mechanisms, a process that in effect can restrict those issues that can be addressed and those actors who can be held accountable. Even the 'alternatives' to the ICC are framed in terms of individualised post-conflict accountability for the worst violence. In monopolising the discourse of justice in Africa, the ICC has placed certain fundamental issues outside the scope of what can be defined as unjust and thus subject to challenge and contestation through the practice of justice. In doing so, it has put outside of contestation many of the structural causes of conflict in the continent, which need to be addressed if sustainable peace is to be realised. The political consequences of the naturalisation of the ICC's discourse on global justice are seen in the inherent limitations of that particular discourse, leading to the ICC's tendency to discipline the practice of global justice itself.

This limitation and its consequences can be seen in the ICC's subject matter jurisdiction: the forms of violence, repression and inequality that can be challenged as 'unjust' are restricted to the most spectacular forms of overt violence. Less spectacular forms of domination, repression and violence – such as economic exploitation, Western sponsorship of violent and anti-democratic political forces, internationally enforced disparities in access to medicines, trade regimes that undermine development and food security, daily violence during so-called peacetime – none of these can be challenged through the pursuit of global justice when global justice is defined by the ICC. Global justice is exclusively associated with punishing the 'most serious crimes of concern to the international community as a whole', conceived of as mass atrocities, while those crimes that *serve* the interests of the 'international community' are conveniently outside the ICC's scope. Mass atrocity is naturalised as the most pressing form of injustice globally, and its prevention and punishment is naturalised as the most pressing issue for the pursuit of justice, trumping all other concerns. The 'international community' is constructed as the agent of global justice, not as its subject.

On an even more fundamental level, the ICC's discourse of global justice has convinced us that *global* justice is something that can be and should be struggled for and realised, even if only partially. In critiquing the ICC's restriction of global justice to criminal justice, we imply that global justice is itself a real political project that can be meaningfully striven for by political actors. But is this the case? What is the agent of global justice? Does talk of global justice simply distract us from examining those sites from which power is really exercised, where injustice is in fact institutionalised? Does it distract us from forms of political organisation and action that take place within existing political communities and that might help lead to peace, and steer us instead towards empty actions that can lead only towards a chimerical global justice? Perhaps this is the ultimate illiberal consequence of the ICC – making people believe in the domestic analogy, believe in a global justice that has the possibility of being realised, regardless of whether the ICC is seen as its agent or its nemesis.

Notes

1 Akhavan (2001); for an exposition of the declared objectives of international criminal law, see Drumbl (2007).

2 A good example of this are the statements of William Pace, the Convener for the Coalition for the International Criminal Court (CICC); see for example his public statement at 'Enhancing Civil Society Participation in the ICC Review Conference: International Symposium on Stocktaking Processes', 27–28 May 2010, Hotel Africana, Kampala.

3 Statement made by Luis Moreno-Ocampo in the ICC Review Conference General Debate, Kampala, 31 May 2010.

4 For an assessment of the claims concerning prevention, see Tallgren 2002.

5 See for example, OTP Press Conference on Kenya, Prosecutor Moreno-Ocampo's Statement, 1 April 2010. Available at http://www.icc-cpi.int/menus/icc/structure%20of%20the%20court/office%20of%20the%20prosecutor/reports%20and%20statements/statement/20100401.

6 See Drumbl (2007) and Simpson (2007).

7 Qtd. in Zolo (2009).

8 Video Clip, Invisible Children Website, http://www.invisiblechildren.com/videos/5429085. See also 'Ambassador: U.S. moving to support international court', CNN U.S. on-line, 24 March 2010.

9 Government of Uganda, 'Referral of the Situation Concerning the Lord's Resistance Army', Kampala, 2003. On file with author.

10 As one example, see public statement by Attorney General Amama Mbabazi at the Uganda Human Rights Commission's conference on 'The Implications of the ICC Investigations on Human Rights and the Peace Process in Uganda', Kampala, 5 October 2004.

Bibliography

Akhavan, P. (2001) 'Beyond Impunity: Can International Criminal Justice Prevent Future Atrocities?', *American Journal of International Law* 95(1): 7–31.

Akhavan, P. (2005) 'The Lord's Resistance Army Case: Uganda's Submission of the First State Referral to the International Criminal Court', *American Journal of International Law* 99(2): 403–421.

Arendt, H. (1963) *Eichmann in Jerusalem: A Report on the Banality of Evil*, London: Faber & Faber, New York: Viking.

Atkinson, R. (2010) '"The Realists in Juba?": An Analysis of the Juba Peace Talks', in T. Allen and K. Vlassenroot, *The Lord's Resistance Army: Myth and Reality*, London: Zed Books, pp. 205–222.

Chandler, D. (2002) *From Kosovo to Kabul: Human Rights and International Intervention*, London and Sterling, VA: Pluto.

Chandler, D. (2009) *Hollow Hegemony: Rethinking Global Politics, Power and Resistance*, London: Pluto.

Clark, P. (2008a) 'If Ocampo Indicts Bashir, Nothing May Happen', from http://blogs.ssrc.org/sudan/2008/07/13/if-ocampo-indicts-bashir-nothing-may-happen/.

Clark, P. (2008b) 'Law, Politics and Pragmatism: The ICC and Case Selection in Uganda and the Democratic Republic of Congo', in N. Waddell and P. Clark, *Courting Conflict? Justice, Peace and the ICC in Africa*, Royal African Society: 37–45.

De Waal, A. (1997) 'Becoming Shameless: The Failure of Human Rights Organizations in Rwanda', *Times Literary Supplement* 21: 3–4.

Drumbl, M. A. (2007) *Atrocity, Punishment, and International Law*, Cambridge: Cambridge University Press.

Koskenniemi, M. (2001) *The Gentle Civilizer of Nations: The Rise and Fall of International Law, 1870–1960*, Cambridge: Cambridge University Press.

Koskenniemi, M. (2002) 'Between Impunity and Show Trials', *Max Planck Yearbook of United Nations Law* 6(1): 1–32.

Mamdani, M. (2008) 'The New Humanitarian Order', *The Nation* 29.

Perrot, S. (2010) 'Northern Uganda: A "Forgotten Conflict," Again? The Impact of the Internationalization of the Resolution Process', in T. Allen and K. Vlassenroot, *The Lord's Resistance Army: Myth and Reality*, London: Zed Books, pp. 187–204.

Simpson, G. J. (2007) *Law, War and Crime: War Crimes Trials and the Reinvention of International Law*, Cambridge: Polity.

Snyder, J. and L. Vinjamuri (2004) 'Trials and Errors: Principle and Pragmatism in Strategies of International Justice', *International Security* 28(3): 5–44.

Sriram, C. L. (2007) 'Justice as Peace? Liberal Peacebuilding and Strategies of Transitional Justice', *Global Society* 21(4): 579–591.

Tallgren, I. (2002) 'The Sensibility and Sense of International Criminal Law', *European Journal of International Law* 13(3): 561.

Teitel, R. G. (2001) 'Humanity's Law: Rule of Law for the New Global Politics', *Cornell International Law Journal* 35: 355.

Žižek, S. (1997) 'Repeating Lenin', available at http://www.lacan.com/replenin.htm, accessed 3 January 2011.

Zolo, D. (2009) *Victors' Justice: From Nuremberg to Baghdad*, London: Verso.

8

Civil Society beyond the Liberal Peace and its Critique[1]

Thania Paffenholz

Introduction

Civil society is an important part of the liberal peace and statebuilding agenda, though peacemaking and statebuilding were for a long time seen as affairs of states. This changed with the evolving international peace and statebuilding discourse starting in the early 1990s. In light of the helplessness of the international community in the face of increased international peace and statebuilding failures such as Somalia, Rwanda or the Balkans, support for civil society was seen to be an alternative and a supplement to diplomatic and peacekeeping efforts. The policy and non-governmental organisation (NGO) practitioner communities, as well as many researchers, almost undisputedly concluded that civil society was a key actor in peace and statebuilding essential for achieving and sustaining peace.[2] Consequently, civil society has established its place in the conceptual framework of the liberal peace. This led to a massive rise in civil society peace and statebuilding initiatives with sufficient donor funding in place.

Civil society's role in peace and statebuilding has also been in the spotlight of the critics of the liberal peace. Their main claim is that civil society is part of an externally driven agenda that provides few real benefits in terms of social change or everyday peace for people in conflict settings (Bendaña 2003; Paris 2004; Richmond 2005; Heathershaw 2008).

Both the pro-civil society liberal peace as well as its critique are missing a systematic and substantial contribution that civil society actors can make to peace and statebuilding. The liberal peace proponents present an idealistic picture, while the critics present an exceedingly narrow picture of the contributions and limitations of civil society during and in the aftermath of armed conflict and war.

Liberal Peace and Civil Society

For a better understanding of the role of civil society within the framework of the liberal peace, we need to first discuss the role of peacebuilding within this framework in order to then analyse the role of civil society therein.

The roots of the liberal peace

Although the term *peacebuilding* was first introduced by Johan Galtung (1975: 282–304), its main proliferation began with its use in the 1992 UN Secretary-General report, *An Agenda for Peace*. In Galtung's understanding, peacebuilding achieves positive peace by creating structures and institutions of peace based on justice, equity and cooperation (Galtung 1975: 297–304). The evolving understanding of *liberal peacebuilding* starting with *An Agenda for Peace*, on the other hand, focuses mainly on the democratic rebuilding of states after armed conflict. This presents a much more narrow focus than Galtung's original definition.

Historically, the roots of the liberal peace debate can be traced back to the understanding of democracy building in modern Europe going back to the works of Immanuel Kant and Adam Smith as well as earlier modern European political philosophers.

In his work of 1795 *Zum Ewigen Frieden* ('On Perpetual Peace'), Kant laid the foundation for understanding peacebuilding between states based on democratic values (Senghaas 2007). He argued that the democratic constitution of states correlates with their relatively peaceful behaviour vis-à-vis other states. Confirming Kant's arguments, a mountain of quantitative research makes a clear positive causal linkage between democracy and peace (Chan 1997; Ray 1998; Russett and Starr 2000). Democracies do not fight each other (Doyle 1983a and 1983b; Small and Singer 1976), because democracies' shared norms of compromise and cooperation prevent conflicts of interests from escalating into violence. Rummel (1997) extended this research to armed violence *within* states, coming to similar conclusions: democracies have by far the lowest level of internal armed conflict. Interestingly, repressive authoritarian states also have a relatively low level of armed violence, but for different reasons. States in the transitional phase between authoritarian and inclusive democratic governance have the highest levels of armed violence (Hegre et al. 2001).

In his book *An Inquiry into the Nature and Causes of the Wealth of Nations*, Smith (1904) suggested a possible correlation between democracy, economic liberalisation, and peace (i.e. the higher the level of a free-market economy in combination with a democratic political system, the higher the chances for peace). While there is a great deal of research to support the democratic peace theory, the evidence for Smith's theory is sparse and disparate. There are a number of quantitative studies confirming a positive correlation between armed conflict, peace, economic growth or globalisation. Collier and colleagues (Collier and Hoeffler 1998 and 2002; Collier et al. 2003) suggest that economic growth has a direct positive effect on violence reduction, as well as an indirect effect because it generates income that positively correlates with violence reduction. Bussmann and Schneider (2007) come to the conclusion that economic liberalisation reduces the risk of armed conflict, but the process towards global economic integration increases the chances of armed conflict.

Today, the 'liberal peace' proposition is an integral part of the 'democratic peace' debate (Xenias 2005: 360) as most democracies are also liberal market economies. In a widely debated study, Roland Paris (2004) analysed the consequences of the application of liberal peace policies (i.e. consolidating peace in war-shattered states through a quick transformation of these countries into free market democracies). He found that the limited success of many post-conflict processes is based on the destabilising effects generated by rapid political and economic liberalisation processes in post-conflict societies that lack the necessary preconditions. His findings do not contradict 'liberal' or 'democratic peace' but question the process and timeframe of their application in post-conflict countries.

Democracy theorists, especially transitologists,[3] analyse transitions from authoritarian to democratic rule. Transitions from war to peace are treated as one sub-category in the first stage of transition[4] (Merkel 1999). Different preconditions for successful transitions are presented in the literature: elite pacts (O'Donnell et al. 1986; Burton et al. 1992), power-sharing arrangements (Linder and Bächtiger 2005), negotiated agreements (Colomer 1991), the problem-solving capacity of the society (Almond and Powell 1988), economic conditions (Lijphardt 1968 and 1977), international and regional climate of coexistence (Merkel 1999) and cultural factors (Linder and Bächtiger 2003). Whether and how civil society should participate in the transition process is also part of this debate.

The above look at the historical development of the liberal peace debate demonstrates that while the 'end stage' of liberal democratic societies is desirable from a peace perspective, the core problem that remains, however, is the transition to that state. These transitions occur over long periods of time, are extremely prone to violence and are subject to long-term instabilities and regression.

Civil society's role in the liberal peace

What role should civil society play in transitions to the liberal peace? We find different roles attributed to civil society within the relevant development cooperation, democratisation and peacebuilding debates. All of these debates are characterised by an intertwined relationship between academic and practitioner discourses.

In development cooperation, discussions of and support to civil society gained momentum in the 1980s, which can be attributed to the neoliberal development model (Debiel and Sticht 2005: 9). This was spurred on by scepticism toward the state and an expressed preference for privatisation of state welfare and infrastructure services. In response, development NGOs took on new assignments, especially within social sectors, for which the state had previously been responsible. They increasingly took over operational tasks, in line with efforts to reduce the role of the state when state weakness became pervasive (Abiew and Keating 2004: 100–101). A series of UN world conferences during the 1990s encouraged the formation of new NGOs and the expansion of existing ones. NGOs were presented as alternative implementers of development assistance when states and governments in partner countries were weak or performing poorly. The ascendance of NGOs was due to their perceived political independence, their flexibility and their effectiveness in reaching beneficiaries, relative to the bureaucratic state apparatuses. The funding of official development assistance channelled through NGOs increased from an average of US$3.1 billion from the Organisation for Economic Cooperation and Development (OECD) countries in 1985–1986 to US$7.2 billion in 2001 (Debiel and Sticht 2005: 10).

In the democratisation discourse, civil society gained momentum at the beginning of the 1990s as a means to improve governance and democratisation. As the Cold War ended, an opportunity arose to establish principles of good governance, respect for human rights and the rule of law. A vibrant civil society was considered an important pillar for establishing democracy, and support for it became an obvious aim of democratisation (Schmidt 2000: 312). Almost all international donors mention the importance of civil society's ability to 'influence decisions of the state' (BMZ 2005: 3), also highlighting civil society's responsibility for a democratic state and its 'dynamic role . . . in pushing for social, economic and political change' (DfID 2005) or stressing its role in encouraging open debates on public policy (USAID 2005).

Research in democratic system transformation (i.e. transitology) identifies different roles for civil society in the various stages of democratisation. In the first stage of immediate transition, which often occurs through a revolution or armed conflict, civil society plays the role of opposition to the established authoritarian system. This occurred in Latin America in the 1980s as well as in Eastern Europe in the early 1990s. Here, strong civil society movements were the relevant agents of change (Merkel 1999, 2000; Lauth 2003; Birle 2000).[5] A vibrant civil society was also considered to support the consolidation of a successful democracy by monitoring state institutions, developing civic culture and supporting social cohesion (Almond and Powell 1988; Putnam 1993; Merkel 1999, 2004).

Civil society became prominent in the peacebuilding discourse in the mid-1990s. Civil society peacebuilding was not new, however. The Quakers and other religious actors had always worked with and supported civil society. However, most official mediation efforts prior to the 1990s were an affair of state diplomacy. This changed with major international peacebuilding failures in the early 1990s (i.e. Rwanda, the Balkans and Somalia) when civil society started to be seen as an alternative or supplement to international diplomatic efforts.

Three of the schools of peacebuilding theory – conflict management, conflict resolution and conflict transformation[6] – attribute different roles for civil society. In the realist-inspired conflict management school, civil society usually plays a limited role because non-state issues are mostly ignored (Richmond 2005: 89; Paffenholz and Spurk 2006: 18). Nonetheless, this school does give attention to efforts by international civil society organisations who act as mediators, such as the Comunità di Sant'Egidio in the Mozambique peace negotiations or the Geneva Centre for Humanitarian Dialogue in the first Aceh peace negotiations. When civil society actors become official mediators, their actions and behaviour are not different from official governmental mediators (Paffenholz 1998: 213–215; Paffenholz 2010: 56–58). Civil society, however, rarely has a seat at the negotiation table, on the basis of the assumption that the smaller the number of actors involved, the easier it is to reach agreement (Paffenholz et al. 2006). Global civil society can also play an important role by exerting pressure on donors in their home countries to address specific issues of international peacebuilding, to protect national civil society through international awareness or to support their functioning through knowledge transfer and funding (Kaldor 2003).

Civil society actors are the key protagonists both in the idealist-inspired conflict resolution and in the conflict transformation schools. These two schools focus on the roots of conflict and on relationships among conflict parties and society. The understanding within both is that such issues can best be addressed by non-state actors. The main difference between the two schools is that the conflict resolution school tends to focus on external actors as peacebuilders, whereas the conflict transformation school looks mainly at internal actors.

As of the mid-1990s, peacebuilding practice was strongly influenced by Lederach's conflict transformation approach. Although Lederach offered a complex, comprehensive approach to peacebuilding (Lederach 1997), donors and international NGOs mainly focused on his middle–out approach. Here, Lederach identifies mid-level individuals and groups and empowers them to build peace and support reconciliation. Empowerment of the middle level is assumed to influence peacebuilding at the macro and grassroots levels. Lederach's focus on the empowerment of the mid-level leadership has had considerable influence on the practice of civil society peacebuilding. It has lead to a mushrooming of conflict resolution training and dialogue initiatives for mostly urban middle and upper-class NGOs, executed by international and national NGOs, which receive the majority of funding. Civil society is assumed to be the 'good society', inevitably contributing to peacebuilding in a positive way (Paris 2004; van Tongeren et al. 2005; Aal 2007).

Civil Society as Seen by the Critics of the Liberal Peace

The critiques of the liberal peace deconstruct international peacebuilding and show that the conceptual and practitioner discourse is trapped in the 'liberal imperative' (Richmond 2005: 208) as only one model for peacebuilding is normatively accepted, that is, the liberal peace. Most authors claim that this kind of peacebuilding has become a self-referential system, which long ago lost its connection to the real world and the needs of people. A. B. Featherstone and Alexandro Bendaña deliver the most radical interpretations. Through a power analysis based on Foucault, Featherstone considers the peacebuilding schools as 'part of an apparatus of power which attempts to discipline and normalize' (Featherstone 2000: 200). On the basis of an analysis of Southern voices, Bendaña comes to similar conclusions by emphasising that peacebuilding becomes an inherently conservative undertaking, which seeks managerial solutions to fundamental conflicts over resources and power. Peacebuilding thus attempts to modernise and relegitimise a fundamental status quo that is respectful of a national and international market economy (Bendaña 2003: 5).

Within this alternative discourse no meta-alternative[7] is presented. Instead, authors point to the need to refocus on the everyday peace of ordinary local people (Featherstone 2000; Bendaña 2003; Mac Ginty 2006: 33–57; Richmond 2005). Peacebuilding, hence, should be transformative in the sense that it leads to a post-hegemonic society (Featherstone 2000: 213–214), in which oppressed voices are listened to and respected. It therefore also implies structural changes and the acknowledgment that peacebuilding is mainly a Western enterprise that needs to engage in a serious South–North dialogue.

Civil society plays an important role within the critiques of liberal peacebuilding. Here, more emphasis is put on grassroots emancipation, cultural, gender and other differences, and on structural changes through international dialogue and possibly also revolution. An emancipated civil society becomes a change agent through social movements and public communication.

Studies analyzing the practice of civil society peacebuilding with explicit reference to liberal peacebuilding (Paris 2004, 2006: 425; Richmond 2005; Heathershaw 2008, 607–609, 616–618; and Bendaña 2003) come to the conclusion that civil society organisations are part and parcel of the liberal peacebuilding grand narrative, as they serve the purpose of implementing the liberal peacebuilding agenda. Heathershaw states that in holding to the principle of impartiality, understood pragmatically as 'do no harm,' civil society organisations have lost their ability to advocate for radical social change (Heathershaw 2008: 609). Bendaña notes that 'liberal donors and accompanying NGOs have evolved sufficiently to now recognize that short and medium term "conflict-sensitive development" do [sic] not, in and of themselves, bring us closer to sustainable engagement of long term structural problems and attainment of positive peace' (Bendaña 2003, 20). Roland Paris, nevertheless, opts for promoting 'good civil society' alongside statebuilding (Paris 2004: 194–196).

Other critiques focus on the 'NGOisation' of civil society peacebuilding. Funding for civil society has concentrated mainly on NGOs. These NGOs are less independent from governments than is assumed by donors, and their accountability to local people and communities is weak (Debiel and Sticht 2005: 11). Funds are channelled from donor governments to Northern NGOs, which then subcontract project implementation to Southern NGOs (Neubert 2001: 61). The modern Southern NGO represents a new type of organisation: nonprofit, but acting like a commercial consulting firm (Neubert 2001: 63) financed by external mandates. This has led to crowding out of local efforts and actors (Belloni 2001, 2006: 21; Orjuela 2004; Pouligny 2005: 499). These national urban NGOs are also criticised for their weak membership base (Orjuela 2004: 256; Debiel and Sticht 2005: 16–17; Neubert 2001: 63). They attain their prominence often at the expense of other civil society actors that have broader membership (Stewart 1997: 26). For example, trade unions and other mass membership organisations could guarantee more participation than urban NGOs with a very limited membership base. Some critics fear that the commercialisation of civil society, especially of those that carry out advocacy or public policy work, discourages more legitimate local actors who, in turn, do not receive funds from doing this work or become more active (Pouligny 2005: 499). Civic engagement is therefore at risk of being dominated by commercial urban NGOs, which in the long run weakens the development of a vibrant civil society. Hence, one could argue that donor-driven NGO civil society initiatives have limited the capacity of other types of civil society to create domestic social capital and ownership for the peace process (Belloni 2006: 21–22).

Beyond assumptions: what does civil society really contribute to peace and statebuilding?

Although some of the aforementioned critiques of liberal civil society peace and statebuilding are based on individual case studies, none of them are based on a systematic comparative assessment of civil society roles in transitions from war to peace. In response to this gap, in 2006, a four-year project was started by the Centre on Conflict, Development and Peacebuilding at the Graduate Institute of International and Development Studies in Geneva.[8] Based on a common framework, the project conducted a meta-analysis of the role of civil society in thirteen case study countries.[9] This framework outlined seven possible peacebuilding functions that civil society performs to support democracy building and related activities during the various stages of armed conflict and peacemaking. These functions are: *protection, monitoring, advocacy, socialisation, social cohesion, facilitation* and *service delivery* (Paffenholz and Spurk 2010: 65–76). This functional approach allows for a systematic assessment of all relevant civil society activities and, hence, a broader look at all existing social forces that can contribute to peacebuilding, rather than the common narrow focus on well-known pro-peace NGOs. Table 8.1 explains each function within democratisation and statebuilding (left side) and peacebuilding (right side).

Table 8.1 Comparing civil society functions in statebuilding and peacebuilding

Civil society functions	Understanding in democratisation and statebuilding	Understanding in peacebuilding
1. Protection	Against attacks from state against freedom, life and property	Protection against attacks from all armed actors
2. Monitoring	Monitoring and controlling state activities and citizens' rights	Monitoring of human rights violations or implementation of peace agreements
3. Advocacy	Articulating interests and bringing relevant issues to the public agenda	Articulating interests and bringing relevant issues to the public agenda as well as the negotiation table
4. Socialisation	Forming democratic attitudes and habits, promoting tolerance and trust	Attitude change for inculcating 'culture of peace' and reconciliation
5. Social cohesion	Building social capital, bridging societal cleavages and adding to social cohesion	Building bridging ties across adversary groups
6. Facilitation	Facilitating interests between citizens and the state	Facilitating between all kinds of different actors
7. Service delivery	Providing basic needs-oriented services to citizens	Seen as serving as important entry point to other functions for peacebuilding in cases where actors are aware of the potential

Overall, the results of this meta-analysis stress that civil society has the potential to play an important and effective role in peacebuilding during all stages of conflict and in the aftermath of large-scale violence, and has often done so. Nonetheless, a careful look at civil society's engagement in peacebuilding, compared to the involvement of other actors, reveals that civil society's role is not necessarily decisive, but rather supportive in most instances. The central impetus for peacebuilding comes mainly from political actors – above all, from the conflict parties themselves. This is often reinforced by strong regional actors like the European Union in Europe and the Mediterranean, or India in South Asia. Nevertheless, this research has found that civil society's supportive role can make a difference when performed in an effective way at the right time. Civil society groups have contributed effectively to the reduction of violence, negotiated settlements, and sustaining peace after large-scale violence has ended.

This research also found that the peacebuilding relevance of the aforementioned seven civil society functions differs tremendously between the four phases analysed: (1) war, (2) armed conflict, (3) windows of opportunity, (4) statebuilding after large-scale violence, as does civil society's peacebuilding and statebuilding potential in these phases. In general, we found a significant imbalance between the level of civil society activities and their relevance for peacebuilding. On the one hand, even when a function was likely to be highly relevant in a particular phase of conflict, it was not necessarily performed. The most striking examples are protection, socialisation and social cohesion. While protection was always highly relevant during armed conflict and war, it was only performed in one third of the cases. On the other hand, functions which were not found to be highly relevant during violent phases of conflict were implemented widely, especially during windows of opportunities for peace agreements. Such was the case for the social cohesion and socialisation functions, which included dialogue initiatives, conflict resolution workshops, exchange programmes or peace education projects.

Though this meta-analysis does not analyse the phase of *prevention* prior to the outbreak of violence, it has an interesting finding in this regard. In all the cases analysed, the attention of international and local peacebuilders focused on the main conflict lines even though disregarding other cleavages and tensions has proven to be dangerous in some of these cases and has led to outbreaks of violence. The case of the violent uprising in the Southern Nepali Terrai region immediately after the comprehensive peace agreement in 2006 is one case in point.

This research also demonstrates that although the *effectiveness* of the seven different functions can vary tremendously, it does not make sense to identify more or less effective functions. The effectiveness of civil society activities within each function depends entirely on context- and function-specific variables:

Context variables: Obviously, the context of the country or case strongly influences the space for civil society to act and thus strengthens or limits its effectiveness. The main context factors considered were: the behaviour of the state, the level of violence, the role of the media, the behavior and composition of civil society itself (including diaspora organisations), and the influence of external political actors and donors (Paffenholz et al. 2010).

Function specific variables: Study of the effectiveness of the functions shows the following patterns. *Protection* is effective in many instances, especially when performed by local (often traditional and religious) actors in local contexts. The work of professional protection NGOs shows high levels of effectiveness when combined with monitoring and advocacy campaigns that had been picked up by media and international networks.

The monitoring that was studied centred on human rights violations during armed conflicts. This type of monitoring is carried out by local and national professional organisations and research institutions which are often linked to international human rights organisations. The effectiveness of monitoring is fairly high in most cases, but usually not as a stand-alone function. Rather, monitoring worked best when it was a precondition for protection and advocacy.

The research found that *advocacy* is one of the most effective functions during all phases of conflict. In addition to advocating on protection-related issues, civil society groups advocate for the inclusion of relevant issues into peace agreements (e.g. refugee return in Bosnia, or truth and reconciliation commissions) and for the legal recognition and implementation of rights for marginalised groups. The advocacy of women's groups is often successful in putting minority and gender issues on the agenda. Our research found that if targeted advocacy campaigns are combined with monitoring, media attention and support from international networks, their effectiveness is highest.

We found that *socialisation of the population at large* on democratic and peace values has little effect in times of armed conflict and war. We find in all cases that existing socialisation institutions in society are key factors influencing how people learn democratic and conflict behaviour. Such institutions include schools, religious and secular associations, clubs, workplaces and families. In all cases, these institutions tend to reinforce existing divides, often to an extent that fosters radicalisation. Overall, the majority of NGO peace education and training work that we studied was ineffective. Deep radical in-group identities within existing institutions cannot be counterbalanced by a few local or national NGO initiatives that take place outside of these institutions.

On the other hand, we found that *in-group socialisation* of underprivileged groups in asymmetric conflict situations proved effective in many instances, as demonstrated by the empowerment of a generation of civic leaders through training and capacity-building (e.g. Maya activists in Guatemala and Dalit organisations in Nepal). However, the strengthening of group identity can also have negative effects, such as through the reinforcement, and sometimes even radicalisation, of existing conflict lines as demonstrated by some ethnic groups in the Democratic Republic of the Congo.

We found that *inter-group social cohesion* is influenced by the effectiveness of conflict resolution workshops, dialogue projects and exchange programmes. In the cases we studied, we found that the overall effectiveness of initiatives aiming to promote intergroup social cohesion was relatively low for a number of reasons; these included radicalisation within society that hinders counteracting peace work, the often scattered, short-term and fragmented nature of most NGO initiatives, the focus on attitude change as opposed to behaviour change and the apolitical nature of most initiatives,. Moreover, these initiatives focus almost exclusively on well-known conflicts with obvious adversary groups, such as the Protestants and Catholics in Northern Ireland, the different group identities in Bosnia, and the Singhalese and Tamils in Sri Lanka. This narrow focus often ignores other conflict lines within societies (e.g. radicals and moderates, geographical regions). Deep cleavages in other societies with less clearly identifiable group conflicts (e.g. Guatemala and Afghanistan) are also often ignored. On the positive side, we found that marginalised groups are often empowered through their participation in such initiatives. Moreover, we found that intergroup social cohesion activities that were not directly related to peacebuilding, such as initiatives that brought together people from different professional groups, were more successful than the peace-related activities.

In our case studies, *facilitation* by civil society at the local level seems to be one of the most commonly performed functions, although the availability of data on this point is limited across our case studies. Nevertheless, many facilitation initiatives are effective when undertaken. With effectiveness contingent upon context, however, it is difficult to pinpoint successful patterns. We found that *national facilitation* by civil society between the main conflict parties is a lesser task. Its importance depends on the existence of eminent persons within civil society, including religious, political and other leaders, who can effectively pave the way for official negotiations and support official mediators during times of stalemate.

Across all case studies, *service delivery* was by far the most commonly performed activity, receiving most of the external funds. When aid initiatives were systematically used for peacebuilding, for instance, they often created entry points for protection, monitoring and social cohesion, although these projects were few in number.

When assessing the effectiveness of different civil society actors, we found several trends. On the whole, based on the reality on the ground, civil society consists of much more than NGOs. Although NGOs can often be effective in providing protection and in conducting targeted advocacy campaigns, established *associations with broader membership* (even though their record is spotty thus far) have far greater potential to promote socialisation and social cohesion, even if their record so far has not been positive. *Traditional and local entities* are effective in local facilitation and have shown positive results when providing protection, and *eminent civil society leaders* can be effective in preparing the ground for national negotiations. Leaders can also help parties break a stalemate in negotiations. *Women's groups* are effective at supporting gender, women's and minority issues and can be effective in bridging existing divides. It is also clear that broader change requires the uniting of all available change-orientated *mass movements*. *Aid organisations*, if they are aware of their peacebuilding potential and make systematic use of it, can support protection, monitoring and social cohesion.

Finally, general support for civil society cannot replace political action. It is clear from the case studies that the major enabling and disabling conditions for civil society arise from coercive states and high levels of violence. Thus, the engagement of the international community in any initiative that reduces violence, enhances protection, increases dialogue and puts pressure on repressive governments facilitates the fundamental preconditions for civil society to fulfil a role in peace and statebuilding.

Confronting liberal peace and its critique with case study evidence

Comparing the results of the aforementioned meta-analysis with the assumptions and analysis about civil society as presented within the liberal framework shows that civil society is neither a homogeneous entity nor always the 'good society'. Civil society is comprised of many more actors than Western supported NGOs; this broad range of actors perform many different roles and their peacebuilding and statebuilding relevance and effectiveness varies according to the stage of the transition as well as the way activities are performed within each context. The narrow understanding of the role that civil society can play within peace and statebuilding is misleading and has led donors to fund a pre-selected set of activities carried out by urban elite-based NGOs, whereas relevant activities, such as mass mobilisation and other social change activities, carried out by more locally grounded organisations have been largely ignored.

Consequently, our research shows that the critics of the liberal peace are correct in their critique of the NGOisation of peacebuilding. The focus on urban NGOs ignores oppressed voices and does not put an emphasis on structural changes in conflict systems that support for existing social movements and advocacy likely would have. Nonetheless, the critics of liberal peace have, ironically, also focused narrowly on Western NGOs and their local, primarily urban elite, partners. As a result, the critics fail to transcend the liberal peace realm that they denounce. They barely analyse oppressed voices and have an uncritical view of the 'local' that is as glorified as 'good society' is by proponents of liberal civil society. Although the liberal peace critics' focus on 'everyday peace' (Richmond 2005) offers a good change in perspective, it lacks ideas on how to best get there without being, once again, ignorant of the conditions on the ground. Power, gender and hierarchy that are presented in different forms in various geographical contexts (cast, class, ethnicity, religion) also prevail in 'everyday peace' on the local level, making *the local* as 'good' or 'bad' as the society in which she or he lives.

Conclusions: Civil Society beyond the Liberal Peace and its Critics

Civil society is an important protagonist within the framework of liberal peace. Civil society is the guarantor of human rights and a civic culture through socialisation and social cohesion. It also provides services to people when the state is weak. There is a great deal of theory and evidence that civil society plays these roles in the everyday reality of working democracies.

Liberal peacebuilding is, however, taking place within states in transition from war to peace, often generations away from working democracies. The main problem within the liberal peacebuilding endeavour is that it takes all elements of the 'end stage' of a working liberal democracy as the model for peace and statebuilding, instead of reflecting the needs of the transition phase these countries are undergoing. Liberal peace- and statebuilders thereby may risk stabilising instabilities that otherwise would have been only transitional phases.

This tendency to support stabilisation, rather than true liberalisation, is also reflected in the way civil society is supported. Funders and proponents of civil society who aim to support liberal peacebuilding, often view it uncritically as the 'good society'. They see local NGOs only as peace- and statebuilders while ignoring their true potential as well as their limitations. And they are ignorant of the broad range of other civil society actors, such as membership-based professional associations, unions, or faith-based or traditional actors. Liberal peacebuilders also pay little attention to the potential relevance and effectiveness of the potential breadth of civil society in different phases of peace and statebuilding at the same time as they overwhelmingly ignore the interaction that civil society groups have with political actors and the difficult context in which they operate.

The critics of the liberal peace do not fare much better. They advance a general critique of the liberal framework, while failing to analyse or understand the alternative, oppressed actors for whom they advocate. The main focus of these critical studies is the liberal peace and the international community (i.e. Western governments and NGOs, the UN, etc.), which seems to be an inherent contradiction to the very alternative discourse for which these authors advocate. Their focus on 'everyday peace' and the 'good local' also misses a critical assessment of the potential and limitations of many different local actors that operate in a specific political and societal context where all sorts of power relations prevail.

In conclusion, both liberal peace and its critics fail to provide an empirically based critical analysis of the role that civil society can play in long-term war-to-peace transitions. As a result, the liberal model presents uniform answers to very context specific problems, while its critics provide a narrow picture of reality that focuses mainly on Western NGOs and their local urban-elite partners.

A discussion that extends beyond the liberal peace and its critics that is characterised by a holistic and distinct analysis of all civil society actors within a given political and societal transition is therefore necessary.

Notes

1 The empirical evidence in this chapter is generated from the project 'Civil Society and Peacebuilding' that is based on thirteen case studies (Guatemala, Northern Ireland, Bosnia-Herzegovina, the Kurdish conflict in Turkey, Tajikistan, Cyprus, Israel/Palestine, Afghanistan, Nepal, Sri Lanka, Somalia, Nigeria and DR Congo) and can be found in Paffenholz (2010).

2 See the references and chapters on civil society in major donor, UN and NGO publications such as OECD/DAC 1997, UN 2005, UN 2009 or van Tongeren et al. 2005.

3 See Zinecker 2009 for an explanation of terminology and the issues debated.

4 According to Merkel 1999 there are three phases of transition: liberalisation, democratisation and consolidation.

5 For a summary see Spurk 2010: 10–11.

6 I am only discussing these three schools here; elsewhere I present five schools and a more detailed overview of all schools, see Paffenholz 2010: 50–58.

7 'Meta-alternative' refers to an overall normative theoretical explanation of the world, like idealism, realism or Marxism.

8 The main publications of the project's results are Paffenholz 2010 and 2009.

9 See note 1.

Bibliography

Aall, P. (2007) 'The Power of Nonofficial Actors in Conflict Management', in H. A. Croker, *Leashing the Dogs of War: Conflict Management in a Divided World*, Washington DC: United States Institute of Peace Press.

Abiew, F. K. and Keating, T. (2004) 'Defining a Role for Civil Society', in T. Keating and W. A. Knight (eds) *Building Sustainable Peace*, Edmonton: University of Alberta Press, pp. 93–117.

Almond, G. A. and G. B. Powell (1988) *Comparative Politics Today: A World View*, 4th edn, Glenview, IL: Scott, Foresman/Little, Brown College Division.

Almond, G. A. and S. Verba (1963) *The Civic Culture: Political Attitudes and Democracy in Five Nations*, Newbury Park: Sage.

Belloni, R. (2001) 'Civil Society and Peacebuilding in Bosnia and Herzegovina', *Journal of Peace Research* 38(2): 163–180.

Belloni, R. (2006) 'Civil Society in War-to-Democracy Transitions', in A. Jarstad and T. Sisk (eds) *War-to-Democracy Transitions: Dilemmas of Democratization and Peacebuilding in War-Torn Societies*, Cambridge: Cambridge University Press.

Bendaña, A. (2003) 'What Kind of Peace is Being Built? Critical Assessment from the South', discussion paper prepared on the occasion of the tenth anniversary of 'An Agenda for Peace', Ottawa: International Development Research Centre.

Birle, P. (2000) 'Zivilgesellschaft in Südamerika. Mythos und Realität', in W. Merkel (ed.) *Systemwechsel 5. Zivilgesellschaft und Transformation*, Opladen: Leske and Budrich, pp. 231–271.

Bundesministerium für wirtschaftliche Entwicklung und Zusammenarbeit (BMZ) (2005) *Förderung von Demokratie in der Deutschen Entwicklungspolitik* [Support for democracy in German Development Cooperation], position paper, Bonn: BMZ.

Burton, M., R. Gunther and J. Higley (1992) 'Introduction: Elite Transformations and Democratic Regimes', in R. Gunther and J. Higley (eds) *Elites and Democratic Consolidation in Latin America and Southern Europe*, Cambridge: Cambridge University Press, pp. 1–37.

Bussmann, M. and G. Schneider (2007) 'When Globalization Discontent Turns Violent: Foreign Economic Liberalization and Internal War', *International Studies Quarterly* 51(1): 79–97.

Chan, S. (1997) 'In Search of Democratic Peace: Problems and Promise', *Mershon International Studies Review* 41: 59–91.

Collier, P. and A. Hoeffler (1998) On Economic Causes of Civil War, *Oxford Economic Papers* 50(4): 563–573.

Collier, P. and A. Hoeffler (2002) *Greed and Grievance in Civil War*, Working Paper CSAE WPS02002–01, Oxford: Centre for the Study of African Economies.

Collier, P., A. Hoeffler, L. Elliot, H. Hegre, M. Reynal-Querol and N. Sambanis (2003) *Breaking the Conflict Trap Civil War and Development Policy*, Oxford and Washington DC: Oxford University Press and World Bank.

Colomer, J. M. (1991) 'Transitions by Agreements: Modeling the Spanish Way', *American Political Science Review* 85(4): 1283–1302.

Debiel, T. and M. Sticht (2005) 'Towards a New Profile? Development, Humanitarian, and Conflict-Resolution NGOs in the Age of Globalization', Report No. 79, Duisburg: Institute for Development and Peace.

Department for International Development (DfID) (2005) *Civil Society* (online), available at www.dfid.gov.uk.

Doyle, M. (1983a) 'Kant, Liberal Legacies, and Foreign Affairs', *Philosophy and Public Affairs* 12(3): 205–235.

Doyle, M. (1983b) 'Kant, Liberal Legacies, and Foreign Affairs Part 2', *Philosophy and Public Affairs* 12(4): 323–353.

Featherstone, A. B. (2000) 'Peacekeeping, Conflict Resolution and Peacebuilding: A Reconsideration of Theoretical Frameworks', *International Peacekeeping* 7(1): 190–218.

Galtung, J. (1975) 'Three Approaches to Peace: Peacekeeping, Peacemaking, and

Peacebuilding', in J. Galtung (ed.) *Peace, War, and Defense: Essays in Peace Research*, Copenhagen: Christian Ejlers.
Heathershaw, J. (2008) 'Unpacking the Liberal Peace: The Dividing and Merging of Peacebuilding Discourses', *Journal of International Studies* 36(3): 597–621.
Hegre, H., T. Ellingsen, S. Gates and N. P. Gleditsch (2001) 'Toward a Democratic Civil Peace? Democracy, Political Change, and Civil War, 1816–1992', *American Political Science Review* 95(1): 33–48.
Kaldor, M. (2003) *Global Civil Society: An Answer to War*, Cambridge: Polity.
Lauth, H. (2003) 'Ambivalenzen der Zivilgesellschaft in Hinsicht auf Demokratie und Soziale Inklusion', *Nord-Süd Aktuell* 2: 223–232.
Lederach, J. P. (1997) *Building Peace: Sustainable Reconciliation in Divided Societies*, Washington, DC: United States Institute of Peace Press.
Lijphart, A. (1968) 'Consociational Democracy', *World Politic* 4(1): 207–225.
Lijphart, A. (1977) *Democracy in Plural Societies*, New Haven, CT: Yale University Press.
Linder, W. and A. Bächtiger (2005) 'What Drives Democratisation in Asia and Africa?', *European Journal of Political Research* 44: 861–880.
Mac Ginty, R. (2006) *No War, No Peace: The Rejuvenation of Stalled Peace Processes and Peace Accords*, Basingstoke: Palgrave.
Merkel, W. (1999) *Systemtransformation. Eine Einführung in die Theorie und Empirie der Transformationsforschung* [System transformation. An introduction into theory and empiricism], Opladen: Leske and Budrich.
Merkel, W. (2000) *Systemwechsel Band 5. Zivilgesellschaft und Demokratische Transformation* [System change. Civil society and democratic transition], Opladen: Leske and Budrich.
Merkel, W. (2004) 'Embedded and Defective Democracies', in A. Croissant and W. Merkel (eds) 'Consolidated or Defective Democracy? Problems of Regime Change', Special Issue of *Democratization* 11(5): 33–58.
Merkel, W. and Lauth H. J. (1998) 'Systemwechsel und Zivilgesellschaft. Welche Zivilgesellschaft Braucht die Demokratie?' [System change and civil society. What kind of civil society does democracy need?], *Politik und Zeitgeschichte* 6(7): 3–12.
Neubert, D. (2001) 'Die Globalisierung eines Organisationsmodells: Nicht-Regierungsorganisationen in Afrika', in U. Bauer, H. Egbert, and F. Jäger (eds) *Interkulturelle Beziehungen und Kulturwandel in Afrika*, Frankfurt A. M.: Peter Lang, pp. 51–69.
O'Donnell, G., P. C. Schmitter and L. Whitehead (1986) *Transitions from Authoritarian Rule: Prospects for Democracy*, Baltimore, MD: Johns Hopkins University Press.
OECD/DAC (1997) *Guidance on Conflict, Peace and Development*, Paris: OECD/DAC.
Orjuela, C. (2003) 'Building Peace in Sri Lanka: A Role for Civil Society', *Journal of Peace Research* 40: 195–212.
Orjuela, C. (2004) 'Civil Society in Civil War, Peace Work, and Identity Politics in Sri Lanka', Ph.D. dissertation, Department of Peace and Development Research, University Göteborg, Sweden.
Paffenholz, T. (1998) *Konflikttransformation durch Vermittlung. Theoretische und Praktische Erkenntnisse aus dem Friedensprozess in Mosambik (1995–1996)* [Conflict transformation via mediation. Theory and evidence from the Mozambican peace process] Mainz: Grünewald.
Paffenholz, T. (2009) 'Civil Society and Peacebuilding: Summary of Results of a Comprehensive Research Project', CCDP Working Paper 4, Geneva: Graduate Institute of International and Development Studies.

Paffenholz, T. (2010) (ed.) *Civil Society and Peacebuilding. A Critical Assessment*, Boulder: Lynne Rienner.

Paffenholz, T. and C. Spurk (2006) *Civil Society, Civic Engagement, and Peacebuilding*, Social Development Papers, Conflict Prevention and Reconstruction Paper No. 36. Washington, DC: World Bank.

Paffenholz, T. and Spurk, C. (2010) 'A Comprehensive Analytical Framework', in T. Paffenholz (ed.) *Civil Society and Peacebuilding. A Critical Assessment*, Boulder, CO: Lynne Rienner.

Paffenholz, T., D. Kew and A. Wanis-St. John (2006) 'Civil Society and Peace Negotiations: Why, Whether and How they Could be Involved', policy paper prepared for the 4th Oslo Forum for Senior Mediators, 25 May 2006, Geneva: Centre for Humanitarian Dialogue.

Paffenholz, T., C. Spurk, R. Belloni, S. Kurtenbach and C. Orjuela (2010) 'Enabling and Disenabling Factors for Civil Society Peacebuilding', in T. Paffenholz (ed.) *Civil Society and Peacebuilding. A Critical Assessment*, Boulder, CO: Lynne Rienner.

Paris, R. (2004) *At War's End: Building Peace After Civil Conflict*, reprint 2006, Cambridge: Cambridge University Press.

Pierce, J. (1998) 'From Civil War to "Civil Society": Has the End of the Cold War Brought Peace to Central America?', *International Affairs* 74(3): 587–615.

Pouligny, B. (2005) 'Civil Society and Post-Conflict Peacebuilding: Ambiguities of International Programmes Aimed at Building "New" Societies', *Security Dialogue* 36(4): 495–510.

Putnam, R. (1993) *Making Democracy Work: Civic Traditions in Modern Italy*, Princeton, NJ: Princeton University Press.

Ray, J. (1998) 'Does Democracy Cause Peace?', *Annual Review of Political Science* 1: 27–46.

Richmond, O. (2005) *The Transformation of Peace*, London: Palgrave Macmillan.

Rummel, R. J. (1997) *Power Kills: Democracy as a Method of Nonviolence*, New Brunswick, NJ: Transaction Books.

Russett, B. and H. Starr (2000) 'From Democratic Peace to Kantian Peace: Democracy and Conflict in the International System', in M. Mildarsky (ed.) *Handbook of War Studies*, Ann Arbor: University of Michigan Press, pp. 93–128.

Schmidt, S. (2000) 'Die Rolle von Zivilgesellschaften in Afrikanischen Systemwechseln' [The role of civil society in system transformation in Africa], in W. Merkel (ed.) *Systemwechsel 5. Zivilgesellschaft und Transformation*, Opladen: Leske and Budrich, pp. 295–334.

Senghaas, D. (2007), *On Perpetual Peace: A Timely Assessment*, New York: Berghahn.

Small, M. and J. Singer (1976) 'The War Proneness of Democratic Regimes, 1816–1965', *Jerusalem Journal of International Relations* 1 (Summer): 50–69.

Spurk, C. (2010) 'Understanding Civil Society', in T. Paffenholz (ed.) *Civil Society and Peacebuilding. A Critical Assessment*, Boulder, CO: Lynne Rienner, pp. 3–27.

Stewart, S. (1997) 'Happy Ever After in the Marketplace: Non-Governmental Organizations and Uncivil Society', *Review of African Political Economy* 24(71): 11–34.

Swedish International Development Agency (SIDA) (2007) *SIDA's Support to Civil Society in Development Cooperation*, Stockholm: SIDA.

United Nations (1992) *An Agenda for Peace: Preventive Diplomacy, Peacemaking and Peace-keeping*, Report of the Secretary-General, New York: United Nations.

United Nations (2005) *In Larger Freedom. Towards Development, Freedom and Human Rights for All*, Report of the Secretary General, New York: United Nations.

United Nations (2009) *Peacebuilding in the Immediate Aftermath of Conflict*, Report of the Secretary General, New York: United Nations.
USAID (2005) 'Increased Development of a Politically Active Civil Society', available at www.usaid.gov/our_work/democracy_and_governance/technical_areas/civil_society.
Van Tongeren, P., B. Malin, M. Hellema and J. Verhoeven (2005) *People Building Peace II: Successful Stories of Civil Society*, Boulder, CO: Lynne Rienner.
Xenias, A. (2005) 'Can a Global Peace Last Even if Achieved? Huntington and the Democratic Peace', *International Studies Review* 7(3): 357–386.
Zinecker, H. (2009) 'Regime-Hybridity in Developing Countries: Achievements and Limitations of New Research on Transitions', *International Studies Review* 11(2): 302–331.

PART III

Rethinking the Critique: What Next?

9

Alternatives to Liberal Peace?[1]

Roland Paris

Introduction

Based in part on the critiques of liberal peacebuilding which were outlined and discussed earlier in this collection (Roland Paris, 'Critiques of Liberal Peace'), there has been much written in recent years on the need to promote 'alternative versions of peace' that are not rooted in liberal peacebuilding models (for example, Mac Ginty 2008: 159; further examples are engaged with below). On the surface, such writers appear to reject the idea of liberal peacebuilding, but on closer examination many actually embrace variants of liberal peacebuilding. Few critics endorse terminating the practice of peacebuilding altogether, or abandoning its broadly liberal orientation.

The persistent appeal of liberal peacebuilding, even among many of its purported challengers, reveals two things. First, there is greater potential for conceiving of reforms within the liberal approach to peacebuilding than some of its critics seem to concede. If many of the proposed 'alternative' strategies (such as increasing the ability of local authorities to challenge the decisions of international officials) are themselves based in liberal principles, it follows that much of the critical literature is actually espousing variations within, rather than alternatives to, liberal peacebuilding. Liberalism is a broad canvas that can accommodate a wide range of political and economic structures as well as diverse methods for engaging with the inhabitants of war-shattered societies. Indeed, I suggest in this chapter that there is no realistic alternative to some form of liberal peacebuilding strategy.

Second, the apparent disjuncture between the discourse and content of many liberal peacebuilding critiques raises troubling questions about the current critical scholarship in this field. Is the rejection of liberal peacebuilding substantive or ritualistic? Is this rejection now considered a prerequisite of any 'genuinely' critical peacebuilding analysis? One hopes not. Critical scholarship is crucial to helping us understand the 'prevailing order' and how this order is reproduced (see Cox 1986: 208), including in the realm of peacebuilding. But in the absence of self-criticism, critical theory can devolve into dogmas that can be just as unthinking as other unquestioned orthodoxies.

While the turn to critical theory in this field has generated important insights over the past decade, nothing in the recent critical literature provides a convincing rationale for abandoning liberal peacebuilding or replacing it with a non-liberal or 'post-liberal' alternative. The literature does, however, reinforce the case for reforming current approaches to peacebuilding, without disavowing the broadly liberal orientation of these missions. Clarifying these points seems important, both for scholars of peacebuilding and for broader debates about the future of international assistance to war-torn states.

Liberals in Disguise?

Consider, for example, Michael Barnett's intriguing discussion of a possible 'republican' approach to peacebuilding, which he portrays as a much-needed 'alternative' to the liberal approach (2006). Republicanism is a better model for stabilising post-conflict states, he argues, because it prioritises substantive and continuous deliberation among members of the society. Deliberation need not be limited to democratic elections; in fact, it needs to take place between elections in order to encourage 'individuals to consider the views of others, generalize their positions to widen their appeal, find a common language, articulate common ends, demonstrate some detachment from the self, and subordinate the personal to the community' (ibid.: 98). This could have a taming effect on factional tensions, Barnett argues. Republicanism also emphasises the importance of representation, but in contrast to liberalism it is open to a wider variety of methods and types of representation than elected legislatures. Together, these and other features of republicanism offer a better basis 'for post-conflict stability by establishing the process for creating a legitimate state that is restrained in its ability to exercise arbitrary power and can minimize conflict among factions' (ibid.: 96).

All of this makes good sense, but whether Barnett's vision is truly an alternative to liberal peacebuilding is questionable. The distinction between liberalism and republicanism is, in reality, one of nuances. As Barnett notes, both philosophies rest on the values of 'liberty and the need to check the power of the sovereign through elections, representation, constitutions, and laws' (ibid.: 94). He is not calling for disengagement from war-torn states, nor for authoritarian forms of governance, nor for state-socialist forms of economic planning.

Barnett's vision is one of improved political participation and representation, all rooted in principles of individual freedom and accountable government. Thus, while his proposed strategy is interesting and compelling, it represents much less of an alternative to liberal peacebuilding than he suggests. In fact, Barnett hints at this when he acknowledges that liberalism and republicanism are frequently conflated and 'with good reason' (ibid.: 93).

David Chandler's critique of peacebuilding was described above ('Critiques of Liberal Peace', this volume). International actors, he argues, have taken a 'high handed approach' which has 'restricted . . . political party competition and policymaking by elected representatives' in the 'tiny postwar state of Bosnia' (2006b: 480). The result has been 'a situation where there is little accountability for the policy results of external rule' (2006a: 125). One of Chandler's central concerns, therefore, is not the liberal orientation of peacebuilding, but the illiberal behaviour of international administrators, including their relatively unconstrained and unaccountable exercise of power and methods that discourage local political activity and participation. Such criticisms are rooted in a distinctively liberal set of values, emphasising self-government, political participation and representation, and limitations on governmental power. Although he does not offer specific policy prescriptions, one apparent implication of his analysis is that peacebuilders should honestly acknowledge the gap between their stated liberal principles and their less-than-liberal actions, and that they should live up to the liberal principles they purport to espouse. Nevertheless, his writing has been wrongly interpreted as providing evidence that 'the liberal peace is in crisis' (Cooper 2007: 606).

Such misinterpretation would be less likely if Chandler and other deeper critics clearly explained what kinds of peacebuilding they would find more acceptable or effective. The purpose of seeking such clarification would not be to push every researcher into a 'problem-solving' mode of analysis,[2] but simply to clarify the nature and scope of each critique. If, for example, a given analyst's preferred alternative turned out to be another mode of international intervention that still embraced and promoted liberal values, this critique should not be interpreted as a rejection or indictment of either 'liberal peacebuilding' or the 'liberal peace'. Misinterpreting such critiques can have real effects: it may unnecessarily delegitimise the idea of liberal peacebuilding rather than focusing attention on the mode or methods of liberal peacebuilding.

Some responsibility therefore rests on individual authors to clarify their views on what, if anything, would constitute a better approach to peacebuilding. For example, what exactly would 'emancipatory' peacebuilding involve in practice (Duffield 2007: ch. 9; Pugh 2005)? Mark Duffield describes an emancipatory approach as one that enhances the 'solidarity of the governed' (2007: 234). Michael Pugh, for his part, suggests that it would involve greater 'participation of local actors' and more 'pro-poor engagement with local populations', which he contrasts to the 'subjugation' of the prevalent liberal model (2005). Who could disagree with appeals for emancipation, phrased in such vague terms? If these authors offered more specific recommendations, it would be possible to evaluate these alternative approaches in greater detail. It would also allow us to understand the degree to which these emancipatory approaches are genuinely distinct from liberal peacebuilding.

To confuse matters further, not all of the proponents of the emancipatory approach view it as distinct from liberal peacebuilding. Oliver Richmond, for instance, argues that the goal of 'emancipation' is actually integral to liberalism, but he maintains that current liberal approaches place insufficient weight on 'bottom up' policies and do not adequately empower individuals or free them from 'domination, and hegemony, as well as want' (2007: 461). When Richmond turns to prescriptions, however, he offers little more by way of detail than either Duffield or Pugh. Emancipatory peacebuilding, he says, would focus more on 'social welfare and justice' (2006: 301, 311) and embrace the ethic of 'human security' (2007). More precision would be welcome.

In spite of this lack of clarity, there are good reasons to take the concept of emancipatory peacebuilding seriously. Richmond correctly points out that 'liberal peacebuilding cannot succeed unless it achieves a broad consensus among its target population', and this may ultimately be connected to the idea of emancipation, depending on how the term is defined (2007: 460). As I shall argue below, more research is needed on the sources of local legitimacy in peacebuilding, including the challenge of incorporating mass publics and non-elites into post-conflict political and economic structures and directly into the management of international peacebuilding operations themselves. The concept of emancipatory peacebuilding may provide a framework for pursuing such efforts, but we will not know until this concept is elaborated and specified. When this happens, we may also discover that emancipatory peacebuilding is not really opposed to liberal peacebuilding at all.

Is There an Alternative to Liberal Peacebuilding?

In fact, there seems to be no viable alternative to some version of liberal peacebuilding. Consider, first, the question of whether international peacebuilding should be continued at all. Some commentators including Jeffrey Herbst (2003) and Jeremy Weinstein (2005) have suggested that conflicts should sometimes be allowed to burn themselves out, and that large-scale 'impartial' intervention (even after a ceasefire agreement) risks locking in conditions that are not sustainable or compatible with long-term peace. There is some logic to this approach, since wars ending in military victory may produce longer-lasting peace than those ending in negotiated settlements. But this strategy could also involve huge risks and costs: The victors might decimate the losers, or alternatively some wars might grind on for years or decades without resolution, all the while producing humanitarian crises before one side finally achieves victory. In the meantime, conflicts could spread to neighbouring territories, as several have done in Africa in recent years. On balance, then, failing to provide assistance when it is possible to do so, and when it is requested by local parties, would seem a short-sighted and dangerous solution to the shortcomings of these operations; just as suspending the practice of post-conflict peacebuilding would be a significant overreaction to the various problems that these missions have experienced and caused. Nor is there any sign of declining demand for new operations, given the increased trend for civil conflicts to end in negotiated settlements in recent years (HSP: 2008).

But why, in this case, must peacebuilding be liberal? The simple answer is that alternative strategies – that is, strategies not rooted in liberal principles – would likely create more problems than they would solve. One approach, for example, might be for international agencies to establish permanent trusteeships over war-torn states – that is, externally run governments that have no intention of ceding their authority to local actors. This option is not unlike the formula proposed by Stephen Krasner, who called for direct international governance of dangerously fragile states 'for an indefinite period of time' (2004). The main problem with this approach is that it would come very close to colonial-type control – indeed, much more so than even the most long-lasting and interventionist post-settlement missions that have been conducted to date. Maintaining such an arrangement over the long term would likely require permanent suppression of domestic political activity within the host state. As David Edelstein points out, even when foreign military deployments are made at the invitation of local parties, they face a problem of an 'obsolescing welcome' whereby elements of the local population tend to grow increasingly resentful of a powerful external presence in their society (2009). Continuing to embrace the objective of transferring full sovereign powers to local actors may thus be the single most important strategy for addressing this problem and for widening the 'window' of time available for peacebuilders to assist in strengthening domestic institutions within the host state. By contrast, establishing permanent foreign rule would reduce the time available for peacebuilders to do their work before local resentment begins to build and the peacebuilding mission becomes an obstacle to, rather than a facilitator of, the consolidation of a stable peace.

A second alternative to liberal peacebuilding might be for international agencies to identify local leaders who could rule as undemocratic strongmen over their society. This would, at least, provide a means for peacebuilders to scale back their presence quickly, as long as they continued to offer various types of support (financial, material, etc.) to the ruling person or party. Indeed, this was roughly that strategy that the US and Soviet Union pursued with their respective patrons in many parts of the world during the Cold War. However, one of the practical problems with this approach is that authoritarian regimes created and sustained by external parties have often turned out to be more fragile than they appear, in part because they tend to lack domestic legitimacy and therefore remain in power only by repressing or buying off their internal rivals. This was one of the lessons learned at the end of the Cold War, when a reduction or cessation of immense flows of superpower assistance led to the collapse of authoritarian regimes in Somalia, Zaire/Congo and elsewhere, followed by a violent scramble for power. Furthermore, in a country just emerging from civil war, where two or more factions were engaged in large-scale killing, a post-conflict 'strongman strategy' would risk alienating unrepresented groups that might choose to resume violence rather than living under the new regime. Some measure of power-sharing, or at least a reasonable prospect of gaining power through an unrigged political process, generally helps to mitigate this danger (Jarstad and Nilsson 2008; Goldstone and Ulfelder 2004).

A third alternative to liberal peacebuilding might be to rely on traditional or indigenous practices of peacemaking and governance, rather than elections and other accoutrements of liberal democracy. Roger Mac Ginty has usefully highlighted the limited space provided for such approaches in existing peacebuilding models, which tend to be 'highly standardized' and rooted in a sense of the 'superiority of Western approaches to peace-making' (2008: 144, 151). In contrast to the more formalistic and legalistic approaches, traditional and indigenous methods tend to focus on 'consensus decision-making, a restoration of the human/resource balance, and compensation or gift exchange designed to ensure reciprocal and ongoing harmonious relations between groups' (ibid.: 149). Because they reflect local customs, he adds, these techniques may 'hold the potential to achieve a grass-roots legitimacy that may be lacking from more technocratic "alien" forms of dispute resolution that form the mainstay of Western-funded and designed peace-support programs and projects' (ibid.: 155).

While Mac Ginty makes a strong case for adapting policies to local conditions and traditions (using examples such as Afghanistan's Loya Jirgas, or tribal assemblies, which played an important role in that country's initial transition from Taliban rule), he does not recommend relying exclusively on such techniques. On the contrary, he wisely warns of the danger of romanticising traditional or indigenous practices – not least because they may serve to reinforce 'the authority of existing power-holders' and to impose 'social conformity', sometimes in brutal ways (ibid.: 150). Tanja Chopra's analysis of local peacebuilding initiatives in Kenya offers a cautionary tale illustrating these dangers. Efforts to tap into traditional conflict-resolution techniques through community-level 'peace committees' in Kenya have shown some success, but in some cases they have also served to 'deepen existing rifts between communities' and 'reinforce divisions' while also undermining concurrent efforts to strengthen respect for the rule of law at the national level (2009). Traditional and bottom-up approaches, in other words, should be part of peacebuilding, but they are no panacea.

There are other reasons to be cautious before embracing traditional governance methods. Those who believe that doing so will eliminate or reduce the intrusion of foreign peacebuilders in the domestic affairs of the host state fail to recognise that peacebuilders will still need to make crucial choices, whether they wish to do so or not. No society has a single, unambiguous set of governance structures (traditional or otherwise) that can be automatically activated. Consequential decisions must therefore be made to privilege some structures and not others – and, as much as peacebuilders might view themselves as referees in such decisions, in fact they will always be 'players' simply by virtue of their relative power in the domestic setting of a war-torn state (de Waal 2009). In any event, some measure of external influence may be necessary and desirable: if the post-conflict society could organise its own governance arrangements without international assistance, there would have been no need or demand for peacebuilding in the first place.

Given all this, consider the implications if international agencies were to adopt a general policy of relying on indigenous governance structures in post-conflict countries. Very likely, any political outcomes of this process would be questioned and contested due to perceived international 'interference', no matter how well-meaning and diligent the peacebuilders were in seeking to remain neutral. Further, in cases where one individual or group dominated such a process, the result could be the equivalent of the second alternative to liberal peacebuilding discussed above – strongman rule – with all the problems associated with that option. These are all real concerns that counsel caution. Yet in spite of these risks and complexities, experience in Afghanistan, Cambodia and elsewhere suggests that more research attention needs to be devoted to the topic of hybrid arrangements in countries recovering from conflict, or approaches those that blend formal, informal, modern and customary methods of governance and conflict resolution (Debiel et al. 2009; Roberts 2009; Zinecker 2009).

It is also interesting that Mac Ginty argues that one of the benefits of customary arrangements could be to enhance 'political participation', while he also warns against the dangers of authoritarianism. Such arguments suggest that Mac Ginty, like other commentators discussed above, is less concerned with the liberal orientation of current peacebuilding approaches than he is with their relative rigidity and lack of adaptability to local conditions. In fact, there is nothing in the idea of the 'liberal peace' or 'liberal peacebuilding' that mandates such inflexibility. Liberal polities come in many different styles and forms, from group-based 'consociational' proportional representation arrangements to Anglo-American-style plurality systems, and there is nothing to prevent liberalism from accommodating new models. Nor does support for liberal political principles stand in the way of pursuing any number of complementary initiatives and goals, including those focusing on post-conflict reconciliation (Baglione 2008), social welfare and justice (Richmond 2006: 311; Tadjbakhsh 2009: 648), extensive public deliberations at the national and local levels (Papagianni 2009), or the empowerment and inclusion of women and other marginalised groups (Lidén 2009: 621). The key principles of liberalism – individual freedoms, representative government and constitutional limits on arbitrary power – offer a broad canvas for institutional design and creative policymaking.

Without clear alternatives, some version of liberalism therefore remains the most sensible foundation for post-conflict peacebuilding. The overarching goal of such missions should be to create the conditions for representative self-government, not only because such an outcome is the least morally objectionable goal for peacebuilding, but also for the practical purpose of facilitating the eventual departure of peacebuilders through the restoration of domestic sovereignty over the territory. Further, while the importance of elections alone should not be exaggerated, they remain a crucial tool for populations to constitute their own governments, not only during the period of peacebuilding, but on an ongoing basis (Sisk 2009). While it is true that encouraging elections itself involves an external intrusion in the internal affairs of the host state, surely we can differentiate between more and less acceptable intrusions – including the fact that elections are meant to facilitate the society's ability to shape its own destiny and exercise self-government, so that the peacebuilders themselves can leave. Elections alone cannot achieve this goal; nor do elections equal democracy. But of all the possible ways in which international actors can influence the domestic politics of a country, the idea of promoting self-government is one of the least troubling – and, from the standpoint of not overstaying an 'obsolescing welcome', it may be a pragmatic necessity.

Similarly, while certain economic liberalisation strategies can be destabilising (see Paris 2004: 166–168, 199–205), is there really an alternative to some version of market-oriented reform in states emerging from war? The second half of the twentieth century demonstrated that centrally planned and state-dominated development strategies – including not only Soviet-style communism but also import substitution strategies pursued in many parts of Latin America and Africa – generally produced lower levels of economic growth than market-oriented development strategies. Debates continue about the appropriate balance between the market and the state in economic development, including greater regulation of financial institutions and the like, but there is near-universal agreement today that non-market-oriented economic policies (or those that do not give the market a primary role in allocating scarce resources) are too inefficient to generate sustained economic growth. Most of those who have criticised the economic dimensions of liberal peacebuilding (including this author) have called for less aggressive adjustment strategies in order to reduce the destabilising effects of rapid marketisation, but have not rejected the idea of economic liberalisation itself – in part because economic growth is important to the long-term success of peacebuilding (Sambanis 2008). Although there is no guarantee that states pursuing market-oriented development policies will become richer, there is a near guarantee that those pursuing non-market-oriented strategies will stay poor.

There is no single, market-oriented model appropriate for all peacebuilding cases. Rather, there are countless variations of liberal economic policies that can be explored and pursued (Williams 2005: 170). But all share one thing in common: a primary orientation toward markets as a foundation for long-term growth. If existing economic policies have been ill-suited to the needs of war-torn states, it is not because these policies have been 'liberal' or market-oriented in the broad sense of these terms, but rather, because they have paid too little attention to the particular vulnerabilities of countries just emerging from destructive and divisive conflicts, including the potentially destabilising effects of 'shock therapy' adjustment policies (Stewart 2006). Addressing such problems primarily involves altering and customising, not abandoning, the economically liberal elements of peacebuilding.

Conclusion: Saving Liberal Peacebuilding

If there is no realistic or preferable alternative to broadly liberal approaches, what can be done in the face of the current 'crisis' of liberal peacebuilding? The first step is to question the extent to which this crisis is real or imagined. Earlier in this volume ('Critiques of Liberal Peace'), I attempted to show that some of the most sweeping critiques of liberal peacebuilding have rested on dubious claims and logic, including the conflation of post-conquest and post-settlement peacebuilding; un-nuanced analogies of peacebuilding and colonialism or imperialism; definitions of the liberal peace that are too broad; mischaracterisations of the peacebuilding record; and oversimplifications of the moral complexity of peacebuilding.

The 'crisis' of liberal peacebuilding has therefore been much exaggerated. The challenge today is not to replace or move 'beyond' liberal peacebuilding, but to reform existing approaches within a broadly liberal framework. This enterprise has both conceptual and policy elements. Peacebuilding remains ripe for theoretical treatments that shed light on the meaning and effects of these operations. In other words, the peacebuilding literature need not, and should not, be limited to narrowly policy-oriented or 'problem-solving' analyses. In the 1990s, most of the peacebuilding literature was preoccupied with practical policy issues and paid little attention to the relationships between peacebuilding and larger phenomena in international politics. The rise of more critical analysis since then has been part of a welcome broadening of the field, which now places greater emphasis on exploring the theoretical underpinnings and implications of these missions. The great strength of critical approaches has always been their focus on exposing and dissecting widely held assumptions and orthodoxies. But critical scholarship can lose its intellectual and empirical moorings if it fails to be self-reflective and self-critical – that is, if its logic, evidence and implications are not themselves subject to scrutiny and challenge. Nothing in the recent critical literature offers a convincing rationale for abandoning liberal peacebuilding, rather than reforming it. If anything, the rise of what I have called hyper-critical scholarship – and particularly its dubious yet seemingly ritualised rejection of liberal peacebuilding – has served to cloud rather than clarify our understanding of what peacebuilding is, and what it does.

Of course, there is no single 'best' way of analysing these missions or the broader phenomenon of international peacebuilding. This field of research is – and hopefully will remain – a diverse bazaar of different theoretical and empirical approaches, open to discussion and debate across intellectual traditions and methodologies. This chapter has sought to contribute to this debate by arguing for a rethinking and rebalancing of liberal peacebuilding critiques. In contrast to the unconvincing hyper-criticism of today, or the irrational exuberance of earlier years, a more constructively critical approach might build on the recognition that: (1) both liberalism and liberal peacebuilding are deeply problematic concepts – in theory and application – and their internal contradictions play themselves out in peacebuilding, sometimes in troubling and destructive ways; (2) liberally oriented peacebuilding can, in principle, accommodate a great deal of internal variation and adjustment, including many of the specific changes proposed by many critics; (3) scholars who repudiate liberal peacebuilding or call for 'alternative' strategies should be expected to reflect carefully on the normative underpinnings of their own arguments and to clarify the alternatives they may be proposing, including the moral and practical implications of pursuing these alternatives. The third point should be particularly important for those who believe that critical peacebuilding scholarship has a useful contribution to make to the field – and that the recent turn towards a reflexive antiliberalism has diminished the force of these critiques.

Adopting a constructively critical orientation does not mean accepting the current practices of peacebuilding. It does not mean that peacebuilding must be 'top-down' instead of 'bottom-up' – that is a criticism of centralism, not liberalism. It does not mean that peacebuilding should be fixated on formal institutions to the exclusion of informal or customary methods of governance – that is a criticism of formalism, not liberalism. It does not mean that peacebuilders should adopt a 'fixed, non-negotiable concept of what the state should eventually look like' (Eriksen 2009: 663) – that is a criticism of institutional isomorphism, not liberalism. Nor does it mean that peacebuilders should assume that liberalisation will necessarily foster peace – that is a criticism of naïve Wilsonianism, one variant of liberalism (Paris 2004). Addressing all of these real problems may entail probing the internal tensions of liberalism, but it does not require a sweeping rejection of liberal peacebuilding.

In fact, there are many recent examples of constructively critical research that raise important theoretical and practical questions, some of which challenge liberal premises without making the mistake of discarding the baby with the bathwater. For instance: what are the sources and dynamics of 'legitimacy' in international peacebuilding (Talentino 2009; Mitchell 2008; Coleman 2007)? What obligations, if any, do international actors have in rebuilding societies after conflict (Gheciu and Welsh 2009)? What are the limits of external democracy promotion efforts (Tansey 2007; Ohlson and Kovacs 2009)? How might 'non-elite' populations of host states be included more directly into peace negotiations and post-conflict institutional reform (Papagianni 2009; Zartman 2008; Samuels 2009)? What is the relationship between power-sharing arrangements and peace (Norris 2008; Jarstad and Nilsson 2008; Jarstad 2008; Hartzell and Hoddie 2007)? How might ideas of 'local ownership' be developed in a manner that avoids simplistic bromides about the need for greater local ownership or emancipation (Goodhand and Sedra 2010; Donais 2009; Chesterman 2007; Narten 2009)?

Other questions include: How do 'discursive frames' and organisational procedures shape the design and conduct of peacebuilding in practice (Autesserre 2009; Paris 2003; Barnett 1997)? How can peacebuilding agencies learn from experiences across missions without falling into the trap of assuming that 'technical' knowledge is readily transferrable across diverse local circumstances (Piiparinen 2007; Barnett 2005)? Why does the UN seem to make peacebuilding commitments that it subsequently fails to fulfil in practice (Lipson 2007)? What are the economic impacts of peacebuilding operations (Carnahan et al. 2007; Cramer 2009)? What is the relationship between 'peace conditionalities' in economic assistance and the durability of the ensuing peace (Emmanuel and Rothchild 2007)? How can economic liberalisation be pursued in ways that minimise the dangers of strengthening black markets (Rose-Ackerman 2008)? Under what circumstances should peacebuilding missions end, and how should they 'exit' (Caplan 2006; Zaum 2007)?

This is just a small sampling of research questions that represent a broad mix of normative approaches. They point to even larger unresolved questions, including the crucial issue of how one should define peacebuilding 'success' (Call 2008). Many of these research efforts also offer the possibility of making peacebuilding operations more effective, and more just, in the future.

In the end, however, whichever research paths one may choose to follow, those engaged in constructively critical analysis have an immense task ahead of them: peacebuilding is tremendously complex and prone to unanticipated consequences, yet it is also too important to lose or abandon. As long as both scholars and practitioners embrace an open discussion of peacebuilding's merits and flaws, without descending into unwarranted hyper-criticism, there is still hope of improving both the conception and delivery of international assistance to societies embarking on difficult transitions from war to peace.

Notes

1 An extended version of this chapter was published as 'Saving Liberal Peacebuilding', *Review of International Studies*, 36 (2010), pp. 3337–3365, and the material is republished with kind permission.

2 In principle, however, there is no reason why 'critical' theorising cannot provide useful insights into 'what to do' questions (see Price 2008).

Bibliography

Autesserre, S. (2009) 'Hobbes and the Congo: Frames, Local Violence, and International Intervention', *International Organization* 63: 249–280.

Baglione, L. A. (2008) 'Peacebuilding: A Time to Listen and Learn from Reconciliationism', *Polity* 40(1): 120–135.

Barnett, M. N. (1997) 'The UN Security Council, Indifference, and Genocide in Rwanda', *Cultural Anthropology* 12(4): 551–678.

Barnett, M. N. (2005) 'Illiberal Peacebuilding and Liberal States', paper presented at the Roundtable on Humanitarian Action, New York, Social Science Research Council, 8 February.

Barnett, M. N. (2006) 'Building a Republican Peace: Stabilizing States After War', *International Security* 30(4): 87–112.

Call, C. T. (2008) 'Knowing Peace When You See It: Setting Standards for Peacebuilding Success', *Civil Wars* 10(2): 173–194.

Caplan, R. (2006) 'After Exit: Successor Missions and Peace Consolidation', *Civil Wars* 8(3): 253–267.

Carnahan, M., S. Gilmore and W. Durch, W. (2007) 'New Data on the Economic Impact of UN Peacekeeping', *International Peacekeeping* 14(3): 384–402.

Chandler, D. (2006a) *Empire in Denial: The Politics of Statebuilding*, London: Pluto.

Chandler, D. (2006b) 'Back to the Future? The Limits of Neo-Wilsonian Ideals of Exporting Democracy', *Review of International Studies* 32(3): 475–494.

Chesterman, S. (2007) 'Ownership in Theory and Practice: Transfer of Authority in UN Statebuilding Operations', *Journal of Intervention and Statebuilding* 1(3): 3–26.

Chopra, T. (2009) 'When Peacebuilding Contradicts Statebuilding: Notes from the Arid Lands of Kenya', *International Peacekeeping* 16(4): 531–545.

Coleman, K. P. (2007) *International Organisations and Peace Enforcement: The Politics of International Legitimacy*, Cambridge: Cambridge University Press.

Cooper, N. (2007) 'Review Article: On the Crisis of the Liberal Peace', *Conflict, Security and Development* 7(4): 605–616.
Cox, R. (1986) 'Social Forces, States and World Orders: Beyond International Relations Theory', in R. O. Keohane (ed.) *Neorealism and Its Critics*, New York: Columbia University Press, pp. 204–254.
Cramer, C. (2009) 'Trajectories of Accumulation through War and Peace', in R. Paris and T. D. Sisk (eds) *The Dilemmas of Statebuilding: Confronting the Contradictions of Postwar Peace Operations*, London: Routledge, pp. 129–148.
De Waal, A. (2009) 'Mission without End? Peacekeeping in the African Political Marketplace', *International Affairs* 85:1: 99–113.
Debiel, T., R. Glassner, C. Schetter and U. Terlinden (2009) 'Local State-Building in Afghanistan and Somaliland', *Peace Review* 21(1): 38–44.
Donais, T. (2009) 'Empowerment or Imposition? Dilemmas of Local Ownership in Post-Conflict Peacebuilding Processes', *Peace and Change* 34(1): 3–26.
Duffield, M. (2007) *Development, Security and Unending War*, London: Polity.
Edelstein, D. (2009) 'Foreign Militaries, Sustainable Institutions, and Postwar Statebuilding', in R. Paris and T. D. Sisk (eds) *The Dilemmas of Statebuilding: Confronting the Contradictions of Postwar Peace Operations*, London: Routledge, pp. 81–103.
Emmanuel, N. and D. Rothchild (2007) 'Economic Aid and Peace Implementation: The African Experience', *Journal of Intervention and Statebuilding* 1(2): 171–188.
Eriksen, S. S. (2009) 'The Liberal Peace Is Neither: Peacebuilding, State Building and the Reproduction of Conflict in the Democratic Republic of Congo', *International Peacekeeping* 16(5): 652–667.
Gheciu, A. and J. Welsh (eds) (2009) 'Postwar Justice and the Responsibility to Rebuild', special issue, *Ethics and International Affairs* 23(3).
Goldstone, J. A. and J. Ulfelder (2004) 'How to Construct Stable Democracies', *Washington Quarterly* 28(1): 9–20.
Goodhand, J. and M. Sedra (2010) 'Who Owns the Peace: Aid, Reconstruction, and Peacebuilding in Afghanistan', *Disasters* 34(1): 78–102.
Hartzell, C. and M. Hoddie (2007) *Crafting Peace: Power Sharing and the Negotiated Settlement of Civil Wars*, University Park, PA: Penn State University Press.
Herbst, J. (2003) 'Let Them Fail: State Failure in Theory and Practice: Implications for Policy', in R. I. Rotberg (ed.) *When States Fail: Causes and Consequences*, Princeton, NJ: Princeton University Press.
HSP (2008) Human Security Project, *Human Security Brief 2007*, Vancouver, BC: Simon Fraser University, Human Security Project.
Jarstad, A. K. (2008) 'Power Sharing: Former Enemies in Joint Government', in A. K. Jarstad and T. D. Sisk (eds) *From War to Democracy: Dilemmas of Peacebuilding* Cambridge: Cambridge University Press, pp. 105–133.
Jarstad, A. K. and D. Nilsson (2008) 'From Words to Deeds: The Implementation of Power-Sharing Pacts in Peace Accords', *Conflict Management and Peace Science* 25(3): 206–223.
Krasner, S. D. (2004) 'Sharing Sovereignty. New Institutions for Collapsed and Failing States', *International Security* 29(2): 85–120.
Lidén, K. (2009) 'Building Peace between Global and Local Politics: The Cosmopolitical Ethics of Liberal Peacebuilding', *International Peacekeeping* 16(5): 616–635.
Lipson, M. (2007) 'Peacekeeping: Organized Hypocrisy?', *European Journal of International Relations* 13(1): 5–34.

Mac Ginty, R. (2008) 'Indigenous Peace-Making Versus the Liberal Peace', *Cooperation and Conflict* 43(2): 139–163.

Mitchell, C. (2008) 'The Limits of Legitimacy: Former Loyalist Combatants and Peace-Building in Northern Ireland', *Irish Political Studies* 23(1): 1–19.

Narten, J. (2009) 'Dilemmas of Promoting Local Ownership: The Case of Postwar Kosovo', in R. Paris and T. D. Sisk (eds) *The Dilemmas of Statebuilding: Confronting the Contradictions of Postwar Peace Operations*, London: Routledge, pp. 252–283.

Norris, P. (2008) *Driving Democracy: Do Power-Sharing Institutions Work?*, Cambridge: Cambridge University Press.

Ohlson, T. and M. S. Kovacs (2009) 'Peace Through Democracy? The Challenges of Post-War Democratization in Weak and War-Torn States', in A. Swain, R. Amer and J. Öjendal (eds) *The Democratization Project: Challenges and Opportunities*, London: Anthem Press, pp. 165–182.

Papagianni, K. (2009) 'Transitional Politics in Post-Conflict Countries: The Importance of Consultative and Inclusive Political Processes', *Journal of Intervention and Statebuilding* 3(1): 47–63.

Paris, R. (2003) 'Peacekeeping and the Constraints of Global Culture', *European Journal of International Relations* 9(3): 441–473.

Paris, R. (2004) *At War's End: Building Peace After Civil Conflict*, Cambridge: Cambridge University Press.

Piiparinen, T. (2007) 'Putting the Cart before the Horse: Statebuilding, Early Warning and the Irrationality of Bureaucratic Rationalization', *Journal of Intervention and Statebuilding* 1(3): 355–378.

Price, R. (2008) 'Moral Limit and Possibility in World Politics', *International Organization* 62: 191–220.

Pugh, M. (2005) 'The Political Economy of Peacebuilding: A Critical Theory Perspective', *International Journal of Peace Studies* 10(2): 23–42.

Richmond, O. P. (2006) 'The Problem of Peace: Understanding the "Liberal Peace"', *Conflict, Security and Development* 6(3): 291–314.

Richmond, O. P. (2007) 'Emancipatory Forms of Human Security and Liberal Peacebuilding', *International Journal* 62(3): 459–477.

Roberts, D. (2009) 'The Superficiality of Statebuilding in Cambodia: Patronage and Clientelism as Enduring Forms of Politics', in R. Paris and T. D. Sisk (eds) *The Dilemmas of Statebuilding: Confronting the Contradictions of Postwar Peace Operations*, London: Routledge, pp. 149–169.

Rose-Ackerman, S. (2008) 'Corruption and Government', *International Peacekeeping* 15(3): 328–343.

Sambanis, N. (2008) 'Short- and Long-Term Effects of UN Peace Operations', *World Bank Economic Review* 22(1): 9–32.

Samuels, K. (2009) 'Constitutional Choices and Statebuilding in Postconflict Countries', in R. Paris and T. D. Sisk (eds) *The Dilemmas of Statebuilding: Confronting the Contradictions of Postwar Peace Operations*, London: Routledge, pp. 173–195.

Sisk, T. D. (2009) 'Pathways of the Political: Electoral Processes after Civil War', in R. Paris and T. D. Sisk (eds) *The Dilemmas of Statebuilding: Confronting the Contradictions of Postwar Peace Operations*, London: Routledge, pp. 196–223.

Stewart, F. (2006) 'Policies towards Horizontal Inequalities in Post-Conflict Reconstruction', World Institute for Development Economics Research, UN University, Research Paper, No. 2006/149, November.

Tadjbakhsh, S. (2009) 'Conflicted Outcomes and Values: (Neo)Liberal Peace in Central Asia and Afghanistan', *International Peacekeeping* 16(5): 635–651.

Talentino, A. K. (2009) 'Nation Building or Nation Splitting? Political Transition and the Dangers of Violence', *Terrorism and Political Violence* 21(3): 378–400.

Tansey, O. (2007) 'The Concept and Practice of Democratic Regime-Building', *International Peacekeeping* 14(5): 633–646.

Weinstein, J. (2005) "Autonomous Recovery and International Intervention in Comparative Perspective', Working Paper 57, Washington, DC: Center for Global Development.

Williams, P. D. (2005) 'International Peacekeeping: The Challenges of Statebuilding and Regionalization', *International Affairs* 81(1): 163–175.

Zartman, J. (2008) 'Negotiation, Exclusion and Durable Peace: Dialogue and Peacebuilding in Tajikistan', *International Negotiation* 13(1): 55–72.

Zaum, D. (2007) 'The Politics of Exit: Transition and Exit from Post-Conflict Statebuilding Operations', paper presented at the annual conference of the American Political Science Association, Chicago, IL, August.

Zinecker, H. (2009) 'Regime-Hybridity in Developing Countries: Achievements and Limitations of New Research on Transitions', *International Studies Review* 11(2): 302–331.

10

The Uncritical Critique of 'Liberal Peace'[1]

David Chandler

Introduction

Since the late 1990s, commentators have developed critical frameworks of the 'liberal peace' to understand the new, more interventionist, approaches to the problems of post-conflict rebuilding and the threat of state failure (see, for example, Duffield 2001; Paris 2002; Pugh 2005; Richmond 2005; Richmond and Mac Ginty 2007). In essence, the 'liberal peace' is held to go beyond traditional approaches of conflict prevention, or 'negative peace': towards the external engineering of post-conflict societies through the export of liberal frameworks of 'good governance', democratic elections, human rights, the rule of law and market relations (see Richmond 2008a). As Alex Bellamy summarises: 'The principal aim of peace operations thus becomes not so much about creating spaces for negotiated conflict resolution between states but about actively contributing to the construction of liberal polities, economies and societies' (Bellamy 2008: 4–5). The critical discourse of the liberal peace flags up the problem that, under the guise of universalising Western liberal frameworks of democracy and the market, the needs and interests of those subject to intervention are often ignored, resulting in the maintenance of inequalities and conflicts and undermining the asserted goals of external interveners. The critique of international intervention and statebuilding, framed by the construction of the liberal peace, has been highly effective in challenging assumptions of easy fixes to post-conflict situations (see, for example, Chesterman et al. 2005; Dobbins et al. 2007; Paris and Sisk 2009a).

This chapter seeks to forward an alternative framework and to question the use of the 'liberal peace' rubric to describe and analyse post-conflict and international statebuilding interventions in the post-Cold War period. It will be argued that the critique of liberal peace bears much less relation to policy practice than might be assumed by the critical (radical and policy) discourses and, in fact, appears to invert the relationship between the critique of the liberal peace and the dominant policy assumptions. The shared desire to critique the liberal peace leads to a set of assumptions and one-sided representations that portray Western policy-interventions as too *liberal*: too fixated on Western models and too keen to allow democratic freedoms and market autonomy. It will be explained here that this view of 'liberal' interventions transforming post-conflict societies through 'immediate' liberalisation and 'rapid democratization and marketization' is a self-serving and fictional policy narrative (Paris 2004: 235). This narrative fiction is then used, in the frameworks of policy-orientated critiques, as the basis upon which to reflect upon Western policy and to limit policy expectations (while often extending regulatory controls) on the basis that the aspirations of external interveners were too ambitious, too interventionist and too 'liberal' for the states and societies which were the subject of intervention.

It is unfortunate that this policy narrative can appear to be given support by more radical critiques of post-Cold War intervention, similarly framed through the critique of liberal peace. For example, Oliver Richmond is not exceptional in re-reading the catastrophe of the invasion and occupation of Iraq in terms of an 'attempt to mimic the liberal state', which has 'done much to discredit the universal claims of the transferability of the liberal peace in political terms' (Richmond 2008b: 458). Michael Barnett argues that 'liberal values' clearly guide peacebuilding activities and that their 'explicit goal' is 'to create a state defined by the rule of law, markets and democracy' (Barnett 2006: 88). Beate Jahn has argued that 'the tragedy of liberal diplomacy' lies in the ideological drive of liberalism, in which intervention is intensified despite the counter-productive results (Jahn 2007a, 2007b). Foucaultian-inspired theorists, Michael Dillon and Julian Reid, similarly reinforce the claims that the key problematic of intervention is its liberal nature in their assertion that we are witnessing a liberal drive to control and to regulate the post-colonial world on the behalf of neoliberal or biopolitical power, seeking 'to globalize the domesticating power of civil society mechanisms in a war against all other modes of cultural forms' (Dillon and Reid 2009).

This view of a transformative drive to regulate and control the post-colonial world on the basis of the liberal framings of power and knowledge stands in stark contrast to the policy world, in which, by the end of the Cold War, leading policy institutions were already highly pessimistic of the capacities of non-liberal subjects to cope with liberal political, economic and social forms and suspicious of even East and Central European states coping with democracy and the market, let alone those of sub-Saharan Africa. Bringing the critique back in relation with the policy practices seems to suggest that the policy critics of the liberal peace offer succour and consolation to the policy-makers rather than critique. This leads to the concern of this chapter that more radical critiques of the liberal peace may need to ensure that they are not drawn into a framework in which their critical intentions may be blunted.

There are many different approaches taken to the critique of liberal peace approaches; nevertheless, for heuristic purposes, it will be useful to frame these diverse critiques within two broad, distinctive, but often interconnected, approaches, which are here categorised as the radical, 'power-based', and the more policy-orientated, 'ideas-based', critiques. The former approach tends to see the discourse of liberal peace as an ideological and instrumental one, arguing that the rhetoric of freedom, markets and democracy is merely a representation of Western self-interest, which has little genuine concern for the security and freedoms of those societies intervened in. The latter approach suggests that rather than the concepts being misused, in the discursive frameworks of the projection of Western power, the problem lies less with power relations than with the universal conceptualising of the liberal peace itself.

The 'Power-based' Critique

In this framework, the liberal peace is critiqued on the basis that it reflects the hegemonic values and the political, economic and geo-strategic needs of Western states. This critique focuses on the role played by the interests of Western powers in shaping policy and the impact of the economic and structural inequalities of the world economy. It also pays attention to the naturalising of policy assumptions based upon this perspective. There are three main versions of this power-based perspective.

Firstly, there is a critical approach which tends to engage with a Left or neo-Marxist structural critique of liberal peace approaches. This framing suggests that Western intervention is inevitably reproducing hierarchies of power due to the structural constraints of neoliberal market relations – opening up societies and economies through the demands for democratisation and the free market (for example, Pugh 2005; also Pugh et al. 2008). This approach focuses on the problems of neoliberal economic policies for the reconstruction of post-conflict societies and suggests that, in serving the interests of dominant Western powers and the international financial institutions, the policies of the liberal peace inevitably reproduce the conditions and possibilities for conflict (see also Abrahamsen 2000; Barbara 2008; Cramer 2006; Jacoby 2007).

This approach often draws upon Robert Cox's critical theory to suggest that the narrow problem-solving approach taken by Western policy-makers is problematic as it takes for granted the interests of these actors and treats market-based economic solutions as merely technical 'problem-solving' approaches to address problems of post-conflict development (see Cox 1981). These critical approaches to the liberal peace suggest that it is necessary to reflect on these assumptions to reveal the power interests that lie behind them and to question the presentation of these policies in policy-neutral technical terms (see, for example, Bellamy 2008). Michael Pugh, for example, has consistently highlighted how neoliberal economic practices are naturalised as technical solutions to development and reconstruction, marginalising or preventing political discussions of economic alternatives better suited to post-conflict societies (2005; also Pugh et al. 2008).

Secondly, there is a more Foucaultian structuralist approach, which critiques the 'liberal peace' not so much on the liberal basis of its interventionary policies per se as on the interests behind these policies: understood as perpetuating the needs and interests of liberal, neoliberal or biopolitical capitalism in the West. Mark Duffield has pioneered this approach in his 2001 book *Global Governance and the New Wars*. Here the focus is less on the opening up of non-Western economies to the world market and more on the reshaping and transformation of these societies in order to prevent instability. In his 2001 work, Duffield argued that the project of 'liberal peace reflects a radical development agenda of social transformation' with the aim 'to transform the dysfunctional and war-affected societies that it encounters on its borders into cooperative, representative and, especially, stable entities' (2001: 11).

This transformative liberal intervention has necessitated the radicalisation of both development and security discourses, giving the external institutions of global governance new mandates to: 'shift the balance of power between groups and even to change attitudes and beliefs' (2001: 15). In his later work, Duffield expands on this framework of the projection of liberal interests in stabilising 'zones of conflict' through the use of the Foucaultian conception of biopolitics, where intervention is understood as saving, developing, or securing the Other, at the same time legitimising and extending external regulatory control (Duffield 2007; see also Dillon and Reid 2009; Jabri 2007). Duffield argues that in the interests of stabilising the neoliberal economic order, the divisions between the 'developed' and the 'undeveloped' world are reproduced through policies of containment such as 'sustainable' or 'community-based' development.

The third approach engages from the approach of critical theory and human security. Like the first approach, it highlights that 'liberal peace' policies should be seen as political and power-based, rather than as purely technical solutions (for example, Bellamy, 2008). However, the focus is less on the assumptions about market relations or securing the needs of global neoliberal or biopolitical power and more on the assumptions made about the political and institutional framework and positivist and rationalist forms of Western knowledge. For writers such as Alex Bellamy, a central concern is the problematic focus on the rebuilding of Westphalian state forms; for Oliver Richmond, the focus is on the liberal assumptions of political community assumed in the approach of 'liberal peace', which tends to ignore vital local concerns of identity and culture (for example, Richmond 2008a).

The power-based approaches in this third category clearly take on board the concerns over universalising Western liberal assumptions which will be dealt with in the following section, sketching the 'ideas-based' critiques. However, they are classed within the first category as the conception of Western 'power' still plays a vital role. Unlike the first two approaches, these more subjective or constructivist frameworks of critique suggest that frameworks of liberal peace, projected through Western power, can be successfully challenged by other more reflective, emancipatory or 'bottom-up' approaches to liberal peace; suggesting that there is not necessarily a clash of interests between those intervening and those intervened upon (Richmond 2008b: 462). Some commentators from within this perspective would argue that elected Western politicians could pursue alternative polices by constructing their interests in a more enlightened way, for example, through pursuing more human security orientated policies, which could be conceived as in Western self-interest, in a globalised and interconnected world, or that non-state actors may be able to intervene in ways which engage more equally and empathetically with those on the ground (see Tadjbakhsh and Chenoy 2007; Maclean et al. 2006).

The 'Ideas-based' Critique

The 'ideas-based' critique of liberal peace presents itself as a critique of the grounding universalising assumptions of the liberal policy discourse itself, rather than merely as a critique of the forms of its implementation. These critics of liberal peace advocate less liberal frameworks of intervention, with less attention to the reconstruction of sovereign states, democracy and the free market. While upholding the values of democracy and the free market aspirationally, these critics argue against the liberal peace approach on the basis that it is unsuitable in the context of post-conflict states and situations of state failure.

This approach tends to focus on the problem of Western interventionist 'ideas' or 'values' rather than on interests or power relations. While their critique of the liberal peace thesis therefore may appear to be more radical, their intentions can also be understood as more conservative or policy-orientated. Rather than problematising relations of power or the interests behind policymaking, there is a tendency to view the liberal peace approach as a projection of Western ideals in a context where they can be counterproductive. This critique has been developed by Jack Snyder (2000), Fareed Zakharia (2003), Stephen Krasner (2004, 2005), Robert Keohane (2002, 2003), and Roland Paris (2004), amongst others, who argue that liberal peace assumptions have undermined the effectiveness of international statebuilding.

One of the core liberal assumptions problematised in this approach is that of sovereign statehood. These critics argue that focusing on (re)constructing sovereign states is unlikely to solve the problems of post-conflict societies, merely to reproduce them. Krasner argues that sovereignty is problematic for many states because they lack the capacity for good governance and require an external regulatory framework in order to guarantee human rights and the rule of law (2004: 89; see also Fearon and Laitin 2004). Robert Keohane forwards a similar perspective with differing levels of statehood applicable to different levels of governance capacity: 'We somehow have to reconceptualise the state as a political unit that can maintain internal order while being able to engage in international co-operation, without claiming exclusive rights . . . traditionally associated with sovereignty' (2003: 277).

Pursuing a similar approach, Paris argues that the assumptions of the liberal peace – that democracy and the free market will ensure social progress and stability – neglect to consider the problematic nature of transition. Questioning the assumption that 'liberalization fosters peace', Paris advocates less emphasis on interventionist policies which promote democracy and the market, both of which can encourage competition and conflict without adequate institutional frameworks (2004: 40–51). Instead, Paris advocates a policy of 'Institutionalization before Liberalization' in order to establish the regulatory frameworks necessary to ensure that post-conflict societies can gradually (and safely) move towards liberal models of market democracy (ibid.: 179–211; see also Huntington 1968; Chandler 2006b).

These critics of liberal peace do not argue that they are anti-liberal; merely that liberalism, as projected in liberal peace frameworks, has to take into account the non-liberal context in which intervention takes place. Fareed Zakharia, for example, argues that while in the West we have historically associated liberalism and democracy, in much of the non-Western world we have to make a choice between liberalism and democracy as, without the institutional framework of limited government, 'elections provide a cover for authoritarianism' and are 'merely legitimized power grabs'; in this context, therefore, 'what Africa needs more than urgently than democracy is good governance' (2003: 98–99; see also Snyder 2000).

This critique of the liberal peace is that, rather than being based on the needs and interests of Western hegemonic powers and international financial institutions, the problem is one of projecting an idealised understanding of the West's own historical development; one which tends to naturalise the smooth working of the market and understand liberal political frameworks as an organic product of democratic processes such as free elections. For these critics, the founding assumptions of the liberal peace are the problem: attempts to universalise Western models in non-liberal contexts will merely reproduce, and maybe even exacerbate, the problems of conflict and instability.

A 'Critical' Consensus?

This chapter seeks to argue that the radical intent of the critics of interventionist Western policies has been blunted by their articulation within the problematic of a 'liberal peace', enabling their critique to be assimilated into the policy discourse of how policy might be reformed and legitimated in the wake of the discrediting of the claims of Western policy-making after the debacles of Iraq and Afghanistan. The two fairly distinct critical framings of the 'liberal peace' stem from very different methodological perspectives and political and policy intents. While the 'ideas-based' critics tend to seek to defend and legitimate regulatory external intervention, the 'power-based' critics tend to challenge and oppose these frameworks as the projection of Western power and interests. Nevertheless, in critiquing Western policy interventions, developed since the end of the Cold War, within the problematic of 'liberal peace' it seems that there is often much less distance between the radical approaches and the policy approaches than might be assumed on the basis of political intent and occasionally there is a surprisingly large area of confluence.

The critique of liberalism as a set of assumptions and practices seems to be driving the approach to the study of post-Cold War interventions in ways which have tended to produce a fairly one-sided framework of analysis in which the concept of liberalism is ill-equipped to bear the analytical weight placed upon it and appears increasingly emptied of theoretical or empirical content. Liberalism appears to be used promiscuously to explain a broad range of often contradictory policy perspectives and practices across very differing circumstances and with very differing outcomes. In this sense, it appears that liberalism operates as a 'field of adversity' (see Foucault 2008: 106) through which a coherent narrative of post-Cold War intervention has been articulated both by critical and policy-orientated theorists. The promiscuous use of liberalism to explain very different policy approaches is, of course, facilitated by the ambiguous nature of the concept itself.

It is this ambiguity which enables liberalism to be critiqued from opposing directions, sometimes by the same author at the same time. Good examples of this are Roland Paris and Timothy Sisk who criticise 'liberal' peacebuilding for being both too laissez-faire and too interventionist in its approach to the regulation and management of conflict. In the peacebuilding literature today, the experience of the early and mid-1990s and the 'quick exit' policies of the 'first generation' peacebuilding operations in Namibia, Nicaragua, Angola, Cambodia, El Salvador, Mozambique, Liberia, Rwanda, Bosnia, Croatia and Guatemala have been repackaged as evidence that Western interveners had too much faith in the liberal subject (see, for example, Paris and Sisk 2009b). Similarly, the ad hoc responses to the problems of the early 1990s in the development of 'second generation' peacebuilding with protectorate powers in Bosnia, Kosovo and East Timor have been criticised as liberal hubris, on the assumption that international overlords could bring democracy, development and security to others. It seems that, rather than adding clarity, the critique of the 'liberalism' of intervention tells us very little.

The mechanism through which these liberal framings have been facilitated and critiqued is that of the discursive centring of the non-liberal Other; on whose behalf the policy critics assert the need for different policy practices. In this way, the policy critics of past policy approaches evade a direct critique of liberal assumptions about equality, autonomy and transformative capacity, arguing instead that the non-liberal Other (in various ways) invalidates, challenges or resists (passively as well as actively) policy practices which may otherwise have been less problematic.

Rather than criticising liberalism for its inability to overcome social, economic and cultural inequalities, both the policy, 'ideas-based', critique of the liberal peace and the more radical, 'power-based', critiques argue that social, economic and cultural inequalities and differences have to be central to policy practices and invalidate universalising liberal attempts to reconstruct and rebuild post-conflict societies. In this context — in which the dichotomy between a liberal policy-making sphere and a non-liberal sphere of policy intervention comes to the fore — there is an inevitable tendency towards a consensual framing of the problematic of statebuilding or peacebuilding intervention as a problem of the relationship between the liberal West and the non-liberal Other.

The rock on which the liberal peace expectations are held to crash is that of the non-liberal Other. The non-liberal Other increasingly becomes portrayed as the barrier to Western liberal aspirations of social peace and progress; either as it lacks the institutional, social, economic and cultural capacities that are alleged to be necessary to overcome the problems of liberal peace or as a subaltern or resisting subject, for which liberal peacebuilding frameworks threaten their economic or social existence or fundamental values or identities. The 'critique' becomes apology in that this discursive focus upon the non-Western or non-liberal Other is often held to explain the lack of policy success and, through this, suggest that democracy or development are somehow not 'appropriate' aspirations or that expectations need to be substantially lowered or changed to account for difference.

International Statebuilding and the Critique of Liberalism

It would appear that the assumptions held to be driving liberal peace approaches are very much in the eye of their critical beholders. The most obvious empirical difficulty is that international policy regarding intervention and statebuilding seems to have little transformative aspiration: far from assumptions of liberal universalism, it would appear that, with the failure of post-colonial development, especially from the 1970s onwards, international policy-makers have developed historically low expectations about what can be achieved through external intervention and assistance. The lack of transformative belief is highlighted by one of the key concerns of the policy critics of the liberal peace – the focus on capacity-building state institutions and intervening to construct 'civil' societies. The focus on institutional solutions (at both the formal and informal levels) to the problems of conflict and transition is indicative of the narrowing down of aspirations from transforming society to merely regulating or managing it – often understood critically as the 'securitising' of policy-making. This is a long way from the promise of liberal transformation and the discourse of 'liberating' societies economically and politically.

In fact, it is the consensus of opinion on the dangers of democracy which has informed the focus on human rights and good governance. For the policy and radical critics of liberal peace, liberal rights frameworks are often considered problematic in terms of the dangers of exclusion and extremism. Today's 'illiberal' peace approaches do not argue for the export of democracy – the freeing up of the political sphere on the basis of support for popular autonomy. The language of illiberal institutionalist approaches is that of democratisation: the problematisation of the liberal subject, held to be incapable of moral, rational choices at the ballot box, unless tutored by international experts concerned to promote civil society and pluralist values. In these frameworks, the holding of elections serves as an examination of the population and the behaviour of electoral candidates, rather than as a process for the judgement or construction of policy (which it is assumed needs external or international frameworks for its production).

The focus on institutionalism does not stem from a critique of liberal peace programmes; institutionalist approaches developed from the 1970s onwards and were rapidly mainstreamed with the end of the Cold War. From 1989 onwards, Western governments and donors have stressed that policy interventions cannot just rely on promoting the freedoms of the market and democracy, but need to put institutional reform and 'good governance' at the core (see, for example, World Bank 1989, 1992, 1997, 1998). Even in relation to Central and Eastern Europe it was regularly stressed that the people and elected representatives were not ready for freedom and that it would take a number of generations before it could be said that democracy was 'consolidated' (for example, Dahrendorf 1990). The transitology literature was based on the critique of liberal assumptions – this was why a transitional period was necessary. Transition implied that markets and democracy could not work without external institutional intervention to prevent instability. While markets needed to be carefully managed through government policy-making it was held that civil society was necessary to ensure that the population learnt civic values to make democracy viable (see, for example, Fukuyama 1995; Schmitter and Karl 1991; O'Donnell 1996; Gunther et al. 1996).

It was through the engagement with 'transition' and the problematic negotiation of European Union enlargement that the discursive framework of liberal institutionalism – where human rights, the 'rule of law', civil society and anti-corruption are privileged over democracy – was programmatically cohered. It was also through the discussion of 'transition' that the concept of sovereign autonomy was increasingly problematised, initially in relation to the protections for minority rights and then increasingly expanded to cover other areas of domestic policy-making (see, for example, Cordell 1998). It would appear that the key concepts and values of the 'liberal peace' held to have been promoted with vigour with the 'victory of liberalism' at the end of the Cold War were never as dominant a framing as their radical and policy critics have claimed.

Rather than attempting to transform non-Western societies into the liberal self-image of the West, it would appear that external interveners have had much more status quo aspirations, concerned with regulatory stability and regional and domestic security, rather than transformation. Rather than imposing or 'exporting' alleged liberal Western models, international policy making has revolved around the promotion of regulatory and administrative measures which suggest the problems are not the lack of markets or democracy but rather the culture of society or the mechanisms of governance. Rather than promoting democracy and liberal freedoms, the discussion has been how to keep the lid on or to manage the 'complexity' of non-Western societies, usually perceived in terms of fixed ethnic and regional divisions. The solution to the complexity of the non-liberal state and society has been the internationalisation of the mechanisms of governance, removing substantive autonomy rather than promoting it.

While it is true that the reconstruction or rebuilding of states is at the centre of external projects of intervention, it would be wrong to see the project of statebuilding as one which aimed at the construction of a liberal international order: the states being constructed in these projects of post-conflict and failed state intervention are not liberal states in the sense of having self-determination and political autonomy. The state at the centre of statebuilding is not the 'Westphalian state' of classical IR theorising. Under the internationalised regulatory mechanisms of intervention and statebuilding the state is increasingly reduced to an administrative level, in which sovereignty no longer marks a clear boundary line between the 'inside' and the 'outside' (see Walker 1992). Whether we consider EU statebuilding, explicitly based on a sharing of sovereignty, or consider other statebuilding interventions, such as those by the international financial institutions in sub-Saharan Africa, it is clear that the state is central as a mechanism for external coordination and regulation rather than as a self-standing actor in so-called 'Westphalian' terms (see Ghani and Lockhart 2008; also Harrison 2004; Chandler 2006a).

Too Liberal?

Empirically, the radical critics of liberal peace may be correct to argue that external policies of intervention – which operate at the formal level of exporting human rights frameworks, the rule of law and mechanisms of 'good governance' – marginalise the people of these societies. This, however, is not the same as arguing that this is because the frameworks of intervention are too *liberal*. At the empirical level it is unproblematic to argue that the result of these external programmes of intervention might be seen as 'façade democracy' or as 'reproducing state failure' (Chopra 2003; Bickerton 2007) or to highlight that Western policy aspirations have little purchase on very different realities and often therefore result in 'hybrid polities' where the state formally accords to Western norms but informally still operates on the basis of traditional hierarchies and exclusions (Roberts 2008).

Where this critical discourse becomes problematic is in the confidence with which its proponents assert that the reasons for these policy failings can be located in the liberalism of the interveners or the illiberalism of the subjects of intervention. Roland Paris, for example, argues that 'there is no logical requirement for international agencies to resurrect failed states *as states*, rather than [as] some other type of polity', and argues that this is the 'latest chapter in the globalisation of the Westphalian state', where this state form is being propped up despite its failings (Paris 2002: 654). Paris argues that just as the non-liberal Other cannot deal with the liberal state form, they are similarly ill-suited to handle electoral democracy, warning particularly against the holding of elections in post-conflict situations. It is asserted that holding elections when societies are still divided or segmented will be counterproductive, often giving enhanced legitimacy to warring parties and bolstering the legitimacy of the forces successful in conflict. Often the solutions advocated by the policy critics are along similar lines with regard to both sovereignty and democracy: the need for greater international engagement in the state institutions, under the guise of guaranteeing that no voices are 'excluded' and the need to constrict the autonomy of elected authorities. Under the rubric of the critique of the liberal peace, these critics of the liberal peace often advocate the reform of policy interventions away from the focus on liberal rights frameworks and electoral democracy.

When it comes to aspirations of development and modernisation, there has been a similar lowering of horizons through the discursive critique of liberal universalism, similarly centred on allegedly empowering and giving 'voice' to the needs and concerns of the non-liberal Other. In this regard, it is often difficult to tell the policy perspectives apart from the viewpoints of some of the more radical critics of the liberal peace. There is a danger that liberalism is criticised not for its inability to universalise economic growth and overcome the problems of combined and uneven development, but for the aspirations of development itself. For example, Michael Pugh asserts that rather than the 'economic rationalism of (capitalistic) entrepreneurship', other, 'non-liberal', values need to be taken into account. Following the work of those critical of liberal development models, such as Amartya Sen (see Sen 1999), he argues that in non-liberal societies:

> Inequalities and non-physiological needs are considered more significant than either absolute poverty or, beyond a survival point, physiological needs. This means that provided people are not destitute . . . they may choose to live humbly in order to be fulfilled. Such an approach recognises that the paths to modernisation may not be convergent at all, and the marginalised peoples of the world are entitled to choose the extent to which, and how, they integrate in the global economy. (Pugh 2005: 34)

It would seem that at the core of the policy and radical critiques of the liberal peace is a critique of liberal aspirations rather than a critique of international interventionist policies and practices. The critique reflects the ease with which liberalism has become a 'field of adversity', through which both policy reform and critical claims for theoretical advance can both be made. The construction of a liberal 'field of adversity' seems to have little relation to policy realities. This is reflected in the fact that, while there is a consensus on the view that Western policies are problematic in that they are too liberal, there is much less attention to how the problems of the post-colonial world might be alternatively addressed. Here, as discussed below, the discursive critique of the liberal peace unfortunately has very little to offer in ways that go beyond present policy perspectives.

Beyond the Critique of the Liberal Peace?

It would appear that the ostensibly more radical critics, those who draw out the problematic nature of power relations – the 'power-based' critiques above – in fact, have very little to offer as a critical alternative to the current policies of intervention and statebuilding, other than a scaling back of the possibilities of social change. The leading critics of the liberal peace, like Mark Duffield, Michael Pugh and Oliver Richmond, working through critical theoretical frameworks which problematise power relations and highlight the importance of difference, suggest that the difference between the liberal West and the non-liberal Other cannot be bridged through Western policy-making. For Pugh, as we have seen above, taking critical theory to its logical conclusion, capitalist rationality is itself to be condemned for its universalising and destabilising impulses. Similarly, for Duffield, it seems that the problem of hegemonic relations of power and knowledge cannot be overcome, making any projection of the ideals of development or democracy potentially oppressive (see 2007: 215–234). Oliver Richmond has systematised this perspective, highlighting the problems of the disciplinary forms of knowledge of 'liberal peace' approaches and suggesting that while it may be possible to go beyond them through the use of post-positivist and ethnographic approaches – enabling external interveners to have a greater access to the knowledge of 'everyday life' in non-liberal societies being intervened in – any attempt to know, rather than merely to express 'empathy', is open to hegemonic abuse (2008a: 149–165).

It would appear that, without a political agent of emancipatory social change, the radical 'power-based' critics of liberal peace who draw upon the perspectives of critical theory cannot go beyond the bind which they have set themselves, of overcoming hegemonic frameworks of knowledge and power. In fact, it could be argued that these critical approaches, lacking the basis of a political subject to give content to critical theorising, ultimately take an uncritical approach to power. Power is assumed rather than theorised, making the limits to power appear merely as external to it. It is assumed that there is an attempt to transform the world in liberal terms and that the failure to do so can therefore be used to argue that liberal forms of knowledge are inadequate ones. The critique is not essentially of power or of intervention but of the limited knowledge of liberal interveners. The alternative is not that of emancipatory social transformation but of the speculative and passive search for different, non-liberal, forms of knowledge or of knowing. This comes across clearly in the conclusions reached by Duffield, Richmond and others, and highlights the lack of a critical alternative embedded in these approaches.

The more ostensibly conservative critics of the liberal peace, drawn largely to the policy-making sphere, have much clearer political aims in their critique. This is manifest in their focus on institutional reform, understood as a way of reconciling non-liberal states and societies both to the market and to democratic forms. This, like the transitology discourse before it, is a radical critique of classical liberal assumptions. In their advocacy of these frameworks, discursively framed as a critique of the 'liberal peace', they have a clear point of reference, although, as highlighted above, this point of reference is a fictional one: a constructed narrative of post-Cold War intervention, which enables them to ground the scaling-back of policy expectations against a framework of allegedly unrealistic liberal aspirations.

The institutionalist discourse of intervention and regulation is not one of liberal universalism and transformation but one of restricted possibilities, where democracy and development are hollowed out and, rather than embodying the possibilities of the autonomous human subject, become mechanisms of control and ordering. Institutionalisation reduces law to an administrative code, politics to technocratic decision-making, democratic and civil rights to those of the supplicant rather than the citizen, replaces the citizenry with civil society, and the promise of capitalist modernity with pro-poor poverty reduction. To conceptualise this inversion of basic liberal assumptions and ontologies as 'liberalism' would be to make the word meaningless at the same time as claiming to stake everything on the assumed meaning and stakes involved in the critique of the 'liberal' peace.

Conclusion

The critique of the liberal peace is based upon the assumption that Western intervention is too 'liberal'. The fact that it is too liberal is alleged to be revealed in its lack of success on the ground: in its failure to achieve liberal outcomes. For the policy critics, the sources of this failure are held to be located in the non-liberal nature of the societies intervened in. In the dominant policy framing of interventionist agendas, this failing is because of the lack of capacity of domestic societies and political elites; for more radical readings, the problematic impact of external policy-making is often re-read as the resistance of indigenous ways of life and knowledges, which should instead be understood and empathised with.

If the critique of intervention is for its liberalism, then it suggests that the self-image of the West is being projected where it cannot work. The critique can easily flatter the self-understanding of liberal interveners that if they are incapable of transforming the post-conflict societies and failing states that they are engaged with, it is merely because they cannot easily be anything other than liberal and because the societies being intervened in are not ready for liberal frameworks of governance. This critique, can, in fact, result in the reproduction of the ideological binary of the civilisational divide between the interveners and the states intervened in, which is seen to be confirmed the more that interventionist approaches appear to have little impact and to have to be scaled back.

There are a number of problems with the critical construction of 'liberal peace'. These stem not merely from the fact that the interventionist policies being critiqued seem to be far from 'liberal'. Of greater concern is the way that the term 'liberal' appears to have become an easy and unproblematic assertion of critical intent. The critique of the 'liberal peace' – and its ability to encompass both policy advocates and radical critics of intervention – appears to reveal much more about the problematic state of radical and liberal thought than it does about the policies and practices of intervention and statebuilding. The ostensible framework of the 'liberal peace' – of the transformative dynamic ontology of the universal rational subject – had already long since been critiqued and displaced by the framework of governance and regulatory power. It is peculiar, in these circumstances, that the dominant policy discussion and the radical discursive framing of post-Cold War intervention should both therefore take this form.

While apologetic intent can perhaps be reasonably applied to some critics working within policy-making circles and attempting to justify the continuation and revamping of current policy framings, this charge cannot so easily be placed at the feet of those articulating more 'power-based' critiques of the liberal peace. The fact that the radical critique of the 'liberal peace' should reproduce framings similar to those of the policy-orientated institutionalist critique of liberal peace highlights the use of the liberal paradigm as a 'field of adversity' to give coherence to radical frameworks of critique. However, in focusing on the target of liberalism rather than on the policy practices and discourses themselves, there is a danger that radical criticism can be enlisted in support of the institutionalist project, which seeks to rewrite the failures of post-Cold War intervention as a product of the universalising tendencies of a liberal approach and suggests that we should give up on the liberal aspirations of the past on the basis of an appreciation of the irreconcilable 'difference' of the non-liberal subject.

Notes

1 An extended earlier version of this article was published as 'The Uncritical Critique of Liberal Peace', *Review of International Studies* 36 (2011) Special Issue: Evaluating Global Orders, pp. 37–155, and the material is republished with kind permission.

Bibliography

Abrahamsen, R. (2000) *Disciplining Democracy: Development Discourse and Good Governance in Africa*, London: Zed Books.
Barbara, J. (2008) 'Rethinking Neo-liberal State Building: Building Post-Conflict Development States', *Development in Practice* 18(3): 307–318.
Barnett, M. (2006) 'Building a Republican Peace: Stabilizing States after War', *International Security* 30(4): 87–112.
Bellamy, A. (2008) 'The "Next Stage" in Peace Operations Theory', in A. Bellamy and P. Williams (eds) *Peace Operations and Global Order*, London: Routledge, pp. 17–38.
Bickerton, C. J. (2007) 'State-building: Exporting State Failure' in C. J. Bickerton, P. Cunliffe and A. Gourevitch (eds) *Politics without Sovereignty*, London: University College Press, pp. 93–111.

Chandler, D. (2006a) *Empire in Denial: The Politics of State-Building*, London: Pluto Press.
Chandler, D. (2006b) 'Back to the Future? The Limits of Neo-Wilsonian Ideals of Exporting Democracy', *Review of International Studies* 32(3): 475–494.
Chesterman, S., M. Ignatieff and R. Thakur (eds) (2005) *Making States Work: State Failure and the Crisis of Governance*, New York: United Nations University Press.
Chopra, J. (2003) 'Building State Failure in East Timor', in J. Milliken (ed.) *State Failure, Collapse and Reconstruction*, Oxford: Blackwell, pp. 223–243.
Cordell, K. (ed.) (1998) *Ethnicity and Democratisation in the New Europe*, London: Routledge.
Cox, R. W. (1981) 'Social Forces, States and World Orders', *Millennium: Journal of International Studies* 10(2): 126–155.
Cramer, C. (2006) *Why Civil War Is Not a Stupid Thing: Accounting for Violence in Developing Countries*, London: Hurst.
Dahrendorf, R. (1990) *Reflections on the Revolution in Europe: In a Letter Intended to Have Been Sent to a Gentleman in Warsaw, 1990*, London: Chatto & Windus.
Dillon, M. and J. Reid (2009) *The Liberal Way of War: Killing to Make Life Live*, London: Routledge.
Dobbins, J., S. G. Jones, K. Crane and B. Cole DeGrasse (2007) *The Beginners' Guide to Nation-Building*, Santa Monica, CA: RAND Corporation.
Duffield, M. (2001) *Global Governance and the New Wars: The Merging of Development and Security*, London: Zed Books.
Duffield, M. (2007) *Development, Security and Unending War: Governing the World of Peoples*, Cambridge: Polity.
Fearon, J. D. and D. D. Laitin (2004) 'Neotrusteeship and the Problem of Weak States', *International Security* 28(4): 5–43.
Foucault, M. (2008) *The Birth of Biopolitics: Lectures at the Collège de France 1978–1979*, Basingstoke: Palgrave Macmillan.
Fukuyama, F. (1995) 'The Primacy of Culture', *Journal of Democracy* 6(1): 7–14.
Ghani, A. and C. Lockhart (2008) *Fixing Failed States: A Framework for Rebuilding a Fractured World*, Oxford: Oxford University Press.
Gunther, R., N. P. Diamandouros and H.-J. Puhle (1996) 'Debate: Democratic Consolidation: O'Donnell's "Illusions": A Rejoinder', *Journal of Democracy* 7(4): 151–159.
Harrison, G. (2004) *The World Bank and Africa: The Construction of Governance State*, London: Routledge.
Huntington, S. (1968) *Political Order in Changing Societies*, New Haven, CT: Yale University Press.
Jabri, V. (2007) *War and the Transformation of Global Politics*, Basingstoke: Macmillan.
Jacoby, T. (2007) 'Hegemony, Modernisation and Post-War Reconstruction', *Global Society* 21(4): 521–537.
Jahn, B. (2007a) 'The Tragedy of Liberal Diplomacy: Part One', *Journal of Intervention and Statebuilding* 1(1): 87–106.
Jahn, B. (2007b) 'The Tragedy of Liberal Diplomacy: Part Two', *Journal of Intervention and Statebuilding* 1(2): 211–229.
Keohane, R. O. (2002) 'Ironies of Sovereignty: The European Union and the United States', *Journal of Common Market Studies* 40(4): 743–763.
Keohane, R. O. (2003) 'Political Authority after Intervention: Gradations in Sovereignty', in J. L. Holzgrefe and R. O. Keohane (eds) *Humanitarian Intervention: Ethical, Legal and Political Dilemmas*, Cambridge: Cambridge University Press, pp. 275–298.

Krasner, S. (2004) 'Sharing Sovereignty: New Institutions for Collapsing and Failing States', *International Security* 29(2): 5–43.
Krasner, S. (2005) 'The Case for Shared Sovereignty', *Journal of Democracy* 16(1): 69–83.
Maclean, S. M., D. R. Black and T. M. Shaw (eds) (2006) *A Decade of Human Security: Global Governance and New Multilateralisms*, Aldershot: Ashgate.
O'Donnell, G. (1996) 'Illusions about Consolidation', *Journal of Democracy* 7(2): 34–51.
Paris, R. (2002) 'International Peacebuilding and the "Mission Civilisatrice"', *Review of International Studies* 28(4): 637–656.
Paris, R. (2004) *At War's End: Building Peace after Civil Conflict*, Cambridge: Cambridge University Press.
Paris, R. and T. D. Sisk (eds) (2009a) *The Dilemmas of Statebuilding: Confronting the Contradictions of Postwar Peace Operations*, London: Routledge.
Paris, R. and T. D. Sisk (2009b) 'Introduction: Understanding the Contradiction of Postwar Statebuilding', in R. Paris and T. D. Sisk (eds) *The Dilemmas of Statebuilding: Confronting the Contradictions of Postwar Peace Operations*, London: Routledge, pp. 1–20.
Pugh, M. (2005) 'The Political Economy of Peacebuilding: A Critical Theory Perspective', *International Journal of Peace Studies* 10(2): 23–42.
Pugh, M., N. Cooper and M. Turner (eds) (2008) *Whose Peace? Critical Perspectives on the Political Economy of Peacebuilding*, Basingstoke: Macmillan.
Richmond, O. P. (2005) *The Transformation of Peace*, Basingstoke: Macmillan.
Richmond, O. P. (2008a) *Peace in International Relations*, London: Routledge.
Richmond, O. P. (2008b) 'Reclaiming Peace in International Relations', *Millennium: Journal of International Studies* 36(3): 439–470.
Richmond, O. P. and R. Mac Ginty (eds) (2007) Special Issue 'The Liberal Peace and Post-War Reconstruction', *Global Society* 21(4).
Roberts, D. (2008) 'Hybrid Polities and Indigenous Pluralities: Advanced Lessons in Statebuilding from Cambodia', *Journal of Intervention and Statebuilding* 2(1): 63–86.
Schmitter, P. C. and T. L. Karl (1991) 'What Democracy Is . . . and Is Not', *Journal of Democracy* 2(3): 4–17.
Sen, A. (1999) *Development as Freedom*, Oxford: Oxford University Press.
Snyder, J. (2000) *From Voting to Violence: Democratization and Nationalist Conflict*, New York: W. W. Norton.
Tadjbakhsh, S. and A. M. Chenoy (2007) *Human Security: Concepts and Implications*, London: Routledge.
Walker, R. B. J. (1992) *Inside/Outside: International Relations as Political Theory*, Cambridge: Cambridge University Press.
World Bank (1989) *Sub-Saharan Africa: From Crisis to Sustainable Growth: A Long-Term Perspective Study*, Washington, DC: World Bank.
World Bank (1992) *Governance and Development*, Washington, DC: World Bank.
World Bank (1997) *The State in a Changing World: World Development Report, 1997*, New York: Oxford University Press.
World Bank (1998) *Assessing Aid: What Works, What Doesn't, and Why. A World Bank Policy Research Report*, New York: Oxford University Press.
Zakharia, F. (2003) *The Future of Freedom; Illiberal Democracy at Home and Abroad*, New York: W. W. Norton.

11

A Reality Check for the Critique of the Liberal Peace

Shahar Hameiri

Introduction

Arguably, few ideas in history have reached a hegemonic status on par with the liberal peace thesis in the early years of the post-Cold War era. While dating back to early Enlightenment thinkers like Kant, Locke and Adam Smith, the notion that liberal-democratic polities are both internally and internationally pacific had experienced an incredible revival in the closing decades of the twentieth century. The liberal peace thesis was updated and expounded by a slew of eminent scholars (Doyle 1986; Russett 1993) and publicly endorsed by many national and international policymakers in the post-Cold War era, most notably United Nations (UN) Secretary-General Boutros-Ghali (1992) in *An Agenda for Peace*. Perhaps more importantly, however, the liberal peace thesis is strongly reflected in the stated objectives of peacebuilding and statebuilding interventions, which have become ubiquitous since the 1990s (Paris and Sisk 2009).

The challenge to the liberal peace thesis began as a trickle in the early years of the new millennium, with Duffield's (2001) and Chandler's (2002) scathing critiques of Western humanitarian interventions and development assistance. In the past five or so years, however, the critique of liberal peacebuilding has turned into a veritable flood (e.g. Paris 2004; Chesterman 2005; Richmond 2005; Bellamy et al. 2004; Pugh 2005). These scholars have investigated the validity of the core assumptions of the liberal peace thesis, variously criticising its normative, political and empirical claims, while highlighting the contradictions inherent in the liberal peace project as reflected in the international peacebuilding agenda.

Indeed, liberal peacebuilding appears to be in crisis (Paris 2010; Cooper 2007). With the majority of peacebuilding and statebuilding interventions apparently failing to meet their objectives (OECD 2006), it could be argued that the critique has been so successful as to become the new mainstream – peacebuilding's own post-Washington consensus. The ideological decline of the liberal peace is manifested in the public pronouncements of leading policymakers from the world's major states and international organisations. Strident proclamations of a new world order have more recently been replaced with cautious, even anxious deliberations on the limits of Western power (Chandler 2009). Nevertheless, the premises of the post-liberal peacebuilding consensus, if there is one, remain far from clear, as critics are in fundamental disagreement over whether the values and assumptions of liberal peacebuilding are inherently flawed or whether it is only implementation that has to be improved (Newman et al. 2009: 13; Cooper 2007: 606; Richmond 2009: 61).

The critique of the liberal peace has played an essential and important role in debunking what was always an ideologically constituted and ahistorical argument. In this manner it has opened up important debates over the desirability and form of international interventionism, as well as over the very nature of peace and how it could (or should) be realised. Yet, where the critique of the liberal peace has failed is in explaining the social and political outcomes of contemporary interventions. So concerned have the critics been with deconstructing the liberal peace that they have almost invariably focused on what is *not* occurring – the liberal peace, or one or other alternative to it they would prefer – rather than on what *is* occurring through contemporary interventions. There is generally a deficit of analytical rigour applied to theorising the actual forms of political rule emerging through interventions. Any discussion of alternative pathways must be established, however, on an analysis of how these interventions affect state, society and political agency in both intervening and intervened countries, which itself requires a historically grounded analysis of how these modes of intervention have developed. Indeed, rather than understanding the outcomes of statebuilding interventions in terms of a failed liberal peace or statehood, we need a different vocabulary that does not portray situations on the ground as deficient specimens of something else, but as deserving explanation in their own right. To understand how these interventions affect political rule we must not assume a priori that they are simply vehicles for delivering liberal governance to non-liberal states and societies. We must also break free from the 'methodological nationalism' or 'territorial trap' that underlies the concepts used in the critique.

I begin with the observation that whether or not peacebuilding or statebuilding interventions achieve their stated objectives they are transformative of both targeted and intervening states, leading to the emergence of a transnationalised and transnationally regulated form of statehood. This new kind of disaggregated statehood is not a temporary or easily reversible phenomenon, but the product of historical processes associated with the shift in the West from the post-war Keynesian settlement to the neoliberal regulatory state, of which contemporary statebuilding interventions are both manifestation and facilitator. Indeed, because contemporary interventionism is associated with the contested emergence of anti-competitive forms of governance within Western states, it is problematic to view this phenomenon in terms of the idea of the liberal peace. Furthermore, I argue that it makes little sense to think of these interventions in terms of a clash between external and domestic actors, institutions and values, seen mainly through the 'liberal' versus 'non-liberal' prism. Rather, spaces of interventions are located within the governing and policy apparatus of the state and are therefore part of the state. Contemporary interventions are also typically very diffuse, involving a very large number of actors – public, private and nongovernmental. This complexity creates a problem of description and analysis that is compounded by the unfortunate disjuncture between state theory and the literature on peacebuilding and statebuilding.

To overcome this problem I define contemporary interventions through the concept of 'multilevel regime' (Hameiri 2010: 50–57). The notion of regime refers to historically specific constellations of social and political forces, institutions and ideas that work to routinise particular political outcomes (Pempel 1998; Jayasuriya and Rosser 2006). The intervention regimes I examine are not internal to one state but are simultaneously found within and outside the state, comprising several levels of intervention at once. These regimes have emerged due to the contradictory efforts of interveners to preserve the formal sovereignty of states while simultaneously seeking to limit the political choices available to domestic leaders and citizens. What the concept of multilevel regime highlights is that notionally 'domestic' actors, institutions or social and political forces can be part of this regime at particular historical moments, and that various, even seemingly unlikely, coalitions can emerge around particular issues. Therefore, the main fault-line of conflict shaping the political outcomes of contemporary peacebuilding or statebuilding interventions is not between outsiders and locals, but between competing regimes within the state (Hameiri 2010).

The significance of this observation is apparent if we examine the case of Cambodia – one of the longest-running cases of international intervention. The statebuilding agenda is often seen to challenge the powerful patronage networks that support the Cambodian government. Yet, Prime Minister Hun Sen and his followers have been very adept at using it to marginalise social and political oppositions and strengthen an increasingly authoritarian form of political rule, which combines far-reaching patronage networks with internationalised policymaking processes. Hun Sen has turned the donors' emphasis on building state capacity, which critics have rightly argued allows for the exercise of power without accountability (Chandler 2009; Pender 2007), into a political advantage. With donors increasingly preoccupied with programme coherence and being seen to support country-ownership, Hun Sen and his cohorts in government have been able to argue that the failure of particular projects and programmes results from donors' incoherent aid delivery. Ultimately we see that in Cambodia both patronage and statebuilding regimes are highly complementary in curbing political pluralism.

Critiques of the Liberal Peace and their Limitations

In the past decade the liberal peace thesis and liberal peacebuilding have come under increasing critical scrutiny. This critique could be crudely divided into two main camps roughly along the lines of Cox's (1981) famous distinction between 'problem-solving' and 'critical' approaches. On the one hand there are scholars like Paris, Sisk and Newman who are generally comfortable with the liberal peace as a goal for interveners but are nevertheless critical of the notion that it could be easily or even fully implemented in post-conflict or war-torn societies. On the other hand, there are those, like Richmond, Pugh and Cooper who are sceptical of the fundamental assumptions of liberal peacebuilding. This schism has also been translated into diverging research agendas. While the first group has sought to develop ways of refining the implementation of liberal peacebuilding programmes, the other has attempted to move beyond liberal peacebuilding altogether and develop new ways of engaging post-conflict states and societies. The 'critical' camp also includes scholars such as Herbst (2004) and Atzili (2006–2007) who argue that international interventions to support weak states are inherently problematic and counter-productive. This group has not so much attempted to offer alternatives to the liberal peace, but has more generally sought to make the point that war is crucial to state-making.

One of the earliest and loudest shots in the debate over the liberal peace was fired by Roland Paris (2004) in *At War's End*. In his influential book, Paris sets out to criticise the assumptions of peacebuilders in the 1990s, who generally attempted, he argues, to marketise, democratise and leave post-conflict states as quickly as possible. Paris claims that in post-conflict situations, economic and political liberalisation, while ultimately desirable, should be delayed until after the establishment of functioning governance institutions, such as the rule of law. Though he initially sets himself up as a critic of the liberal peace thesis, it becomes clear very quickly that it is not the core premises of the liberal peace that Paris intends to dispute but the ways in which these have been implemented in practice in supposedly non-conducive environments. Paris and others who share his viewpoint therefore attempt to not so much replace the liberal peace but find ways of making it, at least in part, a reality (e.g. Paris 2009).

What distinguishes current 'critical' problem-solvers from earlier, 'uncritical' work on liberal peacebuilding is that the former recognise the potential contradictions between the various objectives of the liberal peace thesis and therefore discuss at length the trade-offs required in order to build the peace in practice (see Paris and Sisk 2009). They contend that earlier interventions were 'too' liberal in attempting wholesale liberalisation. In contrast they argue that not all good things go together and that in some cases, for instance, social and political stability has to precede or even delay indefinitely the promotion of liberal markets. In a similar vein, numerous other scholars have argued that particular aspects of liberal peacebuilding should be explored and bolstered if interventions are to succeed. Some of the suggestions made in that respect include emphasising reconciliation, welfare, consultation and inclusive political processes, or the empowerment of civil society and marginalised groups. These issues are not incompatible with the ideal of the liberal peace, as liberalism is a very broad church, but have arguably been peripheral to peacebuilders in practice (Paris 2010).

While problem-solving critics continue to refine the liberal peacebuilding paradigm, authors from the 'critical' camp have questioned the desirability of all or parts of the exercise. The critical camp could be divided into two main groups. On the one hand, scholars like Herbst (2004) and Atzili (2006–2007) argue that peacebuilding is likely to fail and that in most cases lasting solutions to internal conflicts result from allowing one warring faction to attain military victory over its rivals. Others, however, have taken a normative position attacking liberal peacebuilding as a form of domination, or even imperialism (Bain 2006; Cooper 2007). Mark Duffield (2007), for example, argues that statebuilding is manifestation of a fundamentally racist biopolitics, designed to secure the borders of Western civilisation from the dangerous 'underdeveloped' masses beyond. Michael Pugh (2005) has argued liberal peacebuilding is part of a broader hegemonic project, associated with neoliberalism (also Bendaña 2005). Oliver Richmond (2009: 54), one of the most articulate critics of liberal peacebuilding, has argued that while academics and practitioners have equated the liberal peace with the establishment of the institutions necessary for the liberal governance of society, economy and politics, in reality, due to local resistance, there are mostly hybridised forms of the liberal peace and other non-liberal variants, creating a perception that the former fails to meet expectations.

Indeed, one of the main themes of the stronger critique is that liberal peacebuilding leads to the development of weak, internationalised states in which state and society are not organically connected. Chesterman (2005), for example, has argued that the aims of international administration – establishing self-governing liberal democracies – are at odds with the means: imposed international rule. David Chandler, though not a critic of the liberal peace as such but of the undemocratic nature of statebuilding interventions (see Chandler 2010) – has arrived at similar conclusions in his study of intervention in the Balkans. International administrators, he argues, are loath to be held to account for the policies they pursue or the outcomes of their interventions into the political process. At the same time, local actors are denied the political autonomy to reach their own compromise solutions and assume accountability themselves. (Chandler 2005: 314)

He concludes that although the international administration in Bosnia and Herzegovina has been able to meet the 'externally decided needs of good governance', it has been unable to build the institutions of government, without which legitimate statehood is impossible (Chandler 2005: 319). Ottaway (2003: 247) further explains:

The externally-led or donors' model demands a transition from the collapsed *de jure* state to the Weberian *de facto* state; the internally-led model more modestly accepts a transition from the collapsed *de jure* state to a raw power *de facto* state that slowly develops institutions, though not necessarily democratic ones. The latter process is closer to the way in which states have developed historically.

One of the resulting preoccupations for many, though not all (e.g. Chandler 2010), of the authors in the critical camp has consequently been developing models of hybridised liberal and non-liberal governance, values and institutions that would hopefully better combine peaceful outcomes, local legitimacy and even social justice (Boege et al. 2009; Richmond and Franks 2007; Mac Ginty 2008; Cooper 2007). Richmond (2009: 55), for example, argues that the failure of the liberal peace to build 'united polities' in many countries indicates a 'need for a reform of the liberal model for peace, or to establish a capacity for it to coexist with other alternatives, or to replace it'. Because replacement is not currently feasible, Richmond argues that the objective of peacebuilding should be developing a 'liberal-local hybrid' form of peace. Richmond (2009: 72) further claims that 'backsliding is actually the renegotiation of the liberal peace to reflect key political, economic, social and cultural dynamics in their local context'.

There are at least two related problems with both the 'problem-solving' and 'critical' critiques. First, they are focused on evaluating the idea of the liberal peace and the extent to which it could or should be realised. Yet, as Chandler (2010) observes, this preoccupation leads to a false dichotomy between the 'liberal' intervener and the 'non-liberal' other, which implicitly serves to corroborate the view that the failure of liberal peacebuilding results from the capacities and characteristics of the intervened. Second, the two approaches fail to develop a conceptual and theoretical framework from which to develop a 'positive' assessment of peacebuilding/statebuilding that is not focused on what these interventions fail to achieve but on the nature, dimensions and development of actual forms of political rule under contemporary modes of international and transnational intervention. Critics often use expressions such as 'shadow state', 'virtual peace' (Richmond 2009) and 'alien rule' (Bain 2006) that essentially contrast what they observe with an ideal-typical 'peace' or 'state' that is not there. Indeed, the idea of hybrid peace or hybrid political order (Richmond 2009; Boege et al. 2009) is based on pre-existing notions of 'purer' forms of peace or political order to which existing situation are compared. This built-in comparison in turn shapes questions researchers ask and the way in which particular situations are understood. The common critique that state-building creates 'weak' states, for example, is premised on an idea of what a state is. Yet, the 'prototypical' Western state has itself undergone a process of transformation in recent decades, which suggests that stateness is always a moving target (see Nettl 1968).

Regrettably, the peacebuilding literature has largely tended to ignore the literature on state theory, and particularly the branch associated with Poulantzas (1978) and Jessop (2007) that focuses on the role of social and political conflict in not only shaping political outcomes, but in transforming the state itself. For the most part, students of peacebuilding have tended to examine the impact of these interventions on targeted states and populations, but without looking back at the intervening states to see how contested political processes there affect and are affected by interventions (Chandler 2009 is an exception). As a result, this scholarly debate creates the wrong impression that peacebuilding/statebuilding is essentially a struggle between competing and generally coherent paradigms of 'liberal' or 'non-liberal' peace, institutions and values. As we shall later see, however, contemporary interventions are both products and facilitators of broader and historically specific processes of change in statehood fought out within the institutional spaces of both intervening and intervened states. This results not in 'hybrid', but in *new* forms of political rule and statehood.

Liberal Peacebuilding or State Transformation?

The scope of this chapter does not allow for a full articulation of my approach to the study of contemporary interventions (see Hameiri 2010). Below I provide a very brief summary of the argument, particularly with the aim of demonstrating its utility for avoiding the limitations of the existing critique. To reiterate, my aim is not to provide an alternative critique of the liberal peace, but to move beyond this project altogether towards a framework that treats the social and political relations emerging through intervention as deserving explanation in their own right.

As a starting point, it is problematic to view contemporary interventions within the narrow sphere of peace operations and their development. In this I do not so much echo the prevalent argument that these interventions are an attempt to extend a hegemonic neoliberal project globally (see Pugh 2005; Bendaña 2005). Rather, I argue that statebuilding interventions are a new mode of governance whose development is both outcome and facilitator of a broader and contested process of transformation in the global political economy and statehood that is still being played out. Statebuilding as we see it today is related to four historical processes: (a) the perception that the 'marketise-democratise-leave' interventions of the early 1990s had failed (Paris 2004); (b) the evolution in market-led approaches to development associated with advances in the economic theory of institutions and its ascendance in the donor community after the upheaval caused by the structural adjustment programmes and several large-scale financial crises in the 1980s and early 1990s; (c) the transformation of the Western state, associated with the rise of neoliberalism from the late 1970s; and (d) the assumed emergence of transnational and potentially existential security risks and the associated reorientation of policymaking towards managing and containing the risks of an interconnected world, particularly after the 11 September 2001 terrorist attacks (Hameiri 2010: 64).

While all of the above have played an important role in the development of statebuilding, the most important historical development for our purposes is the one associated with the shift in the West from the post-war welfare state towards the regulatory state, or more concretely from government and the politics of interest-representations towards governance and the politics of values. That process began with the crisis of Western capitalism in the 1970s and the subsequent rise to power of Thatcher and Reagan (Harvey 2005). While neoliberalisation has initially consisted mainly of attacks on Keynesian and welfarist institutions, from the 1990s onwards, in response to strong political resistance and several financial crises, the reform agenda has shifted towards the attempted construction of broader social and political coalitions and an expanded regulatory role for the state (Peck and Tickell 2002).

A crucial aspect of the shift from the Keynesian to the regulatory state has been the systematic marginalisation of political claims based on material cleavages, which were highly institutionalised in the state apparatus and in political party structures in Western states in the post-war period. The marginalisation of the politics of class, which is often contested and usually incomplete, has been attempted through the incremental reduction of the sphere of political contestation played out in the institutions of representative democracy. At the same time and partly in response to governance failures, a wide range of specialist, unelected regulatory agencies and private sector actors began to take part in public policymaking and implementation under the broad supervision (or meta-governance) of the executive arm of government (Jayasuriya 2006). As a consequence, functions previously within the ambit of the national state apparatus have increasingly been shifting below, above and beside the traditional centres of policymaking power. This is a process variously described as state disaggregation or multilevel governance (Hooghe and Marks 2003), yet it is crucial to remember that it is not a natural progression of government but a manifestation of a contested political project.

The upshot of this very quick historical overview of state transformation in the West is that contemporary forms of regulatory statehood, of which state-building interventions are part, are not easily reversible because their emergence is part of a long-term shift and not simply a matter of policy associated with one government or another.

Importantly, the domestic compact between capital and labour was also reflected in an international order of 'embedded liberalism', designed to enable the governments of the main Western states to protect this settlement (Ruggie 1982). The domestic imperative had therefore underpinned the existence of harder forms of national sovereignty and authority and a more pluralist international society. These domestic and international orders were also supported by the ideological dominance of the modernisation paradigm and particularly by the geopolitics of the Cold War (see also Hobsbawm 1994).

The collapse of both the Keynesian domestic compact and the geopolitical constraints of the Cold War has led to a transformation of domestic political contestation from a politics of interest-representation, typically organised along capitalist class division, towards an emphasis on 'good governance' and values (see Chandler 2009). The main line of disagreement between 'conservative' and 'progressive' political parties in most Western states in recent years has been on issues of culture and values. The politics of values at times clashes with the politics of 'good governance', but both are compatible in that they are viewed as post-political and beyond the grubby politics of interest-representation and compromise. The result has been a shift in the way liberalism is understood and practised, from a pluralist version that emphasises negotiation between competing interest to an anti-pluralist depiction of liberalism as a set of values and a way of life (Jayasuriya 2005). This understanding of liberalism has both (neo)conservative and progressive manifestations, in that progressive critics of liberal interventions would at times depict these as 'too liberal' for 'non-liberal' intervened societies (Chandler 2010). The 'idealisation' of liberalism, as Chandler (2009: Ch. 8) persuasively argues, is a manifestation of the weakness, not strength, of political elites in the West, stemming from their disconnection from broad societal support-bases. As we have seen, this disjuncture is not incidental but one of the outcomes of the shift from the post-war state, in which politics was socialised, to the regulatory state of our time, in which the market is socialised (Jayasuriya 2006).

In tandem, the increasing number of financial and political crises associated with capitalist expansion since the 1980s has led to a reorientation of state action towards the management of transnational risk, blurring the distinction between 'domestic' and 'international'. Yet, the way in which risk has been defined and managed cannot be separated from the processes of state transformation discussed above. Risk has mainly come to be viewed as related to the absence or inadequate functioning of regulatory frameworks and institutions for liberal markets. The emphasis on institutions was related to the intellectual ascendance of new institutional economics (NIE), in the wake of major financial crises in Mexico, Russia and Asia in the 1990s. The growing currency of the idea that to function well markets require a particular and broadly conceived institutional set of regulations was of course related to the overall attempt on the part of governments to discredit the claims of distributional coalitions. In turn, because political demands of a particular kind are seen as illegitimate, risk management has come to be associated with a new kind of political logic, in which policy-making is justified on the basis of expertise and good management (see Furedi 2009), beyond the institutions of representative democracy.

Under these conditions, the emphasis on evaluating and supporting the 'capacity' of political, economic and social institutions in the developing world has become a staple of development policy from the late 1990s, becoming known as the post-Washington consensus. Yet, particularly after September 11, capacity building has become securitised due to the perception that institutional weakness is not only a development problem, but potentially a source of global security concerns too. As a result, various development and security experts have acquired key roles in identifying 'risky' states and in managing the risk through various interventions designed notionally to improve governance, but more substantively to limit the spectrum of political choices available to the governments and societies of intervened states. For the most part, however, these interventions do not involve the long-term abrogation of the formal sovereignty of intervened states (see Chandler 2010). Rather, what we see is a multitude of more or less coordinated interventions by 'experts' in various areas of governance and government, linked together either via the apparatus of the intervened state or through an especially set-up coordinating mechanism.

Indeed, contemporary interventions are located simultaneously within and outside the state and often at various levels of governance and government at once. To conceptualise this form of governance I employ the term 'multilevel regime'. Regimes are constellations of social forces, institutions and legitimating ideas that work to regularise political outcomes (see Pempel 1998; Jayasuriya and Rosser 2006). Though Pempel (1998) views a regime as a 'tripod' in which the three elements must co-exist, it is argued here that regimes are better understood as a pyramid with social and political coalitions at the base and ideas at the apex (Jayasuriya and Rosser 2006: 263). In other words, rather than seeing institutions as existing in an equal, if complex, relationship with social structures, 'systems of social hegemony [are often] able to transcend different institutional structures' (Robison and Hadiz 2004: 17).

While regimes are typically seen as internal to one state or as an inter-state matter, multilevel regimes of the kind associated with contemporary interventions combine intergovernmental interactions with several bureaucratic-administrative interventions at lower levels of government and governance. This means that they are simultaneously part of the state and outside of it, creating a new kind of transnationalised and transnationally regulated statehood that is not captured by prevalent definitions in international relations and international law. This transformation of the political and institutional spaces of the state occurs irrespective of whether the stated objectives of interveners are met or not. The intergovernmental level, which is essential for maintaining the formal sovereignty of the intervened state, is in most cases where the legal and operational space for intervention is negotiated. Other, functional interventions generally operate independently within the spaces enabled through intergovernmental agreements, because they are defined through and are seen as requiring specialised forms of expertise, for example in finance or policing.

The multilevel nature of statebuilding interventions means that to understand how they operate and are resisted we must examine the relationship between the different scales, as well as conflicts within the various spaces of governance constructed around particular functions. Crucially, all levels of intervention are simultaneously located within every particular space in which intervention occurs at the same time. This means that conflicts at the intergovernmental level may affect power relations around particular issues and the design of the institutions through which power is organised, but this is not necessarily a top-down flow. For example, the Australian Federal Police's (AFP) contingent of the Australian Enhanced Cooperation Package in Papua New Guinea (PNG) was structured as a direct relationship between the AFP and its local counterpart, in which the AFP took on policing and capacity-building roles. This arrangement, in which the AFP had enjoyed considerable operational independence, was enabled by an agreement between the Australian and PNG governments, ratified through legislation by the PNG parliament, which provided legal immunity to AFP officers from PNG laws. However, a constitutional challenge to the immunity provision led to the immediate withdrawal of the AFP in May 2005.

The above discussion contains two implications for the study of particular interventions. First, to understand the agency of local and international actors in contemporary interventions, it is important to locate them in the context of regimes and the power relations within which these are constituted. Examining agency in this way avoids the tendency of liberal peace critics to focus mainly on the role of ideas and legitimacy, as well as evaluate existing situations against non-existing ideal-types such as the liberal peace or other assumed non-liberal cultural predilections. Second, rather than reify the domestic–external dichotomy that informs much of the literature on peacebuilding or statebuilding, particularly when it comes to explaining the effects of intervention, it is more useful to focus on clashes between different regimes within the state and the ways in which these conflicts shape the nature of political rule.

The utility of this approach will be demonstrated in the following section, in which I will look at the ways in which interrelations between regimes of statebuilding and patronage have affected the ways in which political power is organised and resisted in Cambodia.

Intervention and the Consolidation of Authoritarian Rule in Cambodia

Cambodia represents one of the earliest and most extensive cases of international intervention under the rubric of liberal peacebuilding. Though official international supervision had ended along with the departure of the United Nations Transitional Authority in Cambodia (UNTAC) in 1993, Cambodia is still the recipient of vast amounts of international development assistance, at least relative to the official national budget. Cambodia's long experience with international intervention allows us to track the effects of the shift from an earlier, albeit limited, emphasis on political liberalisation and human rights towards an increased focus on capacity building and good governance from the late 1990s. In that time we have seen the emergence of seemingly contending regimes within the state. The first is a regime of patronage, centring on Cambodian Prime Minister Hun Sen but penetrating state and society to the village level. The second is a regime of statebuilding, comprising a variety of governance spaces within state and civil society and primarily associated with the agency of the international donor community, as well as with various Cambodian groups seeking political space independent from the powerful networks of the dominant Cambodian People's Party (CPP).

Though the donors' emphasis on good governance has led to clashes over contentious issues such as public administration reform and demobilisation, Hun Sen and his supporters have become adept at using the statebuilding agenda to transform social and political conflicts relating to the uneven and exploitative nature of economic development in post-communist Cambodia into technical matters framed and managed through the 'international' relationship between the government and donors. This process has been aided by Hun Sen's ability to dominate a new array of aid coordination mechanisms, whose emergence is linked to the aid effectiveness agenda of the Organisation for Economic Cooperation and Development (OECD). The emphasis on state capacity has allowed the Cambodian government to limit the ability of opposition parties and civil society groups to form transnational and international alliances, thereby considerably weakening them.

The persistence of patronage networks in Cambodian political life has led some critics of liberal peacebuilding to argue about the 'superficiality of statebuilding' vis-à-vis deeply ingrained cultural and social structures dating back to pre-colonial times (Roberts 2009). The assumed passivity of Cambodian villagers is often seen to be incompatible with Western notions of democracy, leading to their manipulation by predatory elites. Oliver Richmond and Jason Franks (2007) have also argued that the promotion of the liberal peace in Cambodia has to take into account the Cambodian cultural context; otherwise it remains nothing more than 'hubris'.

Yet, as Caroline Hughes (2003: 60–67) has shown, current patronage networks in Cambodia bear little resemblance to pre-colonial patronage, though attempts have been made by key figures in the Cambodian government to justify it in those terms (Öjendal and Kim 2006; Hughes 2006). Already transformed by colonisation and the emergence of absentee landlords that were not bound by the same social and customary ties as traditional patrons, patronage in Cambodia was further transformed during the post-Khmer Rouge years, particularly by economic liberalisation from 1989, which preceded international peacebuilding. While customary patronage involved dyadic relationships between patron and clients within one community, current forms of 'transformed' patronage consist of three-way relationships in which patrons in government or public office permit others to exploit a third party that is not strictly speaking part of the patronage network. Rather than being the resurrection of cultural tradition, contemporary patronage is a manifestation of the pre-intervention government's effort to develop stronger support-bases, beyond communist ideology, at a time in which few other options were available due to the withdrawal of aid from the Soviet bloc. Its existence also depends on modern methods of control and surveillance and on the availability of markets beyond Cambodian borders for the resources pillaged.

The arrival of UNTAC in 1991 heralded a massive expansion of political space in Cambodia. Hitherto, opposition groups that together with the Khmer Rouge formed the Coalition Government of Democratic Kampuchea depended on international backers to fight the Vietnamese-backed Phnom Penh government from the Thai border area. There were no opposition parties in Cambodia, however, and certainly no civil society groups. UNTAC helped facilitate Cambodia's first national elections in decades and its human rights office directly funded and supported several new human rights NGOs with the idea of democratising Cambodian society from below. Other donors and international NGOs also provided funding and resources to local counterparts, at a time in which they had no other sources of support outside the CPP-dominated patronage networks. Ultimately however, international and transnational support for Cambodian oppositions and civil society groups has led to their reliance on international funding and audiences instead of cultivating Cambodian support-bases able to rival the power of the CPP, particularly in the countryside where most Cambodians live (Hughes 2003).

Though intervention in the early 1990s was crucial to the expansion of political space, donor officials, as well as mostly middle-class Cambodian human rights NGO activists, were generally wary of destabilising 'traumatised' Cambodia and therefore promoted conservative versions of democracy and human rights that discouraged Cambodians from mobilising and acting politically outside of the heavily regulated channel of the ballot. As a result, the official political process was strangely disconnected from the realities of power in Cambodia. While Cambodians were encouraged by donors and NGOs to contemplate the policy agendas of different parties in private and cast their votes accordingly, the more pressing issue for most was the concern that voting for the opposition would invite violent retribution from the government and its supporters in the military (Hughes 2005).

From the late 1990s, however, the limited political space opened up through intervention was reduced further as a result of donors' shifting emphasis from promoting (regulated) political liberalisation to good governance and state capacity. In particular, the emergence of the OECD aid effectiveness agenda has from 2004 been associated with the development of a variety of coordination mechanisms supposedly designed to harmonise aid interventions and align them better with the government's strategic development plans.

The government–donor relationship is now organised around a three-level structure with the Cambodian Rehabilitation and Development Board acting as the main coordinating body and as the secretariat. At the bottom there are technical working groups organised around particular topics, such as public administration reform or public financial reform. Above there is the Government-Donor Coordination Committee, which brings together high-level in-country officials every three months to discuss coordination and broader strategic direction. At the top is the Cambodia Development Cooperation Forum, a high level annual forum usually hosted by Hun Sen and attended by representatives from donor governments and organisational headquarters.

While it is questionable whether this coordination structure has in fact made aid delivery more efficient, it is clear that the new centralised structures have allowed the government to internationalise policymaking, while assuming greater control over who gets to participate in these processes and on what terms. It has allowed the government to frame implementation difficulties, which are typically the result of powerful resistance from interests benefiting from patronage, in terms of lacking capacity or poor coordination between the donors themselves or between them and the government. The upshot has been to turn conflict into a matter for experts and administrators to manage away from the political process – something which the donors are generally at ease with, as we have seen. The government, in turn, has been able to entirely exclude opposition parties and more critical NGOs from the aid coordination fora, because these are defined in terms of 'international' relations, even though they effectively pertain to the negotiation of domestic governance arrangements in Cambodia. In turn, opposition parties, which as we have seen have come to rely on the 'international community' as a substitute for other support-bases, have considerably weakened as a result of donors' emphasis in recent years on building state capacity.

In fact, even the successful implementation of the statebuilding and good governance agenda is unlikely to seriously threaten CPP power. This is because the various administrative and legal mechanisms being promoted, while providing channels for contesting arbitrary executive power, will do little to weaken the CPP's stranglehold over the countryside. Cambodians living in villages are typically very poor and subsistence-dependent and therefore have very little capacity to mobilise politically or to lodge complaints through costly official channels that might undo painstakingly cultivated relationships with local power-brokers. Indeed, despite their apparent incompatibility, both patronage and statebuilding regimes promote anti-competitive visions of social and political organisation as essential for Cambodia's stability and future development, as well as acting in different ways to contain unregulated political mobilisation. To summarise, the interests associated with Hun Sen and his supporters hold sway, but the way power is exercised and resisted is dependent upon a complex relationship of institutions and interests within and beyond the state that have developed through various forms of intervention from the 1990s.

Conclusion

The critique of the liberal peace and of liberal peacebuilding has become a new mainstream in the twenty-first century, accepted even by policymakers and practitioners (see Chandler 2010). Yet this critique, whether problem-solving or critical, remains limited by its framing and evaluation of existing situations in relation to an ideal-typical notion of peace or statehood. The focus for critics is on what is *not* there, rather than on explaining the forms of political rule created through intervention. As a result, many end up proposing hybridisation of peace or statehood as the way out of the implementation failures of liberal peacebuilding, but without gaining sufficient insight into the forces shaping the political outcomes and trajectories of actual interventions.

As we have seen, the exercise of power in Cambodia has been shaped by the historical emergence of 'transformed' patronage networks and the ways in which various forms of interventions have acted to both challenge and promote their consolidation. The transformation of the Cambodian state, associated with the development of an extensive aid coordination apparatus, has enabled the government to further limit the political space in Cambodia that is independent of the patronage networks that sustain its power. The broader conclusion to be drawn from the Cambodian case is that the effects of interventions cannot be understood nor evaluated in terms of disembodied ideas of peace or statehood, but only through a historically informed analysis of the development of the actual social and political forces present, as well as the institutions and spaces through which power is contested.

Bibliography

Atzili, B. (2006–7) 'When Good Fences Make Bad Neighbors: Fixed Borders, State Weakness, and International Conflict', *International Security* 31(3): 139–173.
Bain, W. (2006) 'In Praise of Folly: International Administration and the Corruption of Humanity', *International Affairs* 82(3): 525–538.
Bellamy, A. J., P. Williams and S. Griffin (2004) *Understanding Peacekeeping*, Cambridge: Polity.
Bendaña, A. (2005) 'From Peace-Building to State-Building: One Step Forward and Two Steps Back?', *Development* 48(3): 5–15.
Boege, V., A. Brown, K. Clements and A. Nolan (2009) 'Building Peace and Political Community in Hybrid Political Orders', *International Peacekeeping* 16(5): 599–615.
Boutros-Ghali, B. (1992) *An Agenda for Peace: Preventive Diplomacy, Peacemaking and Peacekeeping*, New York: United Nations.
Chandler, D. (2002) *From Kosovo to Kabul and Beyond: Human Rights and International Intervention*, London: Pluto Press.
Chandler, D. (2005) 'Introduction: Peace without Politics', *International Peacekeeping* 12(3): 307–321.
Chandler, D. (2009) *Hollow Hegemony: Rethinking Global Politics, Power and Resistance*, London and New York: Pluto Press.
Chandler, D. (2010) *International Statebuilding: The Rise of Post-Liberal Governance*, London and New York: Routledge.
Chesterman, S. (2005) 'Transitional Administration, State-Building and the United Nations', in S. Chesterman, M. Ignatieff and R. Thakur (eds) *Making States Work: State Failure and the Crisis of Governance*, Tokyo: United Nations University Press, pp. 338–359.
Cooper, N. (2007) 'Review Article: On the Crisis of the Liberal Peace', *Conflict, Security and Development* 7(4): 605–616.
Cox, R. W. (1981) 'Social Forces, States and World Orders: Beyond International Relations Theory', *Millennium: Journal of International Studies* 10(2): 126–155.
Doyle, M. W. (1986) 'Liberalism and World Politics', *American Political Science Review* 80(4): 1151–1169.
Duffield, M. (2001) *Global Governance and the New Wars: The Merging of Development and Security*, London: Zed Books.
Duffield, M. (2007) *Development, Security and Unending War: Governing the World of Peoples*, Cambridge: Polity.
Furedi, F. (2009) 'Specialist Pleading', *The Australian Literary Review*, 2 September.

Hameiri, S. (2010) *Regulating Statehood: State Building and the Transformation of the Global Order*, Basingstoke: Palgrave Macmillan.

Harvey, D. (2005) *A Brief History of Neoliberalism*, Oxford: Oxford University Press.

Herbst, J. (2004) 'Let Them Fail: State Failure in Theory and Practice: Implications for Policy', in R. I. Rotberg (ed.) *When States Fail: Causes and Consequences*, Princeton: Princeton University Press, pp. 302–318.

Hobsbawm, E. (1994) *The Age of Extremes: The Short Twentieth Century 1914–1991*, London: Michael Joseph.

Hooghe, L. and G. Marks (2003) 'Unraveling the Central State, but How? Types of Multi-Level Governance', *American Political Science Review* 97(2): 233–243.

Hughes, C. (2003) *The Political Economy of Cambodia's Transition, 1991–2001*, London and New York: RoutledgeCurzon.

Hughes, C. (2005) 'Candidate Debates and Equity News: International Support for Democratic Deliberation in Cambodia', *Pacific Affairs* 78(1): 77–93.

Hughes, C. (2006) 'The Politics of Gifts: Tradition and Regimentation in Contemporary Cambodia', *Journal of Southeast Asian Studies* 37(3): 469–89.

Jayasuriya, K. (2005) *Reconstituting the Global Liberal Order: Legitimacy and Regulation*, London and New York: Routledge.

Jayasuriya, K. (2006) *Statecraft, Welfare and the Politics of Inclusion*, Houndmills: Palgrave Macmillan.

Jayasuriya, K. and A. Rosser (2006) 'Pathways from the Crisis: Politics and Reform in South-East Asia since 1997', in G. Rodan, K. Hewison and R. Robison (eds) *The Political Economy of South-East Asia: Markets, Power and Contestation*, 3rd edn, Melbourne: Oxford University Press, pp. 258–282.

Jessop, B. (2007) *State Power*, Cambridge: Polity.

Mac Ginty, R. (2008) 'Indigenous Peace-Making Versus the Liberal Peace', *Cooperation and Conflict* 43(2): 139–163.

Nettl, J. P. (1968) 'The State as a Conceptual Variable', *World Politics* 20(4): 559–592.

Newman, E., R. Paris and O. P. Richmond (2009) 'Introduction', in E. Newman, R. Paris and O. P. Richmond (eds) *New Perspectives on Liberal Peacebuilding*, Tokyo and New York: United Nations University Press, pp. 3–25.

OECD (2006) *Whole of Government Approaches to Fragile States*, Paris: Organisation for Economic Cooperation and Development.

Öjendal, J. and K. Sedara (2006) '*Korob, Kaud, Klach*: In Search of Agency in Rural Cambodia', *Journal of Southeast Asian Studies* 37(3): 507–526.

Ottaway, M. (2003) 'Rebuilding State Institutions in Collapsed States', in J. Milliken (ed.) *State Failure, Collapse and Reconstruction*, Malden, MA: Blackwell, pp. 245–266.

Paris, R. (2004) *At War's End: Building Peace after Civil Conflict*, Cambridge: Cambridge University Press.

Paris, R. (2009) 'Understanding the "Coordination Problem" in Postwar Statebuilding', in R. Paris and T. D. Sisk (eds) *The Dilemmas of Statebuilding: Confronting the Contradictions of Postwar Peace Operations*, London and New York: Routledge, pp. 53–78.

Paris, R. (2010) 'Saving Liberal Peacebuilding', *Review of International Studies* 36(2): 337–365.

Paris, R. and T. D. Sisk (2009) 'Introduction: Understanding the Contradictions of Postwar Statebuilding', in R. Paris and T. D. Sisk (eds) *The Dilemmas of Statebuilding: Confronting the Contradictions of Postwar Peace Operations*, London and New York: Routledge, pp. 1–20.

Peck, J. and A. Tickell (2002) 'Neoliberalizing Space', *Antipode* 36(3): 380–404.
Pempel, T. J. (1998) *Regime Shift: Comparative Dynamics of the Japanese Political Economy*, Ithaca, NY and London: Cornell University Press.
Pender, J. (2007) 'Country Ownership: The Evasion of Donor Accountability', in C. J. Bickerton, P. Cunliffe and A. Gourevitch (eds) *Politics without Sovereignty: A Critique of Contemporary International Relations*, London and New York: University College London Press, pp. 112–130.
Poulantzas, N. (1978) *State, Power, Socialism*, London and New York: Verso.
Pugh, M. (2005) 'The Political Economy of Peacebuilding: A Critical Theory Perspective', *International Journal of Peace Studies* 10(2): 23–42.
Richmond, O. P. (2005) *The Transformation of Peace*, Basingstoke: Palgrave Macmillan.
Richmond, O. P. (2009) 'Beyond Liberal Peace? Responses To "Backsliding"', in E. Newman, R. Paris and O. P. Richmond (eds) *New Perspectives on Liberal Peacebuilding*, Tokyo and New York: United Nations University Press, pp. 54–77.
Richmond, O. P. and J. Franks (2007) 'Liberal Hubris? Virtual Peace in Cambodia', *Security Dialogue* 38(1): 27–48.
Roberts, D. (2009) 'The Superficiality of Statebuilding in Cambodia: Patronage and Clientelism as Enduring Forms of Politics', in R. Paris and T. D. Sisk (eds) *Dilemmas of Statebuilding: Confronting the Contradictions of Postwar Peace Operations*, London and New York: Routledge, pp. 149–169.
Robison, R. and V. R. Hadiz (2004) *Reorganising Power in Indonesia: The Politics of Power in an Age of Markets*, London and New York: RoutledgeCurzon.
Ruggie, J. G. (1982) 'International Regimes, Transactions, and Change: Embedded Liberalism in the Postwar Economic Order', *International Organization* 36(2): 379–415.
Russett, B. (1993) *Grasping the Democratic Peace: Principles for a Post-Cold War World*, Princeton, NJ: Princeton University Press.

12

Hybrid Peace: How Does Hybrid Peace Come About?

Roger Mac Ginty

Introduction

This chapter proposes the concept of hybridity as a way of capturing the interaction between internal and external actors in contexts experiencing internationally sponsored peacebuilding and statebuilding operations. The concept is recommended for five reasons. Firstly, it encourages us to move beyond some of the debates on liberal peacebuilding that merely criticise or defend the liberal peace (Paris 2010). Such debates resemble a World War One battle in which each side shells the other from prepared positions. The result is a predictable stalemate with little real engagement between each side. Secondly, the concept of hybridity encourages us to question the boundaries between categories. Many of our descriptions and analyses of peacebuilding rely on the notion of reasonably discrete sets of actors that are often grouped as oppositional binaries: internal versus external, traditional versus modern, good versus evil. The concept of hybridity allows us to look at the interstices and sites of cooperation and conflict between these apparently discrete categories and reappraise notions that boundaries are fixed. Thirdly, and related to the last point, the concept of hybridity recommends that we look inside categories themselves and question the extent to which they are homogeneous or united. Terms like 'international community', 'NATO' or 'Taliban' are often used promiscuously and conceal a good deal of diversity.

The fourth reason to recommend the concept of hybridity is that it manages to capture the complexity and fluidity of internationally supported peacebuilding situations. The model of hybridisation proposed in the chapter is based on the notion of variable geometry, or the sense that all the actors, institutions and ideas that combine to create peacebuilding are in permanent flux.

Importantly, the notion of hybridity is in tune with the conflict transformation literature that encourages us to examine relationships between actors, and questions the fixity of identities and worldviews (Lederach 1995, 1999). Finally, the notion of hybridity is deployed as it encourages us to examine all levels of actors involved in peacebuilding. This moves us beyond state- and institution-centric international relations approaches that tend to concentrate on formal actors. Hybridity works at all levels of society, and so it is important that we examine the formal and the informal, and the interactions between both and the ways that they change.

The chapter is an exercise in conceptual scoping and is primarily interested in attempting to capture the actuality of peacebuilding contexts. It draws on previous work by the author that was interested in the interaction between top-down and bottom-up approaches to peacemaking and peacebuilding (Mac Ginty 2006, 2010a, 2011). The chapter will proceed by first conceptualising the notion of hybridity. Just as it is important to say what hybridity is, it is also important to say what it is not. It is proposed that processes of hybridisation occur as a result of the interaction of four elements: the coercive power of the liberal peace; the incentivising power of the liberal peace; the ability of local communities to resist, negotiate with and subvert the liberal peace; and the ability of local communities to create and maintain alternatives to the liberal peace. The third section of the chapter examines hybridity in action, and specifically the hybridisation of core pillars of liberal peacebuilding: security, economic reform, statebuilding and constitutional reform, governance and civil society.

Hybridity

Hybridity is taken as the composite forms of social thinking and practice that emerge as the result of the interaction of different groups, practices and worldviews. In terms of internationally supported peacebuilding contexts, we can take hybridity as the summation of actions and worldviews by a series of actors. It involves a series of explicit and implicit actions and reactions. It is both a condition and a process, and involves a complex dynamic of conflict, cooperation and coalescence. Much academic and policy literature on violent conflict and peacebuilding is tempted to see 'systems' and rational patterns in the midst of conflict. This is understandable from the perspective of a need to find a way of comprehending conflict. Yet, such an approach risks being overly reductionist; it distorts conflicts into ways that are easily understood by outsiders but are not necessarily an accurate reflection of the lived experience of conflict or peacemaking. As a result, this work favours a notion of hybridity that recognises that conflict and peacemaking are messy and awkward.

The concept of hybridity also encourages us to move away from thinking about vertical 'silos' of interaction whereby there is a straightforward top-down chain of power and resources from the international actors, to national governments and thence downwards to municipalities, local communities and individuals in societies attempting to emerge from violent conflict. Certainly, in liberal peacemaking contexts, international actors are capable of marshalling significant material and moral power, of co-opting local actors, and of projecting their power through military, economic or cultural means. But such a vertical and linear picture is overly simplistic. There is a real danger that such a view overlooks the agency of local actors and their power to ignore, subvert, sit-out, exploit and resist external interventions. So top-down movement is augmented by bottom-up movement as well. Rather than a top-down system of exclusive north-to-south and international-to-local tutelage, the liberal peace experiences distortion and blowback through indigenous and local agency.

It is important in this regard not to romanticise all things local, traditional, indigenous and customary (Mac Ginty 2010b). Some of the critical literature on peacebuilding suffers from a 'last native syndrome', or the sense that the most effective and sustainable ways of finding peace can only be known and experienced by indigenous peoples unaided by external interference. The purpose of the proposing the concept of hybridity is not to 'rescue' indigenous or traditional peacebuilding just as Roland Paris (2010) has sought to 'rescue' liberal peacebuilding. Instead, the purpose is to propose a more accurate view of the dynamic and multifarious nature of actors, ideas and practices that contribute to peacebuilding. For the purposes of this chapter, hybridity is a composite and fusion of multiple factors. It is *not* the grafting together of two separate entities to create a third entity. Instead, it is assumed that actors, norms and practices are the result of prior hybridisation (Canclini 2005: xxv). This compels us to question narratives that might prefer to see discrete or pristine actors that are 'polluted' by encounters with international actors. The novelty of globalisation is much over-stated: human societies have long traditions of mixing, conflict, cooperation and co-option.

Consider, by way of a rather micro-local example, the cemetery just along the road from the author's study. It is situated on the edge of a village of 79 people in southern Scotland. The surrounding area is predominantly agricultural and is 'off the beaten track'. It is over fifty miles to the nearest city, university or large hospital. Yet, the cemetery illustrates a community with a long history of globalisation: a son who died in Gallipoli fighting in the New Zealand military but is marked on his parents' gravestone; a husband who died on the western front in 1917; an Australian-born artist who retired to the area; a Polish soldier who came to Scotland in the Second World War, settled, had a family and is buried with his Scottish wife; a son who died as a colonial administrator in India and is remembered on his parents' gravestone. The chief point is that the communities that we might want to label as 'local', 'isolated' or 'remote' are rarely as immune from globalised trends as we may imagine (Davis 2001). Social interaction and negotiation is the stuff of human society, and has been occurring for millennia. There is a significant danger that much analysis of peacebuilding too readily and neatly separates actors and worldviews into discrete categories.

Hybridisation

Having outlined the utility of the concept of hybridity, the chapter now seeks to explain the process whereby hybridity is produced and reproduced. A four-part model of hybridisation is proposed. Like all models, this is an abstraction and is unable to capture the full complexity of actors and actions in societies emerging from armed conflict and experiencing international peace-support interventions. Yet the model is an aid to our understanding of the complex interactions that combine to forge new forms of peace and politics. The four parts of the model are:

- the ability of liberal peace actors, structures and networks to impose their version of peacemaking;
- the ability of liberal peace actors, structures and networks to incentivise local actors to cooperate with the liberal peace;
- the ability of local actors, structures and networks to negotiate with, subvert, exploit, and resist the liberal peace;
- the ability of local actors, structures and networks to create and maintain alternatives to the liberal peace.

The interaction between the four parts of this model can be characterised as hybrid forms of peace and politics. Clearly such a model needs to be swathed in caveats. Not all parts of the model will have equal weighting. Instead, the emphasis on each variable will change from context to context and over time. Moreover, the four parts of the model need to be placed in a wider structural context which recognises the economic and coercive power of certain actors and trading regimes.

Each part of the model requires elucidation. The first part, the ability of liberal peace actors, structures and networks to impose their version of peacemaking, recognises the coercive power of the liberal peace. This coercion can be explicit as evidenced through the democratisation at gunpoint adventurism by the United States and its allies in Afghanistan, or through the use of economic instruments to compel actors to act in particular ways. The powers of coercion are often implicit and take the form of complex and near hegemonic systems of economic, diplomatic and security rules and mechanisms that compel states to act in certain ways. Thus, for example, leading states in the global north control the World Bank and International Monetary Fund (IMF) and have been able to use this power to discipline states through the use of aid conditionalities, structural adjustments and poverty reduction strategies papers. National governments in societies coming out of civil war or authoritarianism are often left in little doubt that they must accept the advice of their international mentors. In this way, the national government becomes an agent of the liberal peace, and in turn compels municipalities and citizens to adopt prescriptions that were ultimately recommended by international bureaucrats whose loyalty and legitimacy lie outwith the target country. While international liberal coercion is often cloaked in the language of emancipation, it has also been boosted by the securitisation of post-war reconstruction and development (Duffield 2002). This has been particularly the case in the post-9/11 era.

The second part of the model, the incentivising or encouraging aspects of the liberal peace, reminds us of the multiple faces of liberalism (Gray 2000). Just as liberalism can be forceful and coercive, it is also capable of constructing a very attractive narrative of emancipation and progress. The liberal rhetoric paints a picture of autonomous individuals and communities free to chart their own course in life, protected and enabled by plural mechanisms. While critics of the liberal peace point out that ultimately the form of liberalism on offer from the liberal peace is ethnocentric and restrictive, there is no doubting that the liberal peace has been able to provide an impressive set of incentives. Again, critics will say that these incentives must be measured against the coercive powers of the liberal peace. Nevertheless, international actors have engaged in a good deal of old-fashioned Keynesianism in the pursuit of securing their preferred form of peacemaking. Persistent reports of Afghan officials and figures close to the government taking bales and suitcases of US dollars out of Afghanistan attest to the generosity of liberal internationalism to some sectors in some contexts (Gabbatt 2010).

More generally, champions of the liberal peace have promoted notions of 'trickle down' security, politics and economics: an elite bargain between warring factions will allow for local security and refugee repatriation; a new nationally agreed constitution will allow for a power-sharing government through which resources and respect can be shared; an efficient private sector unfettered by state interference will be internationally competitive and allow citizens to prosper through their own entrepreneurialism. The beguiling nature of liberal rhetoric is not to be under-estimated, especially given how international actors are capable of extending their material power into moral power. For example, in a number of societies attempting to extricate themselves from civil war, international actors were able to construct powerful, near-hegemonic narratives that 'there is no alternative', that warring factions 'must move on', that 'the past must be put behind us', and that nationalism and particularism must be replaced in 'a new beginning'.

The third part of the four-part model is the ability of local actors, structures and networks to negotiate with, subvert, exploit and resist the liberal peace. The chief point here is the need to recognise the agency of local actors in societies undergoing internationally supported peacebuilding. International interventions tend to subjectify local populations into what are often broad and static categories: victims, combatants, beneficiaries, etc. Such conceptualisations often presuppose that people have one mode of operation (that is, as a victim, combatant or beneficiary, etc). Yet, such a one-dimensional view overlooks the ability of local actors to adopt multiple strategies during the course of a civil war, peace process and peace implementation programme. These strategies need not be consistent: a farmer in Kosovo may be thankful to the international community for the physical security it has facilitated, but be disdainful of the economic uphill struggle created by international markets. Moreover, groups that outsiders may regard as homogeneous may include significant diversity.

International peace-support actors suffer from a major drawback in that they often access information in ways that reflect their own cultural biases. Thus, for example, there has been a trend towards the collection of data in formal ways for the construction of indicators (Suhrke and Samset 2007). Such formal metrics may allow contexts and situations to be 'read' and quantified by donor governments and international non-governmental organisations (INGOs), yet these formats are not necessarily faithful to the lived experience of local people. Moreover, the donor community may restrict itself to metropolitan areas, and most of its interactions may be with the cosmopolitan political and NGO elite in the country. In short, international actors may be poorly placed to observe and understand the full breadth of local agency. Politics in a society undergoing a war-to-peace transition may not conform to Western-looking templates. Political activity may not be principally organised according to formal political parties. Instead, family dynasties or ethnic bonds may take predominance. Yet, observers from Western contexts may be acculturated to 'reading' politics through the frame of political parties and other formal indicators.

Agency by local actors whereby they negotiate with, subvert or exploit international peace-support actors and structures is not necessarily akin to outright resistance. In most cases it can be most usefully seen in terms of local communities attempting to get on with their lives and maximise their own security. Resistance can also take subtle forms such as 'sitting out' an international intervention in the knowledge that international attention towards a particular country will likely shift away after a few years.

The fourth part of the hybridisation model emphasises the ability of local actors, structures and networks to create and maintain alternatives to the liberal peace. International actors are often very successful in creating the impression that the internationally mandated peace is 'the only game in town'. In this view, alternative forms of peace are regarded as illegitimate or somehow deviant. Yet local actors may prioritise types of peace, and ways of achieving peace, that differ from the internationally 'approved' type of peace. One of the prominent features of the internationally supported liberal peace is the extent to which it is state-centric. In many cases, it can be said that peacebuilding has been reduced to statebuilding. Liberal peace interventions often revolve around rebuilding the state, reforming the state, managing how the state controls the economy, and managing how the state accommodates different factions within a society. In essence, the state is the focal point of many liberal peace interventions. Yet the reach of the state is often limited, leaving many other sectors of the polity, economy and society in which people can create and maintain their own forms of peace and politics. These alternative forms of peace may not always be consciously created as a local form of peace or reconciliation. Rather than being a well-meaning social experiment imposed from the outside, alternative forms of peace and co-existence may be the bi-product of a business venture or the coming together of communities to exploit a local resource. (Meredith 2010). Such alternatives may simply take the form of people attempting to get on with their lives by earning a living, sending their children to school, and engaging in social diversions. In some cases this might involve forging new relationships (both in-group and out-group), or recognising that co-existence is required if everyday social goals are to be achieved. In some circumstances, these new relationships and recognition of the need for co-existence (even if it is grudging co-existence) can be called 'peace'.

There are, of course, conscious attempts to create alternative forms of social and political space that are removed from the orthodox forms of peace and order. For example, Hezbollah has been adept at organising its own reconstruction and social provision initiatives in Lebanon. These initiatives are often more efficient that those provided by the Lebanese state, but they can also be seen as part of a wider political struggle in which Hezbollah seeks to maintain a distance between its Shiite constituency and the Lebanese state (Harb and Fawaz 2010; Alamuddin 2010). But conscious attempts to create alternatives often occur on the margins of the polity, or in geographical spaces deemed inaccessible by those in metropolitan centres.

As already mentioned, state-centric approaches to peacemaking that are supported by the international community often take the form of technocratic interventions that may be formulaic. Such interventions may not always pay particular attention to the cultural needs and aspirations of communities. It may be the case that communities experiencing internationally sponsored peacemaking do not find externally imposed forms of peace legitimate or culturally appropriate. Such forms of peacemaking often emphasise the recalibration of formal political and bureaucratic relationships (for example, the institution of a power-sharing assembly) but do little to foster meaningful connections at the local and everyday levels. Importantly, attitudes towards peace and conflict often operate at the affective level (something that technocratic approaches are poor at engaging with). Local pacific or socially inclusive initiatives may have the benefit of engaging with cultural expectations of what peace and reconciliation should 'look like'.

It should be stressed that the 'reach' of the liberal peace can be extensive, and that the space for alternatives to the liberal peace are often constrained or time-limited. Away from conscious attempts at statebuilding or reconciliation, the liberal peace's main reach is in the form of globalised capitalist economics. The market has been able to shape relationships, attitudes and behaviours in multiple subtle and not-so-subtle ways. The space for fully fledged alternative forms of peacemaking is often very marginal, yet in some contexts populations retain respect for forms of peacemaking and reconciliation that draw on customary, indigenous and traditional practices and beliefs. The continuing appeal of customary and indigenous reconciliation and dispute resolution practices may be linked to four factors. Firstly, they may be regarded as legitimate and able to connect with locally mandated practices and expectations. Secondly, they may work more effectively than imported forms of peacemaking. Thirdly, an issue or area may remain outside of the reach or interest of formal liberal peace initiatives, and so local people may have few alternatives but to fall back on local practices. Fourthly, elements of the international community may seek to promote customary and indigenous forms of peacemaking, recognising them as effective, low-cost and a way of easing the exit or responsibility of international actors. The extent to which such approaches are truly indigenous or traditional can be debated (Mac Ginty 2008, 2010a, 2010b), but that is of secondary importance to the efficacy of such approaches.

In the interstices between the four parts of the model is a hybrid form of politics that may, in certain circumstances, be called a hybrid peace. What becomes clear in this model is that no actor is able to chart and maintain a unilateral course of action. Instead, all actors must take into account the positions and strategies of others. Especially important in this regard is a realisation that international actors, despite the enormous material power that is often at their disposal, are usually unable to force their will on others. Instead, all strategies are likely to encounter some form of distortion as they are refracted and bent by the actions and stances of others. Crucially, the distortion does not only apply to the stances and discourse of actors, it also applies to the very constitution of actors. Through their interaction with other actors, they will be exposed to ideas and practices that will encourage change. This change may be minor and imperceptible, but it does encourage us to reappraise notions of the unchanging actor in conflict areas. It also helps underscore the extent to which peacemaking environments are marked by dynamism and a complex interactionism through which the actions of one party result in responses by others.

Hybridisation in Action

Processes of hybridisation take place across all aspects of peace process and peace accord implementation environments. The interaction between internal and external actors will differ from issue to issue and from context to context. It is worth re-stressing that terms such as 'internal' and 'external' must be exercised with care and it is useful to think of them as porous and shifting. To aid comprehension, it is possible to conceive of five peace implementation sectors in a society emerging from violent conflict with assistance from international actors: security; economy; statebuilding and constitutional reform; governance; and civil society. Each of these sectors will be a site of conflict, cooperation, negotiation, collaboration and subversion as actors engage with one another or seek ways to enhance their own position. This section will review these five sectors with reference to reconstruction or peacebuilding in a specific context (hybrid security in Afghanistan, hybrid economic development in Iraq, hybrid statebuilding in Bosnia, hybrid governance in Lebanon, and hybrid civil society in Northern Ireland).

In terms of security, it is possible to see interaction between the local and the international, and the top-down and bottom-up in many contexts. Afghanistan provides a good example of how neither Western nor Afghan actors have been able to provide their preferred kind of security in the post-Taliban era. Liberal peace prescriptions of a monopoly of violence held by a democratic state have failed to materialise. Instead warlords and militia commanders have been incorporated into the Western-backed post-Taliban government. The warlords control private armies, raise their own 'taxes', and offer limited loyalty to Kabul (Giustozzi 2005; Schetter et al. 2007). The severity of the Taliban threat, however, has meant that Western states – and the United States in particular – have ditched much of their liberal emancipatory rhetoric and co-opted less-than-liberal actors into the defence of the post-Taliban protectorate. Contemporary Afghanistan provides a context in which there is cooperation and cohabitation between a modernist statebuilding worldview and one based on feudal armies. It is a context of hybrid security and is illustrative of the multiple compromises found in societies emerging from conflict. Importantly, the Afghan example is not a simple case of discrete Western and non-Western actors and practices coming together to create a fusion polity and composite form of security. The process is much more complex, as actors are neither consistent nor homogeneous.

In terms of the economic dimension of liberal peacebuilding environments, it is possible to see the hybridisation of economies. All economies are hybrids, and are composed of a mix of types of economic activity and management, as well as different sizes of enterprises. The peculiar circumstances of societies emerging from violent conflict and subject to internationally supported peacebuilding interventions can accelerate and distort much of this hybridity. In the case of Iraq, we can see how the invasion and occupation introduced a unique set of distortions to the already hybridised Iraqi economy. The policy choices of top-down and bottom-up actors were severely constrained by the actions of the other. No actor, not even the new masters of Iraq who had swept aside Saddam Hussein's regime in 41 days, had full autonomy (Phillips 2005). Instead, all economic actors were forced to deal with obstacles and opportunities presented by others. Coalition-led attempts to rehabilitate the oil industry and to privatise state-owned enterprises met with failure (Herring and Rangwala 2006; Herring 2008). The bottom-up informal economy of survival thrived through necessity. The top-down and bottom-up economies shaped each other, even though – theoretically – they represented two very different economic spheres; on the one hand a capital-intensive, highly globalised resource extraction industry, and on the other an economy of everyday survival through low-level trade, 'corruption' and smuggling.

All four elements of the hybridisation model were in evidence in relation to the attempt by the liberal peace powers to 'reboot' the Iraqi economy. Liberal peace coercion was evidenced by the economic restructuring impositions and edicts by the Coalition Provision Authority (Alkadiri and Mohamedi 2003; Lacher 2007). Liberal peace incentives were in place through reconstruction grants and loans. Local resistance, subversion and alternatives to the liberal peace came in the form of the informal economy. Everyday economic survival by Iraqis was rarely a conscious act of resistance. The necessity of 'getting by' restricted the ability of many Iraqis to engage in explicit resistance or alternative-making, while the security situation added another impediment. Iraq's post-invasion hybrid economy reveals the limits of liberal peace projection and the agency of local actors in subverting and distorting the liberal peace.

In relation to the third pillar of liberal peacebuilding interventions, statebuilding and constitutional reform, it is clear that many liberal interventions have sought to recast the state in the liberal Weberian mode. Constitutions have been re-written in ways that emphasise individual rights and political notions usually associated with the global north. Yet despite the rhetoric of a 'clean break' and a 'fresh start' that often accompanies liberal statebuilding and constitutional reform, states and constitutions cannot be formed from scratch. In all cases there is some legacy from the past resulting in a hybrid state. This applies in cases of regime change or even the creation of a new state arising from secession.

Consider the example of Bosnia-Herzegovina, which was formed as a result of the 1995 Dayton Accords that sought to bring the wars in Yugoslavia to an end. The liberal statebuilders of 1995 were merely the latest in a long line of political leaders who sought to 'create' a 'new' state that would accommodate the region's competing nationalisms. The result, like the political constructions before it, was a hybrid that reflected past experience, existing boundaries, demography, battlefield gains, international strategic calculations, international legal and economic norms, and emotional decisions on how some actors should be rewarded and others punished. The 'new' state of Bosnia-Herzegovina was a distortion of liberal ideas melded with nationalism, realism and a socialist legacy. It was hybridised in its conception, design and implementation. Hybridisation also became evident in the operation of the new state, as nationalists, the old socialist nomenclature and others grappled with internationally imposed governance norms.

Hindess (2007: 326) notes a 'tendency to treat belonging to the past as a bad thing, that is, as a kind of cultural and moral failure'. Citizens in societies emerging from violent conflict are often bombarded by the international community and local centrist politicians with inanities along the lines of 'put the past behind you', 'it's time to move on', and 'we must all look to the future'. Nationalist histories may be frowned upon, and new approved histories – perhaps emphasising a fictional prelapsarian multi-ethnic idyll – are endorsed (Grodach 2002). Yet, despite facing inconvenient and awkward situations, societies must contend with what is dealt to them – not the situations liberal peacebuilders would like them to have. Bosnia-Herzegovina experienced a series of continuities that stretched from the days of the monarchy and the socialist era. The most significant of these was the continuing relevance of nationalism to many of its inhabitants. Nationalism and ethnicity remained the principal political referents for the majority of the population of Bosnia-Herzegovina in the post-Dayton era, and attempts to establish a civic, plural Bosnian 'nationness' foundered (Nikiforou 1997: 84; Donais and Pickel 2003: 19). Post-Dayton nationalisms were not exact replicas of pre-war nationalisms, but they were powerful enough to bend the new state and distort its attempts to create a fresh start. It was a hybridised context. Baskin (2007: 261) reminds us of the importance of a long-term historical perspective: 'The nasty war in Bosnia-Herzegovina that took place from 1991 to 1995 was one act in the failed drama of the Yugoslav transition from one-party socialism to a liberal, democratic order.'

The fourth sector of liberal peacebuilding that deserves coverage is governance. Such reforms are often driven by external actors, and so it is possible to develop a narrative of governance as a top-down, technocratic process through which Western administrative values and practices are injected into a war-torn society as part of an international peace-support intervention. While governance interventions are indeed largely top-down and externally driven, the picture is not always so clear-cut. Hybrid forms of governance abound in which endogenous and exogenous forms of governance conflict, co-exist and cooperate. In the case of post-civil war Lebanon it is possible to see how the World Bank, IMF, United Nations Development Programme (UNDP), the European Union and others embarked on intrusive and highly political projects under the guise of 'efficiency' and 'participation'. Many of these interventions have been without finesse, and it has been very clear that they have a one-way dynamic in which Western 'best practice' is 'recommended' to target states in ways that they find difficult to refuse (Hamieh and Mac Ginty 2009).

Three points are worth making in relation to Lebanon's experience of 'good governance' interventions. Firstly, the governance interventions were extremely political in nature. They went far beyond technocratic reforms concerned with administrative efficiency, and involved issues such as electoral reform, improving the quality of criminal investigations, and inter-communal dialogue – all extremely political issues. Secondly, it is clear that the governance agenda was set by external actors. The EU, IMF, World Bank, OECD and UNDP were the donors of governance advice and resources while Lebanon was the recipient. Governance-related documents from international organisations do not even pay lip-service to the notion that local actors in Lebanon would have anything to contribute to governance programming by way of knowledge, values or practices. Old-school pedagogy runs through these documents; they have a hectoring tone that makes it clear that Lebanon is deficient and that only rapid conformity to international standards will suffice. Thirdly, although governance reforms were conducted in the name of the Lebanese people, these interventions were largely conducted without consultation. A good example comes from the World Bank's urging that Lebanon's nationalised water utility be privatised, that consumers are made to pay for water, and that the national water service be broken up into several companies (Catafago 2005: 80–81). There was no public appetite for this change, nor did the initiative for it come from the Government of Lebanon.

Despite the very obvious Western imprint on governance interventions, there was one aspect of the governance agenda on which many Lebanese actors were active: anti-corruption. Perpetrators of governance interventions often develop a comforting and self-affirming narrative that non-Western governments and practices are corrupt and require rectification under Western tutelage. Of course, such narratives are oblivious to the corruption associated with Western polities and enterprises (the UK parliamentary expenses scandal and the state 'regulated' casino capitalism that led to the global financial crisis in 2008 spring to mind). In Lebanon, a wide range of local political and civil society actors were interested in governance reform. Evidence of sustained government corruption, inefficiency, discrimination and incapacity was not difficult to find. Some Lebanese actors were co-opted by external actors and willingly enjoined the externally driven governance reform agenda. Many were compelled to cooperate with the governance reforms: given the economic leverage held by international actors the Lebanese government had little choice but to take on board governance advice. In some cases, a mix of internal and external forces combined to improve governance. The Lebanese Transparency Association (LTA), for example, is the local chapter of the INGO Transparency

International. While having a local membership and being well represented in Lebanese civil society, the LTA also cooperates with external organisations such as Mercy Corps, UNDP and the Center for International Private Enterprise. The organisation's mission is in tune with those of many international good governance organisations and programmes, thus raising questions on the extent to which LTA's agenda can be judged to be Lebanese.

Aside from the more obvious anti-corruption NGOs and INGOs, there was one actor in Lebanon with a sustained interest in tackling corruption, and this actor held many views that were antithetical to those held by the champions of the liberal peace. Hezbollah's opposition to government corruption was largely independent of the internationally driven good governance agenda. Liberal peace agents and Hezbollah chose very different methods to tackle corruption. For the former, corruption could be tackled via good governance programmes that sought to modify state mechanisms and tutor state functionaries in 'modern' and transparent means of governance. Liberal peace governance interventions have largely been about reinforcing the Lebanese state and moulding it in the likeness of a preferred Western model of the Weberian state. Hezbollah also judges the Lebanese state to be deficient, equating it with many of aspects of Lebanese society that it would wish to change: corruption, weakness in the face of Israel and an over-eager orientation towards the West.

Hezbollah worked hard to exploit the corruption issue. Its growth in popularity within the Shiite population was initially fuelled by frustration with the Amal movement who were seen as venal, corporeal and ineffective (Norton 2000: 24). It juxtaposed the efficiency of its own social services with those of the state. This was particularly the case during reconstruction following the 2006 war when state reconstruction efforts were seen to be slow, overly bureaucratic and corrupt (Hamieh and Mac Ginty 2009). Hezbollah made a show of the speed and efficiency of its reconstruction programme. In multiple interviews with the author, personnel from INGOs, NGOs and the Lebanese bureaucracy attested that Hezbollah's approach to reconstruction was superior to that shown by the state and many international organisations. Within the political system, Hezbollah have stressed the importance of addressing corruption. Shanahan (2005: 4) observed that Hezbollah members 'are meticulous about maintaining a public reputation for financial probity and an active opposition within government.' Norton (2000: 32) noted that 'Hizballahi deputies have earned a reputation for acumen and flexibility. They have also sustained a singular reputation for integrity.'

A hybridisation of the Lebanese context is visible through the extent to which political actors with very different worldviews have been forced to accept the existence of the other. UN, EU and INGO officials working on governance issues must deal with Hezbollah politicians and officials, especially at the municipal level. Indeed, at the time of writing in 2011, a Hezbollah minister is in charge of the Ministry of Administrative Reform and thus is the key link person between the Lebanese government and international organisations like UNDP and the EU that promote the good governance agenda. Governance reforms in Lebanon are exemplars of hybridisation.

The final sector commonly found in internationally supported peacebuilding interventions revolves around civil society. Internationally supported civil society is regarded as a bulwark against nationalism and as a service provider that may be more efficient than the state. Northern Ireland during its peace process (from 1994 onwards) provides a good example of hybridised civil society. In this case, the British and Irish governments, who acted as guardians of the peace process, encouraged organisations associated with the two sides in Northern Ireland to become involved in pro-peace process civil society initiatives. This encouragement was aided by enormous sums of European Union peacebuilding funding. Almost €2 bn will have been spent when peacebuilding funding comes to an end in 2013. The result was the creation of a peacebuilding political economy which distorted pre-existing civil society and led to the creation of many new groups. Some of these groups were sincere in their desire for peacebuilding. Others were not and were primarily motivated by the funding. The key point is that a hybridised form of civil society developed in which actors that could not be described as 'plural' or 'inclusive' were admitted to the government-recognised civil society sector. The exigencies of the peace process meant that the British and Irish governments directed funding towards sectarian organisations with a record of exclusion and, in some cases, violence. Civil society was hybridised, not only as a set of organisations and practices, but also as a notion. It became a mix of the liberal and the non-liberal.

Concluding Discussion

The notions of hybridity and hybridisation have been deployed as a way of 'bringing the local back in' to our studies. They encourage us to look beyond the overly neat silos or transmission chains whereby liberal peacemaking is something that it 'done to' local communities. As well as co-option and cooperation, it involves 'blowback' or local actors pushing back against international peace interventions, which in turn has consequences on liberal peace progenitors. It also involves local actors creating and maintaining their own space for political, economic and cultural interaction that is largely removed from the agendas and resource streams created by liberal peace actors.

It should be noted that this chapter does not advocate hybridity *per se*. Hybridity is often problematic and not necessarily pacific. We have seen hybrid forms of war and injustice, as well as hybrid forms of sharing and tolerance. So it is worth differentiating between 'hybrid peace' or forms of hybridity that encourage inclusion, tolerance, and sustainable approaches from wider forms of hybrid politics, economics and security.

A worldview patterned by the liberal peace might be tempted to negatively frame local action in the face of liberal peace interventions; unless, of course, those actions conform to 'approved' types of action. Resistance might be viewed as an inherently negative activity. Such a view is presupposed on the righteousness of hegemonic approaches to peacemaking. Yet much 'resistance' is simply people getting on with their lives, opting out of the formal structures and norms offered by the liberal peace, and creating their own solutions to local issues. It is often a process of individuals and societies and finding an equilibrium between various pressures. As such, it is a form of conflict management. Much of it is to be celebrated as it contains the types of 'ownership' and 'sustainability' that internationals often try to create. Of course, we must not romanticise resistance and hybridity as 'plucky locals standing up to the nasty international'. Resistance can be sectarian and motivated by selfish interests. But in some cases, resistance and hybridity lead to a better form of peace: a peace that is more comfortable and sustainable for the communities that must live that peace. A great difficulty is that many international actors and perspectives are unable to accept such hybrid forms of peace as 'peace'.

Bibliography

Alamuddin, H. (2010) 'Wa'd: The Reconstruction Project of the Southern Suburb of Beirut', in H. Al-Harithy (ed.) *Lessons in Post-War Reconstruction: Case Studies from Lebanon in the Aftermath of the 2006 War*, London: Routledge, pp. 47–70.

Alkadiri, R. and F. Mohamedi (2003) 'World Oil Markets and the Invasion of Iraq', *Middle East Report*, 227: 20–31.

Baskin, M. (2007) 'Interim Notions of Statehood in Bosnia-Herzegovina: A Permanent Transition?', in K. Guttieri and J. Piombo (eds) *Interim Governments: Institutional Bridges to Peace and Democracy* Washington, DC: United States Institute of Peace Press, pp. 257–280.

Canclini, N. G. (2005) *Hybrid Cultures: Strategies for Entering and Leaving Modernity*, Minnesota: University of Minnesota Press.

Catafago, S. (2005) 'Restructuring Water Sector in Lebanon: Litani River Authority – Facing the Challenges of Good Water Governance', in A. Hamdy and R. Monti (eds) *Food Security under Water Scarcity in the Middle East: Problems and Solutions*, Bari: CIHEAM-IAMB, pp. 75–93.

Davis, M. (2001) *Late Victorian Holocausts: El Nino Famines and the Making of the Third World*, London: Verso.

Donais, T. and A. Pickel (2003) 'The International Engineering of a Multiethnic State in Bosnia: Bound to Fail, yet Likely to Persist', paper prepared for presentation at the CPSA Annual Conference, Halifax, Nova Scotia, 1 June.

Duffield, M. (2002) 'Reprising Durable Disorder: Network War and the Securitization of Aid', in B. Hettne and B. Odén (eds) *Global Governance in the 21st Century: Alternative Perspectives on World Order*, Stockholm: Almqvist and Wiksell, pp. 74–105.

Gabbatt, A. (2010) 'US to Cut $4bn in Afghan Aid after Corruption Allegations', *Guardian*, 1 July.
Giustozzi, A. (2005) 'The Debate on Warlordism: The Importance of Military Legitimacy', Crisis States Research Centre discussion paper 13, London School of Economics.
Gray, J. (2000) *Two Faces of Liberalism*, Cambridge: Polity.
Grodach, C. (2002) 'Reconstituting History and Identity in Post-war Mostar, Bosnia-Herzegovina', *City* 6(1): 61–82.
Hamieh, C. S. and R. Mac Ginty (2009) 'A Very Political Reconstruction: Governance and Reconstruction in Lebanon after the 2006 War', *Disasters: The Journal of Disaster Studies, Policy and Management* 34(1): 103–123.
Harb, M. and M. Fawaz (2010) 'Influencing the Politics of Reconstruction in Haret Hreik', in H. Al-Harithy (ed.) *Lessons in Post-War Reconstruction: Case Studies from Lebanon in the Aftermath of the 2006 War*, London: Routledge, pp. 21–45.
Herring, E. (2008) 'Neoliberalism Versus Peacebuilding in Iraq', in M. Pugh, N. Cooper and M. Turner (eds) *Whose Peace? Critical Perspectives on the Political Economy of Peacebuilding*, Basingstoke: Palgrave Macmillan, pp. 47–64.
Herring, E. and G. Rangwala (2006) *Iraq in Fragments: The Occupation and Its Legacy*, London: Hurst.
Hindess, B. (2007) 'The Past Is Another Culture', *International Political Sociology* 1(4): 325–338.
Lacher, W. (2007) 'Iraq: Exception to, or Epitome of Contemporary Post-Conflict Reconstruction', *International Peacekeeping* 14(2): 237–250.
Lederach, J. P. (1995) *Preparing for Peace: Conflict Transformation across Cultures*, Syracuse, NY: Syracuse University Press.
Lederach, J. P. (1999) *Building Peace: Sustainable Reconciliation in Divided Societies* Washington, DC: United States Institute of Peace.
Mac Ginty, R. (2006) *No War, No Peace: The Rejuvenation of Stalled Peace Processes and Peace Accords*, Basingstoke: Palgrave.
Mac Ginty, R. (2008) 'Indigenous Peacemaking Versus the Liberal Peace', *Cooperation and Conflict* 43(2): 139–163.
Mac Ginty, R. (2010a) 'Hybrid Peace: The Interaction between Top Down and Bottom Up Peace', *Security Dialogue* 41(4): 391–412.
Mac Ginty, R. (2010b) 'Gilding the Lily? International Support for Indigenous and Traditional Peacebuilding', in O. P. Richmond (ed.) *Palgrave Advances in Peacebuilding: Critical Developments and Approaches*, Basingstoke: Palgrave, pp. 347–366.
Mac Ginty, R. (2011) *International Peacebuilding and Local Resistance: Hybrid Forms of Peace*, Basingstoke: Palgrave.
Meredith, F. (2010) 'The Shop around the Corner', *Irish Times*, 18 December.
Nikiforou, A. (1997) 'Bosnian Futurology', *Cambridge Review of International Affairs* 11(1): 81–91.
Norton, A. R. (2000) 'Hizballah and the Israeli Withdrawal from Southern Lebanon', *Journal of Palestinian Studies* 30(1): 22–35.
Paris, R. (2010) 'Saving Liberal Peacebuilding', *Review of International Studies* 36(2): 337–365.
Phillips, D. (2005) *Losing Iraq: Inside the Postwar Reconstruction Fiasco*, New York: Basic Books.
Richmond, O. P. (2009) 'A Post-liberal Peace: Eirenism and the Everyday', *Review of International Studies* 35(3): 557–580.

Schetter, C., R. Glassner and M. Karokhail (2007) 'Beyond Warlordism: The Local Security Architecture in Afghanistan', *Internationale Politik und Gesellschaft* 2: 136–152, available at: http://www.fes.de/IPG/inhalt_d/pdf/10_Schetter_US.pdf, accessed 18 December 2010.

Shanahan, R. (2005) 'Hizballah Rising: The Political Battle for the Loyalty of the Shi'a of Lebanon', *Middle East Review of International Affairs* 9(1): 1–6.

Suhrke, A. and I. Samset (2007) 'What's in a Figure? Estimating Recurrence of Civil War', *International Peacekeeping* 14(2): 195–203.

13

Resistance and the Post-Liberal Peace

Oliver P. Richmond

Introduction

It has recently become clear that a fourth generation (Richmond 2002) of peacebuilding has not been achieved by liberal peacebuilding approaches. They have instead reaffirmed territorial sovereignty, hierarchical epistemologies and the sovereign limits of modernisation. Recent experiences of statebuilding and liberal peacebuilding indicate the need to begin to look beyond liberalism. Liberal forms of peacebuilding have become subservient to statebuilding and romanticise the non-liberal self. They operate at many levels of denial: cultural, structural, economic and physical (Darby 2009). Critical research agendas for peace (Richmond 2007a, 2009a) have shown that the liberal peace has been troublingly diverted in the relatively new testing grounds of post-conflict environments. This has been towards states, elites, international actors, security issues, and liberal institutions and norms. Worse, internationals have blamed local actors and communities for this diversion in a classical move, reminiscent of an essentialising and romanticising 'colonial gaze'. This erases their own apparently ineffective hegemony and their responsibility to others (Kapoor 2008: xiv; 26–27). It is notable how documents like 'Responsibility to Protect' or doctrines such as 'do no harm' are internationalised rather than localised and fail to engage with everyday life other than in basic emergency and narrow security terms (ICISS 2001; Anderson 1999).

Attention has been diverted away from local contexts, communities and agencies.[1] Much academic and policy work has become complicit with this tendency. This is also true of the older projects of internationalism, peacebuilding and conflict resolution. These have been diverted away from individual and community conditions of peace, in the context of the international and the local, to sovereign peaces organised around states and their territories. This follows on from a hegemonic liberal peace directed by a Western core of states and international organisations.[2] Peacebuilding's focus and derivation from social advocacy and action, from the citizen, the informal sector, and on the most marginalised, has been deferred in favour of the state and bureaucratic, political and business elites. Statebuilding has become the aim even as contemporary IR has problematised the state, sovereignty, embedded liberalism and the international system itself. The most marginalised, the individual, community, kinship, agency and context have been subsumed. At best they are only recognised rhetorically.

Key liberal sites have been captured, ideologically and materially, by those who have more direct access to such institutions or to the liberal international edifice. This has been used unreflexively as a technology of power and legitimacy for the territorial state, not as a technology of the self (Martin et al. 1988: 16–49). The liberal peace has also failed to negotiate with far more entrenched practices, commonly thought of in terms of custom and communalism, and everyday life. This is a classically colonial intellectual move designed to distance the everyday lives of post-conflict individuals (and those in 'development' settings) so that inequality can be effectively justified by non-liberal alterity. However, the liberal framework is deeply entrenched in IR and its related disciplines, and with some good reason: in that individual freedom, social prosperity, and peace are commonly shared political objectives. Yet IR is now interdisciplinary and transnational, not disciplinary and national.

Unsurprisingly, the age-old dynamics of colonial anxiety and local resistance have re-emerged in liberal modernity. This is present in the relationship between mainstream IR and the work of international institutions in liberal peacebuilding and statebuilding, and more critical versions and praxis of both. In response, it is often claimed that the common requisition of post-structural insights to understand emerging resistance to liberal modernity and its emancipatory claims actually undermines the latter's stable, rational agencies, and so 'reduce [s] politics to critique and "resistance"' (Kapoor 2003: 568).

In these struggles, a possibility of a post-liberal peace emerges, in which everyday local agencies,[3] rights, needs, custom and kinship are recognised as discursive 'webs of meaning'. This move away from 'imperious IR' (Agathangelou and Ling 2004: 21) and a willingness to emphasise local context and contingency lays bare those paradoxes and tensions derived from territorial sovereignty, the overbearing state, cold institutionalism, a focus on rights over needs, distant trustee style governance, and a hierarchical international system in which material power matters more than everyday life.

The post-liberal form of peace, and its politics, denotes a hybrid local-liberal peace. Agencies are expressed that contaminate, transgress and modify both the international and the local. They enable political mobilisation to deal with everyday issues and to build representative institutions and locally resonant forms of statehood. Of course, the difficulties of saying 'no' to the hegemonic discourse must be borne in mind (Spivak 1988: 75). Moving beyond liberal peacebuilding does not mean the end of the liberal peace but enabling its reconnection with its subjects in widely divergent contexts. Nor should it romanticise the capacity, resistance and agency of the local (Richmond 2008, 2009a, 2009b, 2009c). At the same time, it should be recognised that 'metropolitan time' (meaning Western modernity) – or the liberal peace – may not set suitable standards for the evaluation of non-Western time (Bhabha 1995: 47–61) (meaning context, custom, tradition and difference in its everyday setting).

This is a partial response to the recent claims about a 'critical impasse' between orthodox liberal debates and the critics of statebuilding or liberal interventionism. Indeed, these claims are premature: the mainstream has not moved to address many of the issues that have been raised by its own 'incomplete modernity' (Chatterjee 1998: 67) in any concrete way (other then via rhetoric about 'local participation' or 'ownership' or ideological defences of liberal universalism and its brethren). Local agencies, whether resisting aspects of statebuilding or co-opting it, have begun to find ways of claiming ownership of a politics that respond to needs and identity issues, appropriating liberal peacebuilding, ignoring it or modifying it.

This chapter discusses what an IR and peacebuilding praxis located around the everyday might look like in terms of the hidden agencies that might emerge. It outlines the general contours of any discussion of the everyday and the local, and the hybridity that ensues. This can be seen as an inevitable post-colonial response to the failings of political liberalism and its use as a universal template.[4] This clarifies the ongoing renegotiation of the liberal peace via local agency and its resistances (Kapoor 2008: 56).

Sites of Knowledge for Peace

The rejection of the state – the de-centring of power – is not enough to justify the now well-known critique of the liberal peace, without the development of alternative or modified understandings of political agency, which do not dilute the capacity of the political subject. It must also respond to the paradox that the state, sovereignty and territory and their associations with the grand project of international order have generally displaced the subject through war and securitisation, institutions and the market, and often counteracted the gains made through peace, human rights, enfranchisement and welfare (Chandler 2009: 56; Kapoor 2003: 568).

The everyday is a space in which local individuals and communities live and develop political strategies in their local environment, towards the state and towards international models of order. It is not civil society (often a Western-induced artifice) but it is representative of the deeper local–local. It is often transversal and transnational, engaging with needs, rights, custom, individual, community, agency and mobilisation in political terms. Yet, these are often hidden or deemed marginal by mainstream approaches. The everyday entails a recognition of just how crucial such dynamics are, even at higher levels of politics, but of course it does not confirm the state in its formal positivist, territorial form. Clearly some form of the state and of institutions which represent the interests of political subjects is necessary but this should include rather than exclude the everyday. The everyday is often seen in a range of literatures as a site of dynamics including resistance and politicisation, solidarity, local agency, hybridity, and also of passivity and depoliticisation. Resistance indicates the potential of the everyday for repoliticisation, as well as the potential of institutions and a state shaped around the everyday.

The move towards the 'local', defined as an alternative space, has been developing in many areas of study. This opposes the focus on the international, the state or governments, or indeed on 'locals' as ill-trained liberals or non-liberals. It also has methodological implications that require researchers to consider the implications of 'taking part' (even if they do not actually do so) in the everyday lives of the societies, regions, states and systems they study, not merely contributing to policy (which has often been determined beforehand). What is more, there is also the issue of whether and what the local and everyday should gain from research, and which and how local voices are selected (Eckl 2008: 187–190). In this context, the latter's relations with the everyday, local, custom and culture need to be understood in the context of material inequalities and imbalances. Gate keepers need to be uncovered, and assumptions and stereotypes need to be interrogated (ibid.: 196). The dynamics of 'studying down', from privileged positions towards those of the marginalised, poor, oppressed and conflict ridden (as opposed to the normal habits of 'studying up' towards states and institutions), need to be more widely understood, falling as they may somewhere between 'going native' or co-option and the tendency to move towards ethical or universalising responses (ibid.: 197). This process should not establish another set of binary oppositions, this time between the everyday and local and the international/state, the non-liberal other and the liberal. Instead the everyday is a site where these meet and are negotiated, leading variously to repulsion, modification or acceptance, and hybridity. Here, hidden everyday agencies renegotiate the liberal peace. It should be noted that the concept of hybridity is taken by Bhabha (one of its leading exponents) to include the way in which even in domination the coloniser invokes hybridity, reproducing a colonial relationship (Bhabha 1994: 33). To see through this, the 'labour of translation' needs to be undertaken (Butler 2002: 52). Otherwise, any engagement with the everyday will be skewed towards the currently predominant 'liberal' mode and, limited by the 'grid of the nation state system' (Chatterjee 1998: 59), this sort of hybridity would instead enable institutional agency.

Rather than reproducing Foucaultian patterns of liberal contradiction (leading to resistance) incorporating the everyday may enable an understanding of how local agency is also producing hybridity (Richmond 2009b). A contextual empathetic, and everyday form of peacebuilding and commensurate theory and methodology would prevent an 'unbecoming liberalism', whereby subjects engage in almost inevitable resistance (even though it may offer them more sophisticated rights).[5] As a result, liberal agents resort to coercion, which effectively undermines liberalism's offerings. As with previous and more directly colonial experiences, this is also unsettling for its agents, who were in the past colonial administrators and today may well be officials or employees of the UN, UNDP, World Bank, EU, OSCE, donor agencies, NGOs or the state (Hindess 2001: 353). Often, they may be concerned that the policies and approaches they follow do not live up to liberal standards – a kind of 'colonial anxiety' (Guha in Hindess 2001: 363).

The hybridity that emerges between the liberal and the local may avoid such anxieties and engage in a mutual remediation of political space, both overcoming and maintaining boundaries between them. Indeed, in the context of a *longue durée* perspective of debates on peace, in its positive and ambitious forms the everyday has always been a crucial part of IR for precisely this reason. It has been common for critical post-colonial, and post-structuralist thought to invoke the everyday in their relationship with a broad range of areas and disciplines. Indeed, most of the major developments in peace praxis have connected closely with everyday issues. Certainly, democracy, the rule of law and human rights connect the everyday to an institutional setting, and human security was a way of reconnecting security to the everyday and the local while maintaining liberal institutions after the state-centricity of Cold War politics (Acharya 2004). Concepts aimed at 'hearts and minds' operations, local ownership, civil society, or capacity-building approaches have emerged, implying intimate conversations between the local and the international in full acknowledgement of implicated power relations.[6]

Yet, these have failed to represent the everyday. In particular, they have failed to recognise local capacity, agency and resistance, as well as local elite co-option of the shallow neoliberal states that emerged from current international statebuilding practice. Most liberal philosophers associated with developing concepts such as internationalism, democracy, the social contract, human rights and rule of law saw this in the context of liberal peoples who used land 'productively' (Harvey 2005). The indigenous, local, nature and 'other', has been excluded and masked by a discussion of interests, norms and rights. This has laid the theoretical basis of a very powerful Foucaultian critique (Foucault 1991) and a discussion of identity, culture, representation and the 'local'. This is a more suitable site for an emancipatory or ethical form of peace or order in response.[7]

The Implications of the Everyday

In both Western and non-Western contexts, the everyday is a site of perceived subaltern agency, of resistance to depoliticisation, of activism, agonism and alterity – of both radical passivity and activity as well as passive and active radicality.

Much liberal, cosmopolitan and constructivist theory, recently actualised through documents such as 'Agenda for Peace' or 'Responsibility to Protect' or the 'High Level Panel Report', reaches implicitly for both the legitimacy of the everyday and the emancipation and facilitation of the everyday (Boutros Ghali 1992; United Nations 2004). Such work differs not on whether the everyday is significant at all but whether it is uniform across the world in its most basic sense of needs and rights, and whether it should and can be facilitated, guided and protected from above, via an *a priori* rights-based approach or should emerge as a result of individual and local agency and self-government. The politics of the everyday have generally been seen in juxtaposition to the conservative politics that preserve existing power relations between classes, social economic groups, identity groups, or the liberal politics which focuses on the institutional structures of governance that preserve state frameworks (large or small) for the benefit of communities and individuals. In this sense, they are associated with solidarity. Such positions are also often consistent with attempts to oppose meta-narratives, which essentialise the everyday, politics and identity (de Certeau 1984: xi; Plant 1992: 157–158).

This approach captures a 'place of hybridity' resting on such critiques and translations, leading through dissensus, alterity and otherness to an agonistic process of negotiation (Bhabha 1994: 35–37). Hybridity is produced by colonialism but is also a sign of resistance rather than a mere mimicry (though it may be more mimicry than resistance) (ibid.: 159–163). It is not aimed at reproducing 'civility' in its liberal and heterogeneous sense. Neither does it reproduce an indigenous golden era. Its locality is complex and multifaceted, focused on the 'contest for political and social authority within the modern world order' – read over liberal standards for political culture (ibid.: 245). This move rests partly on the reconstruction of IR using the discursive critique of post-colonialism, and the material critique of dependency theory (Kapoor 2002: 647–664). If a sovereignty is to be found that reconstructs the state, it is one emerging through de-territorialised democracy, cognisant of culture and custom, of alterity, liminality and of time lag vis-à-vis modernisation-based theories (Bhabha 1994: 274). The agonistic politics of representation, of needs, and rights, and of identities, open up a bridge between difference, based upon empathy, in an everyday context in spite of its agonism. Indeed, it is agonism itself that presents the possibility of empathy, and requires an engagement with the everyday (Connolly 1991). What Bhaba refers to as the 'in-between space' represents the emergence of cultural hybridity, and translation from and to an interface between the everyday and the international even despite the latter's liberal tendency towards claims of the universal, timeless, hegemonic fixity of a dominant Western, customary praxis. In the latter lie the telltale signs of governmentality (Bhabha 1994: 56) as opposed to the vox populi of an everyday context.

Post-colonial approaches reveal the subtleties of hegemony (or the liberal peace) in subverting alterity, the everyday, and making them appear abnormal or insignificant. Its response is sometimes ambivalent about local agency (Kapoor 2002: 661). From this perspective, local agency is best recognised as limited and ambivalent about its derivation in colonial or hegemonic power as opposed to the local (Kapoor 2003: 563). Even post-colonial approaches see the local as often to be found in the 'language of the master', which also itself become hybrid via the local (Bhabha 1994: 33). These agencies may be more than mimicry, but they offer a politics less than local self-determination, and may reconfirm hegemonic power.

Ethnographic approaches have also been widely seen in IR and related disciplines as enabling a clearer engagement with the local, with alterity, and with the everyday in the name of emancipation (Vrasti 2008: 280). The ethnographic turn has the everyday at its heart, if only in comparison to the failure of IR to enable the very qualities it often assumes in its liberal guise: i.e. democracy, human rights and development (ibid.: 283).

The concept of human security, which developed at the end of the Cold War, in part is a way of allowing such a move (Newman and Richmond 2001). Broadening security to include a range of political, social and economic factors allowed for the consideration of security in the context of everyday life in order to facilitate local agencies. This was soon attacked and labelled as implausible and unable to be operationalised (Paris 2001; Tadjbaksh 2005). As it was adopted by various states and international organisations it developed into a liberal institutionalist form, rather than the emancipatory form that was envisaged (Richmond 2007b). Everyday forms of peacebuilding may, in contrast, draw the concept of human security towards an emancipatory focus (see also Begby and Burgess 2009).

Democracy is crucial in this respect, but not necessarily in the institutional form that is encapsulated by a state (and often has been regarded procedurally as drained of substance) (Cerny 2009: 780) or in cosmopolitan form (Held 1997). To enable everyday agency it requires a 'broader attitude towards governance, political community, and life in general' (Chou and Bleiker 2009: 674). This might be in terms of the communicative turn that Aradau and Husymans have recently outlined (Aradau and Huysmans 2009: 587), or might be in terms of the 'democracy to come' outlined by Derrida, Newman and Connolly (Newman 2007). The aspiration for democracy and self-determination cannot be satisfied purely by state institutions; it must also incorporate the everyday so it may operate transnationally, informed by independent and radical agencies beyond mere rationalism and sovereignty (Chou and Bleiker 2009: 662). Democracy reaches for self-government on everyday, contingent terms, rather than institutionalism and a 'tyranny of the majority' (de Tocqueville 1945). This is reminiscent of deterritorialised democracy, agonistic respect and critical responsiveness, especially for the most marginalised, that Connolly has proposed, or the agonistic democracy of Mouffe, or to a lesser degree the deliberative vision of Habermas (Connolly 1991: 123–127; Mouffe 2000; Habermas 1998).

It also requires a conception of human rights, a framework for wealth, redistribution or social welfare, and a rule of law in a constitutional setting in order to guarantee the political agency of the individual in its everyday and community setting, not just in terms of formal state institutions. In these terms, this would represent a post-liberal development for both democracy and human security, through connection with the everyday with the liberal peace model. Implicitly, democracy is also about agency and resistance in a variety of forms, implying a tension with the liberal peace's technocratic, institutional, statist and bureaucratic tendencies (Newman 2007: 228). This emphasises the tensions within the liberal peace and also within the liberal-local hybrid now emerging in many locations, in which resistance and radical political agencies (or perhaps more appropriate, non-Western, non-developmental, subaltern agencies) are emerging. As Melucci argues, social movements and agency arise not just because of opposition to ideological hegemony or state power, but also as an expression of the cognitive, affective and creative relationships between people, which then translates into social action, which may also take the form of resistance.

Calls to describe an alternative paradigm of 'peace', or to enable its operationalisation, miss the point completely. Contextually reconstructing IR and its related peacebuilding or statebuilding enterprise cannot be achieved in general theory. To engage with the everyday and recognise local agency, contextual theory is required, which needs to be written obliquely, cognisant of time-lag, of aporias, of catechisms, of alterity, and sensitive to the many subalterns, without whom legitimacy cannot be achieved. Here the task of politics is to undercover local, everyday agencies, and to make each capable of translating, engaging, recognising, assisting and negotiating, without reverting to older colonial and racist patterns of understanding. This also means problematising the 'modernisation' of politics that has undermined the sphere of the everyday in favour of territorial sovereignty and institutionalism. The everyday is where formal explanatory capacity loses its abilities, and where inductive and critical approaches gain traction; it is also where the 'vague' and 'fuzzy' concepts associated with everyday life by rational thought are most apparent. Yet, for the critical thinker, the everyday is real, clear, sharp and precise, and is where IR often begins. To think in such terms offers the possibility of de-romanticising the local, and demystifying the international, and enabling the very 'critical agency' at stake in all political intervention (Chandler 2009).

Thus, the everyday represents the rebalancing and re-occupation of IR by real and lived experiences rather than merely as the empty and virtual residual space specific to powerful states and elites. It offers an opportunity for empathetic relations to emerge between the international and the everyday. It offers a balancing framework for say, Habermasian discourse ethics, where its impulse might be to valorise liberal values, a field site for post-structuralist scholars, and of course, uncovers a conveniently forgotten level of analysis for more orthodox approaches ranging from realism to constructivism. A sociology and ethnography of IR is required to balance the securitised and institutionalised responses of realist and liberal approaches. But, this would not, as with constructivism or critical theory, begin with the core assumptions of realism and liberalism, but instead with those conceptual, theoretical, methodological and ontological puzzles offered by the everyday in its international and regional contexts. In particular, this would enable a better understanding of how local actors fulfil their needs and maintain their institutions and identities, while appearing to conform to the strategic institutions of biopolitical governance (Foucault 2008).

One of the key liberal responses to this phenomena has to been to incorporate local actors and dimensions more closely into international attempts to deal with security, to establish liberal institutions, to promote development, human rights, human security, civil society and the rule of law. This was partly in response to local movements for more self-determination in the peace processes in Kosovo and Timor Leste, among many others. It has become customary for local partners, politicians, officials, local employees of agencies and NGOs, or local NGOs, social movements, cultural movements or religious groups to maintain their connection with international donors while also trying to maintain their autonomy and identity, as well as their priorities. While the donors have moved further into the terrain of donor-driven project development, local actors have often played along whilst also maintaining their own agendas. In Afghanistan, for example, the Tribal Liaison Office aimed at bridging the local and international has seen both agreement and confrontation. In Iraq, tribal politics were soon understood to be both the cause of and solution to the violence during US and UK attempts at liberal statebuilding. In sub-Saharan Africa, there has been a serious attempt to incorporate customary forms of law and governance even though donor positions on corruption, decentralisation, democracy and liberal institutions are often in tension with these attempts (Comaroff and Comaroff 1999; Ucko 2008; Schmeidl 2009; Boege et al. 2008). These reactions – spanning an incorporation of custom and traditional structures and the elevation of local voices and agencies – can be read both as examples of the reinsertion of local agency into IR and as a liberal realisation of its own failings. Here, the interface between the liberal and the local is producing hybridity often in ways which represent the international more than the local. Yet, the ambitions of the liberal peace and the legitimacy of liberalism itself have been significantly moderated by such dynamics, illustrating the hidden agencies of the everyday and their unexpected capacities.

The everyday is one of the main realities of IR. The local, empathy, the everyday, society, and the needs and agency of communities and individuals become to a large extent exempt from the interests of orthodox IR theory (as well as the issue of well-being, welfare, and 'class', among other everyday issues). The concept of the everyday has reappeared in post-colonial, sociological, and anthropological literatures for precisely these reasons (Spencer 2008: 44, 75). This arises from the legitimacy of ritualistic popular participation in democratic processes, which provide it with the sorts of legitimacy that the institutions of democracy cannot obtain if they are 'empty' (i.e. hijacked or manipulated by elite interests and distant from, and unable to assist, local populations) (ibid.: 78). It raises the question of what is necessary to achieve an everyday state (of peace) rather than merely a liberal state (ibid.: 118). The broader politics of the everyday thus engenders agency (and sometimes resistance) from which a local–liberal interface arises. This produces hybridity and ultimately a post-liberal peace in which liberal institutions and norms are modified in each different context.

Resistance and Post-liberal Peace

Beyond the confines of mainstream IR, peacebuilding may now be seen as partially a site of international assistance, via social, political and economic engineering. It is also partially a site of local acquiescence, local co-option, and of multiple and often hidden forms of resistance. There are international and local public and hidden transcripts at play here, which expose the tension between the international and the local in terms of acquiescence, domination and resistance (Scott 1990: xxii). Both local and international offer a public transcript framed in mutually understandable language about how each may help each other, but there is a hidden transcript which betrays a lack of understanding, care or agreement, and antagonistic relations of domination and resistance (ibid.: 41). Both reject each other as a natural order of things but also attempt to naturalise themselves, which also has the effect of spurring internal and external critiques of international and local practices, where they are deemed to interfere with autonomy and agency (ibid.: 72, 103).

Peacebuilding as resistance appears, at least from the local level, to offer the main avenue through which to shape the emerging political environment, though this is predicated on the ability to resist overwhelming technical superiority, and to modify it marginally, or to mimic it. This occurs through a range of 'minute, individual, autonomous tactics and strategies' (Foucault in Scott 1990: 29), the constant everyday forms of resistance through which local agency may be expressed despite overwhelming authority. This is a resistance to the central claims of liberal peacebuilding and statebuilding, its celebrations of pluralism-as-liberalism, its claimed rights to adjudicate and manipulate material resources, its universal legitimacy, its underlying celebration of individualism and deference to the market, its underlying claims that agency (in this instance meaning self-help) is always present even for the most marginalised, and its validation of national identities, sovereignty, rights and justice in prior forms. It may involve becoming 'modern' or becoming 'liberal' but in heavily or subtly modified ways, rather than merely rejecting fully the liberal peace model and romanticising either local resistance or international authority. Local forms of peacebuilding are reconstituting themselves as resistance to the relatively empty signification of doctrines such as responsibility to protect or 'do no harm' as well as liberal peacebuilding itself, and its assumption of liberal state creation. Resistance at the local level provides a site from which a new peace begins to be imagined in contextual and everyday terms, perhaps reconstituting a social contract and a state, or even moving beyond Westphalia.

Peacebuilding as resistance represents a form of agonism between the liberal and the local, experienced mainly at the level of the everyday, rather then via revolutionary alterity (Shinko 2008). It is often through resistance to peacebuilding, statebuilding, development, the market, or to modern or normative praxes that a civil society and a social contract comes into being in agonistic terms, overcoming the distancing that liberal peacebuilding tends to bring about. Thus, peacebuilding as resistance may lead to emancipation (as well as to more dubious forms of politics, for which a balance must be found). This can be seen in two ways: either peacebuilding as resistance revitalises the liberal social contract and gives these externally constructed states substance, or it enables a more proactive encounter between the liberal peace and its others, in which the hegemonic weight of the liberal peace project is finally countermanded.

This process is only now becoming clear. In many post-conflict or conflict environments, the everyday is ignored mainly because it is seen as a site of alterity and of resistance, or worse of apathy: or perhaps, as problematic. As Scott argued in another context, local actors, intentions and processes silence themselves in the interests of maintaining their remaining space (Scott 1990:

301), or are simply muted by international dominance and a liberal aversion of non-liberal symbolic productions. Yet, engaging the local with peacebuilding requires engaging with local understandings which may well entail resistance to modernity, to modernisation, to centralised state power, sovereignties outside of limited communities, liberal norms and institutions, the market and conceptions of rights over needs. Peacebuilding as resistance may prioritise self-determination, community, agency, autonomy, sometimes democracy and a sense of nation, and sometimes the materiality of liberal states.

Thus, there are parallels between liberal peace frameworks and cosmopolitan or internationalist aspirations, but there are also acute tensions, some of which play out agonistically or lead to blockages in the negotiating process between the two. Until recently, the tendency has been for the international to take priority because of the older bias of IR, but this has disenfranchised the very populations it sought to govern. Peacebuilding needs to incorporate local discourse founders (Foucault 1979), as well as received international wisdom. Even without overt cooperation, together they produce new political subjects in post-conflict environments via a complex mixture of agency, autonomy, resistance and acceptance. This requires the recognition of the transversal, transnational and translocal agencies expressed in the everyday, and an assessment of their capacity to move between such situations, as they create autonomy themselves and their politics and avoid technologies of power, reductionism and totalising praxes that endanger freedom and self-determination.

Peacebuilding cannot just be reduced to localised resistance of course, but the latter's relationship with liberal statebuilding needs to be problematised (indeed, in the field, it is notable how today many members of the 'international civil service' of peacebuilders privately resist aspects of liberal peacebuilding themselves). Of course the programmes introduced by liberal peacebuilding generally remove or constrain local agency as resistance in various, often unintended, ways. Both disarmament, demobilisation and reintegration and security sector reform remove weapons and concentrate them in the hands of armies. Marketisation removes protectionism making competition and so livelihoods very difficult for new post-conflict entrants in the market system. Democratisation focuses politics on the party system and their general and often nationalist agendas. Human rights supplant human needs. The rule of law endorses all of this and protects private property and may even entrench socio-economic inequality and a class system. International support, loans, grants, advice, companies, peacekeepers, agencies and NGOs are supposed to compensate for this removal of agency in these areas, and to focus on empowering civil society, citizens and the state to operate in their confines. This sleight of hand is what makes the everyday so important, and is what leads to the paradox of civil society and localised forms of peacebuilding becoming platforms for deep, local–local resistance, however marginal, and for the development of an agonism between the liberal and the local. On a positive note this may form the basis of a new social contract.

At the very least, considering the everyday in both IR and in peacebuilding praxis requires that, rather than being policy-driven, elite-driven and externally driven, both are 'context-driven'. Here, the repoliticisation and enabling of relatively autonomous agency necessary for democracy, rights, needs, justice and culture and identity may occur. Contextually driven approaches require an empathetic response between 'liberals' and 'locals' over their mutual and separate everyday norms, interests, and lives. They require a detailed and ethnographic, not just securitised, or institutional, or statistical or trend-based understanding of each other's positions and contexts. They open up the world of the local to IR, and to peacebuilding approaches, also perhaps reinvigorating an emancipatory notion of human security. It requires, at the very least, a thin version of the Habermasian approach to discourse theory on the part of those engaged in what they see as a liberal, cosmopolitan project (Linklater 2005: 154; Connolly 1991: 218) but preferably an engagement with the less easily essentialisable offerings of Connolly on deterritorialisation, on the avoidance of othering and narcissistic difference, or on the reconstruction and pluralisation of exclusive communities. IR should 'stop operating on the assumption that observable diversity is but a veil over fundamentally similar processes' (Chabal and Daloz 2006: 327), where the state, peace and agency might be easily uncovered. The site of the everyday is probably not a place to reconstruct a single cosmopolitan everyday or to aspire to communitarian boundaries, but instead represents pluralities, which meet, interact, integrate, react, resist, mediate and negotiate.

Conclusion: The Infrapolitics of Peacebuilding

Everyday engagements with peacebuilding around the world are often aimed at claiming autonomous agency at the local or national level. This indicates resistance is often relatively hidden or very explicit, which can be seen from Timor Leste to Afghanistan. Often these resistances take place in the 'blind spots' of the liberal peace (caused by its problem-solving and epistemic frameworks), and are framed as liberation discourses, either for community or national projects. They may well be marginal, but they are having a significant impact in that they are producing hybrid forms of peace, which are indicative of a post-liberal evolution.

One of the most interesting aspects of the 'post-liberal peace' is that it rescues and reunites both the liberal and the local. It does not aim to depoliticise the local or to remove politics from the international, but to highlight the evolving relations between them. Of course, liberalism is actually a form of customary political community, derived from the Western experience (i.e. the West's own 'local'). The liberal–local hybrid can represent either a combination of very negative political practices (for example, rigorously determined liberal institutionalism and market development solutions with patriarchal, feudal, communal or sexist practices). It can be more positive, in that it connects complementary practices related to self-determination and agency, democracy, human rights and needs, and a rule of law, with customary social support networks and customary forms of governance and political order. It can connect both negative and positive practices (meaning both the liberal and the locally developed elements of attraction and rejection). Though the problem posed here might be that liberalism and customary forms of governance are mutually exclusive, empirical research suggests that this is not always the case (Richmond 2011). Liberalism, more specifically, is less likely to recognise the local, the contextual, and customary order. Liberalism is more likely to actively marginalise the local than the local is to marginalise the liberal. This is partly due to the power-relations between liberalism and the local, which inevitably favour liberal political orders.

The liberal–local hybrid represents a long-term process of political evolution towards a post-liberal form via the everyday, which might be taken as a 'post-conventional contextualism' (Benhabib 1993). This everyday is not a benign space, but a tense episteme requiring understanding and translation (not mapping, explaining or essentialising). Through this, other voices can attain agency and represent themselves, so that the subaltern may speak in and to IR, even if only to try to explain their predicament (Spivak 1988: 104). This is where the 'infrapolitics' of peacebuilding lie – and a relatively hidden realm of IR: where culture, identity, agency and structure *from beneath* have a significant effect on its more visible mainstream dynamics such as the development of institutions and states (Scott 1990: 183–184).

A post-liberal peace requires that international actors use a range of methods that enable local actors and the most marginalised to engage with a discussion of their own requirements for needs provision and their own understandings of rights and institutions. What are often thought of as informal institutions, processes and modes of subsistence, as well as actors who are relatively insignificant in modern understandings of state formation, play a role in peacebuilding and the development of the state. In each context, this means that democracy and the formation of state institutions is at least partially determined and expressed by local voices expressing the full range of everyday issues and processes. This then takes the form of a negotiation between the range of local actors and international actors over the processes, institutions and aims of political organisation and mobilisation for peace.

It would see the co-existence and re-negotiation of liberal versions of democracy, the rule of law, human rights, development and the market, all contained by the modern state with customary forms of governance. It would include the recognition of the dynamics of the everyday, from the needs of communities and citizens in subsistence and customary settings, of tradition, history and non-liberal identities, of customary law, hereditary and tribal institutions, different notions about the use and ownership of land and property, to the role of the state, market or community/collective in providing services, and so forth.

A post-liberal form of peace may include the possibility of states or institutions emerging that are representative of a desire for the more equitable redistribution of wealth, of customary processes and non-rational forms of politics and society, including over land use and distribution, of collective rights as well as individual rights. It may also be indicative of a desire on the part of local stakeholders for international peacebuilding to play a facilitative rather than a directive role, to allow the post-liberal peace to emerge in a range of spaces which internationals may not fully understand because of their lack of contextual knowledge. It may require them to respond more urgently to material deficiencies that destabilise day-to-day life, rather than maintaining their current focus on elites, governance, politicians, and a business class housed within a formal state.

Institutions, and potentially states, designed in this more sensitive manner by local actors and facilitated by external actors would make a much better job of shaping participation and rights, of democracy and inclusion, and be much more empowering than at present. They might also escape elite predation and corruption to a greater degree, and facilitate political mobilisation without a nationalist state project or gross inequality emerging as an unintended consequence of international intervention, statebuilding or development.

Peacebuilding as resistance represents a complex mix of international hegemony, local resistance, mimicry, agency and subversion.[8] Beyond governmentality and biopower/politics, beyond essentialised notions of culture and identity, lies a range of hybrid processes – the often marginal modification of hegemonic praxis by hitherto hidden local agencies. The everyday captures these dynamics and spaces where a new politics may emerge beyond the liberal peace. The infrapolitics of peacebuilding and the resultant local-liberal hybrid make a post-liberal space for peace already a reality. As Fanon argued, a critical consciousness is required that is 'freed from colonialism and forewarned of all attempts at mystification, inoculated against all national anthems' (Fanon 1967 [1963]: 147).

Notes

1 Henceforth, I use the term 'the local' to denote what international actors normally perceive as a range of actors and terrains spanning their partners for liberal peacebuilding and

statebuilding at the elite level (whilst also acknowledging that many local actors may have extensive transnational and transversal experience of liberal politics) and civil society. The term 'local-local' would indicate the existence and diversity of communities and individuals that constitute political society beyond this often liberally projected artifice who may also have transnational and transversal exposure. The latter is where the everyday is at it most powerful as a critical tool. I do not equate the everyday/local with either non-liberalism, illiberalism or liberalism necessarily. On the local and its interconnections see Massey 1994; de Sousa Santos 2007.

2 The same might also be said of cosmopolitan forms of liberalism, such as that of David Held; Marxist-flavoured forms, such as that of Andrew Linklater; and post-modern versions of liberalism, as in Richard Rorty's work. See in particular, Rorty 1991: 209.

3 Thanks to Necati Polat for pointing out that agency is an Enlightenment concept, and my claim to facilitate it locally situates my work in this tradition. For key thinkers on everyday life see: Blanchot 1993; Lefebvre 1991; Debord 1999; de Certeau 1984.

4 I am indebted to Kristoffer Lidén for this link with post-colonial theory.

5 See, for a discussion of similar accusations aimed at Habermasian discourse theory, Linklater 2005.

6 Among others, Jean Paul Lederach is well known for making such arguments, and Jarat Chopra has made similar suggestions (Lederach 1997; Chopra and Hohe 2004). Such participatory approaches have been the subject of well-placed criticism, however, that they simply advocate international approaches at the local level rather engaging with local agency.

7 Such analyses often draw on Geertz's understanding of culture as an historically transmitted system of symbols, conceptions, knowledge and attitudes. This is, of course, fluid, and also plays out within and through politics (Geertz 1973: 89).

8 Here, I note Pinar Bilgin's argument that even mimicry can disguise subtle forms of agency (Bilgin 2007: 6).

Bibliography

Acharya, A. (2004) 'How Ideas Spread: Whose Norms Matter? Norm Localization and Institutional Change in Asian Regionalism', *International Organization* 58(2): 239–275.

Agathangelou, A. and L. H. M. Ling (2004) 'The House of IR', *International Studies Review* 6(4): 21–49.

Anderson, M. B. (1999) *Do No Harm: How Aid can Support Peace – or War*, Boulder, CO: Lynne Rienner.

Aradau, C. and J. Huysmans (2009) 'Mobilising (Global) Democracy: A Political Reading of Mobility between Universal Rights and the Mob', *Millennium: Journal of International Studies* 37(3): 583–604.

Begby, E. and J. P. Burgess (2009) 'Human Security and Liberal Peace', *Public Reason* 1(1): 91–104.

Benhabib, S. (1993) *Situating the Self*, Cambridge: Polity.

Bhabha, H. (1994) *The Location of Culture*, London: Routledge.

Bhabha, H. (1995) 'Freedom's Basis in the Indeterminate', in J. Rajchman (ed.) *The Identity in Question*, New York: Routledge, pp. 47–61.

Bilgin, P. (2007) 'Thinking Past Western IR', *Third World Quarterly* 29(1): 5–23.

Blanchot, M. (1993) *The Infinite Conversation*, Minneapolis: University of Minneapolis Press.
Boege, V., M. A. Brown, K. P. Clements and A. Nolan (2008) 'States Emerging from Hybrid Political Orders – Pacific Experiences', The Australian Centre for Peace and Conflict Studies (ACPACS) Occasional Papers Series.
Boutros-Ghali, B. (1992) *An Agenda for Peace: Preventative Diplomacy, Peacemaking and Peacekeeping*, New York: United Nations.
Butler, J. (2002) 'Universality in Culture', in M. Nussbaum (ed.) *For Love of Country?*, Boston, MA: Beacon Press, pp. 45–52.
Cerny, P. (2009) 'Some Pitfalls of Democratisation in a Globalising World', *Millennium: Journal of International Studies* 37(3): 767–790.
Chabal, P. and J.-P. Daloz (2006) *Culture Troubles*, Chicago: Chicago University Press.
Chandler, D. (2009) 'Critiquing Liberal Cosmopolitanism? The Limits of the Biopolitical Approach', *International Political Sociology* 3(1): 53–70.
Chatterjee, P. (1998) 'Beyond the Nation? Or Within', *Social Text* 56(3): 57–69.
Chopra, J. and T. Hohe (2004) 'Participatory Intervention', *Global Governance*, 10(2): 289–305.
Chou, M. and R. Bleiker (2009) 'The Symbiosis of Democracy and Tragedy: Lost Lessons from Ancient Greece', *Millennium: Journal of International Studies* 37(3): 659–682.
Comaroff, J. and J. Comaroff (1999) *Civil Society and Political Imagination in Africa*, Chicago: University of Chicago Press.
Connolly, W. (1991) *Identity/Difference*, Minneapolis: University of Minnesota Press.
Darby, P. (2009) 'The Alternative Horizons of Ashis Nandy', unpublished paper.
De Certeau, M. (1984) *The Practice of Everyday Life*, Berkeley: University of California Press.
De Sousa Santos, B. (2007) 'Human Rights as an Emancipatory Script', in B. De Sousa Santos (ed.) *Another Knowledge Is Possible: Beyond Northern Epistemologies*, London: Verso.
De Tocqueville, A. (1945) *Democracy in America*, Vintage Books.
Debord, G. (1999) [1967] *Society of the Spectacle*, New York: Zone.
Eckl, J. (2008) 'Responsible Scholarship after Leaving the Veranda', *International Political Sociology* 2(3): 185–203.
Fanon, F. (1967) [1963] *The Wretched of the Earth*, London: Penguin.
Foucault, M. (1979) 'What Is An Author?', in J. V. Harrari (ed.) *Textual Strategies: Perspectives in Post-Structuralist Criticism*, Ithaca, NY: Cornell University Press, pp. 141–160.
Foucault, M. (1991) 'Governmentality', in G. Burchell, C. Gordon and P. Miller (eds) *The Foucault Effect: Studies in Governmentality*, Hemel Hempstead: Harvester Wheatsheaf, pp. 87–104.
Foucault, M. (2008) *The Birth of Biopolitics: Lectures at the Collège De France, 1978–1979*, Basingstoke: Palgrave Macmillan.
Geertz, C. (1973) *The Interpretation of Cultures*, New York: Basic Books.
Habermas, J. (1998) *The Inclusion of the Other*, Cambridge, MA: MIT Press.
Harvey, D. (2005) *A Brief History of Neoliberalism*, Oxford: Oxford University Press.
Held, D. (1997) 'Democracy and Globalisation', *Global Governance* 3(3): 251–267.
Hindess, B. (2001) 'Not at Home in the Empire', *Social Identities* 7(3): 363–377.
ICISS (2001) International Commission on Intervention and State Sovereignty, *The Responsibility to Protect*, December.
Kapoor, I. (2002) 'Capitalism, Culture, Agency: Dependency versus Postcolonial Theory', *Third World Quarterly* 23(4): 647–664.

Kapoor, I. (2003) 'Acting in a Tight Spot: Homi Bhabha's Post-Colonial Politics', *New Political Science* 25(4): 561–577.
Kapoor, I. (2008) *The Post-Colonial Politics of Development*, London: Routledge.
Lederach, P. (1997) *Building Peace: Sustainable Reconciliation in Divided Societies*, Tokyo: United Nations University Press.
Lefebvre, H. (1991) *Critique of Everyday Life*, London: Verso.
Linklater, A. (2005) 'Dialogic Politics and the Civilising Process', *Review of International Studies* 31(1): 141–154.
Martin, L. H., H. Gutman and P. Hutton (eds) (1998) *Technologies of the Self: A Seminar with Michel Foucault*, London: Tavistock.
Massey, D. (1994) *Space, Place and Gender*, Minneapolis: University of Minnesota Press.
Mouffe, C. (2000) *The Democratic Paradox*, London: Verso.
Newman, E. and O. P. Richmond (2001) *The United Nations and Human Security*, London: Palgrave.
Newman, S. (2007) 'Connolly's Democratic Pluralism and the Question of State Sovereignty', *British Journal of Politics and International Relations* 10(2): 227–240.
Paris, R. (2001) 'Human Security: Paradigm Shift Or Hot Air?', *International Security* 26(2): 87–102.
Plant, S. (1992) *The Most Radical Gesture*, London: Routledge.
Richmond, O. P. (2002) *Maintaining Order, Making Peace*, London: Palgrave.
Richmond, O. P. (2007a) 'Critical Research Agendas for Peace: The Missing Link in the Study of International Relations', *Alternatives* 32(2): 247–274.
Richmond, O. P. (2007b) 'Emancipatory Forms of Human Security and Liberal Peacebuilding', *International Journal*, Summer.
Richmond, O. P. (2008) 'Reclaiming Peace in International Relations', *Millennium: Journal of International Studies* 36(3): 439–470.
Richmond, O. P. (2009a) 'Eirenism and a Post-Liberal Peace', *Review of International Studies* 35(3): 557–580.
Richmond, O. P. (2009b) 'Becoming Liberal, Unbecoming Liberalism: The Everyday, Empathy, and Post-Liberal Peacebuilding', *Journal of Intervention and Statebuilding* 3(3): 324–344.
Richmond, O. P. (2009c) 'The Romanticisation of the Local: Welfare, Culture and Peacebuilding', *International Spectator* 44(1): 149–169.
Richmond, O. P. (2011) *A Post-Liberal Peace: The Infrapolitics of Peacebuilding*, London: Routledge.
Rorty, R. (1991) *Objectivity, Relativism, and Truth*, Cambridge: Cambridge University Press.
Schmeidl, S. (2009) '"Prêt-A-Porter States": How the McDonaldization of State-Building Misses the Mark in Afghanistan', in M. Fischer and B. Schmelzle (eds) *Peace in The Absence of States: Challenging the Discourse on State Failure*, Berghof Handbook for Conflict Transformation Dialogue Series, Issue No. 8.
Scott, J. C. (1990) *Domination and the Arts of Resistance*, New Haven, CT: Yale University Press.
Shinko, R. E. (2008) 'Agonistic Peace: A Postmodern Reading', *Millennium: Journal of International Studies* 36(3): 473–491.
Spencer, J. (2008) *Anthropology, Politics, and the State*, Cambridge: Cambridge University Press.
Spivak, G. C. (1988) 'Can The Subaltern Speak?', in C. Nelson and L. Grossberg (eds) *Marxism and the Interpretation of Culture*, Basingstoke: Macmillan.

Tadjbakhsh, S. (2005) 'Human Security: Concepts and Implications', Les Etudes du CERI, No. 117–118.

Ucko, D. (2008) 'Militias, Tribes, and Insurgents: The Challenge of Political Reintegration in Iraq', *Conflict, Security and Development* 8(3): 341–373.

United Nations (1948) *Declaration of Human Rights*, New York: United Nations.

United Nations (2004) *Report of the Secretary-General's High Level Panel on Threats, Challenges, and Change*, New York: United Nations.

Vrasti, W. (2008) 'The Strange Case of Ethnography and International Relations', *Millennium: Journal of International Studies* 37(2): 279–301.

14

Situated Critiques of Intervention: Mozambique and the Diverse Politics of Response

Meera Sabaratnam

I belong irreducibly to my time. (Fanon)

Introduction

For those investigating the state of international relations today, there can be few more valuable sites of study than the practice of statebuilding interventions around the world. It is at these points where, away from the formal niceties of the diplomatic circus, the political, economic, social and sometimes military forces of the so-called Great Powers rub up against both each other and those of the global South, under conditions of seemingly relative permissiveness and invisibility from the eyes of the Northern media. To see and understand the lived nature of the global state of affairs, then, one might be better advised to visit Kigali or Phnom Penh than Washington or Brussels. The contemporary debate about statebuilding interventions and the liberal peace should therefore not be considered as a niche interest within the discipline of IR or peace studies; rather it is constitutive of the major problematics that have concerned theorists of all hues for decades: hegemony, globalisation, empire, sovereignty, human rights and so on.

A number of critical theorists within the discipline have rightly latched onto this thought, and have developed analyses that mobilise different theoretical perspectives to frame the problematic. A global critique has developed around the notions of statebuilding interventions as an international 'neo-imperial' 'liberal peace' or 'neoliberal governance' project that is characterised principally by its intention of spread Western ideologies and capitalism in the non-West. Many of these critiques are majorly influenced by Foucault's work on discourse as the association of knowledge and power, his notion of biopolitics, by the Gramscian concept of hegemony, or indeed both plus others. The application of these streams of thought to the question of statebuilding has been extremely valuable in opening up different theoretical, political and ethical questions around the practice, and indeed has reinvigorated critical theory itself within the discipline.

Yet, as Hobson notes, it is not impossible for critical theory to reinforce a Eurocentrism in thought through a monological account of 'winners' and 'losers' in the international system (2007). I argue that this has also happened, with qualifications, in the realm of critical theories of the liberal peace, and is compounded by a fairly consistent, if apologetic, division of the world into 'liberal/neoliberal' and 'local/non-liberal/traditional' halves that are characterised by adherence to particular ideologies and knowledge structures, plus a general pessimism about the preponderance of the former. As a potentially emancipatory project, this tendency is disturbing on a number of levels, not least including the frequent omission, downgrading or ignoring of the substance of politics at the sites of supposed domination that might themselves be the basis of an alternative politics of interaction. Furthermore, it seems to accept at face value the account of the extent of the liberal transformation of post-conflict societies.

This chapter proposes an alternative way of exploring a case of intervention that is inspired by anticolonial critiques of empire, which builds on and challenges a number of the insights of critical analysis thus far. It does this through a situated exploration of the politics of intervention in Mozambique, based in fieldwork techniques that attempt to capture observations and responses to intervention as seen by various actors both involved and not involved in the process. It argues these situated, embedded aspects can help the study of international politics by going beyond the problematic of alterity employed in current framings and into distinct concrete political questions in the relationship.

Critiques of the (Neo)liberal Peace

Critical theorists working on the question of how international agencies intervene in post-conflict spaces have largely been concerned to develop a more or less global picture of a system driven by a particular logic or logics to exert a particular universalising transformative effect at different sites of intervention. The existing critical literature does this through three related analytic moves. The first is the expansion of the notion of liberalism through attaching the label 'liberal' to a broad set of contemporary intervention activities, which implies a structural relationship between these activities in that they have roots in liberalism. A second aspect of this has been the association of this 'liberal' ideology with agencies, organisations and actors coming from 'the West'. The third face of this is the understanding of this relationship between through the lens or metaphor of 'imperialism'.

Together these three angles – the ideas of liberalism, the agency of the West and the structure of imperialism as the analogy for the relationship – form the foundation of a powerful, insightful and productive critique of 'the liberal peace'.[1] The literature on this is extremely rich in terms of commentary, detail and observation. However, as I will argue, the mode of theorising and research is also limiting in terms of being *critical* theory, that engages and articulates alternative ways of thinking and envisions dimensions of change; in short, the 'formulaic, top-down and ethnocentric' (Mac Ginty 2007: 457) nature of the liberal peace finds some parallels in the analytical framing of its critiques. The next section looks at these features of the existing critique.

The preponderance of the 'liberal' as global formula and narrative

As articulated by Mac Ginty and Richmond, the liberal peace 'represents an increasingly formulaic synthesis of Western-style democratisation, "good governance", human rights, the rule of law, and developed, open markets' that become the hallmarks of post-conflict intervention (Mac Ginty and Richmond 2007: 491). A key claim of much of this critique is that the liberal peace is 'the *new ideology*, upon which life, culture, society, prosperity and politics are assumed to rest' (2007: 493, emphasis added). The 'liberal peace' for Richmond is an expansive, and perhaps all-encompassing, characterisation of post-conflict interventions. It can be broken down into gradations, which can be conservative/realist, orthodox or emancipatory in nature, depending on which discourse of liberal peace is most favoured from the four strands that comprise it (Richmond 2005). Despite the multiplicity of components and emphases that the discourses and practices of post-war interventions can have, which Richmond himself acknowledges can be 'theoretically rather incoherent' (Richmond 2008: 15), the central motif of the work is that it can be *usefully understood* as the 'liberal peace project' – a 'blueprint for stability and sustainability' (Richmond and Franks 2007: 44) adhered to by peacebuilders across the spectrum. This includes military interventions that focus on the 'conservative' aspects of a liberal peace as well as NGOs that envision an 'emancipatory' version of the liberal peace.

Duffield's critique of contemporary post-war and developmental intervention makes much bolder claims about the role of liberalism now and historically, seeing it as fundamentally shaping both security and development, and therefore relations between North and South. Adapting Foucault's application of the notion of 'biopolitics' to the Third World, Duffield argues that '[l]iberalism is a technology of governance that supports freedom while governing people through the interconnected natural, social, and economic processes that together sustain life' (2007: 6). In its contemporary guise, it supports the joining of development and security discourses to secure a form of liberal governance that is modernity's solution to the problem of the 'surplus' life required and produced by capitalism (ibid.: 10). As such, a rethinking of 'whether liberalism itself, rather than being seen as a solution, is counted as one of the problems' is required in order to improve the situation (ibid.: 31).

Whilst, of course, some form of simplification is a legitimate course of action for any theorist of the international system to take, what emerges from all of these critiques, individually and as a whole, is that an expansive, inclusive ideological programme identified as 'the liberal peace', 'liberalism' and/or 'neoliberalism' is the key feature of intervention in the South by international agencies. This creates the narratives of a single hegemonic interventionary framework that is ideologically unitary, if not coherent, and intentionally driven according to this ideology.

The ideology-origin problematic, cultural inappropriateness and 'hybridity'

With different degrees of qualification and variegation, the tendency in the critical literature is to associate this ideology very generically with 'the West', and to disassociate it from the spaces of intervention, where 'traditional' or 'local' values are narrated as opposed to those of liberal political structures. This consciousness underpins a number of critiques of the liberal peace which highlight the incompleteness or ineffectiveness of trying to impose an alien system on another society.

The notion of 'hybridity' has, however, emerged as an assessment of the results of liberal peacebuilding, whereby 'indigenous' or 'local' actors have combined and/or adapted post-conflict institutions to fit other 'traditional' patterns of legitimation. For example, in his discussion of Cambodia's statebuilding project, Roberts notes that various political structures and processes, such as the Senate and land reform, were 'indigenized', representing a continuation of traditional forms of rule and politics within the statebuilding experience (2009: 165). Roberts sees the Cambodian case being one where statebuilding had 'a superficial impact on very resilient indigenous societies and polities' (ibid.: 163), but argues that essentially this may have been a good thing from the point of view of being both 'culturally appropriate [and] pragmatically necessary' (ibid.: 167). Whilst Roberts recognises the inherent dangers of 'Othering' other states by normalising 'liberal democracy', it is clear that there is a basic division that underpins the argument between the 'indigenous' and the 'democratic'.

Other theorists have grappled with the problematic also, warning against the dangers of romanticising or essentialising the 'local' (Richmond 2009a), but do not dispense with it as the key distinction within analysis. Richmond, in a discussion visualising a 'post-liberal peace' argues that:

A research agenda is needed which engages with an understanding of the dynamics of the relationship between the *liberal and the local*, and of the interface between the two in terms of everyday life for local communities and actors, as well as for more abstract institutional frameworks. This *'liberal-local interface'*, and the nature of peace that it suggests requires extensive and ongoing consultation and research in order to develop these ideas (2009b: emphasis added).

One of the questions that is being identified here is that of the diverse origins of interveners and recipients as leading to a basic alienation from the ideas of intervention on the part of the latter. The implication that statebuilding/ the liberal peace needs to find a way of developing a type of meeting point between the liberal and the local depends on the claim that they are basically different.[2] As Chandler (this volume) argues, the problematisation of alterity underpins both the power-based critiques of liberal peace such as these, as well as the more technocratic approaches that seek to limit the liberal nature of the practices.

The limits of global critique

Whilst both interesting and powerful, many contemporary critiques of intervention remain distant from the sites of intended 'emancipation' – that is the 'recipients' or objects of domination, hegemony and empire. I do not mean this in a physical or geographical sense – increasingly fieldwork and familiarity with context and cases is becoming better used within the literature – but in an unwillingness to attempt the use of other embedded epistemological standpoints to act as a counterpoint, understood in a Saidian sense, to the dominant narrative of global 'liberalism' or 'neoliberalism', rather than purely re-inscribing its force through a critique from a similar viewpoint (Chowdry 2007: 101). The narrative of a liberal-imperial-West as the principal intervener in the Third World, shaping it into a formulaic liberal image through its actions, is the principal thrust of much current critique. Whilst it is plausible and useful in a general sense, I argue that this formulation itself, if interrogated more deeply, also becomes problematic at precisely the site of attempting to engage with the 'local' or 'indigenous', which is constructed as the opposite of the 'liberal'.[3]

It must firstly be noted that the label 'liberal' is used so variously throughout and within the critical literature and used interchangeably with 'neo-liberal', that it is hard to argue that it has a consistent meaning. In Richmond's formulation, the 'liberal' peace is also a hybrid of different strands, including militarism, orthodox conservatism and emancipatory politics. In short, 'liberalism' becomes a breadth of different political positions and activities that characterise interventions by a broad group of actors. This is perhaps a formally valid move in the sense that between political philosophers, there are deep divisions as to what constitutes 'liberalism' and who its true heirs are, as well as political differences between the values of polities that are thought to have 'liberal' foundations.

However, given the way that it is used, and particularly when it is used as a quality distinct from the 'local' or the 'non-Western', it seems clear that it denotes a marker of origin as much as a marker of political philosophy. As such, the West is narrated as liberal, and liberal ideas are narrated as Western. This is also the case in Duffield, whose account of liberalism strongly ties it to Western domination and imperialism as a technology of government. What he means is that liberalism is a set of ideas and beliefs that has been used to exercise and legitimate control over various parts of the non-Western world.

Such accounts of liberalism draw a boundary of an ideology-power-origin problematic of the liberal peace, that is for Richmond overcome through a pluralist Eirenism that demonstrates 'empathy' for the 'local' (2009b). Such a formulation is intended to respect difference and not erase it, as has supposedly been the tendency of the liberal peace. However, the conception of 'difference' is one that seems to rest on the liberal-local binary, which, despite the various deconstructions that the critiques of the liberal peace do, is not one which is subjected to sufficient scrutiny. Whilst 'othering' is challenged in the discourses of intervention, it is not fundamentally challenged within the critiques themselves, which seek to reconstruct the structural impasse, albeit in a more emancipated way. This construction also reflects either epistemological humility or epistemological scepticism, or both, when it comes to analysing, narrating or 'knowing' the post-conflict environment and people that live within it. As such, there is usually a deferral against articulating anything more specific than either the origin of people ('local'/'indigenous'), although this sometimes also becomes 'non-liberal' or 'non-Western'.

The risks of such a 'solution' to the 'liberal peace' become clearer when trying to actually execute the principles of engaging 'the everyday' empathetically. What emerges is that the ethical and political problems of 'liberal' interventions are not in and of themselves a clash with the 'local' or the 'indigenous' as abstract or concrete forms. In many formerly colonial states, the meaningfulness of the 'local' or 'indigenous' is as problematic as the meaning of the 'liberal' is amongst the interveners. Indeed, the Todorovian Encounter that seems to haunt critical engagement with today's global South feels misplaced. But if critique remains in a principally abstract form, it seems inevitable that it will reproduce these categories. A related critique might be made of Duffield's appeal to the notion of 'the governed' which underpins his appeal for a 'practical politics of solidarity' (2007). Whilst he is keen to focus on the similarities between people rather than the differences, the very broad level of his critique – entirely directed at the ideas underpinning liberalism and development – does not permit him to go there in any substantive way. As such the meaning of 'the governed' as a class of peoples amongst which solidarity might be constructed seems to dissipate in context.

Situated Revolt: Intellectual Inversion, Immanent Critique and Creativity in Anti-colonial Protest

When thinking about whether the liberal peace is imperial – a term frequently used in the critiques – it is worth remembering that historically many anti-imperial thinkers and activists did not focus their intellectual attacks on imperialism and colonialism as a *European or liberal ideology per se*. They certainly made trenchant critiques of imperial and capitalist economic exploitation, and attacked the racist foundations of rule.[4] However, in many cases this was not so much derived from the principles of an underlying *fundamental* alterity or 'local' character as the differentiated, violent and unjust *experience* of life under colonial rule. Intellectually and politically, it was articulated strongly in terms of universalist and immanent critiques of the existing order, around which solidarist and internationalist political coalitions were formed (Jones 2010).

As such, the relevant response to the question of empire was a forceful concretisation and articulation of its problematic effects. Beyond structural economic analysis, thinkers identified and described a range of problems, including racism, dispossession, psychological control and violence of many forms, through seeking to engage the experiences of the colonised. It was this situated critique of the *experience* of empire that undermined its claims to being a 'civilising' influence; what became nakedly apparent was that it was a system of violence, exploitation and instrumentalisation despite its own propaganda.

Indeed, an important part of this critique of colonialism was their failure to extend the application of universal rights to peoples under their rule:

> And that is the great thing I hold against pseudo-humanism: that for too long it has diminished the *rights of man,* that its concept of those rights has been – and still is – narrow and fragmentary, incomplete and biased and, all things considered, sordidly racist . . . that at the very time when it most often mouths the word, the West has never been further from being able to live a true humanism – a humanism made to the measure of the world. (Cesaire 1972, emphasis in the original)

Cesaire's critique is stinging because it turns ideas about domination back on their proponents as a means of critique. This suggests that an immanent critique[5] of 'European' ways could be a sincere, provocative and useful way to engage others on common political terrain. The major themes then become about deliberate exclusion from these processes, and a denial of the humanity of the colonised as a basis for a much more ambitious pan-African vision. This is expressed neatly in Cabral's public declaration against the Portuguese:

> The African anticolonialist organisations of the Portuguese colonies representing the legitimate aspirations of their people want to re-establish the human dignity of Africans, their freedom, and the right to determine their own future. These

organisations want the people to enjoy real social development based on fruitful work and economic progress, on African unity and fraternity, on friendship and equality with all peoples, including the Portuguese people. They want peace in the service of humanity. (Cabral et al. 1980: 27)

Indeed, the early post-colonial thinkers acknowledged their various intellectual debts to the West, even as they sought to subvert or expand the frameworks with which they worked, the better to capture what they understood as their realities (Chabal 1981). Their move then becomes not purely an 'ontological' one in the pitting of the rational individual against the forces of production or race, but also a *positional* one to do with the standpoint from which problems are viewed and the experiences in which they are embedded.

This is not to say that these thinkers necessarily validated the universalist discourses which legitimated empire, nor that there were no important differences between them and the universalisms of the anti-colonial movement. The point is that they understood universals as embedded in and productive of a particular kind of politics, and re-thought them accordingly. Simply because forms of power validate themselves in universalist and exceptionalist terms does not mean that they are what they say, nor that successfully opposing them requires a fixation on their imagined opposite. Rather, it might also involve a subversion and redeployment of these ideas to express an alternative idea of politics in a creative manner.

So far, critiques of the liberal peace have not tended to recognise this,[6] although given the politics of inclusion they demand (e.g. 'a practical politics based on the solidarity of the governed' for Duffield) it is clear that such work might usefully complement, help re-think and re-articulate the core problematic of international power in post-war environments. In what follows, I will briefly illustrate the potential of this alternative critical project through an engagement with the recent politics of the 'liberal peace' in Mozambique.

Exploring the Case of Mozambique and the 'Liberal Peace'

Mozambique, whilst often put forward as an example of a 'success story' within both the peacebuilding and development literature, is also put forward as a case of a 'governance state', as discussed by Graham Harrison (2005). Since 1990, and slightly beforehand, it has been subject to large quantities of targeted international intervention and assistance in the name of peacebuilding, governance assistance, capacity building and democratisation, which have sought to transform it away from being a socialist one-party state towards becoming a multi-party democracy. As a example selected to develop a critique of the liberal peace, then, I argue that it represents a important case – one where the intervention of the international community has coincided with the cessation of violent conflict, the holding of regular elections, the rebuilding of state institutions, impressive rates of economic growth and macroeconomic stabilisation, an increase in the numbers and sizes of civil society organisations, the attraction of foreign investment, the awarding of a 'good governance' prize to its former President, a sizeable fall in the level of absolute poverty and so on. It regularly gets cited within policy documents as a representation of precisely what can be achieved through the correct type of engagement (Hanlon and Smart 2008: 5).

Interestingly, neither the critics nor supporters of the liberal peace have engaged with it very extensively within the literature as evidence for their various positions, although there is a growing literature rooted in development and anthropology that deals with Mozambique's trajectory over time. The exceptions to this are Mark Duffield's work on the role of NGOs (2007), which extends his account of global liberal governance, Michel Cahen's assessment of success in the *Making States Work* volume (2005), Roland Paris's analysis in *At War's End* (2004: 135–148) and its inclusion in a new study in this volume (see Zürcher). Duffield shows that NGOs have become part of the governmental process in Northern Mozambique. Cahen, asked to provide an analysis of Mozambique's success for the volume, argues for an only qualified success with regard to societal involvement, and Paris argues that given the shallow domestic roots of the war, it does not provide a basis for assessing the outcomes of liberal peacebuilding, although it can be considered largely successful.

What remains unexplored within the literature on this subject, with the slight exception of the work of Cahen, a sociologist, are the internal processes and politics of Mozambique as they relate to intervention. Within broader debates about development and intervention, as well as emanating from within policy organs themselves, there is a much richer literature on what has happened over the last twenty years, although again, the majority of this is framed by the objectives of interveners or by other particular debates. Work that deals with the ethics and politics of intervention in Mozambique, with a few notable exceptions,[7] is neither sought after nor produced with much frequency.

The rest of this chapter will sketch briefly some selected political critiques made within Mozambique of co-operation with the West which use the critical interpretation of the 'liberal peace' as a set of pervasive social transformations. These viewpoints are drawn from various forms of primary and secondary research collected within and outside Mozambique on the subject of internationally sponsored reform and transformation. These critiques are selected, interpreted and articulated by the author in terms of insights they shed on the liberal peace debate in terms of concretising issues. As such, there is no claim being made that these are statistically representative nor that they in any way exhaust the range of critiques of intervention that are made within Mozambique by various groups. Indeed, given the practical and political problems of reliable access to non-elite and non-urban sources of critique, these are somewhat skewed towards urban and elite critiques. This is a general limitation of the narrative. Nonetheless, they attempt to shed some light on the dynamics of intervention as experienced and understood by its supposed non-liberal Others. As I will argue in the conclusion, these preoccupations suggest a rather different approach to the politics of critical engagement than that hitherto displayed in the debate on the liberal peace. In this sense, the case material is not intended as an ethnographic treatment of the 'everyday', as advocated by Richmond, which I have suggested reproduces discourses of Otherness within critique. In offering these specific critiques as important on their own terms, the chapter seeks to challenge more radically the normal hierarchies of critique between scholars and subjects.

Situating Critiques in Mozambique

Problematising economic neoliberalism

Critiques of the liberal peace suggest that liberal ideology is a key aspect of intervention in the South, and that this is problematic for 'local' communities, whose values are not incorporated (see Richmond, this volume). However, in interpreting responses in Mozambique about the various forms of intervention in the country and the associated relationships with aid partners, there were rarely objections articulated to the ideological principles behind programmes based on 'local' values, even from those who were most exercised about the system as it currently stood. This is not to suggest that there are not distinctive traditions of politics across Mozambique, but it does indicate that it is not their disruption that informs primary objections to intervention.

More commonly, particular principles associated with 'liberal' policy discourses were often selectively redeployed to critique the impact of neoliberal development, which had resulted in deep economic vulnerability. There was a consciousness amongst those that worked in the policy levels in the agricultural sector and more widely that the international financial institutions were conscious that they had been proved wrong over their choices for the cashew industry, errors which stemmed from arrogance and heavy-handedness as much as from policy failure.[8] Those very few that did talk self-consciously about the turn towards capitalism in the late 1980s presented it as an expediency above all else for getting foreign assistance,[9] although not one to which there were sustained objections.

The more prevalent and cutting objection to the economic reform agenda was that it did not either reflect any historical pattern of development, nor was it fair in how it was set up:

But economic activity must be public before it is private. If you look at the USA in the 30s, the EU until today – they are giving subsidies, they have the biggest force in innovation and technology, in product quality. So Mozambique, if it follows the rules, couldn't compete. So we were still poor, because we didn't make the rules.[10]

The critique here of neoliberal economics is much more blunt than that it is inappropriate or incomprehensible – it is that it is a basically false model for development. The same was echoed in discussions with low-income farmers in rural Nampula, who wanted 'above all, markets' for their crops, but despite reforms lacked access to ones in which they could compete.[11] In both cases, it is the promises of free markets and development which are turned against the actual effects of reform.

Visible public anger of recent years has focused on discontent with rising food and fuel prices, which have in the last three years resulted in unprecedented political riots and a restoration of the subsidies that donors had encourage the government to remove. Within the context of these riots have been articulated resentment of visibly rising inequalities and widespread unemployment, for which the extravagant wealth of the political elite has become a focal point.[12]

What is of note for the liberal peace debate is that it is *policies* themselves that are being contested politically, for their incoherence and failure to generate the promised well-being. In the case of the price riots at least it is clear that anger is directed towards Mozambican political and business elites much more so than towards the general presence of international intervention, although the specific role of international financial institutions is noted by some. Importantly, though, the axes of critique – unfairness, inequality, hypocrisy – are not the assertions of a fundamental alterity but appeals to values associated with universal relevance.

International assistance and the suppression of politics

This is not to say that value is not placed on any form of pluralism. Indeed, an important charge levelled against the various forms of international assistance is that it has stifled the political creativity and imagination of elites and blunted their capacity for critique. For example, the director of a civil society organisation focused on accountability and good governance, itself funded by the UK government, argued:

> There is no alternative there – they don't do ideology; they just do what the donors want. Co-operation has really corrupted the thinking of African leaders. They know that they can lose their jobs and consultancies if they are too critical. There are two forces contributing to this – the state: people want an easy life, and the donors.[13]

Another argued that: 'Development needs to be less dependent. If Mozambique accepted this, there would be room to think. But there is not a debate at the moment. There is lots of accommodation . . . we need to think about depending less.'[14]

From these and other commentaries it is clear that a major area of concern was that the perception that donor assistance monopolised the economic, and subsequently political, concerns of ruling elites. From the perspective of government insiders, this situation was not denied but framed as the necessary pragmatism of a poor country – indeed a historic pragmatism that had formed part of the Frelimo political tradition since its pre-Independence struggle. As is now publicly commemorated as part of Frelimo folklore, during the Cold War Frelimo leader Eduardo Mondlane famously received money from the US, Soviet and Chinese governments to fund the anti-colonial war. The receipt of money from a wide range of donors in the present day was justified in similar terms.[15]

Critical political economy approaches to development and aid have often framed this situation as the co-optation of Southern elites through the development of their ability to profit from the proposed reforms. Indeed, this correlates with other accounts in this book of the actual impact of particular forms of transformation (see Hameiri, this volume). Indeed, as these critiques demonstrate, it is a conscious interpretation that is made within Mozambique itself of the behaviour of ruling elites. What is interesting however is that these critiques are made by actors who themselves use the discourses of donors – such as good governance and ownership – to develop force for their own political messages which are critiques of vested power. This is not to claim that therefore these discourses are necessarily emancipatory – it is to point out that they can be and are subverted and redeployed to challenge power as well as maintain it. Critiques of the liberal peace, through an emphasis on the formulaic, liberal character of the discourses nonetheless miss the ways in which they can be leveraged in the service of particular and pointed critique.

Wastefulness and introspection

From the perspective of those implementing projects associated with donor assistance, when discussing the nature of the intervention, the issue of 'imposition' did occasionally arise. Again, this was not articulated as because the substance of the ideas was not comprehensible to 'locals', but because donors wanted to call the shots and prioritise their own requirements. Another substantial issue was that of the waste of resources through the spending of money on things that were not needed and were too expensive, and that these were not having any intended effect:

One thing I feel is not really good; in general, and this is the point of view of the donors. As a Mozambican, I feel that the donors give money but want to control everything . . . Normally when MINAG [Ministry of Agriculture] develops some plan to do themselves, they say no, do outsourcing. But this means that you have to give money to the company – you can't assume it's a better service. But the donors are just happy to subcontract and for someone to do the job in name. But we had experience – we were doing outsourcing in Zambezia and Nampula; the donors say they are happy, but in the end, I'm not happy; the company don't take responsibility like the DPA [Provincial Agricultural Directorate] or MINAG. This contract is signed by MINAG, but you know it's not the decision – it's an imposition. This is a big problem; we impose a lot of things . . . but I don't think this is a good way, and this is why MINAG do some things themselves. Because sometimes they have seen the opportunity to change, add, but the donors don't want. I feel that donors don't really want to reduce poverty. We started with PROAGRI [the common fund] in 1995. There were millions spent on consultant studies – four studies, but if you see how much is going to the farmer, it's just 25% – I say why? Each donor wants to do the study, and to use the money of PROAGRI. And the amount of money they pay for the study is unacceptable. They always want the evaluation, and they contract out – and how much do they support? But the support for the farmers itself, they are not getting a lot. *With one study, you can buy ten tractors, can really solve some problems.* I am not saying that the study is not important, but you need to let them do what they want, let them direct. (emphasis added)[16]

The overwhelming critique within this narrative however is that intervention in this case was fundamentally and obviously disconnected, both from its own objectives – i.e. the improvement of governance and the reduction of poverty – and the recipients – in this case the rural poor. Instead, intervention was more focused on things that could be executed by the donors to their own specifications or around their own needs, particularly those of familiarisation and evaluation. More respondents highlighted the percentages of programme and project budgets that were either spent within institutions on salaries and living costs for international and domestic employees, and the very small percentage that reached the intended recipients.[17] Again, this seems very distant from the critique that 'Western liberal' norms are not appropriate for 'local' populations, or that there is some necessary friction between them. It rather seems that there is a more fundamental lacuna in that projects and programmes are not seen to actually use their money to do very much that has any impact in practice.

A clear issue articulated by those who were the intended targets of programmes was that, whilst extensive training in governance and capacity was offered and given by organisations, very little material was supplied to actually carry out the things that they had been trained to do, whatever the notions underpinning the programmes. Health activists, farmers and religious leaders each mentioned that they had received training ('capacitação') in various skills which they were meant to pass on to others or carry out, but they lacked basic transport such as bicycles to even reach the places where training had to take place.[18] Whilst they worked around this, either by using borrowed means, or undertaking lengthy journeys by foot, it seemed an odd discrepancy that so much could be spent on the front end of the programmes and so little at the back. Overall, the sense was that whilst assistance might be generally welcome, it did not often do very much, its stated objectives being only loosely delivered, and its material focus being largely internal. These aspects of intervention are visible and obvious to those on the receiving end of it. Whilst this image of development has perhaps become something of a cliché, I would argue that it remains a constitutive aspect of the experience of intervention.

In terms of implications for critical theory, it has seemed so far within discussions of the liberal peace that such issues of wastefulness, introvertedness and incomplete, reversible implementation are rather too banal and pedestrian to deal with at the structural level. They operate so much as commonsense both for 'recipients' and those working within the system that trying to understand the politics of this seem overly obvious.

In terms of critique, it does however point towards more distributive issues that fundamentally call into question the nature of intervention if it consistently fails to get near its objectives through a tendency to absorb its own resources. Certainly, amongst quite a few people, such as the respondent above, this set of practices suggested that intervention was not about *really* reducing poverty but about the donor circus, and thus generated a level of cynicism amongst them. This seemed to be a much more obvious and widespread cause of alienation than the fact that practices or values of intervention were in some way 'foreign' to societies. Viewed from this perspective, intervention practices can present themselves as a form of introspective consumption for those involved.

Populism, control, nationalism and resistance; changes in the relationship

Indeed, particular politicians have made a good deal of political capital out of demonstrably resisting the perceived cultures of time-wasting, high foreign earners and kickbacks that are popularly associated with international cooperation. The former Health Minister Paulo Ivo Garrido is one such figure. He was almost universally a figure who caused discomfort amongst both the donor community and some of his colleagues due to his extremely centralised managerial style and forceful personality. However, amongst a large proportion of non-elite respondents, he was something of a hero for preventing his staff from attending various seminars paid for by the international community, with their attendant per diems and catering, for seeming to clamp down on corruption in hospitals, and for performing unannounced visits which often resulted in the dismissal of staff caught not doing their jobs, for which former leader Samora Machel was approvingly remembered. That he is a qualified surgeon also seems to gain him much respect amongst the general public who tend to view him as someone who works hard, does not suffer laziness, knows what he is doing and who stands up for himself.[19]

An incident which occurred in 2009 seemed to demonstrate the ways in which intervention practices play in populist politics. The US Chargé d'Affaires threatened to withdraw a large amount of US aid, including in the health sector, if eleven US health workers were not cleared to work in the Embassy's HIV/AIDS programme.[20] Their visas, similarly to the visas of a large number of other international workers at the present time, were been processed extremely slowly and painstakingly, pending the production of original documentation from medical schools and so on. The Minister said publicly that the Government must be able to determine what kind of health workers they need – the issue quickly became one about control, US high-handedness and 'attempted blackmail'.[21] A number of respondents raised this as an example of US arrogance, a harking back to colonial master–servant relations, the US trying to impose their will and so on.[22] This inspired a certain amount of indignation and resentment about imposition, and became a point for discussions of national control of the agenda. One respondent, however, working for a US-funded NGO, was keen to stipulate that there were no problems in relations, that the whole thing was a misunderstanding and that people didn't know what they were talking about.[23]

The increasing perception that Mozambique had the power to say 'no' to large donors, even if only occasionally, was clearly something that interested a number of respondents, even those critical of the government.[24] Particularly within the government, there was a sense that in recent years Mozambique had entered a new era of co-operation, whereby it developed its own plans, was in control of its own agenda and so forth. Even with the international financial institutions, small victories such as the allowing of some protection for the sugar industry demonstrate that the government is willing to push the limits of their apparent regulations, and, in the case of the national development bank, completely side-step them through co-operation with another donor.[25]

Of course, as is well documented, the impact of new co-operation initiatives with partners such as China, Brazil and India has given African governments more options in terms of financing without political conditions, and this is not less true in Mozambique. In the context of the relations with Northern donors, a Government Minister interviewed argued:

> This is the major impact of Brazil, India, China . . . We don't waste months or years negotiating. You say what you want; you do it now and the road is there. You see the results immediately. We want results, not processes. We do not want to waste

time discussing conditionality. There is no interference. The EU and US say that China is not democratic, it doesn't respect human rights, but that is not our business. What we want is the agreement and to fulfil it. If they keep their obligations, that is ok. We are not changing their internal policies – that is not our business. We will not ask Zimbabwe to change its policies – it's their business. They will ask for something – here we will ask them to accept our constitution. This principle of non-interference with India and China is better. It is not because we are against human rights. But we understand that they have their own systems and intelligence. It is not our business. We wouldn't go to the US, to try and change the face of A and B. We would never go to Europe and ask for a President to be taken to court. We are not the champions of democracy. But in our relationships with China, we say what we want.[26]

It is clear that politically, it is important to the government to try to assert control over its development and intervention agenda as far as possible. This type of resistance is something which has played well with the public – current President Guebuza's critique of Chissano's laxity (*deixa-andarismo*) in dealing with donors and internal corruption seemed to be one with which people could identify, and one which gained momentum going into the 2004 and 2009 Presidential elections.

These examples suggest that open resistance to aspects of co-operation has an important political value and role for various actors in Mozambique – a greater value than one might have expected from reading the critiques of statebuilding. Moreover, there seem to be successful instances of general control. However, it is important to note that this is not a resistance against all foreigners, or against interventions from the outside, or even of liberalism – what seemed to be important was the ability to negotiate and choose the types of intervention and the kind of relationship it has with partners. This indicates that there is a politics about the relationship between Mozambique and the outside world, but it is not one marked by rejectionist attitudes so much as the desire to control and choose the means of equitable engagement.

Conclusions

Whilst the global critiques of the liberal peace have opened up, quite rightly, a number of ethical and political questions that need addressing, I argue that their emphasis on the origins of ideas and practices, and the division between the liberal and the local fundamentally obscures the concrete politics of intervention, and in particular the counter-claims and critiques being made by its intended objects. However, I argue that in beginning to move towards a situated critique of intervention, we engage in analysis that can be more politically challenging, policy-relevant and more radical in terms of its calls for reform. The situated critiques show that not only is there a disconnect between theory and policy, but between both of these and the concrete issues raised through experience.

Experience in this case suggests that there are the beginnings of immanent critiques of intervention taking place within sites of intervention whereby the claim that intervention consists of transformative practices which operate to improve the host state and society is fundamentally dubious. The emerging critiques made by the intended objects of aid in Mozambique – that assistance is often wasteful, ineffective, ill-informed, introspective, illiberal, repetitive and capricious – are not just operational critiques regarding implementation from people that have been co-opted into a particular ideological system. I argue that they can also, and should, be read as political critiques that reveal much about the nature of the experience of intervention.

Given the material situation of a country like Mozambique, these critiques are not surprising. When one considers the complaints about waste, it is clear that this is the flip-side of a politics of survival – what seems to accompany the international community's rhetoric of alleviating poverty for subsistence and survival is a practice of internally maximising resource consumption and self-protection, which also reinforces the instrumentalisation of the process and alienation from it amongst recipients. The popularity of seeming to assert control and strength over the co-operation process however also indicates the significance of a sense of autonomy and direction that is not reducible to output and material benefits.

Fanon's account of racialised existential angst and violence, and Cabral's focus on the 'reality of the land' expressed and animated a situated and 'humanist' response to the practices of colonialism that contributed to a wider consciousness of its problems. I argue that critical theories of intervention in IR can gain much by thinking in a similar way, in order to fully engage and understand the dysfunctionality or otherwise of the system. Such a focus can open up areas for contestation and debate that are currently hidden or ignored, such as the problems of insularity, hypocrisy, waste and resentment. These issues in a sense more radically challenge the mythologies of liberal intervention through systematically undercutting its self-image as competent, efficient bringers of peace and development. It is through engaging these important aspects of intervention's lived experience that critics might be best placed to realise Duffield's ambition for a 'practical politics of the solidarity of the governed'.

Notes

1 For more detail, see the Introduction and chapter 1 of this volume.
2 Richmond grapples further with this problem in his chapter in this volume, as does

Mac Ginty, but I would suggest that it may not be resolved. However it is beyond the scope of this chapter to engage with these frameworks in detail.

3 A somewhat nuanced and complex exception is the work of Graham Harrison, who discusses the 'embedding' or internalisation of 'neoliberal' policy mechanisms in governance states (2005).

4 See Fanon (1963) and Cabral et al. (1980) as key examples.

5 By use of the term 'immanent critique' I do mean a critique based on analysing the contradictions within the current system; however, I do not mean to imply anything about its role as a dialectic in history.

6 With a few exceptions, e.g. Heathershaw (2007).

7 In terms of work published in English, the work of Joseph Hanlon in Mozambique spans several decades, and has been critically engaged with the problems of developmental intervention since its inception. See Hanlon (1984, 1990, 1996), Hanlon and Smart (2008).

8 See Hanlon (2000). This incident was mentioned to me independently by, at least, a senior journalist (interview, Beira, 6 July 2009), a major civil society activist (Maputo, 21 August 2009) and a senior agronomist (Nampula, 19 August 2009).

9 Interview with a junior Minister for Planning and Development, Maputo, 11 July 2008; interview with a senior agriculture NGO official, Nampula, 14 August 2009.

10 Interview with a senior adviser for co-operation, Provincial Government of Nampula, 12 August 2009.

11 Interview with a farmers' savings and credit association, Monapo, 7 August 2009.

12 J. Langa, 'Editorial', *O Pais,* 1 September 2010.

13 Interview with a director of a major national development NGO, 17 August 2009, Maputo.

14 Interview with the director of a major civil society organisation, 22 August 2009, Maputo.

15 Interview with a junior Minister for planning and development, Maputo, 11 July 2008.

16 Interview with a Mozambican agronomist working with a European development agency, Sofala, 7 July 2009.

17 Interview with a Mozambican secondary school teacher, 17 June 2009, Maputo.

18 Interviews with: a health NGO worker, Beira, 10 July 2009; a farmers' savings and credit association, Monapo, 7 August 2009; a Methodist priest, 6 August 2009, Nampula.

19 Diary notes, various.

20 Reported widely, see AllAfrica: 'Employ Our People or No Money, Says US Embassy', 22 May 2009, http://allafrica.com/stories/200905220822.html. Accessed 17 October 2009.

21 Ibid.

22 Interview with a newspaper editor, Sofala, 6 July 2009; conversation with a young theatre director, 12 June 2009, Maputo; interview with a junior Minister, 19 August 2009, Maputo.

23 Interview with a Mozambican doctor working for an American NGO, 6 August 2009.

24 Interviews with a high school teacher, 17 June 2009, Maputo and a former civil servant in the Ministry of Health, 17 June 2009, Maputo.

25 See BBC, 'Mozambique's sugar faces a new threat', 16 November 2004: http://news.bbc.co.uk/1/hi/business/4002529.stm. Accessed 17 October 2009. And Net News,

'Mozambique, Portugal, agree to set up $500m investment bank', http://www.netnews-publisher.com/mozambique-portugal-agree-to-setup-500m-investment-bank/. Accessed 17 October 2009.

26 Interview with a junior Minister, 19 August 2009, Maputo.

Bibliography

Antonio, R. J. (1981) 'Immanent Critique as the Core of Critical Theory: Its Origins and Developments in Hegel, Marx and Contemporary Thought', *British Journal of Sociology* 32(3): 330–345.

Cabral, A. (1980) *Unity and Struggle: Speeches and Writings*, trans. by M. Wolfers, texts selected by Partido Africano da Independência da Guiné e Cabo Verde, African Writers series, London: Heinemann Educational.

Cahen, M. (2005) 'Success in Mozambique?' in S. Chesterman, M. Ignatieff and R. Thakur, *Making States Work: State Failure and the Crisis of Governance*, Tokyo and New York: United Nations University Press.

Césaire, A. (1972) *Discourse on Colonialism*, New York: Monthly Review Press.

Chabal, P. (1981) 'The Social and Political Thought of Amilcar Cabral: A Reassessment', *Journal of Modern African Studies* 19(1): 31–56.

Chandler, D. (2006) *Empire in Denial: The Politics of State-building*, London: Pluto Press.

Chowdhry, G. (2007) 'Edward Said and Contrapuntal Reading: Implications for Critical Interventions in International Relations', *Millennium: Journal of International Studies* 36(1): 101.

Duffield, M. R. (2007) *Development, Security and Unending War: Governing the World of Peoples*, Cambridge: Polity.

Fanon, F. and C. Farrington (1965) *The Wretched of the Earth*, London: MacGibbon & Kee.

Hanlon, J. (1984) *Mozambique: The Revolution under Fire*, London: Zed Books.

Hanlon, J. (1991) *Mozambique: Who Calls the Shots?*, Bloomington: Indiana University Press.

Hanlon, J. (1996) *Peace without Profit: How the IMF Blocks Rebuilding in Mozambique*, Oxford: James Currey.

Hanlon, J. (2000) 'Power without Responsibility: The World Bank and Mozambican Cashew Nuts', *Review of African Political Economy* 27(83): 29–45.

Hanlon, J. (2010) 'Mozambique 167', E-bulletin, 2 September.

Hanlon, J. and T. Smart (2008) *Do Bicycles Equal Development in Mozambique?*, Woodbridge, UK and Rochester, NY: James Currey.

Harrison, G. (2005) 'Economic Faith, Social Project and a Misreading of African Society: The Travails of Neoliberalism in Africa', *Third World Quarterly* 26(8): 1303–1320.

Heathershaw, J. (2007) 'Peacebuilding as Practice: Discourses from Post-Conflict Tajikistan', *International Peacekeeping* 14(2): 219–236.

Hobson, J. M. (2007) 'Is Critical Theory Always for the White West and for Western Imperialism? Beyond Westphilian towards a Post-racist Critical IR', *Review of International Studies* 33(S1): 91–116.

Jones, B. G. (2010) 'Anti-racism and Emancipation in the Thought of Cabral, Neto, Mondlane and Machel', in R. Shilliam, *International Relations and Non-Western Thought: Imperialism, Colonialism and Investigations of Global Modernity*, London: Routledge.

Mac Ginty, R. (2007) 'Reconstructing Post-war Lebanon: A Challenge to the Liberal Peace?', *Conflict, Security & Development* 7(3): 457–482.

Mac Ginty, R. and O. P. Richmond (2007) 'Myth or Reality: Opposing Views on the Liberal Peace and Post-war Reconstruction', *Global Society* 21(4): 491–497.

Paris, R. (2004) *At War's End: Building Peace after Civil Conflict*, Cambridge and New York: Cambridge University Press.

Richmond, O. P. (2005) *The Transformation of Peace*, Palgrave Macmillan.

Richmond, O. P. (2008) *Peace in International Relations*, New York: Routledge.

Richmond, O. P. (2009a) 'The Romanticisation of the Local: Welfare, Culture and Peace-building', *International Spectator* 44(1): 149–169.

Richmond, O. P. (2009b) 'A Post-liberal Peace: Eirenism and the Everyday', *Review of International Studies* 35(3): 557–580.

Richmond, O. P. and J. Franks (2007) 'Liberal Hubris? Virtual Peace in Cambodia', *Security Dialogue* 38(1): 27–48.

Roberts, D. (2009) 'The Superficiality of Statebuilding in Cambodia: Patronage and Clientelism as Enduring Forms of Politics', in R. Paris and T. D. Sisk (eds) *The Dilemmas of Statebuilding: Confronting the Contradictions of Postwar Peace Operations*, Abingdon and New York: Routledge, pp. 149–169.

Index

Abdullah, A. 75
accountability: of peacebuilding organisations 97–8, 100; of Western governments to home audiences rather than Afghan activists 114, 116
adaptation *see* organisational learning and adaptation
advocacy 145, 147
Afghanistan 3, 37, 58, 79, 82, 83, 213, 234; ambiguous Western footprint 114–19; composition of parliament 107–8; Elimination of Violence Against Women law (EVAW) 106, 107–8, 112–14, 117, 118, 119; hybrid security 217; lack of demand for democracy 75–6; legal reforms and promoting women's rights 6, 106–20; Shia Personal Status Law 106, 107–8, 108–12, 116, 117, 118, 119
Afghanistan Independent Human Rights Commission 109, 112
Africa 45, 234–5; ICC and 122, 129–31, 135; *see also under individual countries*
Agenda for Peace, An 14–15, 139, 191, 231
agonism 231–2
aid 78–9, 141; aid effectiveness agenda of the OECD 202, 204–5; aid organisations as civil society actors 149; broken feedback loop of international aid 97–8; donor aid agencies 89, 92, 98; Rwanda 79; situating critiques in Mozambique 254–60, 261; and the suppression of politics 255–6
Akhavan, P. 132
alternatives to liberal peace 7, 159–73; hybridisation model and creating and maintaining 212, 214–16
Amal movement 221
Angola 15, 34, 57
Annan, K. 35
anti-colonial critiques 8, 246, 251–2
anti-corruption agenda 220–1
anti-liberal forces, empowerment of 114, 114–15
'Archimedean' view 63–4
Arendt, H. 125–6
Argyris, C. 93–4
arrest warrants 130, 131–2, 133
Atzili, B. 195
Australian Federal Police (AFP) 201
Autesserre, S. 59–60
authoritarian regimes: consolidation of 202–5; creation of 163–4
autonomous recovery 36–7

Bain, W. 37, 46
Baldwin, D. 61
bargaining 73, 75, 84–5, 212, 214
Barnett, M. 58–9, 60, 97, 98, 160–1, 175
Baskin, M. 219
Bellamy, A. 174, 177–8
Bendaña, A. 38, 143, 144
Bhabha, H. 229, 232
biopolitics 177
Bose, S. 44
Bosnia-Herzegovina 15, 34, 35–6, 77–8, 79–80, 82, 83, 196; hybrid statebuilding 218–19; peacebuilding record 44

266   INDEX

Boutros-Ghali, B. 14–15, 15–16, 191
Brazil 259–60
Britain *see* United Kingdom (UK)
bureaucracies, self-reproduction of 97
Burundi 24, 99–100, 101
buy-in by host state and society 91

Cabral, A. 251–2
Cahen, M. 253
Call, C.T. 13
Cambodia 7, 34, 193–4, 202–5, 205–6, 248
Cambodian Development Cooperation Forum 204
Cambodian People's Party (CPP) 202, 203–4, 205
Cambodian Rehabilitation and Development Board 204
capacity building 200
Carnegie Commission on Preventing Deadly Conflict 17
Central and Eastern Europe 141, 182–3
Cesaire, A. 251
Chandler, D. 35–6, 37, 44, 134, 161, 191, 195–6, 199
change, theories of 90–1
Chesterman, S. 195
China 259–60
Chopra, T. 164
civil society 7, 138–55, 182–3; actors 148–9, 150; as seen by critics of the liberal peace 143–50; beyond the liberal peace and its critics 150–1; contribution to peace and statebuilding 144–9; hybrid peace 217, 222; NGOisation 118; role in the liberal peace 140–3
'Civil Society and Peacebuilding' project 144–50
Clark, P. 133
clientelistic networks 74, 76, 202–5, 205–6
Coalition Government of Democratic Kampuchea 203
Collier, P. 140
colonialism 62, 229–30, 251, 261; colonial anxiety 230; equating peacebuilding with 38, 41–2; *see also* anti-colonial critiques
communitarian critiques 2
complex emergencies literature 22
conflict management 142; intellectual history of 5, 13–30
conflict resolution 142
conflict sensitivity 92, 100–1

conflict transformation 142–3
Congo, the 59
conquest, military 40–1, 43, 162–3
consensus, critical 180–1
constitutional reform 217, 218–19
constructively critical approach 90–3, 168–70
constructivism 2, 177–8
contextual theory 233–4
Convention on the Elimination of All Forms of Discrimination against Women (CEDAW) 107, 110
co-opted peacebuilding 60
corruption 220–1
Cousins, E.M. 13
Cox, R. 176–7, 194
Crawford, N.C. 42
Criminal Law Working Group 112
crisis of liberal peacebuilding 167
critiques of liberal peace 7, 90, 167–8, 174–90; and civil society 143–50, 150–1; critical consensus 180–1; global critique 245–6, 246–50; 'ideas-based' critique 7, 176, 178–80, 180–1, 186–7, 187–8; impasse 5–6, 31–51; mistakes in 40–6; pendulum swing 33–9; 'power-based' critique 7, 176–8, 180–1, 185–6, 187–8; and their limitations 191–2, 194–7, 205
Crocker, C.A. 17, 20–1, 24, 26
cultural bias 214
cultural inappropriateness 248–9
customary practices 164–5, 211, 215–16

Danish, S. 108
Dayton Accords 34, 218
definitional stretching 42–3
demand for democracy 6, 69–88; engagement of peacebuilders and lack of 75, 78–80; local elites and 6, 74–8, 78–9, 82, 83
democracy/democratisation 33, 38, 39, 139–40, 179, 182, 232–3; civil society and democratisation 141, 145; demand for democracy 6, 69–88
depoliticisation 126–7
deterrence 124–5, 128–9, 146
development 184–5, 200; economic 18–19, 167, 217, 217–18; neoliberal model 141
development cooperation 140, 141
development projects 78–9
difference, respect for 4, 8

Dillon, M. 175
domestic analogy 122, 123–5; inapplicability of 125–9
domestic dynamics 60
donor aid agencies 89, 92, 98
double-loop learning 91, 93–4
Duffield, M. 21–2, 45, 93, 161, 177, 185–6, 191, 195, 247–8, 250, 253

East Timor 19, 35, 58, 71, 80–1, 82
Eastern and Central Europe 141, 182–3
Ebrahim, A. 97–8
Eckl, J. 229
economic benefits of peace 45
economic development 18–19, 167; hybrid peace 217, 217–18
economic liberalisation 21, 33–5, 38, 139–40, 166–7, 176–7; problematising neoliberalism 254–5
Edelstein, D. 163
Eden, L. 95
effects of peacebuilding 6, 55–68; omnipotent external actors 55, 56–61; sovereignty, patronage and power 61–5
El Salvador 34
elections 33, 34, 57, 101, 166, 182, 184
Elimination of Violence Against Women law (EVAW) 106, 107–8, 112–14, 117, 118, 119
emancipatory peacebuilding 161–2, 178, 236
embedded liberalism 199
empathy 232
engagement of peacebuilders 75, 78–80
Englebert, P. 36, 60, 62
epistemic communities 65
Ethiopia 130
ethnographic approaches 232
European Union (EU) 219, 220, 222
everyday, the 8, 61, 228–35, 239; implications of 231–5; resistance and post-liberal peace 236–8
'everyday peace' 150, 151
evolutionary narrative 124
exploitation 212, 214
external actors/peacebuilders 55–6; accountability of peacebuilding organisations to 97–8; commitment 85; and the democratic outcome 83–5; engagement and lack of local demand for democracy 75, 78–80; hybridisation model 212–14; illiberal behaviour 161;
objective 73; omnipotent 55, 56–61; relation with local actors 56, 60–5

failed states 15–16, 17–18, 23–4, 32
Fanon, F. 240
Featherstone, A.B. 143
feedback from local population 91
financial crises 199–200
Finnemore, M. 97, 98
Foucault, M. 245–6
Foucaultian structuralist approach 177
frames, organisational 95–6
France 41
Freedom House score 70, 86
Frelimo 81, 256

Galtung, J. 139
Garrido, P.I. 258–9
genocide 125–6
global community 123, 127, 129
global governance 65, 66
global justice 121, 134–6; see also International Criminal Court (ICC)
globalisation 22, 23, 211–12
'good local' 149–50, 151
governance 18–19, 23, 24–5, 62–3, 183, 199; global 65, 66; hybrid peace 217, 219–22; ICC and conformity with good governance 124–5; standards 74; traditional practices 164–5, 211, 215–16
Government–Donor Coordination Committee 204
Gray, J. 38
Guebuza, President 260

Hazaras 108, 111
Heathershaw, J. 13, 143–4
Helman, G. 32
Herbst, J. 36, 37, 162, 195
Hezb-e Islami 108
Hezbollah 215, 221–2
High Level Panel Report 231
Hindess, B. 219
history: intellectual history of conflict management 5, 13–30; organisational learning and 94–6
Hobson, J.M. 246
home audiences, accountability to 114, 116
host government, agency of 99–100
Howard, L. 59, 93, 94
human security 177–8, 232
humanism 251

Hun Sen 193–4, 202, 204, 205
hurting stalemate 82–3
hybrid peace 4, 8, 92, 165, 184, 196–7, 205, 226–44, 248–9; the everyday 8, 61, 228–35, 239; how it comes about 209–25; resistance and 235–8
hybridisation 209–10, 212–22; in action 217–22; four-part model 212–16
hybridity 209–10, 210–12, 229–30, 248–9; implications of the everyday 231–2
hyper-critical school 31–3, 168

'ideas-based' critique 7, 176, 178–80, 180–1, 186–7, 187–8
ideology 21–2; ideology–origin problematic 248–9
immanent critique 251–2
imperialism 41–2, 251; equating peacebuilding with 37–8, 41–2
imposition of liberal peace 256; hybridisation model 212, 212–13; impossibility of 98–102
in-group socialisation 147–8
incentivisation 212, 213–14
India 259–60
indigenous agency see local actors
indigenous practices 164–5, 211, 215–16
individual criminal responsibility 123, 125–6
infrapolitics of peacebuilding 238–40
institutionalisation before liberalisation (IBL) 21, 57–8, 179
institutionalism 182–3, 186–7; and the ICC as an agent of peace 121–2
intellectual history of international conflict management 5, 13–30
interactive nature of peacebuilding 72–3
inter-group social cohesion 145, 148
internal actors see local actors
international administration 19, 46, 161, 195–6; permanent foreign rule 163
international aid see aid
International Commission on Intervention and State Sovereignty (ICISS) 19
International Committee for the Reconstruction of Cambodia 19
International Criminal Court (ICC) 6–7, 121–37; domestic analogy 122, 123–5; inapplicability of the domestic analogy 125–9; Uganda case 129–33; what it actually does 133–6
international organisations (IOs) 65, 89,
92, 98; self-reproduction of 97; see also under individual organisations
International Monetary Fund (IMF) 213, 219, 220
introspection 256–8
Iraq 23, 37–8, 40, 58, 175, 234; hybrid economic development 218
Islam 117; see also Afghanistan, Shia Personal Status Law

Jahn, B. 43, 175

Kant, I. 139
Karzai, H. 75, 79
Kenya 125, 164–5
Keohane, R. 178–9
knowledge, sites of 228–31
Kony, J. 132
Koskenniemi, M. 128
Kosovo 19, 35, 58, 77–8, 79–80, 82, 83
Krasner, S.D. 163, 178–9
Kumar, K. 20

Lacher, W. 38
'last native syndrome' 211
Latin America 141
lawmaking: fragmentation of 118–19; legal reforms in Afghanistan 6, 106–20
learning, organisational see organisational learning
Lebanese Transparency Association (LTA) 220–1
Lebanon 215; hybrid governance 219–22
Lederach, J.P. 20, 142
Levitt, B. 94–5
liberal–local hybridity see hybrid peace, hybridisation, hybridity
liberal–local interface 248–9
liberalisation 57–8; economic see economic liberalisation; political 21, 33–5, 38
liberalism 3–4; as 'field of adversity' 185; preponderance as global formula and narrative 247–8, 249–50; too broad a definition 42–3; variety and style 165–6
Liberia 34
local actors 55, 56, 59–61, 99–100, 101, 211; empowerment and emancipation of 92; feedback from 91; 'good local' 149–50, 151; hybrid peace see hybrid peace, hybridity; hybridisation model 212, 214–16; othering 4, 7, 181,

184–5, 248–9, 250; relation between external actors and 56, 60–5
local elites 62–5, 71; aid and the suppression of politics 255–6; and demand for democracy 6, 74–8, 78–9, 82, 83; objective 73–4
local–liberal hybridity *see* hybrid peace, hybridisation, hybridity
local ownership 2, 35–6, 56, 91, 100
Lord's Resistance Army (LRA) 7, 131–3
Lubanga, T. 124
Ludin, Maulawi A. 108

Mac Ginty, R. 164, 165
Machel, S. 259
March, J.G. 94–5
market-oriented reforms *see* economic liberalisation
Martens, B. 97
mass violence 135; and individual criminal responsibility 123, 125–6; psychology of participation in 128
membership-based associations 148–9
meta-critique 25–6
middle–out approach 142–3
military victory 40–1, 43, 162–3
Mohseni, Sheikh A. 108, 110, 111
Mondlane, E. 256
monitoring 145, 147
moral complexity, oversimplification of 45–6
moral reasoning 129
Moreno-Ocampo, L. 124–5, 130
Mozambique 8, 15, 57–8, 81–2, 252–60; situating critiques in 254–60, 261
mujahedin 114–15
multilevel governance 198–9
multilevel regimes 7–8, 193, 200–2; Cambodia 202–5, 205–6
Museveni, President 131, 133

Namibia 14, 57–8, 80, 82
national agency 99–100, 101
national politics, ICC and 124–5, 127–8
national self-determination 42
nationalism 219, 258–60
NATO intervention in Afghanistan 111, 119; NATO governments' accountability to home populations 116; and polarisation of the political climate 116–17
negotiation 73, 75, 84–5, 212, 214

neoliberal development model 141
neoliberal economics *see* economic liberalisation
neo-Marxist structural critique 176–7
Nepal 124
networks, clientelistic 74, 76, 202–5, 205–6
new institutional economics (NIE) 200
new institutional theory 65–6
Nicaragua 14, 34
9/11 terrorist attacks 23, 37
non-governmental organisations (NGOs) 89, 92, 98, 141, 148, 253; NGOisation 118, 144, 149
non-intervention approach 36–7, 162–3
non-liberal Other 4, 7, 181, 184–5
norms: conforming to global norms 124–5, 127–8; constraints of a normative agenda 98
Northern Ireland 222
Norton, A.R. 221

Obama, B. 107
Office of the High Representative in Bosnia 19
Operation Lightning Thunder 133
Organisation of American States (OAS) 33
Organisation for Economic Cooperation and Development (OECD) 23, 220; aid effectiveness agenda 202, 204
Organisation for Security and Cooperation in Europe (OSCE) 33, 230
organisational frames 95–6
organisational learning and adaptation 6, 59, 89–105; challenges of 94–6; defining learning 93–4; importance 90–3; particular challenges in peacebuilding organisations 96–8
othering 248–9, 250; non-liberal Other 4, 7, 181, 184–5
Ottaway, M. 196
ownership, local 2, 35–6, 56, 91, 100
Oxfam International 45

Papua New Guinea (PNG) 201
Paris, R. 21, 22, 56–7, 57–8, 140, 144, 178–9, 180–1, 184, 194, 253
path dependence 96, 99
patronage 74, 76; sovereignty, power and 61–5; and statebuilding in Cambodia 202–5, 205–6
peace studies 16–18, 26

INDEX

peacebuilders *see* external actors/
 peacebuilders
peacebuilding 24, 26, 31–2, 139–40;
 conditions of birth 40–1; consensus 25;
 early years 14–16; equating with
 imperialism or colonialism 37–8, 41–2;
 historial record 13–21; infrapolitics
 of 238–40; institutionalisation 18–19;
 mischaracterising the record of 44–5;
 reconciliation and healing 19–21;
 as resistance 235–8; role of civil
 society 140, 141–3, 144–50; roots of
 the liberal peace 139–40;
 shortcomings 39–40, 56–7; UN
 principles 14–16
peacebuilding missions/operations 33–5,
 69; and democratic transitions 70–1, 72
peacebuilding organisations 6, 89–105
policy-oriented ('ideas-based') critique 7,
 176, 178–80, 180–1, 186–7, 187–8
political economy of war 22
political elites, local *see* local elites
political infrastructure for
 peacebuilding 63–4
political liberalisation 21, 33–5, 38; *see also*
 democracy/democratisation
politics: ICC and national politics 124–5,
 127–8; polarisation of political
 climate 114, 116–17; political
 consensus 4–5; suppression of 255–6
populism 258–60
positive complementarity 124–5
post-colonial approaches 2, 231–2
post-conquest peacebuilding 40–1
post-settlement peacebuilding 40–1
post-Washington consensus 200
Powell, W. W. 96
power 6; performative aspect 65; relation
 between external and local actors 61–5
'power-based' critique 7, 176–8, 180–1,
 185–6, 187–8
prevention 124–5, 128–9, 146
problem-solving approach 1, 71–2, 90–3,
 194–7
protection 145, 147
Pugh, M. 22, 37, 161–2, 177, 185, 185–6,
 195

Qanooni, Y. 108

radical ('power-based') critique 7, 176–8,
 180–1, 185–6, 187–8

Ratner, S. 32
reconciliation 19–21
regimes, multilevel *see* multilevel regimes
regulatory state 198–9
rehabilitation 20–1
Reid, J. 175
Renamo 81
representation 160–1
republican peacebuilding 58, 160–1
resistance 61, 212, 214, 218, 223, 226–44;
 implications of the everyday 231–5;
 Mozambique 258–60; and post-liberal
 peace 235–8; sites of knowledge for
 peace 228–31
responsibility 19; ICC and Western
 avoidance of 134
Responsibility to Protect, The 19, 231
Richmond, O. P. 2, 25, 43, 61, 162, 175,
 178, 185–6, 195, 196, 247, 248–9, 249,
 250
rights: ICC and 123, 125, 126; women's in
 Afghanistan 6, 106–20
riots 255
risk management 199–200
Roberts, D. 248
Robinson, W. 37
routines 94–6, 99, 100, 100–1,
 101–2; unaltered and peacebuilding
 organisations 96
Rwanda 15, 34, 57, 76–7, 79, 82, 83

Samar, S. 115
Sayyaf, A. R. 109, 115
Scott, J. C. 235–6
security: human 177–8, 232; hybrid 217
security studies 16–18
self-government 166
service delivery 145, 148
Shanahan, R. 221
Sharia 117
Shia Personal Status Law
 (Afghanistan) 106, 107–8, 108–12, 116,
 117, 118, 119
Shinwari, F. H. 115
Sierra Leone 35, 58
single-loop learning 93–4
Sisk, T. 180–1
situational factors 59
Smith, A. 139
Smith, D. 91
Snyder, J. 178
social cohesion 145, 148

INDEX

social constructivism 2, 177–8
social justice 14–15
social transformation 177
socialisation 145, 147–8; in-group 147–8; of the population at large 147
Somalia 15, 130
South West Africa People's Organisation (SWAPO) 80
sovereignty 179, 183; patronage, power and 61–5; as responsibility 19
Srebenica massacre 15
stalemate, hurting 82–3
state–society relations 64
state transformation 192–3, 197–202, 205–6
statebuilding 23–5, 35, 69, 198, 215; civil society functions 145; and the critique of liberalism 181–4; hybridisation model 217, 218–19; and patronage in Cambodia 193–4, 202–5, 205–6
strongman strategy 163–4
sub-Saharan Africa 234–5
subversion 212, 214
success: defining 90; organisational learning, defining and measuring 94
Sudan 99–100, 133
Sudanese People's Liberation Army 133
Sunni Muslim MPs 109–10
Supplement to the Agenda for Peace 15–16, 19–20
Supreme Court of Afghanistan 115
sustainable peace 20
Swidler, A. 63

Tadjbakhsh, S. 2
Tajikistan 77, 82, 83
Taliban 106, 114–15, 217
targets, organisational learning and 94
Taylor, C. 34
technocratic approach to peacebuilding 100, 215–16
terrorism (9/11 attacks) 23, 27
theories of change 90–1
top-down movement 211
traditional actors 149
traditional practices 164–5, 211, 215–16
transformation: conflict 142–3; social 177; state 192–3, 197–202, 205–6
transitional administration 19, 46, 195–6
transitions 140, 141, 150, 182–3
transnational advocacy groups 65

transnationalised and transnationally regulated statehood 192–3
Tull, D. 36, 60, 62

Uganda 3, 7, 124–5, 129–33
Uganda Amnesty Act 132
UNAMA (United Nations Assistance Mission in Afghanistan) 110
UNIFEM (United Nations Development Fund for Women) 110, 111, 112
UNITA (National Union for the Total Independence of Angola) 57
United Kingdom (UK) 41; Department for International Development (DfID) 23
United Nations (UN) 31, 33; field-level learning 93; peacebuilding missions *see* peacebuilding missions/operations; peacebuilding principles 14–16; protectorates in East Timor and Kosovo 19, 58; and Shia Personal Status Law in Afghanistan 110–11
United Nations Charter 62
United Nations Development Programme (UNDP) 219, 220
United Nations High Commissioner on Human Rights 107
United Nations Peacebuilding Commission (UNPBC) 24
United Nations Security Council 59
United Nations Transition Assistance Group (UNTAG) 80
United Nations Transitional Authority in Cambodia (UNTAC) 202, 203
United States (US) 23, 26; aid to Mozambique and high-handedness 259; and the ICC in Africa 130–1, 132–3; invasion of Afghanistan 37, 107; war with Iraq 37–8, 40; war on terror 32, 37
UNRISD War-Torn Societies Project 17
USAID (United States Agency for International Development) 23, 110

values, politics of 199
variable geometry 209
victims of mass violence 123, 126–7
victor's peace 43

war-to-peace trajectory 91
war on terror 32, 37
wastefulness 256–8

Weinstein, J. 36–7, 162
Western donor agencies 89, 92, 98
Western self-interest 176–8
Western footprint, ambiguous in Afghanistan 114–19
Westphalian state 183–4
Williams, D. 18
Women's Affairs Commission (Afghanistan) 112, 113, 114

women's rights in Afghanistan 6, 106–20
women's groups 149
World Bank 18, 23, 213, 219, 220

Young, T. 18

Zakharia, F. 178–9
Zürcher, C. 60